Empirical Model Discovery and Theory Evaluation

Arne Ryde Memorial Lectures Series

Empirical Model Discovery and Theory Evaluation

Automatic Selection Methods in Econometrics

David F. Hendry and Jurgen A. Doornik

The MIT Press
Cambridge, Massachusetts
London, England

For information about special quantity discounts, please email special_sales@mitpress.mit.edu

This book was set in Palatino with the LATEX programming language by the authors. Printed and bound in the United States of America.

Library of Congress Cataloging-in-Publication Data

Hendry, David F.

Empirical model discovery and theory evaluation : automatic selection methods in econometrics / David F. Hendry and Jurgen A. Doornik.

   p.   cm.—(Arne Ryde memorial lectures)

Includes bibliographical references and index.

ISBN 978-0-262-02835-6 (hardcover : alk. paper)

1. Econometrics—Computer programs. 2. Econometrics—Methodology. I. Doornik, Jurgen A. II. Title.

HB139.H454   2014

330.01′5195—dc23

2014012464

10 9 8 7 6 5 4 3 2 1

Contents

About the Arne Ryde Foundation

Arne Ryde was an exceptionally promising student in the Ph.D. program at the Department of Economics, Lund University. He was tragically killed in a car accident in 1968 at the age of twenty-three.

The Arne Ryde Foundation was established by his parents, the pharmacist Sven Ryde and his wife, Valborg, in commemoration of Arne Ryde. The aim of the foundation, as given in the deed of 1971, is to foster and promote advanced economic research in cooperation with the Department of Economics at Lund University. The foundation acts by lending support to conferences, symposia, lecture series, and publications that are initiated by faculty members of the department.

Preface

> *It is thus perhaps inevitable that you will view this (book) as a synthesis.... And yet it is not that, not at all. For synthesis looks back over what we have learned and tells us what it means. While we have indeed learned a great deal, the story I tell is, in fact, as incomplete as it is ambitious. I have used empirical evidence wherever possible, but the evidence available scarcely covers the ground. There are gaping holes that I can only fill in with speculation.*
>
> William L. Benzon, *Beethoven's Anvil: Music in Mind and Culture*, p.xii, Oxford University Press, 2002.

This quote was an apt description of the book when writing it commenced in 2007. Much had been achieved, but major gaps existed, in part because there was little previous literature explicitly on empirical model discovery. The long delay to completion was due to filling in some of those major gaps, such that a clear, coherent and sustainable approach could be delineated. A science fiction writer, who was one of the first individuals to propose satellite communication systems (in 1945), but is perhaps better known for *2001: A Space Odyssey*, provides a more apt quote:

> *Any sufficiently advanced technology is indistinguishable from magic.*
>
> Arthur C. Clarke, *Profiles of The Future*, Gollancz, 1962.

As will be explained, it is astonishing what automatic model selection has achieved already, much of which would have seemed incredible even a quarter of a century ago: but it is not magic.

A discovery entails learning something previously not known. It is impossible to specify how to discover what is unknown, let alone show the "best" way of doing so. Nevertheless, the natural and biological sciences have made huge advances, both theoretical and empirical, over the last five centuries through sequences of discoveries. From the earliest written records of Babylon through ancient Egypt to the Greece of Pericles, and long before the invention of the scientific method in the Arab world during the Middle Ages, discoveries abounded in many embryonic disciplines from astronomy, geography, mathematics, and philosophy to zoology. While fortune clearly favored prepared minds, discoveries were often fortuitous or serendipitous. Advancing an intellectual frontier essentially forces going from the simple (current knowledge) to the more general (adding new knowledge). As a model building strategy, simple to general is fraught with difficulties, so it is not surprising that scientific discoveries are hard earned.

There are large literatures on the history and philosophy of science, analyzing the processess of discovery, primarily in experimental disciplines, but also considering observational sciences. Below, we discern seven common attributes of discovery, namely, the pre-exisiting *framework of ideas*, or in economics, the theoretical context; going *outside* the existing world view, which is translated into formulating a very general model; a *search* to find the new entity, which here becomes the efficient selection of a viable representation; criteria by which to *recognize* when the search is completed, or here ending with a well specified, undominated model; *quantifying* the magnitude of the finding, which is translated into accurately estimating the resulting model; *evaluating* the discovery to check its reality, which becomes testing new aspects of the findings, perhaps evaluating the selection process itself; finally, *summarizing* all available information, where we seek parsimonious models.

However, social sciences confront uniquely difficult modeling problems, even when powerful theoretical frameworks are available as in economics, because economies are so high dimensional, non-linear, inertial yet evolving, with intermittent abrupt changes, often unanticipated. Nevertheless, social sciences make discoveries, and in related ways. Historically, most discoveries in economics have arisen from theoretical advances. Recent approaches derive behavioral equations from "rational" postulates, assuming optimizing agents who face various constraints and have different information sets. Many important strides have been achieved by such analyses, particularly in understanding individual and firm behavior in a range of settings. Nevertheless, the essentially unanticipated financial crisis of the late 2000s has revealed that aspects of macroeconomics have not been as well understood as required by using models based on single-agent theories, nor has ahistorical theory proved well adapted to the manifest time-dependent nonstationarities apparent in macroeconomic time series.

At first sight, the notion of empirical model discovery in economics may seem to be an unlikely idea, but it is a natural evolution from existing practices. Despite the paucity of explicit research on model discovery, there are large literatures on closely related approaches, including model evaluation (implicitly discovering what is wrong); robust statistics (discovering which sub-sample is reliable); non-parametric methods (discovering the relevant functional form); identifying time-series models (discovering which model in a well-defined class best characterizes the available data); model selection (discovering which model best satisfies the given criteria), but rarely framed as discovery. In retrospect, therefore, much existing econometrics literature indirectly concerns discovery. Classical econometrics focuses on obtaining the "best" parameter estimates, given the correct specification of a model and an uncontaminated sample, yet also supplies a vast range of tests to check the resulting model to discover if it is indeed well specified. Explicit model selection methods essentially extend that remit to find the subset of relevant variables and their associated parameter estimates commencing from an assumed correct nesting set, so seek to discover the key determinants of the variables being modeled by eliminating empirically irrelevant possibilities. Even robust statistics can be interpreted as seeking to discover the data subset that would deliver uncontaminated parameter estimates, given the correct set of determining variables. In each case, the approach in question is dependent on many assumptions about the validity of the chosen specification, often susceptible to empirical assessment—and when doing so, proceeds from the specific to the general.

All aspects of model selection, an essential component of empirical discovery as we envisage that process, have been challenged, and many views are still extant. Even how to judge the status of any new entity is itself debated. Nevertheless, current challenges are wholly different from past ones–primarily because the latter have been successfully rebutted, as we explain below. All approaches to selection face serious problems, whether a model be selected on theory grounds, by fit—howsoever penalized—or by search-based data modeling. A key insight is that, facilitated by recent advances in computer power and search algorithms, one can adopt a general-to-specific modeling strategy that avoids many of the drawbacks of its converse. We will present the case for principles like those embodied in general-to-specific approaches, as an adjunct to human formulation of the initial choice of problem and the final summary and interpretation of the findings, greatly extending the range of specifications that can be investigated.

However, a general-to-specific approach ceases to be applicable when there are too many candidate variables to enable the general unrestricted model to be estimated. That must occur when the number of candidate variables, N say, exceeds the number of observations, T, the subject of part III. Nevertheless, even when expanding searches are required, the key notion of including as much as possible at each stage remains, so it is important not to add just one variable at a time based on the next highest value of the given selection criterion.

The methods developed below are an extension of and an improvement upon, many existing practices in economics. The basic framework of economic theory has offered far too many key insights into complicated behaviors to be lightly abandoned, and has made rapid progress in a large number of areas from auction theory through mechanism design to asymmetric information, changing our understanding, and our world. That very evolution makes it unwise to impose today's theory on data—as tomorrow's theory will lead to such evidence being discarded. Thus, one must walk a tightrope where falling on one side entails neglecting valuable theoretical insights, and on the other imposes what retrospectively transpire to be invalid restrictions. Empirical model discovery seeks to avoid both slips. The available theory is embedded at the center of the modeling exercise to be retained when it is complete and correct; but by analyzing a far larger universe of possibilities, aspects absent from that theory can be captured when it is incomplete. There are numerous advantages as we now summarize.

First, the theory is retained when the model thereof is valid. Importantly, the distributions of the estimators of the parameters of the theory model are unaffected by selection, suitably implemented: chapter 14 explains why that happens. Second, the theory can be rejected if it is invalid by the selection of other variables being both highly significant and replacing those postulated by the theory. Third, the theory could be rescued when the more general setting incorporates factors the omission of which would otherwise have led to rejection. Fourth, a more complete picture of both the theory and confounding influences can emerge, which is especially valuable for policy analyses. Fifth, commencing from a very general specification can avoid reliance on doubtful assumptions about the sources of problems like residual autocorrelation or residual heteroskedasticity—which may be due to breaks or data contamination rather than error autocorrelation or error heteroskedasticity—such that correcting them fails to achieve valid inference. Finally, when all additional variables from rival models are insignificant, their findings are thereby explained, reducing the proliferation of contending explanations, which can create confusion if unresolved. Consequently when a theory model is complete and correct, little is lost by embedding it in a much more general formulation, and much is gained otherwise.

The organization of the book is in three parts, covering

I. the principles of model selection,

II. the theory and performance of model selection algorithms, and

III. extensions to more variables than observations.

Part I introduces the notion of empirical model discovery and the role of model selection therein, discusses what criteria determine how to evaluate the success of any method for selecting empirical models, and provides background material on general-to-specific approaches and the theory of reduction. Its main aim is outlining the stages needed to discover a viable model of a complicated evolving process, applicable even when there may be more candidate variables than observations. It is assumed that an econometrics text at the level of say Wooldridge (2000), Stock and Watson (2006) or Hendry and Nielsen (2007) has already been studied.

Part II then discusses those stages in detail, considering both the theory of model selection and the performance of several algorithms. The focus is on why automatic general-to-specific methods can outperform experts, delivering high success rates with near unbiased estimation. The core is explaining how to retain theory models with unchanged parameter estimates when that theory is valid, yet discover improved empirical models when that theory is incomplete or incorrect

Part III describes extensions to tackling outliers and multiple breaks using impulse-indicator saturation, handling excess numbers of variables, leading to the general case of more candidate variables than observations. These developments in turn allow automatic testing of exogeneity and selecting in non-linear models jointly with tackling all the other complications. Finally, we briefly consider selecting models specifically for forecasting.

Acknowledgments

The *Arne Ryde Memorial Lectures*, 2007, on which this book was originally based, mainly presented findings using *PcGets* (see Hendry and Krolzig, 2001), and drew on considerable research with Hans-Martin Krolzig, but was substantially rewritten following the development of *Autometrics* in *PcGive* (see Doornik and Hendry, 2013b). Financial support for the research from the Open Society Foundations and the Oxford Martin School is gratefully acknowledged.

We are indebted to Gunnar Bårdsen, Julia Campos, Jennifer L. Castle, Guillaume Chevillon, Neil R. Ericsson, Søren Johansen, Katarina Juselius, Oleg I. Kitov, Hans-Martin Krolzig, Grayham E. Mizon, John N.J. Muellbauer, Bent Nielsen, Duo Qin, J. James Reade and four anonymous referees for many helpful comments on earlier drafts.

Julia Campos, Neil Ericsson and Hans-Martin Krolzig helped formulate the general approach in chapters 3 and 7 (see Campos, Hendry and Krolzig, 2003, and Campos, Ericsson and Hendry, 2005a); and Hans-Martin also helped develop the methods in chapters 10 and 12 (see inter alia Hendry and Krolzig, 1999, 2005, and Krolzig and Hendry, 2001). Jennifer Castle contributed substantially to the research reported in chapters 8, 18, 19, 20 and 21 (see Castle, Doornik and Hendry, 2011, 2012, 2013, and Castle and Hendry, 2010a, 2011b, 2014a); Søren Johansen did so for chapters 14 and 15 (see Hendry, Johansen and Santos, 2008, and Hendry and Johansen, 2014); chapters 15 and 22 also draw on research with Carlos Santos (see Hendry and Santos, 2010); and chapter 23 includes research with James Reade (Hendry and Reade, 2006, 2008), as well as Jennifer Castle and Nicholas Fawcett (Castle, Fawcett and Hendry, 2009). The research naturally draws on the work of many scholars as cited below and to many other colleagues for assistance with the data and programs that are such an essential component of empirical modeling. Grateful thanks are in order to them all.

The authors have drawn on material from their research articles originally published in journals and as book chapters, and wish to express their gratitude to the publishers involved for granting kind permissions as follows.

Hendry, D. F. and Krolzig, H.-M. 1999. Improving on 'Data mining reconsidered' by K.D. Hoover and S.J. Perez, *Econometrics Journal*, **2**, 202–219. (Royal Economic Society and Wiley: eu.wiley.com)

Krolzig, H.-M. and Hendry, D. F. 2001. Computer automation of general-to-specific model selection procedures *Journal of Economic Dynamics and Control*, **25**, 831–866. (Elsevier: www.elsevier.com)

Campos, J., Hendry, D.F. and Krolzig, H.-M. 2003. Consistent model selection by an automatic *Gets* approach, *Oxford Bulletin of Economics and Statistics*, **65**, 803–819. (Wiley: eu.wiley.com)

Castle, J. L. 2005. Evaluating PcGets and RETINA as automatic model selection algorithms, *Oxford Bulletin of Economics and Statistics*, **67**, 837–880. (Wiley: eu.wiley.com)

Hendry, D. F. and Krolzig, H.-M. 2005. The properties of automatic *Gets* modelling *Economic Journal*, **115**, C32–C61. (Royal Economic Society and Wiley)

Doornik, J. A. 2008. Encompassing and automatic model selection, *Oxford Bulletin of Economics and Statistics*, **70**, 915–925. (Wiley: eu.wiley.com)

Hendry, D. F., Johansen, S. and Santos, C. 2008. Automatic selection of indicators in a fully saturated regression *Computational Statistics*, **33**, 317–335. Erratum, 337–339. (Springer: www.springer.com)

Castle, J. L., Fawcett, N. W. P. and Hendry, D. F. 2009. Nowcasting is not just contemporaneous forecasting, *National Institute Economic Review*, **210**, 71–89. (National Institute for Economic and Social Research)

Hendry, D. F. 2010. Revisiting UK consumers' expenditure: Cointegration, breaks, and robust forecasts, *Applied Financial Economics*, **21**, 19–32. (Taylor and Francis: www.taylorandfrancisgroup.com)

Castle, J. L. and Hendry, D. F. 2010. A low-dimension portmanteau test for nonlinearity *Journal of Econometrics*, **158**, 231–245. (Elsevier: www.elsevier.com)

Hendry, D. F. and Santos, C. 2010. An automatic test of super exogeneity pp. 164–193, Ch.12, in *Volatility and Time Series Econometrics: Essays in Honor of Robert Engle*, edited by Bollerslev, T., Russell, J. Watson, M.W. Oxford: Oxford University Press. (Oxford University Press: www.oup.com).

Castle, J. L., Doornik, J. A. and Hendry, D. F. 2011. Evaluating automatic model selection *Journal of Time Series Econometrics*, **3 (1)**, DOI:10.2202/1941-1928.1097 (De Gruyter: www.reference-global.com).

Castle, J. L. and Hendry, D. F. 2011. Automatic selection of non-linear models In Wang, L., Garnier, H. and Jackman, T. (eds.), *System Identification, Environmental Modelling and Control*, pp. 229–250. New York: Springer. (Springer Science+Business Media B.V.: www.springer.com)

Hendry, D. F. 2011. Empirical economic model discovery and theory evaluation *Rationality, Markets and Morals*, **2**, 115–145. (Frankfurt School Verlag)

Castle, J. L., Doornik, J. A. and Hendry, D. F. 2012. Model selection when there are multiple breaks *Journal of Econometrics*, **169**, 239–246. (Elsevier: www.elsevier.com)

Castle, J. L., Doornik, J. A. and Hendry, D. F. 2013. Model selection in equations with many 'small' effects *Oxford Bulletin of Economics and Statistics*, **75**, 6–22. (Wiley: eu.wiley.com)

Castle, J. L. and Hendry, D. F. 2014. Model selection in under-specified equations with breaks *Journal of Econometrics*, **178**, 286–293. (Elsevier: www.elsevier.com)

Hendry, D. F. and Johansen, S. 2014. Model discovery and Trygve Haavelmo's legacy *Econometric Theory*, forthcoming. (Cambridge University Press: www.cambridge.org)

We are also grateful to Jennifer Castle, Julia Campos, Nicholas Fawcett, Søren Johansen, Hans-Martin Krolzig, and Carlos Santos for their kind permission to use material from those research publications, and to James Reade for permission to draw on Hendry and Reade (2006, 2008).

The book was typeset using MikTex, MacTeX and OxEdit. Illustrations and numerical computations used OxMetrics (see Doornik and Hendry, 2013a).

Glossary

AIC   Akaike information criterion.

Autometrics   General-to-specific algorithm for automatic model selection.

BIC   Baysian information criterion, also called SC for Schwarz criterion.

CMSE   Conditional mean squared error. The MSE conditional on selection, so ignoring coefficients of unselected variables.

Congruence   An empirical model is *congruent* if it does not depart substantively from the evidence. More narrowly, *statistical congruence* is when a model satisfies the underlying statistical assumptions. In that case the model is also called *empirically well-specified*.

DGP   The complicated and high dimensional data-generating process of an economy. In a Monte Carlo experiment it is the precise process generating the experimental data.

DHSY   Davidson, Hendry, Srba and Yeo (1978).

Encompassing   A model *encompasses* a rival model when it can account for the results of that rival model. A model *parsimoniously encompasses* a rival model when it is nested in the rival model, while also encompassing it.

Exogeneity   *Weak exogeneity* requires the parameters of conditional and marginal models to be variation free, and the former to provide the parameters of interest.

Strong exogeneity is when weak exogeneity and Granger noncausality both apply.

Super exogeneity is the concept whereby conditioning variables are weakly exogenous for the parameters of interest in the model, and the distributions of those variables can change without shifting the parameters.

Gauge Retention rate of irrelevant variables in the selected model. Gauge is akin to size, because it accounts for the variables that have been wrongly selected.

Gets General to specific.

Granger non-causality X does not Granger cause Y if X is uninformative for predicting future Y.

GUM General unrestricted model, the starting point for automatic model selection.

HP Monte Carlo experiments based on Hoover and Perez (1999).

IIS Impulse-indicator saturation adds an indicator variable (impulse dummy) for every observation to the set of candidate variables.

LDGP Local DGP: the process by which the variables under analysis were generated, including how they were measured. In other words, it is the DGP in the space of the variables under analysis.

Ox Statistical matrix programming language.

PcGive OxMetrics module for dynamic econometric modeling, incorporating *Autometrics*.

Potency Retention rate of relevant variables in selection. Potency is akin to power, because it accounts for variables that have been correctly selected.

SIS Step indicator saturation, which is adding a step-dummy variable (level shift) for every observation to the set of candidate variables.

UMSE Unconditional mean squared error. The MSE after selection over all coefficients and replications, using coefficients of zero for unselected variables.

Wide-sense non-stationarity occurs when there is any change in the distribution of the process.

Data and Software

We use a number of different data sets to illustrate and motivate the econometric theory. These can be downloaded from the Web page associated with the book, www.doornik.com/Discovery

(a) *UK money data.*
   This set of UK monetary data was collected quarterly for the period 1963:1–1989:2 and seasonally adjusted. These data were first documented in Hendry and Ericsson (1991).

(b) *UK consumption.*
   This set of UK consumption data was collected quarterly, but not seasonally adjusted, for the period 1957:1 to 1976:2. It has been documented and analyzed by Davidson et al. (1978). An extension of this consumption data set is also provided, based on more recent records from the UK Office for National Statistics, www.statistics.gov.uk.

(c) *UK annual macroeconomic data,* 1875–2000.
   This set of annual macro variables for the UK has previously been analyzed by Ericsson, Hendry and Prestwich (1998). It is an extension of the data analyzed by Friedman and Schwartz (1982).

(d) *US food expenditure data,* 1929–2002.
   This set of annual variables for the US was first analyzed by Tobin (1950), and previously investigated by a number of studies reported in Magnus and Morgan (1999), including Hendry (1999), based on the update of the time series in Tobin (1950) to 1989 by Magnus and Morgan (1999). It was extended to 2002 by Reade (2008), with results reported in Hendry (2009).

(e) An extension of the original *PcGive* artificial data set, called dataz.

Most results in the book are obtained using *Autometrics*, which is an Ox class for automatic model selection. *Autometrics* is incorporated in *PcGive*, which in turn is part of the OxMetrics software, see Doornik and Hendry, 2013a.

The data sets used in this book, as well as the Ox programs to replicate most simulation experiments can be found online at www.doornik.com/Discovery. The original code was restructured to make it simpler to use, and all experiments were rerun for this book.

I

Principles of Model Selection

1 Introduction

This chapter provides an overview of the book. Models of empirical phenomena are needed for four main reasons: understanding the evolution of data processes, testing subject-matter theories, forecasting future outcomes, and conducting policy analyses. All four intrinsically involve discovery, since many features of all economic models lie outside the purview of prior reasoning, theoretical analyses or existing evidence. Economies are so high dimensional, evolutionary from many sources of innovation, and non-constant from intermittent, often unanticipated, shifts that discovering their properties is the key objective of empirical modeling. Automatic selection methods can outperform experts in formulating models when there are many candidate variables, possibly long lag lengths, potential non-linearities, and outliers, data contamination, or parameter shifts of unknown magnitudes at unknown time points. They also outperform manual selection by their ability to explore many search paths and so handle many variables—even more than the number of observations—yet have high success rates. Despite selecting from large numbers of candidate variables, automatic selection methods can achieve desired targets for incorrectly retaining irrelevant variables, and still deliver near unbiased estimates of policy relevant parameters. Finally, they can automatically conduct a range of pertinent tests of specification and mis-specification. To do so, a carefully structured search is required from a general model that contains all the substantively relevant features, an approach known as general-to-specific, with the abbreviation *Gets*. This chapter introduces some of the key concepts, developed in more detail later.

1.1 Overview

In many respects, automatic model selection has come of age. This book reports the outcomes of several decades of research into the properties of choosing a model, or models, from a large class of candidates, usually suggested by theoretical ideas and aimed to characterize the available data evidence and extant empirical findings. The properties of such empirical models are determined by how they are formulated, selected, estimated, and evaluated, as well as by the data quality and coverage, the initial subject-matter theory, institutional knowledge and previous findings. All these steps are prone to difficulties, even for experts. Models may be mis-formulated by omitting important determinants, mis-specifying dynamic reactions, choosing incorrect functional forms, or not knowing of substantial structural breaks among many other potential mistakes. They may be mis-estimated because of data contamination, invalid conditioning, or as a consequence of a variety of mis-specifications. And they may change within sample, or over a forecast period.

To state that a model is mis-specified entails that there exists an object for which it is not the correct representation: we refer to that object as the local data generation process (with the acronym of LDGP), namely the process by which the variables under analysis were generated, including how they were measured. Such a process in economics is immensely complicated: economies are high dimensional (involving millions of decisions by its agents, often with conflicting objectives); they evolve from many sources of innovation (legal, social, political, technical, and financial: compare an OECD economy today with itself 1000 years ago); and are non-constant from intermittent sudden shifts in policy and agents' behavior. Discovering the properties of LDGPs through developing viable empirical models thereof is a key objective of many modeling exercises, and selecting a model from the set of possible representations plays a central role in that discovery process.

Models of empirical phenomena are developed for numerous reasons. The most obvious is to numerically characterize the available evidence, often seeking a parsimonious form. Another is to test a theory or less stringently, evaluate how well it does against the evidence on some metrics, such as goodness of fit, and the signs and magnitudes of the resulting parameter estimates. Yet another class of reasons concerns forecasting future outcomes, but here other considerations intrude, including who the users might be, the purposes for which they require forecasts and sudden unanticipated breaks. Policy models have even more demanding requirements if a change in a policy instrument is to alter the desired target in the expected direction, time scale, and magnitude. In each case, the criteria differ for choosing one empirical model rather than another, but all share the common need to select a model. To overly summarize, the aim of our approach is to discover an empirical model that does not depart substantively from the evidence, and that can account for the results of rival models of the same data. The former is called congruence, in that the model matches the evidence—as two congruent triangles match each other. The latter is called encompassing, as the selected model essentially puts a fence round all other contending models, which thereby become otiose. The LDGP would be congruent with its own evidence, and encompass other models thereof, so models which are non-congruent or non-encompassing must be misspecified representations of that LDGP. Thus, only by selecting a congruent encompassing representation can one discover the LDGP, and thereby understand how the chosen data variables were generated.

Selection is essentially inevitable in social sciences and related disciplines, since many features of a model's specification are imprecise, such as special effects due to political or military turbulence, seasonality (or even diurnality depending on the frequency of the data), and evolutionary, or sometimes abrupt, changes in the legislative, technological or social milieu, all affecting aspects of a model on which any theory or prior reasoning is relatively, or completely, silent. All data analyses involve a multitude of decisions about what to model, applied to what choice of data, how to formulate the model class, conditional on which variables, testing or selecting at what significance levels, and using what estimation methods. If valid inferences are to result, other data features such as the serial correlation of the residuals, or the possible non-linearity of reactions, will need empirical investigation, again entailing selection. Correctly allowing a priori for precisely everything that matters empirically is essentially impossible in a social science: consequently, many aspects must be based on the data properties, and sometimes too many features need to be taken into account together to be analyzed by a human.

Automatic selection methods can outperform in these settings, by creating, and then empirically investigating, a vastly wider range of possibilities than even the greatest experts. Prior reasoning, past findings, model selection, evaluation and estimation are all involved in discovery of the LDGP. A general framework within which search is conducted must reflect current understanding, and every postulated model must be critically evaluated and validly estimated to ensure it is a good specification given the evidence. However, not all of the possible candidate explanations will be helpful, so some can be eliminated to keep the final analysis more comprehensible and tractable. This book will explain how automatic modeling methods function in this context, and why they can succeed, illustrating by empirical and simulation examples.

1.2 Why automatic methods?

An automatic method offers a number of advantages over manual

1. *Speed*–with (say) 100 candidate explanatory variables there are too many combinations, or search paths, to explore manually.

2. *Numerosity*–it is easy to create general models that are too large for humans to understand or manipulate.

3. *Complexity*–multiple breaks, non-linearities, dynamics, systems, exogeneity, integrability, interactions, etc., need to be addressed jointly when selecting substantively relevant variables.

4. *Expertise*–software can build in best practice knowledge in an expert framework.

5. *Objectivity and replicability*–an algorithm should always find the same outcome given the same data, initial specification and selection criteria.

The first is simply the next stage up from calculation, exploiting a comparative advantage of computers, and assumes that simplification is justified, so tries to deliver a parsimonious and comprehensible final outcome. A structured path search can be executed quickly and efficiently, and thereby highlight which variables, and combinations thereof, merit consideration. There are $2^{100} \approx 10^{30}$ possible models for 100 variables, each model created by including and excluding every variable in combination. Even computing 1000 regressions per nano second, an investigator would take more than 10^{10} years to estimate every possible model. Thus, an efficient search is imperative. We distinguish between model selection, as just described, and model discovery based on variable selection as in *Gets*, where, since there are only 100 variables, a feasible approach can be developed, as shown below.

The second concerns creating a sufficiently general model to nest the relevant LDGP. Chapter 6 outlines the theory of reduction, which is the basis whereby the complicated and high dimensional data-generating process (denoted DGP) of an economy is reduced to the local data-generating process (the LDGP above), which is the DGP in the space of the variables under analysis. Two distinct stages are involved. The first concerns specifying the set of variables to be investigated: this defines which LDGP is the target. The second concerns the formulation of the general model which nests that LDGP, from which admissible simplifications will be investigated to locate the most parsimonious, congruent and encompassing representation. As we show below, large numbers of candidate variables (of which a much smaller number happen to matter) can be created and handled without too much difficulty by an automatic method, although a human would flounder.

A variable is relevant if it enters the LDGP. However, it is deemed to be *substantively relevant* only if it would be significant for the available sample at a conventional level when efficiently estimating the LDGP. Similarly, a variable is irrelevant if it does not enter the LDGP, and is *substantively irrelevant* if it is not substantively relevant. While sample-size and significance-level dependent, such a pragmatic definition is needed in practice. In essence, substantively irrelevant variables would not be retained even if the form of the LDGP was known but conventional inference was conducted, so their role would not be discovered even in that ideal setting. That does not entail that the effects of omitting such variables are negligible, merely that data evidence cannot discriminate between them and genuinely irrelevant variables, although theory information or institutional knowledge could lead to their retention despite insignificance, as addressed in section 3.13.

The third issue (complexity) confronts most empirical models of economic time series, where the proliferation of difficult formulation problems can daunt even the greatest expert. In particular, since most economic variables are inter-correlated, unmodeled non-constancies can seriously distort outcomes, whether such non-constancies are direct (when parameter changes within a model are not taken into account), or indirect (when important variables that are omitted change). Consequently, the fact that change is the norm in economies entails that almost nothing is correct in a model till everything substantive is included, reinforcing the need for general models as the starting point for empirical analyses, albeit judged by a congruent, parsimonious, encompassing final selection.

The fourth advantage is the possibility of embodying a learning step, since a good algorithm should incorporate new developments. Already, *Autometrics*, an Ox Package implementing automatic *Gets* (see Doornik,

2009d, 2009a) improves over both Hoover and Perez (1999) and Hendry and Krolzig (2001). Various aspects of earlier approaches have been removed as unhelpful, and new steps incorporated, a process that can continue as insights accrue. Indeed, being able to efficiently handle more candidate variables than there are observations, as shown below, is just such an improvement.

The fifth is a natural feature of a deterministic algorithm. However, and much more interesting, in practice the algorithm can find the same result from many different starting general models when all the additional variables are in fact irrelevant. Such an outcome is a final response to John Maynard Keynes's famous jibe in his critique of Jan Tinbergen (1939, 1940):

> ... the seventy translators of the Septuagint were shut up in seventy separate rooms with the Hebrew text and brought out with them, when they emerged, seventy identical translations. Would the same miracle be vouchsafed if seventy multiple correlators were shut up with the same statistical material?
>
> Keynes (1939, 1940)

If any additional variables actually mattered, then a different model should of course be found.

Combining these ideas opens the door to empirical model discovery. An automatic program can formulate a vastly more general model than any human investigator, embedding all available theoretical, institutional, and data knowledge as well as previous findings, allowing for all the potential features of a complicated LDGP, then search for the set of congruent parsimonious-encompassing final selections, revealing aspects not previously considered. To do so successfully, however, requires a carefully structured approach, as we now explain.

1.3   The route ahead

We will focus on the approach underlying *Autometrics*, embodied in the widely-used *PcGive* software, but will also discuss the relative performance of other approaches, which will in turn explain why we prefer *Autometrics*. This part will address the principles of selection. The present chapter summarizes the remainder of the book. Chapter 2 discusses the background in scientific discovery, then section 2.4 considers earlier, sometimes implicit, approaches to empirical model discovery in economics and econometrics.

Chapter 3 sets the scene for the rest of the analysis. When the most general unrestricted model (denoted by its acronym GUM) is estimable from the available data, an unbiased estimate of goodness of fit is obtained for the innovation error standard deviation, which provides a bound on how well the variables under analysis can be modeled. Selection then entails a trade-off between minimizing the presence of irrelevant variables on the one hand, and missing too many relevant variables on the other. However, if every lag and non-linear function of all candidate determinants are to be included from the outset, allowing for possible outliers or shifts at any data point, then there are bound to be more variables, N, in total than the number of observations, T, so the GUM cannot in general be estimated: generality and feasibility conflict. To resolve this conundrum, our analysis proceeds in six stages, briefly described in sections 3.4–3.9, and in greater detail in the ensuing chapters 8–15.

Two new terms are helpful to clarify our approach. First, *gauge* denotes the retention rate of irrelevant variables in the selected model, so a gauge of $g = 0.01$ (say) entails that on average one irrelevant variable in a hundred is adventitiously retained in the final selection. A user sets a nominal significance level, $\alpha = 0.01$ say, for conducting individual selection tests, and one criterion for a good selection algorithm is that the resulting g is close to α, so false retention is well controlled. Second, *potency* denotes the retention frequency of relevant variables in selection. Thus, a potency of 90% means that on average, 9 out of 10 substantively relevant variables are retained. This could correspond at one extreme to 9 always being retained and the 10th never; or at the other to all 10 each being kept 90% of the time. These concepts differ importantly from the *size* and *power* of a single statistical test, both because the context is selection, as well as because insignificant irrelevant or relevant variables may sometimes be retained in a selected model for reasons explained below.

Chapter 4 illustrates the concepts in Chapter 3. An artificial DGP enables what is found when *Autometrics* is applied to be checked against what should have been found. Nine topics noted in Chapter 3 are considered: estimating a system of simultaneous equations, diagnostic checking for a well-specified single equation, parsimonious-encompassing tests, testing for non-linearity, handling more candidate variables than observations in the face of breaks, selecting lag lengths despite collinearity, checking for cointegration, implementing both a correct and an incomplete theory, and testing for exogeneity.

Chapter 5 then considers how to evaluate the success of model selection methods in general, as a key step towards model discovery. The analysis leads to adopting three criteria, namely, we will judge a selection algorithm as successful when for the given data sample it jointly achieves the following

1. The algorithm is able to recover the LDGP starting from an initial general model that nests that LDGP almost as often as when starting from the LDGP itself.

2. The operating characteristics of the algorithm match the desired properties, so gauge is close to the adopted nominal significance level, and potency near the theoretical average power of the associated tests, with near unbiased final coefficient estimates.

3. The algorithm could not select better, in that no other congruent model parsimoniously dominates the one that is selected.

The selection algorithm should satisfy all three criteria. However, selection is not a conjuring trick: if the LDGP is almost never found when it is the postulated model, it will not be selected when commencing with additional irrelevant variables. Moreover, we are concerned to discover the LDGP, and there is no theorem linking doing so to successful forecasting (e.g., Clements and Hendry, 1999, Hendry, 2006), so different approaches need to be considered when the objective is *ex ante* forecasting, as addressed in section 3.16 and chapter 23. Finally, phrases like "almost as often" or "near to" need to be calibrated, which is difficult to achieve theoretically, so we present simulation experiments in different states of nature to evaluate the practical success of *Autometrics*, as well as a simulation approach to evaluating its reliability in any specific application.

Chapter 6 explains the derivation of the LDGP from the overall complicated, high dimensional, and evolving data-generating process of the economy under analysis. A well-defined sequence of reduction operations leads from that DGP to the LDGP, which is the generating process in the space of the variables to be analyzed. The resulting LDGP may be complex, non-linear and non-constant from aggregation, marginalization, and sequential factorization, depending on the choice of the set of variables under analysis. Expanding the initial set of variables induces a different LDGP. A good choice of the set of variables—one where there are no, or only small, losses of information from the reductions—is crucial if the DGP is to be viably captured by the LDGP. Given the chosen set of variables to analyze, the LDGP is the best level of knowledge that can be achieved, so it is the **target** for selection in the empirical modeling exercise. The LDGP in turn is approximated by a general model based on a further series of reductions, such that again there are no (or small) losses of information when the LDGP also satisfies those reductions, and if it does not, evidence of departures can be ascertained by appropriate mis-specification tests, so that such reductions are not undertaken. The resulting general unrestricted model (GUM) becomes the initial specification for the ensuing selection search. Measures of the information losses from reduction stages correspond to mis-specification hypotheses to be tested empirically.

Having clarified the central objective of model selection as discovering the LDGP, chapter 7 then describes *Gets* in more detail, noting six main steps in formulating and implementing a *Gets* approach. First, a careful formulation of the GUM for the problem under analysis is essential. Second, the measure of congruence must be decided by choosing the mis-specification tests to be used, their forms, and significance levels. Third, the desired null retention frequencies for selection tests must be set, perhaps with an information criterion to select between mutually encompassing, undominated, congruent models. Fourth, the GUM needs to be appropriately estimated, depending on the weak exogeneity assumptions about the conditioning variables, which then allows congruence to be assessed. Given that the outcome is satisfactory, multiple-path reduction searches can be commenced from the GUM, leading to a set (possibly with just one member) of *terminal* models, namely models where all reductions thus far are acceptable, but all further reductions are rejected at the chosen significance level. These can then be checked for parsimonious encompassing of the GUM. The reliability of the whole process can be investigated by exploring sub-sample outcomes, and simulating the entire selection approach.

Together, these six chapters provide the lead into part II. Chapter 8 explains the baseline approach, denoted "1-cut", which selects a model of the LDGP in just one decision from an estimable constant-parameter nesting model with any number of mutually orthogonal, valid conditioning regressors when $T \gg N$. A Monte Carlo simulation of 1-cut for $N = 1000$ candidate regressors, where only $n = 10$ actually matter and $T = 2000$, shows the viability of selection in such a setting despite an inordinate number of possible models (more than 10^{300}). The aim of this chapter is to establish that model selection *per se* need not entail repeated testing.

Chapter 9 describes some analytical findings about 1-cut when $N = 2$, which although the simplest possible case—especially given that the model nests the LDGP and is known to be congruent without testing—nevertheless highlights the complexities of the resulting distributions of data-based selection estimators. Some authors have used such results to argue against data-based model selection, but the only alternative requires omniscience on the part of all investigators, which is not credible in any social science. When $N = 2$, there is a minimal amount to be discovered, merely whether none, one or two variables matter, so the real reasons for model selection are left out of the analysis, namely all the issues about the validity of the specification of the LDGP. In any practical setting, the costs of omitting key variables, using inappropriate functional form transformations, and failing to account for breaks, far outweigh any costs from an efficient search, but it is nevertheless important to establish what costs of inference are entailed when selecting.

Chapter 10 develops bias corrections for the estimated coefficients of retained variables after model selection, such that approximately unbiased estimates are delivered. That removes one of the costs sometimes attributed to selection, the so-called "pre-test bias" (see e.g., Judge and Bock, 1978). It transpires that these bias corrections—derived for the conditional distributions of relevant variables' estimated coefficients—also drive the estimated coefficients of irrelevant variables towards the origin, substantially reducing their mean squared errors (MSEs) in both conditional and unconditional distributions. That results in small costs from retaining irrelevant variables, even when the GUM has a large number of potential candidates.

Chapter 11 first describes how the *Autometrics* algorithm is structured in section 11.2, then evaluates its properties compared to 1-cut. Based on a tree search, *Autometrics* explores feasible search paths, eliminating unnecessary searches and checking both parsimonious encompassing of the estimable GUM and congruence of the selected models. The framework remains the same as in chapter 8, namely a congruent, constant-parameter regression model in mutually orthogonal, valid conditioning variables, but unlike 1-cut, *Autometrics* does not require orthogonality. Despite exploring many paths, there is no deterioration in the selection quality, and in some respects *Autometrics* outperforms 1-cut, even when the latter is applicable.

Chapter 12 considers the impact of undertaking diagnostic tests to check the congruence of selections. Doing so is bound to affect the operating characteristics of the *Autometrics* algorithm relative to being certain a priori that the GUM and all selected models are congruent, so we explore the costs of the testing required. The converse costs of not testing are that the selected model may be non-congruent, which might adversely affect inferences during selection.

Chapter 13 examines the role of encompassing in model selection. If there are distinct competing empirical models of some economic phenomena, then all but one must either be incomplete or incorrect—and all may be. Encompassing checks whether one model can account for the results found by the others, so can also be used to evaluate the different empirical models that arise during simplification. Since all empirical models are encompassed by the LDGP—knowledge of that LDGP allows one to account for all their findings, even when some models are not nested with respect to others—it is natural to seek models which encompass the LDGP. That motivates our selection strategy: specify a GUM which aims to nest the LDGP, then simplify it to a final model that is as parsimonious as feasible while still encompassing the GUM. This is called parsimonious encompassing, and helps control the gauge close to the nominal size, while avoiding potency losses from missing important relevant variables.

Chapter 14 considers embedding theory models in the selection process based on Hendry and Johansen (2014). A theory often has relatively clear implications as to which variables are definitely included in a model, even if the precise functional form, location shifts, or lag lengths may be left open. *Autometrics* allows such variables to be classified as *retained*, such that they are never eliminated, irrespective of their significance. A search with retained variables then finds the most parsimonious undominated congruent model which includes those theory variables. However, retained theory variables may or may not be significant in the final model—the search is not restricted to seeking the best model in which they enter significantly. By orthogonalizing all other variables with respect to those to be retained, under the null that the theory model is complete and correct, the parameter estimator distributions are unaffected by selection. Hendry and Mizon (2011) investigate the advantages of retaining theory variables while selecting in a general model compared to imposing that theory model on the data.

Chapter 15 introduces the first instance of more variables than observations ($N > T$) when an impulse indicator (dummy variable) is created for every observation in the model and added to the candidate set. This approach is designed to detect shifts, outliers and data discrepancies, and thereby help ensure near normality to sustain valid inferences and viable bias corrections. The procedure, *impulse-indicator saturation*, is denoted by its acronym IIS below. The T indicator variables are entered (in the simplest case) in blocks of $T/2$: first, add half the indicators, record the significant outcomes, then drop that set of indicators. Now add the other half, selecting significant ones again, noting that indicators are mutually orthogonal. These two steps each correspond to dummying out $T/2$ observations for estimation of the remaining parameters. Now combine the retained indicators and select those that are significant jointly. Since αT indicators will be retained adventitiously on average under the null that none matter, by setting $\alpha \leq 1/T$ (for example) the average false null retention rate will be at most one outlier, equivalent to losing 1 observation, which is a tiny efficiency loss for checking the potential occurrence of outliers at T observations. Formal analyses are feasible in this setting, so the resulting large-sample distributions and efficiencies can be obtained. The theory generalizes to more, and unequal, splits, as well as to dynamic models, and is related to robust estimation (see Hendry et al., 2008, and Johansen and Nielsen, 2009). IIS has demonstrated both the feasibility of handling more variables than observations and the surprisingly small costs of doing so, and will play a crucial role in model discovery, tackling multiple shifts and evaluating the validity of conditioning.

Chapter 16 provides an empirical illustration, re-modeling real aggregate UK consumers' expenditure following Davidson et al. (1978), where some features of the model are not derivable from economic theory or institutional knowledge, including the complete set of explanatory variables, their lag lengths, the form of seasonality, as well as both outliers and policy interventions. We first review the previous findings reported in Davidson et al. (1978), and evaluate how much, if at all, their results might have changed by using recent modeling methods.

Chapter 17 carries out some simulation-based comparisons with a number of other approaches, including step-wise regression, information criteria (such as AIC, Akaike, 1973, or BIC, Schwarz, 1978), the Lasso (e.g., Tibshirani, 1996), and RETINA (see Perez-Amaral, Gallo and White, 2003, 2005, and Castle, 2005), as well as investigating improvements over earlier algorithms such as Hoover and Perez (1999) and *PcGets*. Section 17.2 describes the main Monte Carlo experimental designs used in the book

Part III describes extensions in automatic model selection and empirical model discovery. Chapter 19 investigates the general setting when there are more variables than observations, which can arise both when sample sizes are small, or candidate regressor sets are large. Simulations suggest the outcome is similar to the case of impulse-indicator saturation (IIS), with the cost of examining N additional irrelevant candidate regressors being αN, and hence a small loss in degrees of freedom with a concomitant increase in estimation uncertainty. The choice of α matters, as we show in a simulation experiment where $N > T$, when there is a higher probability of finding the LDGP at a tighter significance level.

Chapter 20 applies IIS to processes with multiple shifts. Chapter 15 considered the theory under the null of no outliers or shifts, and showed that the cost under the null was small, but the objective was to detect and model shifts or outliers when they are present. Simulation experiments examine a range of cases from a single break, through multiple shifts, to many outliers. We also illustrate the practical advantages of IIS, using data on US real interest rates in Garcia and Perron (1996), then extending that data set to a much longer sample to compare IIS with the test in Bai and Perron (1998).

Chapter 21 considers selecting non-linear models. Instead of extending the previous best linear model, which is a specific-to-general approach, we commence from a computable general non-linear approximation. Such a formulation needs to be congruent and identified. The former is achieved by the generality of the approximation, using the low-dimensional portmanteau approach in Castle and Hendry (2010a), applicable even when there are large numbers of potential non-linear regressors (including more than the sample size), and the latter by testing the significance of the non-linear additions. Once a congruent parsimonious non-linear model is selected, one can test whether theory-based functions (such as logistic or squashing) further simplify the model. This approach both avoids a possible lack of identification under the null of linearity when such functions are non-linear in parameters, and encompassing tests check that the postulated functions are a complete characterization of the non-linearity. Again, IIS plays an important role in removing outliers and shifts, which can be confounded with non-linearity, as illustrated by Castle and Hendry (2011b).

Chapter 22 describes an automatically computable test of super exogeneity with null rejection frequencies close to the nominal size, and potency against failures (see Hendry and Santos, 2010). IIS is applied to marginal models of the supposed exogenous variables that enter the conditional model contemporaneously, with all significant indicators recorded. The collected indicators are then added to the conditional model and tested for significance. Under the null of super exogeneity, the test has the correct gauge for a range of nominal significance levels of marginal-model saturation tests, both when those processes are constant, and when they undergo shifts in either or both mean or variance. Failures of super exogeneity from a violation of weak exogeneity are shown to be detectable when there are location shifts in the marginal models. The large sample distribution and potency of the test are derived and simulated, and illustrated by an application to testing super exogeneity in UK money demand.

Finally, chapter 23 discusses the different considerations that matter when formulating, selecting or using a forecasting model, given the prevalence of breaks in economic data processes and the associated forecast failures that result. Practical forecasting methods rely on extrapolating presently available information into the future. No matter how good such methods or models are, they require that the future resembles the present in the relevant attributes, which intermittent unanticipated shifts violate. To date, future shifts have eluded being predicted, although some developments are occurring (e.g., Castle, Fawcett and Hendry, 2010, 2011). Consequently, different considerations matter when formulating, selecting or using a forecasting model when the data processes are wide-sense non-stationary. Technically, strict stationarity requires a distribution to remain invariant over time, but unfortunately, the term non-stationary has been taken as a synonym for integrated, which is indeed a source of non-stationarity, but not the only source. By wide-sense non-stationarity, we refer to any changes in the distribution. If no location shifts ever occurred, then the most parsimonious, congruent, undominated model in-sample would tend to dominate out of sample as well. In practice, the robustness to location shifts of a model formulation is essential for avoiding systematic forecast failure, which may entail selecting from a different class of models that need not even be congruent in-sample. The chapter emphasizes the major difference between selecting a model of the LDGP for understanding or policy—where it is essential to disentangle and model all relevant variables and parameter changes—and selecting a model for forecasting, where only the effects of those changes need to be captured by the relevant device to make useful statements about likely future outcomes. Since automatic *Gets* seeks to locate the LDGP, even complete success at doing so need not improve forecasting. However, by transforming a selected congruent encompassing model to a more robust form before it is used in forecasting, causal information can be retained while avoiding systematic forecast failure. Thus, even in the forecasting arena, discovering the LDGP can be valuable.

2 Discovery

This chapter begins by discussing some of the many ways in which discoveries have been made in physical and biological sciences. There seem to be seven common aspects of such discoveries and their subsequent evaluations. Despite important differences, discovery and evaluation in economics are similar to those of other sciences, and the same seven common aspects can be discerned. The complexity of macroeconomic data intrinsically involves empirical discovery with theory evaluation, as well as requiring rigorous evaluation of selected models to ascertain their viability. Directly fitting a theory-specified model limits the potential for discovery. Retrospectively, covert discovery has been common in empirical econometrics.

2.1 Scientific discovery

We first discuss the general issue of scientific discovery, and how it takes place, then apply that notion to empirical econometrics.[1]

A discovery is learning something previously unknown. Since one cannot know how to discover what is not known, there is unlikely to be a best way of doing so. That does not preclude some ways being better than others—not looking is rarely a good way. Building on ancient Greek philosophers, the scientific method developed in the Arabic world during the early Middle Ages with the works of scholars like Al-Biruni and Ibn Sina (Avincenna), and was formalized in England by Roger Bacon (see, e.g., Hackett, 1997). The scientific method was a major advance, as it highlighted where gaps in knowledge existed, delivered

---

[1]This chapter extends the discussion of the relationship between scientific discovery and empirical econometric modeling in Hendry (1980) and Hendry (1995b), and draws on the discussions in Hendry (2011a) and Hendry (2011b) to set the scene for the concept of empirical model discovery.

a systematic approach to filling those gaps, and in due course consolidated the findings in general theories and formulae. Even so, in both the natural and biological sciences, many discoveries had an element of chance, and most imaginable ways of discovering new knowledge have succeeded in some settings: see Mason (1962), Messadié (1991) and compare Popper (1959).

The progressivity of science is its most manifest feature: empirical evidence is accumulated and matched by broader theoretical ideas that cohere together. We understand much more than the ancient or medieval worlds: electricity lights our world (see Fouquet and Pearson, 2006, on the increases in available lumens since 1300); computers calculate; planes fly; etc. As noted in Hendry (2009), we can predict what changes to computer chips will, or will not, speed up calculations, and what aircraft designs will not fly. The path that leads to a scientific discovery is irrelevant to its validity, and could be serendipity, careful testing, or a theory prediction, whereas stringent evaluation and replicability are crucial. In practice, theories are rarely rejected by evidence alone, and tend only to be replaced when better theories are developed, explaining more and accounting for previous anomalies (see Lakatos, 1974, and the views on "scientific revolutions" in Kuhn, 1962).

Science has often been seen as synonymous with experimentation. Indeed, the examples of discovery through experiments are far too many to list, but systematic experimental exploration of all the alternatives is well represented by Antoine Lavoisier isolating and establishing the properties of oxygen, thereby refuting phlogiston theory (see, e.g., Musgrave, 1976), by Robert Boyle formulating his law of gases (see, e.g., Agassi, 1977), and by Benjamin Thompson, Count Rumford, whose experiments on heat refuted the caloric theory then prevalent, and opened the door to modern thermodynamics (see Brown, 2001). Nevertheless, although frequently an invaluable approach, experimentation is neither necessary (astronomy) nor sufficient (alchemy) to define a science: Harré (1981) provides an excellent analysis of the historical role of great experiments in science.

Luck and serendipity are common sources of discoveries, notwithstanding the intended systematic nature of science. Famous examples include Alexander Fleming's discovery of penicillin (see, e.g., Henderson, 1997), Henri Becquerel's discovery of radioactivity, for which he shared the Nobel Prize with Pierre and Marie Curie,[2] and more recently,

---

[2]nobelprize.org/nobel_prizes/physics/laureates/1903/becquerel-bio.html.

Arno Penzias and Robert Wilson uncovering the background cosmic microwave radiation.[3] In the first two cases, and even more so with, say, Archimedes's Eureka discovery, recognition of the significance of what is found is also crucial (i.e., why raised bath water allowed the assessment of an object's density). However, brilliant intuition can also succeed, as with Michael Faraday's dynamo (see e.g., Holton, 1986)

Discovery has been driven both by false theories, as with Johannes Kepler's attempts to characterize the planetary orbits by regular solids, yet leading to his three famous laws (see, e.g., Holton, 1988); and "correct" theories, as with Arthur Eddington's test of Albert Einstein's theory of relativity by the gravitational effects of the sun bending light (see his own account in Eddington, 1928), or Louis Pasteur's germ theory of disease leading to pasteurization and rejection of Aristotle's notion of spontaneous generation (despite objections that were seemingly valid at the time when thermophiles were unknown: see Waller, 2002).

Pure theoretical reasoning has also been a major force for discovery, with often-cited examples being the immense advances following from Isaac Newton's theory of universal gravitation, and Einstein's theories just noted above. Other classic examples include uniform motion by Galileo Galilei (see Drake, 1980); the electro-magnetic spectrum derived by James Clerk Maxwell (see Harman, 1998); black-body radiation analyzed by Max Planck leading to Planck's constant;[4]; quantum theory proposed by Niels Bohr;[5] the positron predicted by Paul Dirac;[6] and the quark postulated by Murray Gell-Mann.[7] The most recent is perhaps the empirical confirmation of the Higgs Boson, first postulated in 1964 to explain why some particles have mass.[8] Some of these were partly evidence based, as with Newton's knowledge of Kepler's laws of planetary motion, whereas others were pure thought experiments, but all required later independent empirical evaluation.

Conversely, careful observation led to William Harvey's model of the circulation of blood in the human body (see Schultz, 2002), to William Herschel discovering the planet Uranus (see Holmes, 2008), to John Snow's tracking down the water borne source of cholera (see, e.g., Smith, 2002, but contrast McLeod, 2000), and to Edwin Hubble's discovering

---

[3]nobelprize.org/nobel_prizes/physics/laureates/1978/wilson-lecture.html.
[4]nobelprize.org/nobel_prizes/physics/laureates/1918/planck-bio.html.
[5]nobelprize.org/nobel_prizes/physics/laureates/1922/bohr-bio.html.
[6]nobelprize.org/nobel_prizes/physics/laureates/1933/dirac-bio.html.
[7]nobelprize.org/nobel_prizes/physics/laureates/1969/gell-mann-bio.html.
[8]nobelprize.org/nobel_prizes/physics/laureates/2013/higgs-facts.html.

that light from distant astronomical objects was red-shifted in proportion to their distance (see, e.g., Nussbaumer and Bieri, 2009).

The invention of new instruments enabled Galileo Galilei's discovery of the moons of Jupiter by a telescope (see Drake, 1980), and of microbes by Robert Hooke and Antonie van Leeuwenhoek using microscopes (see, e.g., Gest, 2002, and Bennett, Cooper, Hunter and Jardine, 2003). The "natural experiment" of the Second World War reduced, then its termination raised, wheat consumption in the Netherlands, which first dramatically lowered then raised the death rate of young sufferers of celiac disease, and so led to the identification of gluten as the cause (see Fasano, 2009). Often self testing was involved, most recently with Barry Marshall drinking *Helicobacter pylori* to demonstrate that they caused ulcers, followed by antibiotics to show the cure.[9] Finally, trial and error on a vast scale was Thomas Edison's route to producing an incandescent lamp (see Nelson, 1959, albeit the British scientist Joseph Swan had previously invented a workable light bulb).

Other examples abound over time and across countries: there are many systematic and non-systematic ways of making discoveries. Science is systematic only in retrospect. Neverthless, just as this book concerns automatic model selection as part of empirical model discovery in observational disciplines, King et al. (2009) propose to automate science.

2.2   Evaluating scientific discoveries

Science is a deductive, not an inductive, discipline in the important sense articulated by John Herschel (1830) in his distinction between the context of discovery, which we have just discussed, and the context of evaluation, later re-emphasized by Popper (1963). Empirical findings remain anomalies until situated within a theory; and science seeks an interlinked system of theories that mutually support the interpretations of evidence: the dating of fossils, plate tectonics, and geological time frames are a classic instance. Theories are abandoned only when a new theory can cover most of the existing ground and explain some new phenomena, albeit that many empirical discoveries have led to changes in theories, an issue we revisit in section 5.8. The consolidation of evidence plays a crucial role: the classic and perhaps most famous is Einstein's $E = mc^2$, which summarizes a remarkable amount in a simple formula (see, e.g., Farmelo, 2002). Without such summaries, the mass of data

---

[9]Humourously recounted in nobelprize.org/nobel_prizes/medicine/laureates/2005/marshall-lecture.html., which should encourage others to persist with their research despite initial skepticism.

would overwhelm with huge costs of knowledge consumption (Sims, 1996, argues that data reduction is a key attribute of science: also see Friedman, 1974).

The boundary between discovery and evaluation is not always clear cut, but a warrant as to the reality of any claim has to be established independently of the discovery process. Since anything goes in the former, as section 2.1 stressed, stringent evaluation is required in the latter (e.g., Mayo and Spanos, 2006). Not all scientists are totally objective, as egos and dogmatism can combine with career ambitions to go beyond, or even distort, their findings, and fraud is not unknown (e.g., Waller, 2002). However, a key attribute of the scientific process is that blockages and previously undiscovered frauds are relatively temporary, as the same behaviors that created them motivate others to attack and overturn invalid claims.

A warrant therefore has to invoke new data, new evidence, new instruments, or new tests. William Herschel's discoverery of Uranus, the first recorded extension of our knowledge of the solar system, occurred because he had a detailed map of the night sky in his brain, and could perceive change against that map, although some attributed his finding to luck. Nevertheless, he was uncertain himself initially, and the new celestial object was only accorded the status of a planet when it was clear that there was no tail (as comets have), that its orbit was calculated by Anders Lexell to be round the sun, and its sighting was reliably replicated by others (see the excellent account in Holmes, 2008).[10] Chapter 23 discusses some of the difficulties facing the use of forecasts to evaluate models in empirical economics.

2.3   Common aspects of scientific discoveries

Despite the diversity in how discoveries were achieved, including creative theory, ideas inspired through evidence or anomalies, to luck or chance, there are seven aspects in common to all the above examples of discovery. First, the *theoretical context*, or more generally, the pre-existing framework of ideas, which may inhibit progress (phlogiston is a classic example), or be a stimulus (as with quantum theory). Secondly, going beyond, or *outside*, the existing state, by greater generality, a new tool or instrument, a chance innovation, or a broader idea or perspective. Thirdly, the *search* for something: what is found may not have been the

---

[10]Possibly why his son John emphasized the distinction between discovery and evaluation in Herschel (1830).

original aim, though it certainly was on some occasions, but there was an objective from the outset to be discovered. Fourthly, *recognition* of the significance of what is found: the discovery usually relied in part on fortune favoring the prepared mind. Fifthly, *quantifying* what is found, by appropriate measurements or experiments. Sixthly, *evaluating* the discovery to ascertain its reality, sometimes by checking replicability, sometimes by testing in new settings. Finally, *parsimoniously summarizing* all the available information.

2.4   Discovery in economics

To date in economics, most discoveries have arisen from theoretical advances, as histories of economic thought from Schumpeter (1954) to Blaug (1980) emphasize. Histories of econometrics, such as Morgan (1990) and Qin (1993), also focus on its theoretical advances (but see Qin, 2013), and while they discuss applied research as well, are not filled with major empirical discoveries that have stood the test of time. Even so, much of previous econometrics has covertly concerned discovery, as we now explain.

Consider an observable variable, y, which is postulated to depend on a set of candidate explanatory variables x, when a sample of T observations is available denoted $\{y_t, x_t\}$ for $t = 1, \ldots, T$. The economic analysis suggests that:

$$y = f(x), \tag{2.1}$$

where the form of $f(\cdot)$ in (2.1) depends on a range of possible theory choices of (e.g.) the utility or loss functions of agents, the precise formulations of the constraints they face, the information they possess, and the unknown effects of aggregation across heterogeneous individuals with different endowments and parameter values. Moreover, theories rarely exactly specify units of time, so data availability usually determines the length from t to $t+1$. Empirically, successive observations are generally dependent, and lag responses are not known, again possibly differing across agents. The quality of the observed data is never perfect, so observations may be mis-measured or even contaminated, leading to outliers. Nor are the underlying processes necessarily stationary, with evolutionary changes ongoing, leading to integrated series, and abrupt shifts inducing various forms of breaks. Thus, many key features of any empirical model are bound to be unknown at the outset of an investigation, however good the prior theory. Fortunately, as the natural and biological sciences have amply shown, new knowledge can still be acquired: all the answers do not need to be known from the outset, even though some economists insist on an approach that appears to do so.

Discovery and evaluation in economics have tended to be categorized as construction and destruction, where the former has been viewed with suspicion when not simply quantifying a pre-specified theory model, and the latter as an annoyance when pet theories are rejected. Combined, such views have led to a denial of either role for econometrics:

> To criticize or reject a model because it is an abstraction is foolish. All models are necessarily abstractions... In fact, searching within some parametric class of economies for the one that best fits a set of aggregate time series makes little sense...

> Kydland and Prescott (1996)

This approach is distinctly non-scientific, as violating evidence ceases to be a concern. Hendry (1995c) provides a critique of that approach to business-cycle modeling, and the developments in chapter 14 provide a way to nest theory-driven and data-driven methodologies (see Bårdsen, den Reijer, Jonasson and Nymoen, 2012, for a related implementation).

We now consider the implicit role of discovery in the five main extant approaches to econometric modeling for the simplest case of a regression equation, as generalizations to other model classes are fairly straightforward.

2.4.1 Classical econometrics
Here it is postulated that:

$$y_t = \beta' g(x_t) + \epsilon_t, \quad t = 1, \ldots, T, \tag{2.2}$$

possibly after data transformations (such as logarithms) which make linearity reasonable, assuming $g(x_t) = x_t$ or is a known function. The aim is to obtain the best estimate of β, given the correct variables, x, and an uncontaminated set of observations, $\mathcal{T}$. Auxiliary assumptions often include that $\epsilon_t \sim \mathsf{IID}\left[0, \sigma_\epsilon^2\right]$ (denoting an Independent, Identically Distributed random variable), and perhaps a set of instrumental variables $\{z_t\}$ (often the $\{x_t\}$) claimed to be independent of ϵ_t, which determine the choice of estimation method as least squares or instrumental variables, or one of dozens of closely related methods (e.g., Hendry, 1976). Departures from the assumptions underlying (2.2) are treated as problems to be solved, such as residual serial correlation or heteroskedasticity; data contamination, outliers or structural breaks; omitted variables, functional-form mis-specification, etc. Most econometric textbooks provide tests for discovering if such problems are present, often followed by recipes for fixing them. Indeed, unless (2.2) is perfectly pre-specified, all these other issues must be resolved from the data evidence. In practice, such an approach is too often covert and unstructured empirical model discovery, with investigators patching their specifications to avoid the most egregious flaws, then reporting estimates as if they were the first attempt: see the criticisms in Leamer (1983) who parodied this as "The econometric art as it is practiced at the computer terminal involves fitting many, perhaps thousands, of statistical models. One or several that the researcher finds pleasing are selected for reporting purposes".

2.4.2 Model selection

Although the starting point is a model written like (2.2), again given the correct initial x, $g(\cdot)$ and $\mathcal{T}$, a major difference is that x now includes a large set of candidate regressors, which is anticipated to include all the relevant explanatory variables, their functional forms and lags etc., but perhaps also some irrelevant (or small) effects. The aim is to first find the subset of relevant variables, x_t^* say, eliminate the irrelevant, and then estimate the associated parameters, β^*. Thus, the setting is more general than section 2.4.1, and the need to discover the relevant subset of variables is explicitly recognized, but again, auxiliary assumptions may include that $\epsilon_t \sim \text{IID}\left[0, \sigma_\epsilon^2\right]$, with a set of instrumental variables $\{z_t\}$ (again often the $\{x_t\}$) assumed independent of ϵ_t, determining the choice of estimation method as before. As with classical econometrics, departures from the assumptions underlying (2.2) are usually treated as problems to be solved, such as residual serial correlation, heteroskedasticity, or structural breaks etc., although some selection methods simply ignore all such problems to select the best model on their given criterion.

2.4.3 Robust statistics

Despite the differences at first sight, the aim now is to find a robust estimate of β in (2.2) by selecting over $\mathcal{T}$, assuming the correct set of relevant variables x, and $g(x_t)$ known. The key focus is avoiding the problems created by data contamination and outliers, so attention is paid to discovering a sample, $\mathcal{T}^*$, where those are least in evidence. However, other difficulties, such as residual serial correlation or heteroskedasticity, structural breaks, functional-form mis-specification etc., still all need separate tests to be detected, and x rarely includes a large set of candidate regressors to be selected over jointly with $\mathcal{T}^*$, so is essentially assumed to be x^*.

2.4.4 Non-parametric statistics

The objective is again to find a robust estimate of β in (2.2) assuming the correct set of relevant variables x, but not specifying the functional form, $g(\cdot)$, of the relation. The approach seeks to discover $g(\cdot)$ without assuming a specific mathematical function, and possibly also leaving the error distribution unspecified. As before, mis-specification needs to be checked, x rarely includes many candidate regressors, so is once more assumed to be x^*, and data contamination can be pernicious as it distorts the function found, but selection over $\mathcal{T}$ jointly with a non-parametric analysis is uncommon. Most of the literature on robust statistics largely ignores such difficulties (e.g., Maronna, Martin and Yohai, 2006).

2.5 Empirical model discovery in economics

We can now clarify what empirical model discovery entails in economics. Most specifications of models intended to be matched against data are derived from a pre-existing theory. For example, (2.1) in section 2.4 was probably derived from an optimization problem postulated for a single agent, subject to some implicit ceteris paribus conditions. There are many styles of implementation, from tight theoretical specifications to be calibrated quantitatively, to using (2.1) as a guide to the set of variables and the possible form of relationship. To be applicable to the real world, economic theory has to explain the behavior of agents, who create the DGP. The LDGP is a reduction of the DGP to a subset of variables believed still to capture the relevant behavior. However, since so many features of any model are unknown until the data are investigated, it seems crucial to re-frame empirical modeling as a discovery process, part of a progressive research strategy of accumulating empirical evidence. There are two distinct stages.

The first step is specifying $\{y_t\}$ and the N basic variables $\{x_t\}$ defining an LDGP intended to provide useful economic knowledge. That is almost certainly best based on subject-matter theory in the light of past evidence and the institutional background. As the LDGP is the target of the analysis, the choice of x is crucial. In wide-sense non-stationary processes, ceteris paribus does not apply empirically, so too small a set of variables under consideration may make it impossible to establish constant models interpretable by the original theory. The global impact of the late 2000's financial crisis has been a salutary reminder that everything is interconnected in economics. Early theories characterized that as general equilibrium, but a general sequential dynamic dis-equilibrium would be a better description. In either formulation, many variables interact, usually with lagged reactions, and often via well-established channels such as credit, exchange rates, interest rates etc. But a larger set of variables is less likely to exclude what are in fact important influences, at the possible cost of retaining adventitious effects. These are asymmetric costs: the former is an order one error, the latter of order $1/T$. Thus, it seems strongly preferable to err on the side of profligacy at this stage, and over, rather than under, include.

The second stage is to embed the chosen set x in a more general model with $x_t \ldots x_{t-s}$ and non-linear terms $g(x_t) \ldots g(x_{t-s})$, where the longest lag is $s \geq 0$ periods and $g(\cdot)$ denotes the appropriate functions of the subset of the basic variables x, jointly with a set of T indicators for breaks and outliers denoted $1_{\{i=t\}}$, leading to the GUM:

$$y_t = \sum_{j=0}^{s} \beta_j' x_{t-j} + \sum_{j=0}^{s} \kappa_j' g(x_{t-j}) + \sum_{j=1}^{s} \lambda_j y_{t-j} + \sum_{i=1}^{T} \delta_i 1_{\{i=t\}} + \epsilon_t. \qquad (2.3)$$

The aim is to discover the parameters $\{\beta_i^*\}$ associated with the relevant functions $g(x_{t-i}^*)$, including lags and indicators as necessary. Collecting the retained indicators in the vector d, the finally chosen model is the congruent parsimonious-encompassing representation:

$$y_t = \sum_{i=1}^{s^*} \lambda_i y_{t-i} + \sum_{i=0}^{s^*} (\beta_i^*)' x_{t-i}^* + \sum_{i=0}^{s^*} (\kappa_i^*)' g(x_{t-i}^*) + \gamma' d_t + v_t, \qquad (2.4)$$

when v_t is the unexplained component in (2.4), leaving the effective sample $\mathcal{T}^*$ after removing outliers. Such a task also includes establishing the validity of conditioning on any contemporaneous variables, perhaps used as instruments, as well as ensuring that $\{v_t\}$ is an innovation process from valid sequential factorization. Model formulation is needed to specify the functional forms $g(\cdot)$, selection plays a key role in choosing which x_t^* matter, and, because of the need to locate all outliers, will inherently involve more candidate variables than observations, which anyway may arise from the large number of initial functions $g(x_t) \ldots g(x_{t-s})$. Automatic methods are essential in this context, and can undertake model extension, model selection, and evaluation both during selection and of the final choice. A similar formulation applies when y_t is a vector of target variables to be modeled, although we do not address that setting here.

Automatic empirical model discovery can be seen to involve the same seven aspects discussed above as common to discovery in general. Here, the first involves the theoretical derivation of the relevant set x and the relationships between its components, and may entail functional forms, lag reactions, etc. The choice of the N variables to analyze is fundamental, as it determines what the target LDGP is; the other extensions to be discussed (lags, non-linear functions and impulse-indicator saturation, etc.) determine how well that LDGP is approximated. Failure to include substantively important influences will usually lead to nonconstant relationships that are hard to interpret, and will probably soon be dominated by an investigator willing to consider a broader range of determinants.

The second aspect becomes the automatic creation of a more general model than initially envisaged by an investigator. When a model is simply the theory imposed on the evidence, little new can be learned—reaching outside a framework is essential to reveal phenomena that were not originally conceived. Empirical model discovery is not an inductive approach: the prior theory plays a key role in structuring the framework, and is the vehicle for thinking about the basic set of variables, x_t and how they might matter. In macroeconomics, models confront wide-sense non-stationary data, so no theory is likely to cover all aspects, but theory ideas remain important as they can be embedded in the more general model: if correct, they should be retained in the final selected model, perhaps augmented by features where the theory was incomplete, which had such features been omitted, might have led to its rejection. Consequently, theory can be fully incorporated, but usually as a part of the model, not all of it, as section 3.13 and chapter 14 discuss. The additional generality needing created can involve any or all of a larger number of candidate variables, each with a wider class of functions, and of lag lengths, allowing for breaks and outliers. Globally, knowledge perforce proceeds from the simple to the general; but locally, it need not do so. "Keep it simple stupid", the so-called KISS principle, at best applies to the final selection, and not to the initial model.

Thirdly, having created a very general model, efficient selection is needed to find the congruent parsimonious representations to which it can be reduced. Model selection plays a major role, and if the second stage of using a very general, automatically created, starting set of candidate variables has been adopted, then selection has to be automatic as well: the scale of the problem becomes too large for manual labor. An efficient selection should have a small probability of retaining irrelevant variables, and a similar probability of retaining relevant variables as if the LDGP had been specified directly, and inference conducted using the same significance levels. We present evidence that *Autometrics* has such properties.

Next, the algorithm has to recognize when the search is completed, namely when a congruent parsimonious encompassing representation, or perhaps several, have been found of the target LDGP. These are called terminal models below. Multiple mutually encompassing terminals are possible, especially when variables are highly collinear and relatively loose significance levels are used: chapter 23 suggests that when forecasting, there may be advantages to combining these.

Fifthly, to appropriately quantify the outcome requires near unbiased parameter estimates with small mean squared errors, and a near unbiased estimate of the equation standard error. As noted above, chapter 10 develops bias corrections, which also substantially reduce the MSEs of retained irrelevant variables. Near normality is important for the inferences made during the selection of the terminal models, and especially so for the bias corrections—IIS plays an important role in removing breaks and outliers. Throughout, an appropriate estimator is essential, so chapter 22 considers a test of exogeneity in the final model.

The sixth step is evaluating the resulting discovery. Since all the data evidence will have been employed in the first two stages, new data, new tests or new procedures are needed for independent evaluation of the selection. When the initial general model is estimable from the available sample, then its evaluation by mis-specification testing is one of the first activities in empirical modeling. When that is infeasible, an initial reduction to $N < T$ is required before such tests are conducted, although they could still reject the null of congruence at that point. We do not use hold-back samples, partly because the lack of time invariance makes it unclear what is learned if the results differ, partly because when the DGP is constant, doing so is inefficient: see, e.g., Lynch and Vital-Ahuja (1998) and Hendry and Krolzig (2004b). Hold-back also fails to distinguish between a coefficient estimate being insignificant in some of the sub-samples because it is irrelevant, because information varies, or because the parameter is not constant, and sub-samples make it even more difficult to handle non-linearities and dynamics jointly with non-constancies, as discussed in section 7.13.3.

The final step is to summarize the findings parsimoniously in a model that is undominated at the significance level used. This is almost automatic given the selection criterion of a congruent parsimonious encompassing representation—but not quite. Having simplified the model to a size a human can grasp, various further simplifications may suggest themselves, including: combining indicators in a single dummy (e.g., Hendry and Santos, 2005); combining lags of variables into more interpretable forms (e.g., Hendry, 1995a), or combining other groups of variables (e.g., Campos and Ericsson, 1999); replacing unrestricted nonlinear functions by an encompassing theory-derived form, such as an ogive (see chapter 21); and so on.

All seven stages are interweaved below. Chapters 15 and 21 concern two major aspects of creating general models automatically, namely impulse-indicator saturation and functional forms. Increasing the set of candidate variables can only be done by an investigator, and changes the LDGP that is being modeled, whereas creating lags is straightforward, so neither is accorded separate chapters, albeit both are important. Chapters 8–11, 14, 19, 20 discuss the selection process, and 17 compares it with some other approaches. These chapters comprise the centerpiece of the book: without an efficient and powerful search instrument, that has operational properties which match what is anticipated, the generality required could not be implemented. However, chapter 18 discusses underspecified models. Thirdly, chapters 5–7 explain the selection criteria, the derivation of the LDGP which is the search target, and why *Gets* offers a route to its discovery. Next, chapter 10 discusses the postselection bias corrections, and their properties. Estimation is so well developed in conventional econometrics texts that we do not devote much space to the choice of estimator beyond checking the validity of conditioning in chapter 22. Fifthly, chapters 12, 13 and 22 concern various aspects of the evaluation of the terminal models, and chapter 23 considers its application to forecasting. The final step of summarizing the findings parsimoniously is partly intrinsic to the approach, as discussed in chapter 5, partly dependent on the classes of valid reductions (e.g., cointegration, simultaneity, or a specific non-linear function, all of which we address below), and partly can only be done by an investigator.

Given this brief overview of our route ahead, chapter 3 explains in detail the roles of each step in accomplishing the task of finding (2.4).

3   Background to Automatic Model Selection

This chapter explains the background in more detail, to provide a framework for the analysis in the rest of the book. We first note the many criticisms of model selection that have been made. While many of these are valid for some approaches, we will show that almost all are rebutted for general-to-specific (*Gets*) model selection. Many criticisms are based on an assumed level of knowledge where discovery is unnecessary, so fail to address that key issue. The main aim of this chapter is to walk through the six stages leading from simple selection to model discovery in a context where there are more candidate variables than observations. Part II will discuss these stages in detail, after chapter 5 considers the choice of evaluation criteria for selection methods, chapter 6 outlines the theory of reduction, and chapter 7 describes *Gets*. Here, we commence by considering a baseline *Gets* approach, denoted *1-cut*, which can select a model from any number of candidate variables with just one decision for mutually orthogonal, valid conditioning variables in a constant-parameter setting given a sufficiently large sample. Next, we show how to obtain near unbiased estimates after selection, then compare the 1-cut method with the multi-path search approach embodied in *Autometrics*, gradually extending the analysis to include diagnostic checking for the selection being well-specified, then parsimonious-encompassing tests against the initial general formulation, as well as efficiently handling more candidate variables than observations in the special case where an indicator is allowed for every data point. We also note the specific issues of selecting lag lengths, handling integrated data, collinearity, evaluating the reliability of the finally selected model by simulation, data accuracy, and the implementation of theory. We conclude this chapter by sketching the extensions that are the focus of part III, including handling more variables than observations in general, automatically testing for multiple breaks and for super exogeneity, as well as modeling non-linear equations, ending with selecting forecasting models. Solving the impulse-indicator saturation problem opens the door to this new realm of tests and modeling strategies, so separate chapters follow on each topic.

3.1 Critiques of data-based model selection

To date, model selection has not had a good press, being called "data mining", "garbage in, garbage out", "a con trick", "data snooping", "curve fitting", and so on—none complimentary. Criticism is easy, since there is a huge number of ways to select models, most of which are unstructured with unknown costs, so some are bound to be very poor in practice. Consequently, it is natural to seek a structured approach which allows for all the statistical decisions involved in model selection, monitoring their costs and benefits. More importantly, we want a general approach which can tackle empirical model discovery effectively.

On the one hand are legions of critics of earlier methods that sought to choose empirical models from data evidence, including Keynes (1939, 1940) (who saw many other difficulties additional to that noted above: see Hendry, 1980), through Koopmans (1947), Leamer (1978), Lovell (1983) to Pagan (1987) and Hansen (2005), as extensively documented in Hendry (2000a, 2009). We will rebut such criticisms by establishing the theoretical and operational properties of our approach. There are also important technical derivations of the distributions of estimators after model selection, such as Bock, Yancey and Judge (1973) and Judge and Bock (1978) (following pioneering studies like Stein, 1956, and James and Stein, 1961), Pötscher (1991), and Leeb and Pötscher (2003, 2005), which tend to draw rather pessimistic conclusions, such as biased outcomes with the intrinsic estimation uncertainty being understated. While most of these contributions assume that the postulated model essentially coincides with the DGP, so that no discovery process is involved, we will draw on aspects of their findings in chapter 9, and develop an approach to bias correct estimates after selection in chapter 10. However, we will also stress that much the greatest uncertainty concerns the appropriate choice of variables to characterize a useful LDGP, as well as its subsequent approximation, and that the costs of selecting a model thereof, which have to be paid to reduce that uncertainty, are small in comparison. Contributions to such an approach include White (1990), Phillips (1988, 1996), Hoover and Perez (1999) and Hendry and Krolzig (2005) among many others.

On the other hand, model selection is the hidden sin of almost all empirical research, where selection is usually covert, and empirical results are regularly presented as if only one hypothesis was ever investigated, with dozens of trial models simply being forgotten: that problem has undoubtedly not lessened since Leamer (1978) wrote. The common pretence that an abstract theory is so good it can simply be imposed on data and deliver the perfect empirical outcome is a pernicious drawback to a scientific approach to empirical modeling. Instead of a progressive accumulation of knowledge and understanding, fads and fashions prevail, with swings between schools as conditions chance to favor their particular assertions. Establishing an appropriate evidential basis would help resolve such difficulties, so when theoretical ideas advance, previous evidence is not jettisoned because its credibility depended purely on believing the previous theory.

The converse approach to asserting complete prior knowledge of the DGP is to confront the manifest complexity of the economy, and allow at the outset for all the candidate determinants of the variables under analysis, embedding available theory insights as a possible special case should the additional factors prove unnecessary. This approach recognizes that there is uncertainty about almost every aspect of a model and the evidence: which variables are relevant, at what lags, in what functional form transformations, which parameters are constant, and which variables are weakly exogenous, as well as what data mis-measurement or outliers have occurred. Thus, selection is unavoidable and aims to *reduce* many of these uncertainties given the data evidence, and avoid the costs of serious mis-specifications. The converse price to be paid for a large reduction in the widespread uncertainties before selection is a small increase in uncertainty around the critical decision region as to precisely what matters, when it matters, and how it matters. Thus, a reframing of the role of model selection is in order: it is in fact an essential tool to reduce the myriad uncertainties about model specification that are bound to occur in a social science, so is a key ingredient of empirical model discovery.

3.2   General-to-specific (*Gets*) modeling

The long list of features of any economic model that are not uniquely derivable from subject-matter theory alone includes the complete and comprehensive specification of every relevant variable and their possibly non-linear functional forms, all lag reactions including unit roots and cointegration (if time series), the timings and forms of all parameter shifts and outliers, and any interactions, as well as the exogeneity status of potential conditioning variables. Good theories can offer invaluable guidance, but most modeling situations involve uncertainty over all these features, so they must be data-based on the available sample. To successfully determine what matters and how it enters, all substantively important determinants need to be included, since omitting key variables adversely affects the goodness of fit, biases the included factors' effects, and in a world of inter-correlated variables with non-stationarities induced by breaks, leads to estimated models that are non-constant.

3.3   What to include?

A *Gets* approach should include all potentially relevant variables from the outset in a general unrestricted model (GUM), intended to embed all candidate data features. In practice, relevance has to have a lower bound, which may vary with the context, sample size availability, and theoretical or policy considerations. As discussed in Hendry (2009), economic theories rely on many ceteris paribus assumptions that are not applicable to empirical modeling in economics where all data are non-stationary, since other things will not stay equal. Two resolutions are possible. First, a *minor influence* result could demonstrate that all omitted factors can be neglected either because changes in them are of a smaller order of importance than those of included effects, or because they are orthogonal to the effects that matter (compare Boumans, 2005, on *ceteris absentibus* and *ceteris neglectis*). For either claim to be plausible, all the major influences must be included, and it is the aim of general models to allow for all the main theoretical or empirically-known variables, as well as the many historical contingencies that have happened, and possible data outliers. Nevertheless, there remains a choice about defining relevance empirically, which here depends on the nominal significance level α: variables that are less significant will not be retained, whether that is because they do not matter, or because their influence in the given sample is not large enough. Below, we use the shorthand *substantively relevant* for variables that should matter at level α, namely ones that would be significant on average at that level in the LDGP for the available sample size. Chapter 23 addresses factor approaches in forecasting, whereby many small influences may be captured adequately by a few principal components (for example).

When the GUM is estimable from the available data, an unbiased estimate of goodness of fit is obtained for the innovation error standard deviation, σ_ϵ say. Commencing from a well-specified GUM both ensures the fit does not exhibit systematic deviations from the data, and provides a bound on how well the variables under analysis can be modeled. From this GUM, feasible reduction paths are explored, eliminating insignificant variables till only relevant variables are retained. As an analogy to *Deep Blue*, the first computer chess playing program to beat the then reigning world champion Garry Kasparov (as recorded in www.research.ibm.com/deepblue/home/html/b.html), automatic methods can explore many more paths than a human, and hence uncover important relationships that might otherwise not be found.

Alternatively, the process is also analogous to sieving for gold, where the GUM contains many irrelevant variables (the large pile of dirt to be sieved), and the resulting gold is the collection of genuinely relevant determinants of the variables being modeled. "Fools' gold" (iron pyrites) corresponds to spuriously relevant variables, but there is also the possibility that the holes in the sieve are too large so some gold nuggets are missed. That trade-off, minimizing the presence of irrelevant variables without missing too many relevant, is central to the success of the enterprise. However, the "Catch 22" is that if every candidate determinant is to be included, especially possible outliers or breaks at any data point, then there are bound to be more variables, N, in total than the number of observations, T, so the GUM cannot in fact be estimated: generality and feasibility conflict. To resolve this conundrum, the analysis proceeds in six stages, briefly described in sections 3.4–3.9, remembering that more dirt can be sieved for gold than is held in one input to the sieve. Chapter 7 discusses general-to-specific modeling in more detail.

3.4   Single-decision selection

Chapter 8 provides a first explanation as to why *Gets* selection can be efficient for a correctly-specified, constant-parameter regression model in orthogonal, valid conditioning variables, to demonstrate that only one selection decision is required when the GUM is directly estimable, irrespective of the number of regressors provided $N \ll T$. The squared t-tests of the significance of every variables' coefficients are ranked, and those greater than the chosen critical value, denoted c_α, are retained, with the remaining variables being eliminated. Thus, for a given c_α, only one decision is needed to select the final model however many variables N are included (but much smaller than T).

A set of simulation experiments for $N = 1000$, when only $n = 10$ variables are actually relevant, confirms the theoretical analysis underlying the *1-cut* approach. Although there are $2^{1000} \approx 10^{301}$ possible models, only one equation needs to be estimated, and only **one** decision is required to select the final model from the thousand candidate regressors. Thus, repeated testing does not occur, and retention rates for irrelevant variables are close to the chosen nominal significance level, α, for small α (e.g., $\alpha \leq k/N$ where $k = 1, 2, 3$ say), which can be accurately controlled. Moreover, retention rates for each relevant variable are close to the theoretical power for a one-off test at significance level α. When $\alpha = 1/1000$, for example, under the null that no variables matter, so $n = 0$, efficiency is 99.9% as only one variable out of the thousand candidates will be retained by chance on average, costing one degree of freedom to explore a vast range of possible effects.

When divided by their degrees of freedom, estimates of error variances based on residual sums of squares from general models (i.e., before selection) will be unbiased for σ_ϵ^2. However, 1-cut selection could induce either over or underfitting, depending on the choice of α, the former for loose values, the latter for stringent. Thus, overfitting is not an intrinsic property of data-based selection, but depends on the stringency of selection, the importance of the relevant variables, and the number of irrelevant variables.

3.5   Impact of selection

Secondly, the coefficient estimates in the final selected model do not have the same properties as those obtained when estimating the DGP (or LDGP as in chapter 6). Selection here also includes commencing an analysis by correctly postulating the DGP—so search does not arise—but not being certain that the specification is completely correct, so testing the significance of its estimates (say), and dropping insignificant variables. Re-estimation then substantively affects the distributional properties of the final model's estimates. This issue is addressed in chapters 9 and 10. There are a number of costs associated with seeking to select a model even when its specification in fact coincides with the DGP. Although it is not a realistic scenario in economics to assume the initial formulation is perfect, it is important to understand the sources of selection costs, and when they are likely to be large or small.

In chapter 9, we draw on the analysis in Leeb and Pötscher (2003, 2005) to investigate the outcomes for a bivariate model that coincides with the DGP. Their focus is the effect of selection on the estimated parameter of the first variable, which is deemed to be the sole parameter of interest. We consider three settings for the second variable: a fixed nonzero parameter; a zero parameter; and a parameter that is local to zero, although non-zero. In that third case, uniform convergence of selection-based estimators cannot be obtained, with the implication that in finite samples, inference may be unreliable when there is a predefined parameter of interest. That becomes one of many considerations in the discovery process, which may even reveal other parameters to be of interest empirically because of their constancy and invariance.

Generally, by retaining only variables whose coefficients are significant at the desired level in the given sample, selection induces biases in the distributions of the estimated coefficients of retained variables—called the conditional distributions. Some relevant variables will be correctly retained only in some samples, but omitted in others. Also, some retained variables will be irrelevant variables that are adventitiously significant due to the vagaries of sampling. Approximate bias correction can be achieved for an orthogonal formulation once distributions of estimators are near normal (see Hendry and Krolzig, 2005), an issue to which we return in section 3.9 below. Bias correction transpires to be beneficial in several settings: we show that not only are coefficients of relevant variables then almost unbiased estimates of the correct partial derivatives, those of irrelevant variables are driven towards zero. Thus, bias correction can improve overall average mean-squared errors (MSEs) of parameter estimates in both conditional and unconditional distributions. The former measures deviations from the DGP parameter values for the retained variables, which may vary from sample to sample, whereas the latter includes the variables that are eliminated, so their coefficient estimates are zero.

Although this setting is too simple to characterize empirical economic modeling, the 1-cut approach provides a baseline that demonstrates

(a) model selection without repeated testing;

(b) without overfitting;

(c) with retention rates for relevant variables close to their theory maximum for the chosen significance level;

(d) with near unbiased parameter estimates; and

(e) with a small, controlled, efficiency loss despite investigating large numbers of candidate variables.

The natural question is how well such implications extend to more general settings.

3.6 *Autometrics*

Using the same setting, in chapter 11 the 1-cut approach is contrasted with the outcome obtained by the general search algorithm *Autometrics*—which does not depend on the orthogonality of the regressors—to investigate the closeness of their outcomes. We first compare these using $N = 1000$, both to show the feasibility of a general algorithm for selection with a large number of candidate regressors, and to establish that in some respects, *Autometrics* outperforms the 1-cut approach despite searching multiple paths, and not exploiting orthogonality. The benefits of bias correction on MSEs are then illustrated using a much smaller N (namely 10) for $n = 1, \ldots, 10$, so the results can be graphed and compared in detail between the two methods. We draw on independent evaluation simulations by Castle, Qin and Reed (2013) to investigate the performance of *Autometrics* relative to some other approaches.

These experiments are conducted assuming that the GUM nests the DGP, so all the models are well specified, and no mis-specification testing is undertaken. Statisticians use *size* as a measure of the false null rejection rate of a (similar) test. Here we are selecting variables, albeit by testing, so may retain a variable which is insignificant on its associated test because it helps offset an otherwise significant diagnostic test, as we will discuss in chapter 12. Consequently, as noted in chapter 1, we use the term *gauge* to denote the false null *retention* rate in the selection process: a gauge of 1% entails that on average one irrelevant variable in a hundred is adventitiously retained in the final selection. Similarly, *power* denotes the rejection frequency of a test statistic when the null is false, whereas we denote by *potency* the *retention* frequency of relevant variables in selection. It can also happen that a relevant variable is retained, despite being insignificant, to ensure diagnostic tests are satisfied. Always retaining a GUM when it nests the DGP ensures potency is unity, but gauge can be large depending on the initial extent of overspecification. Conversely, always using the null model ensures a gauge of zero, but also potency of zero.

3.7   Mis-specification testing

Fourth, chapter 12 assesses the additional cost of mis-specification testing through its impact on false null retention rates. Automatic *Gets* seeks to commence from a GUM that characterizes the evidence in all relevant respects, which is called congruence. As with congruent triangles, which perfectly match when appropriately placed on top of each other, a congruent model matches the evidence against which it is evaluated. That does not preclude there being other evidence which it would not match—just as a triangle could fit on top of an appropriately cutoff 3-sided pyramid, but only match its 2-dimensional surface. Consequently, an investigator must decide what features define congruence in the relevant context. For conditional models on time-series data, the default in *Autometrics* is to require residuals to be serially independent, homoskedastic, and normal, with constant parameters, and valid functional forms: exogeneity is tested later. That produces five test statistics, which are nearly independently distributed under the null, so each is usually conducted at 1% to make a 5% overall evaluation of congruence (e.g., Godfrey and Veale, 2000). If instrumental variables are used, the Sargan (1964) test of instrument validity is reported.

If the GUM is congruent, then valid reductions should be as well, hence simplified models are evaluated using the same test statistics. Since mis-specification tests can also adventitiously reject, the gauge of *Autometrics* is increased by ensuring that any mis-specification test which is insignificant in the GUM remains insignificant when applied to the selected equation. Below, we document the costs of this aspect of building well-specified models. Of course, the real reason for undertaking such mis-specification tests is to avoid a badly-specified GUM, and help reveal at the start of an analysis that a different formulation is needed. Separately, therefore, the tests being used to that end need to be investigated to evaluate their properties under the null, and examine their power when the relevant null is false, as well as establish the impact of selection on their behavior in the final model. All of these issues are addressed in chapter 12.

If an estimable GUM fails the mis-specification tests, then it needs to be re-specified, although it is rarely obvious in what way, especially given a general initial specification. However, it is also possible for tests to reject at the GUM, and cease to reject as simplification occurs (see, e.g., Fig. 12.1 below), so that route merits checking. An investigator must be careful not to try many alternative GUMs as uncertainty will not then be fully accounted for, and such trials should be reported.

3.8 Parsimonious encompassing

Fifth, we have so far only considered single steps along search paths, such that a variable is eliminated by being insignificant at that stage. However, a group of erstwhile insignificant effects can cumulate to be significant as a group, and lead to a non-dominating model being selected. Chapter 13 discusses encompassing, the property that a given model can account for the results of other models of the same data (see Hendry and Richard, 1982, 1989, Mizon, 1984, Mizon and Richard, 1986, and the papers in Hendry, Marcellino and Mizon, 2008, especially Bontemps and Mizon, 2008, and Doornik, 2008). In particular, parsimonious encompassing checks that a small model can explain the results of a larger model within which it is nested: see Govaerts, Hendry and Richard (1994). Parsimonious encompassing can be shown to be reflexive, anti-symmetric and transitive, so defines a partial ordering across models and can sustain a progressive research strategy (see section 3.17) Thus, parsimonious encompassing tests against the GUM mitigate the problem of cumulating counter evidence by ensuring that a joint test of all the reductions remains insignificant at the chosen level. Again, simulation experiments are used to illustrate this property, and show that encompassing helps control the gauge without much loss of potency.

3.9 Impulse-indicator saturation (IIS)

Sixth, since large numbers of candidate regressors are unproblematic for $N \ll T$, as noted above for $N = 1000$, chapter 15 considers the specific setting of impulse-indicator saturation (IIS). By including an indicator for every observation in the set of regressors to detect and remove multiple shifts, when the T indicators are combined with any other regressors, N must always exceed the sample size. The solution investigated by Hendry et al. (2008), and Johansen and Nielsen (2009) enters indicators in large blocks, two sets of $T/2$ in the basic theory, but in several smaller combinations in practice, so both simplification and expansion steps are in fact used. The first authors establish the impact of IIS on estimating the mean when independently sampling in an identical distribution (IID case). Johansen and Nielsen (2009) also prove that under the null of no outliers or shifts, there is almost no loss of efficiency in testing for T indicators when $\alpha \leq 1/T$, even in dynamic models. While surprising at first sight that one could test the relevance of T candidate variables at low cost, retaining an indicator when it is not needed merely removes one observation, which is all that will happen on average. Thus, efficiency is of the order of $(1 - \alpha)\%$. Since so many variables are involved, and the costs of missing a single outlier are not very large, there are grounds for using tighter significance levels for this stage than for linear regressors.

Monte Carlo experiments have confirmed the null distribution and outcomes just described. Again, the null is not the case of relevance in practice, but rather the aim is to detect multiple outliers and breaks. Chapter 20 shows that IIS is capable of detecting up to 20 outliers in 100 observations as well as multiple shifts, including breaks close to the start and end of the sample. We compare our approach with forward step-wise regression—which can also handle $N > T$—and demonstrate the major gains from *Autometrics*. We consider a fat-tailed distribution as well—namely, a Student t-distribution with 3 degrees of freedom, denoted t_3—to show the potential benefits of using IIS to establish approximate normality in a setting where only the first two moments (mean and variance) of the errors exist.

These six ingredients of the search process all play important roles in helping to ensure a congruent undominated final selection. However, there are eight more issues central to successful empirical modeling that we have not yet discussed, namely, integrated and cointegrated data (section 3.10); selecting the correct lag lengths in time series (section 3.11); collinearity and orthogonality of variables in model formulation (section 3.12); retaining economic theory models (section 3.13); the appropriate functional forms of the regressors (section 3.14); the exogeneity status of explanatory variables (section 3.15); and selecting forecasting models (section 3.16), so we will briefly consider these in turn. Together, these point to the need for a progressive research strategy in an empirically oriented discovery process (section 3.17), in which the reliability of the selected model (section 3.18) and the data accuracy (section 3.19) are evaluated.

3.10 Integration and cointegration

Many economic time series are integrated, often of first order, denoted I(1), so that conventional critical values cannot be relied on for all inference decisions. Indeed, for many years, economists were deeply concerned about the impact of unit roots on modeling, following the findings in Yule (1926) that bivariate regressions between unrelated I(1) variables, y_t and z_t say, will lead to the null being rejected about 70% of the time at a 5% significance level, a difficulty re-emphasized by Granger and Newbold (1974): Phillips (1986) rigorously analyses such "nonsense regressions". However, as shown in Hendry (1977), including lagged values of both y_t and z_t removes that problem under the null, which is now rejected about 5% of the time at $\alpha = 0.05$, and delivers an unrestricted version of a first-order equilibrium-correction model when there is a substantive relation. Recently, Mills (2010) brought to light the pioneering work of Smith (1926), who had effectively solved that problem for I(1) time series by nesting levels and differences, although Smith seems to have been unaware of the distributional implications of I(1) data emphasized by Yule (1926). The attempt to demonstrate that a problem remained, because combinations of I(1) variables had to be I(1), led Granger to the concept of cointegration, as he describes in his Nobel Prize autobiography:[1] also see Hendry (2004b). Davidson et al. (1978) referred to the levels feedback as error-correction because it corrected within equilibria, but it does not do so between. Rather, shifts in equilibrium means are pernicious for modeling and forecasting, so although equilibrium-correction and error-correction are often used synonymously, the equilibrium-correction terminology serves to remind that such feedback terms do not error correct.

Systems of I(1) variables can be reduced to I(0) (non-integrated) by differencing and cointegration transformations to facilitate conventional inference, and create a more orthogonal and interpretable formulation (see, e.g., Granger, 1981, Engle and Granger, 1987, Johansen, 1988, 1995, 2006a, and Phillips, 1991: Hendry and Juselius, 2000, 2001, and Juselius, 2006, provide surveys). Differencing is easy to automate, and we address the latter shortly. Provided all variables are entered before differencing transformations, then Sims, Stock and Watson (1990) show that conventional critical values apply to all decisions except that concerned with the reduction from I(1) to I(0), which needs critical values of the form discussed by Dickey and Fuller (1979, 1981) and Johansen (1988) inter alia: also see Toda and Phillips (1993). When y_t and all $x_{i,t}$ are in (perhaps log) levels with lagged values included in the GUM, the coefficient of y_{t-1} will be relatively close to unity, so the null will almost always be rejected. While there may be no need for unit-root critical values at that stage, a reduction from I(1) to I(0) will be needed for a parsimonious specification, so appropriate critical values are required, and moreover need to be applied correctly by an automatic procedure.

A potentially problematic setting is when several lags of an irrelevant unmodeled I(1) variable are included: once all but one of the lags

---

[1]nobelprize.org/nobel _prizes/economics/laureates/2003/granger-autobio.html.

has been eliminated during selection, a t-test on the last one cannot be written in the way Sims et al. (1990) propose. Thus, slightly tighter critical values seem advisable if that is suspected.

A general automatic solution requires discovering the cointegrated relations as part of an overall selection strategy. In a single equation approach, the *PcGive* unit-root test can be used to check cointegration (see Banerjee and Hendry, 1992, Banerjee, Dolado and Mestre, 1998, and Ericsson and MacKinnon, 2002), as was implemented in *PcGets* Quick Modeller. Implementing the Johansen (1988) procedure for a dynamic system characterizing a vector also seems relatively straightforward, using one of the similar formulations, with restricted trend and unrestricted intercept (e.g., Johansen, 1995). Next, the minimal cointegration vectors can be found following an approach like that in Davidson (1998), who seeks "irreducible" relations, such that eliminating any variable therefrom loses cointegration. Omtzig (2002), Kurcewicz and Mycielski (2003) and Liao and Phillips (2012) have proposed and analyzed algorithms for automatic selection of cointegration vectors. The additional complication of possible I(2) variables would also require prior reductions, or may possibly be testable in the final selection (e.g., Kongsted, 2005). The lag length needs joint selection, as do all the outliers and breaks, which in turn will involve somewhat different critical values when IIS is used (e.g., Nielsen, 1996, 2004, and Johansen, Mosconi and Nielsen, 2000). However, the converse of failing to model breaks is even less appealing. Although the order of proceeding is likely to be important, at present the best, or even a good, order is unknown, so we tackle cointegrating reductions after developing a congruent representation in levels.

Chapter 12 notes the possible impacts on mis-specification tests of models where the variables are I(1).

3.11   Selecting lag length

Modeling economic time series congruently depends not just on the appropriate set of variables, but also on correct specifications of all their dynamic reactions. In one sense, the problem of doing so should be similar to selecting variables, but several special features matter. First, as section 3.10 discussed, economic time series are often integrated. Secondly, economic theory is generally non-specific about measures of time units, so a subscript t might denote any interval from a nano-second (in finance), through weeks, months and years to a decade (long-run growth), leaving investigators to determine lags empirically. Thirdly, highly autoregressive variables generate substantial collinearity between successive lags like z_{t-1} and z_{t-2}, say, especially before reductions to I(0). Precise lags are difficult to determine empirically, as they are all relatively good approximations locally to each other, so it is easy to select an incorrect lag in either direction (e.g., selecting z_{t-1} although z_{t-2} enters the LDGP; or vice versa). Nevertheless, the solved long-run is usually little affected by such mis-selections, the main impact of which is on the apparent timing of effects. Fourthly, the maximum lag length may be too long when set by rules like data frequency+1, which becomes 13 lags on monthly data for all variables, especially when some candidate variables have relatively short lag impacts.

Indeed, one of the earliest applications of *Gets* was to lag-length selection, exploiting the ordered nature of the hypotheses from longest to shortest: see Anderson (1971), extending his analysis in Anderson (1962) to time series. Consequently, lag selection allows a pre-search stage, testing downwards sequentially from the longest lag, say s, on all variables x_{t-s} jointly, until rejection occurs at, say, x_{t-r} for $r \leq s$, albeit usually at a relatively loose significance level.

3.12   Collinearity

As explained for 1-cut selection above, orthogonality is essential to ensure that the ranking of the t^2-statistics on each estimated coefficient correctly represents the significance of the associated variable. When there are non-negligible correlations between candidate variables, that assumption fails. Since *Autometrics* does not require orthogonality of regressors, a natural question concerns its performance as collinearity increases. Four different states of knowledge must be distinguished to ascertain the impact of non-orthogonality on selection, additional to its effects on estimation of a known DGP.

In the first state of knowledge, the DGP is known to the investigator and is known to be perfectly specified. Here, no inference or evaluation is required, simply optimal estimation of its unknown parameters. While wholly implausible in any empirical social science, this is essentially the model of the elementary textbook seeking to teach the rudiments of estimation. Even so, collinearity can induce a wider dispersion of parameter estimates, which establishes that the problem is not purely a selection issue.

In the second state, the DGP is known, but there is uncertainty about its overspecification, so some irrelevant variables may also be included. In this setting, inference about its parameters usually includes testing the null hypothesis that they are zero. When a bivariate model coincides with its DGP, Leeb and Pötscher (2003, 2005) show that if the second variable's parameter is local to zero, a constant, non-zero inter-variable correlation can distort inference about the first parameter, even asymptotically. This occurs because the null hypothesis for the second parameter is only rejected some of the time, so the bivariate model is then retained, and otherwise the univariate model is chosen. As a consequence, the first variable's coefficient estimate is a mixture of an unbiased estimate of the correct parameter and one contaminated by an omitted variable with which it is correlated, but which is not substantively relevant in the given sample. We call such mistakes, *costs of inference* as they occur when the DGP is correctly specified, so search is unnecessary, yet inference is undertaken—the best outcome that could occur is to retain the DGP. Such costs of inference are higher the more that collinearity affects the estimators of the parameters of interest.

The third state is when the DGP is not known, and needs to be discovered from data evidence. In the standard *Gets* formulation, the DGP is nested in the most general model under consideration, so now there are *costs of search* additional to costs of inference. Such search costs include retention of irrelevant variables that are adventitiously significant, as well as possibly lower probabilities of retaining relevant variables than might occur if the DGP was known. Section 3.11 already noted a case where high inter-variable correlations might entail incorrect selection of a lag by a close approximation, and the same phenomenon must occur in general. When x_t and z_t, say, are highly correlated, each approximates the impact of the other, so either might be retained by chance sampling variations, irrespective of which actually enters the DGP. Fortunately, such correlations between variables are rarely constant in economics due to intermittent location shifts, as first noted by Koopmans (1937), and that feature can be used in recursive estimation and constancy testing to discriminate between models in practice, one of the few benefits of structural breaks. The DGP itself is unique over an equivariance class of representations, like the likelihood function, which class includes orthogonal transformations, a point emphasized by Campos and Ericsson (1999). Since collinearity is a property of a given parametrization of a model, not of the model itself, one solution to collinearity is to orthogonalize the variables. The mapping from I(1) levels to I(0) differences and cointegration transformations discussed in section 3.10 is a natural way of achieving that in time series. More generally, however, unless one already knows which variables are relevant and which are not, arbitrary orthogonalizations are likely to combine these sets and hence deliver non-parsimonious outcomes. By first selecting over the variables, then over the principal components of those not selected, some combinations of variables that have small effects may be retained: see e.g., Castle et al. (2013).

The fourth state of nature is when the specification of the DGP is unknown, so needs to be discovered, possibly from a general model, but now the GUM does not nest the generating process, so is mis-specified for the DGP. This may well be the most realistic scenario, and is precisely why mis-specification testing is an essential component of empirical modeling. Chapter 18 discusses model selection in underspecified settings. Despite an investigator seeking to commence an empirical study from a general initial specification that nests the DGP (or LDGP) for the set of variables under analysis, the GUM may be an underspecification, especially when there are multiple breaks or unobserved variables. Moreover, the selection of which variables to analyze could lead to the LDGP being a poor representation of the economic DGP. In this setting, model selection, rather than just fitting a prior specification, may help. In particular, IIS can help correct non-constancies induced by location shifts in omitted variables that in turn alter the intercepts of mis-specified models.

3.13   Retaining economic theory

Empirical model discovery aims to provide an extension of and an improvement upon, many existing practices in applied economics, but is most certainly not a replacement for analytical reasoning or theory. Economic theory from Adam Smith onwards has offered far too many crucial insights into complicated economic behavior to be sidelined in the difficult task of developing models of data evidence. Since his 1776 masterpiece, economics has continued to make rapid progress across a very large number of areas: a small set of recent examples includes auctions, mechanism design, principal-agent theory, incentives, and asymmetric information, changing our understanding of how well markets do, or do not, function. Moreover, while highly abstract, theory can lead to connections being highlighted that would otherwise be unnoticed.

Nevertheless, the combination of that abstractness with its evolution makes it unwise to *impose* today's theory on data: tomorrow's theory may be more complete and different, so lead to earlier theory-based evidence being discarded. Instead, the available theory can be *embedded* in the modeling exercise, to be retained in its entirety when it is complete and correct, while at the same time by including a far larger number of candidate variables which may matter, allows for the possibility that aspects absent from an abstract theory can be captured. There are numerous advantages to adopting this strategy.

First, the theory will be retained when valid. This is essential, as the initial discovery could well be theory based, and the method must ensure that such insights are supported when they correctly represent the state of nature. Thus, the theory variables are always retained, irrespective of their significance at any stage of the search. The additional variables are orthogonalized with respect to the theory variables, so the distributions of the theory-parameter estimates are unaffected by selection. By using reasonably tight significance levels for the remaining decisions, almost no additional variables will be significant by chance, leaving the estimated theory model intact. Chapter 14 provides the analysis.

Second, the theory should be rejected when it is in fact invalid. Such an outcome can occur even when all the theory variables are retained, by their being individually or jointly insignificant in the final model, whereas important effects excluded by the theory are retained. Theory variables could still be significant despite the theory being invalid, with either anticipated signs violated, or theory-based restrictions rejected in the final selection.

Third, a theory could be rescued when a direct fit would have rejected, but the more general setting incorporated factors whose omission would otherwise have led to that rejection. As an example, Hendry and Mizon (2011) analyze time-series data on US food expenditure over 1931–2002 first considered by Tobin (1950). A number of studies were reported in Magnus and Morgan (1999) based on their update of Tobin's data to 1989 (since extended by Reade, 2008). Hendry and Mizon show that even when the underlying theory is essentially correct in what it includes, an empirical model thereof can manifest serious misspecifications when just fitted to the data. In their case, the relative price of food had the wrong sign and was insignificant. Conversely, when the same theory was embedded in a general framework allowing for dynamic reactions and major external events such as wars, recessions and substantial policy interventions, it performed well over the whole time period. An indirect advantage of the general approach is illustrated by the fact that most of the studies in Magnus and Morgan (1999) found their models were non-constant over the combined inter-war and post-war, and so dropped the inter-war data as discrepant, whereas a few impulse indicators (especially for a food program in the depth of the great depression) allow the entire sample to be utilized, thereby bene-fitting from the much greater data variation.

Fourth, a more complete picture of both the theory and confound-ing influences can emerge from a general analysis, which is especially valuable for policy analyses. When a theory encapsulates the main in-gredients, but not all substantive aspects, directly fitting it to data would miss other factors. This is related to the previous point, but in a setting where the theory model would not be rejected, but was nevertheless in-complete in policy-relevant directions.

Fifth, well-specified initial formulations avoid reliance on doubtful assumptions about the sources of problems like residual autocorrelation or heteroskedasticity. In the past, these were often corrected following a recipe (see, e.g., Hendry and Mizon, 1978, and Mizon, 1995), but more recently, heteroskedastic and autocorrelation consistent standard errors (HACSE: see, e.g., White, 1980, and Andrews, 1991) are reported for estimated parameters. It is possible that the problem manifest in the residuals is due to the corresponding phenomenon in the errors (i.e., residual autocorrelation is a sign of error autocorrelation), but equally it may be due to breaks, incorrect functional forms, omitted variables or data mis-measurement inter alia, so that "correction" fails to achieve valid inference. Residuals represent ignorance, not knowledge, and it is hazardous to endow what we do not know with specific properties. Congruence does not entail correctness, but does mean that no system-atic information remains in the residuals.

Finally, explaining the findings of rival models reduces the prolifer-ation of contending explanations, which would create major uncertain-ties if unresolved. A possible example is the debate between Friedman and Meiselman (1963) and Ando and Modigliani (1965) on what was es-sentially Keynesian versus monetary theories of business fluctuations. Both could not be correct—although both could be wrong—but embed-ding both theories in a general model would have allowed a rapid reso-lution of their disagreement, perhaps with neither having the complete answer. In economics, many forces can operate together, or with dif-ferent relative magnitudes at different points in time, so it is far from inconceivable that autonomous or induced changes in investment dominate the explanation in one era whereas changes in money multipliers do in another. In a model of UK inflation over 1875–1991, Hendry (2001b) found that almost every theory—excess demand, monetary, cost push, mark-up, imported, etc.—played a role, but even combined, failed to account for many of the major episodes of inflation and deflation experienced historically.

Thus, little is lost and much is gained by embedding theory models in much more general formulations rather then directly imposing them on data as if they were complete, correct and immutable. In some settings, such as when IIS is used, it can be advantageous to retain the intercept in models despite an absence of theory.

3.14   Functional form

Functional form mis-specifications usually lead to a non-congruent model, and may induce parameter non-constancy. Chapter 21 considers the selection of non-linear models. Often, empirical studies commence from a linear model, both as a convenient approximation, and because the form of non-linearity may be unclear a priori. However, given the ability to handle more variables than observations at high efficiency under the null, versus the substantive costs of mis-specifying the functional form under the alternative, we consider postulating a general non-linear approximation in the GUM (functions that are non-linear in the parameters can be reformulated to be non-linear in variables, albeit not parsimoniously). Such a non-linear specification needs to be identified, congruent, and amenable to search in a reasonable time.

There are two possible approaches. In the first, test that there is substantive non-linearity to be modeled: if that does not reject, a linear model is adopted. The low-dimensional portmanteau test for non-linearity in Castle and Hendry (2010a) can be used even if there would be more potential non-linear regressors than the sample size. Otherwise, postulate a general polynomial augmented with exponentials for the GUM, and select a parsimonious representation that captures the non-linearity. Even with just 10 linear variables, there will be 55 quadratic functions and 220 cubics, making 285 candidates in total as the number of distinct terms is $M_N = N(1 + (N + 1)(N + 5)/6)$. Thus, very large numbers of candidate variables are generated as N increases, requiring tight significance levels to keep $\alpha(M_N + T)$ sufficiently small.

This curse of dimensionality suggests a second approach, which also obviates the need for a pre-test for non-linearity. The potentially huge number of non-linear functions can be greatly reduced by forming the principal components of the basic variables, say $w_{i,t}$, and only including terms like $w_{i,t}^2$, $w_{i,t}^3$, etc. Each of the first involves squares and cross-products of the $x_{i,t}$, and the second adds cubes, squares and up to triple cross-products: see Castle and Hendry (2011b). This creates only $3N$ additional candidates even adding exponentials of each $w_{i,t}$.

The supporting theory is still embryonic, applicable to static models with strongly exogenous regressors, where the GUM nests the LDGP, but already highlights numerous interesting problems such as

(a) what classes of non-linearity to investigate;

(b) handling collinearities between non-linear functions that are slowly changing (analogous to those in time series analyzed by Phillips, 2007);

(c) non-normality leading to non-linear functions capturing outliers (also a potential problem for non-parametric methods);

(d) allowing for more variables than there are observations, as noted; and

(e) finding appropriate tests against specific forms of non-linearity such as logistic or squashing functions suggested by theory, to check if they simplify and clarify the approximation (e.g., Granger and Teräsvirta, 1993).

Joint resolution of these difficulties is essential for a successful algorithm, so solutions to the five problems are discussed

1. Use cubic polynomials augmented with exponentials.

2. Create orthogonalized regressors.

3. Remove outliers by IIS jointly with selecting regressors and functional forms.

4. Select by a multi-stage $N > T$ algorithm.

5. Use encompassing tests against specific non-linear forms. Since non-linearity should be retained only when it is really significant, and hence not adventitious, there are grounds for using tighter significance levels for this stage than for linear terms, as with impulse-indicator saturation.

Neither IIS nor functional form are really just an issue of model selection, namely finding a specific model once a GUM has been specified, but also concern extending the model formulation, seeking to discover features of the LDGP outside the initial formulation. Both can be undertaken automatically, in that an investigator simply clicks on a choice to investigate them, which has both advantages (checking a model against likely LDGP alternatives by including their possibility from the outset), and drawbacks (exploring more candidate variables requires a tighter significance level, so may lower potency). Similar comments also apply as discussed above when selecting lag lengths of dynamic reactions, or handling collinearity.

3.15   Exogeneity

Exogeneity concerns whether it is valid to condition on contemporaneous variables in a regression, or whether one needs a different set of instrumental variables that are weakly exogenous (see Engle, Hendry and Richard, 1983, and the various concepts of exogeneity discussed in Hendry, 1995a: Ericsson and Irons, 1994, reprint many of the key papers). We will consider testing exogeneity in detail in chapter 22. As economic processes seem to intermittently undergo location shifts, and intrinsically to exhibit stochastic trends, these wide-sense non-stationarities put parameter constancy and invariance (i.e., not changing when policy regimes alter) at centre stage. Consequently, super exogeneity is the fundamental concept, whereby conditioning variables are weakly exogenous for the parameters of interest in the model, and the distributions of those variables can change without shifting the parameters. Ericsson and Irons (1995) overview the extensive literature on super exogeneity, and its relation to the so-called Lucas (1976) critique (Aldrich, 1989, discusses the history of autonomy and related ideas, dating back to Frisch, 1938). Chapter 22 considers an automatic test of super exogeneity based on impulse-indicator saturation of the processes for the conditioning variables to detect their location shifts, then tests the relevance of those significant indicators in the conditional model: see Hendry and Santos (2010).

3.16   Selecting forecasting models

Trying to ascertain in advance what the future holds has long had a fascination for humankind, and the English language has more than 25 synonyms for forecasting, often derived from ancient contexts (see Hendry, 2001a). All practical methods rely on extrapolating presently available information into the future, often based on formal models, since crystal balls which show the future are generically unavailable. No matter how good such methods or models are, they require that the future resembles the present in the relevant attributes—precisely what intermittent unanticipated location shifts violate. Once a break has occurred, it can be detected and taken into account in modeling; but future breaks would need to be predicted to avoid forecast failure. That has so far proved an elusive activity, although some progress has been achieved (see inter alia, Pesaran, Pettenuzzo and Timmermann, 2006, and Castle et al., 2011, 2010). Consequently, very different considerations matter when formulating, selecting or using a forecasting model: see Clements and Hendry (1998, 1999) for general treatments of forecasting when the data processes are non-stationary. In a nutshell, forecasting is different.

If one could be certain that there were no location shifts near the forecast origin and that none would occur over the forecast horizon, then the most parsimonious, congruent, undominated model in-sample should dominate out of sample as well. In economics, experience suggests that is not a reliable assumption for forecasting. Rather, the robustness to location shifts of a model formulation can be essential, and may entail either selecting from a completely different class of models (for example, double-differenced devices) which are neither congruent not dominating in-sample; or transforming a selected model before it is used in forecasting (as in Hendry, 2006). Moreover, even when the DGP is known, an estimate thereof need not deliver minimum MSE forecasts (e.g., Clements and Hendry, 2005). Since automatic modeling seeks to locate the LDGP, complete success at doing so need not improve forecasting. Consequently, different considerations and criteria apply, which influences how a selection approach should be judged, as chapter 5 notes. Chapter 23 discusses some of the pertinent issues for selecting forecasting models, and emphasizes the route of using an *Autometrics* selected model for forecasting, switching to its first difference if location shifts are detected near the forecast origin.

3.17   Progressive research strategies

Thus, we have reached the need for a progressive research strategy, in which theory and evidence mutually interact to learn about the DGP. The outcome of an empirical analysis may suggest the need for a more general formulation to better approximate an LDGP, or a larger set of variables in order to define a different LDGP that is more constant and easier to interpret. White (1990) shows that sufficiently rigorous testing with suitable re-specification ensures the selection of an acceptable data representation of a constant LDGP as the sample increases without bound, providing the significance level of the complete testing process is controlled and declines as the sample size grows. That result does not conclusively support a *Gets* approach, as almost any approach could eventually converge to a constant LDGP if extended as evidence accumulated, so the choice between methods becomes a matter of research efficiency, which nevertheless is important: learning in a few days versus many years is not a negligible difference.

Any progressive strategy raises the issue of how to extend a model to accommodate one or more rejection outcomes. Rejecting a null hypothesis against a specific hypothesis generally provides no information about the appropriate alternative to adopt, which is a variant of the Duhem–Quine thesis (e.g., Cross, 1982). Conversely, not testing for model mis-specifications creates the opposite problem of not discovering that a given model class is incorrect (e.g., Mayo, 1981). Thus, commencing from a sufficiently general GUM that nests or closely approximates the LDGP has clear advantages by minimizing the frequency with which an arbitrary extension is required. Moreover, by always working in the class of congruent representations, which chapter 6 shows contains the LDGP, then seeking parsimonious encompassing of successive models sustains a progressive research strategy, as noted in section 3.8.

3.18   Evaluating the reliability of the selected model

Model selection can reduce some major uncertainties about the LDGP at the cost of increasing others. One check on the latter is to examine how often the final model would be selected, by rerunning the entire selection process many times in a Monte Carlo simulation. Using the bias-corrected estimates, the selected model becomes the proximate DGP from which artificial data can be generated conditional on the unmodeled variables. Recommencing the analysis from the original form of GUM with that new data, selection is examined in repeated simulations, and the resulting range of models recorded. Such a procedure is not unlike the Monte Carlo study of Hoover and Perez (1999), who replaced the real-economy data on one variable given the others to evaluate an early version of automatic *Gets*. The reliability of the selection process can be evaluated by the resulting measures of gauge, potency and both conditional and unconditional MSEs: see Doornik (2009b), and Castle (2008).

3.19   Data accuracy

To sustain empirically-based modeling, the data in use must provide reasonably accurate measures of the variables under analysis. At the extreme, if the data are too inaccurate to be of any use, or key variables are unobserved, economics must rely on pure theory, which perforce will remain untested, and cannot be calibrated to provide useful quantitative measures, so theory alone, even if correct, is rarely sufficient. The same bad data would be all that was available for evaluating forecasts, which would not necessarily reveal any mis-matches in stationary processes (e.g., Miller, 1978). Even if policy decisions involved location shifts, so outturns did not match the anticipated measures, that need not entail poor data. Thus, the only solution in this state of nature is to invest in better data collection.

At the other extreme, perfectly accurate data corresponding precisely with the relevant economic concepts are not likely to be common. As there is often a multiplicity of theoretical explanations, all sources of empirical evidence need to be carefully explored taking due account of the inaccuracy of the observed variables. Most observed variables are measured with some errors, so the crucial issue is the extent of the adverse impact of those errors on empirical analyses, which depends on the magnitude of any mis-measurement, and whether it changes over time. We consider these in turn.

Data contamination is any substantive perturbation of the observations from the correct measurements. Such mis-measurements may persist for several periods, and so look like a location shift. Discrepancies may be due to mis-recording or to inaccurate initial measures such as nowcasts, where later revision may improve the accuracy. In each case, a deviation leads to what is sometimes called an additive outlier, since its presence is not intrinsic to the process under analysis. In dynamic processes, additive outliers are hard to distinguish from innovation outliers, which do influence the process. Irrespective of their source, both outliers need to be addressed as they may be due to an inappropriate concept, such as using the wrong measure of opportunity cost in a money demand equation.

Most economic time series must have errors of measurement in levels relative to their conceptual targets. However, macroeconomic data tend to be I(1), often with intermittent superimposed breaks, so the signal is strong. To substantially distort an analysis, measurements thereof would have to suffer I(1) deviations from their theoretical counterparts. Even then, differences would be I(0) with breaks, measured with an I(0) error. In that setting, the relative variance of the measurement error to that of the true data becomes the prime determinant of any resulting distortions: Hendry (2001b) provides an empirical illustration. For estimating a known DGP, textbooks provide theoretical analyses of the impacts of measurement errors on coefficient estimates and their estimated standard errors. Here we are concerned with selection, and little is known about the impacts of measurement errors in that context on distorting which variables are incorrectly selected, although simulation studies can shed some light. Intuitively, measurement errors on relevant variables may lower the probability of retaining them, but have no effect on the chance retention of irrelevant variables, so will generally have adverse effects.

Secondly, changes in measurement accuracy in non-stationary processes can induce non-constancy in estimated econometric models. Over long time time periods, that effect is unavoidable, but in most analyses, such an effect will also occur near the last time period, when only preliminary data are available. The tools developed in this book are applicable to improve the accuracy of flash estimates of aggregates like GDP and inflation, as shown in Castle et al. (2009) and Castle and Hendry (2010b), and we address that issue in section 23.13 (Hendry, 1995a, ch.14, analyses effects of revisions on I(1) time series).

Appropriate formulations of data measures can help create constant-parameter equations (called extended constancy in Hendry, 1996). A well-known example is that price indexes use time-varying weights, and although all of the components might enter a model non-constantly, the index could deliver constancy. A commodity price index highlights this effect, as many of the components today would not have existed 200 years ago, and those most relevant then would not enter today: thus, using individual prices would not be sensible, yet the overall index could have a constant impact on aggregate inflation (say).

The most adverse consequences of measurement errors derive from either large errors or abrupt changes in measurement accuracy. Both can be mitigated by impulse-indicator saturation described in chapter 15. Nevertheless, measurement caveats must be borne in mind when interpreting any reported models.

3.20   Summary

The steps described above are integral to a successful approach to empirical model discovery. The choice of the set of variables that characterizes the LDGP is fundamental if useful knowledge is to be acquired about economic behavior. The data must be sufficiently accurately measured to justify their empirical analysis. The initial general model must be a good characterization of the data evidence suggested by the relevant subject-matter theory, institutional knowledge and past findings, embedding all the potential candidate effects that may matter. Most of the time spent on a research study will be allocated to thinking about the formulation of the LDGP, and checking the corresponding data coverage and quality. The exogeneity status of the putative explanatory variables, as to whether it is valid to condition on them, or on instrumental variables, must be carefully considered.

Issues like functional forms, longest lag lengths, multiple breaks and outliers, and the integrability of the time series need to be addressed in formulating the GUM, but these extensions can be tackled automatically. Next, the GUM must be checked for congruence (possibly at a later stage if there are insufficient observations relative to variables initially), and the reduction search commenced. Usually, impulse-indicator saturation will be included, so congruence can be tested only after some initial reductions. At this point, the feasible GUM can be used as the baseline for parsimonious encompassing. The multi-path search will deliver a set of one or more undominated congruent models, which can be compared by encompassing, and also tested against the feasible GUM. The estimated parameters in the finally selected model are then bias corrected, and the results reported. The reliability of the entire process can be evaluated by using that selection as the proximate DGP from which artificial data can be generated, then embedding the analysis in the original GUM and re-selecting in repeated simulations.

Before moving to a more formal analysis of the first six stages, which are the basis for the later extensions—to when there are more candidate regressors than observations, handling multiple structural breaks and outliers, testing exogeneity, and modeling non-linearity—we first illustrate many of the concepts just discussed, then investigate how to evaluate selection methods in general, the topic of chapter 5.

4 Empirical Modeling Illustrated

This chapter illustrates the discussion in Chapter 3 using *Autometrics* on an artificial data generation process first created almost 30 years ago for an early version of *PcGive*. In a setting where the DGP is known to the investigator, but obviously not to the software, what is found can be checked against what should have been found. The major points of Chapter 3 that are implemented are estimating the system of four simultaneous equations; diagnostic checking for the selection of a single equation being well-specified; parsimonious-encompassing tests of it against its GUM; testing for non-linearities; handling more candidate variables than observations when using IIS; selecting lag lengths despite the ensuing collinearity; checking for cointegrated relationships; implementing both a correct and a partially correct theory; and testing for super exogeneity.

4.1 The artificial DGP

To illustrate the important concepts in an arena where the data generation process (DGP) is known and data accuracy is not in question, so the closeness of the findings to the DGP can be judged, we consider modeling the *PcGive* artificial data set with the four variables CONS, INC, INFLAT and OUTPUT, denoted c, i, Δp, and q. In the DGP, c depends on i and Δp, its own first lag and that of i, based on Davidson et al. (1978) (see chapter 16). Then i depends on the first lags of itself, Δc, q and its lag; Δp depends on its own lag and that of q; and q on its own lag and that of Δp. However, the inflation equation has a location shift which is intended to mimic the effects of an autonomous oil shock, where Δp rises permanently leading q to fall, impacting in turn on c and i. Data were generated for a sample intended to represent quarterly observations over 1953(1)–1992(3), where the simulated oil shock started in

1973(3), with (c_t, i_t) interpreted as the domestic economy and $(\Delta p_t, q_t)$ determined by the world economy.

The 4-equation artificial DGP can be written in equilibrium-correction form as:

$$\Delta c_t = -0.9 + 0.4\Delta i_t + 0.15\,(i - c)_{t-1} - 0.9\Delta p_t + \epsilon_{1,t}, \tag{4.1}$$

$$\Delta i_t = -75.0 + 0.3\Delta c_t + 0.25\,(q - i)_{t-1} + 0.25\Delta q_t + \epsilon_{2,t}, \tag{4.2}$$

$$\Delta p_t = 0.3 + 0.7\Delta p_{t-1} + 0.077\,(q_{t-1} - 1200) + 2S_{1973(3)} + \epsilon_{3,t}, \tag{4.3}$$

$$\Delta q_t = 121.3 - 0.1q_{t-1} - 1.30\Delta p_{t-1} + \epsilon_{4,t}, \tag{4.4}$$

where $\epsilon_{i,t} \sim \mathsf{IN}\left[0, \sigma_i^2\right]$ with $(\sigma_1, \sigma_2, \sigma_3, \sigma_4) = (1.0, 3.0, 0.25, 4.0)$ and zero covariances. The variables are interpreted as $x_t = 100 \log X_t$ $(\forall x)$. Thus, there were 159 observations on $(c_t, i_t, \Delta p_t, q_t)$ with a location shift altering the world economy inflation intercept, equation (4.3), at observation 83 represented by the step indicator $S_{1973(3)}$ which is zero before 1973(3) and unity after. This shift left the system dynamics unaltered and only directly affected Δp_t but indirectly affected all the other variables.

The long-run equilibrium of the system was shifted from:

$$\begin{aligned} \Delta p = 1 &\ \left[1.0\% \text{ per quarter}\right] \quad q = 1213 - 13\Delta p = 1200, \\ c = i - 6\Delta p - 6 &= 888 \qquad\qquad\ \ i = q - 300 = 900, \end{aligned} \tag{4.5}$$

to:

$$\begin{aligned} \Delta p = 2.5 &\ \left[2.5\% \text{ per quarter}\right] \quad q = 1213 - 13\Delta p = 1180, \\ c = i - 6\Delta p - 6 &= 859 \qquad\qquad\ \ i = q - 300 = 880. \end{aligned} \tag{4.6}$$

Thus, equilibrium inflation more than doubled and world output fell by about 20%, with knock-on effects on (c_t, i_t) similar in pattern but much larger than the UK experienced at the time.

Figure 4.1 illustrates this comparison, where panels a & b record the actual UK data denoted $\Delta \log P_t$ and $\Delta \log Y_t$ and panels c & d the corresponding artificial Δp_t and q_t. Other than scale, the main difference is the presence of a trend in UK output, so that variable has been plotted in changes. While the location shift in q_t is evident visually, being roughly $5\sigma_4$, that in Δp_t is somewhat less obvious despite being $6\sigma_3$.

4.2   A simultaneous equations model

Since the properties of *Gets* derive from the theory of reduction (see section 6.4), the selection of linear simultaneous equations systems is just a special case of that theory. The crucial decision is the prior division of

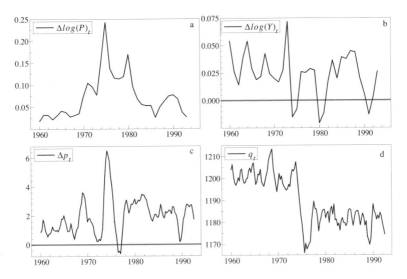

Figure 4.1
UK and corresponding artificial data

all the variables into endogenous variables to model and either weakly exogenous or lagged endogenous non-modeled variables. Here all four variables are initially considered as endogenous, although both Δp_t and q_t are weakly exogenous for the parameters of (4.1) and (4.2). Given that decision, the GUM is the conditional linear statistical system (often called the reduced form), which is always identified and can be tested for congruence as usual, so all later valid reductions should be congruent as well. Once such a specification is established, it is possible to test the hypothesis of super exogeneity using the approach noted in section 3.15, if there are sufficient shifts in the marginal processes of the putative exogenous variables. A parsimonious version of the system is then selected, maintaining congruence, such that all regressor variables are significant at the desired level in their associated equations to avoid spurious identification later (i.e., by including what are actually irrelevant variables). Weak instruments show up as a poorly determined initial system, requiring a loose significance level to retain instruments.

A simultaneous equations system is a reduction of a conditional statistical system characterized by over-identification restrictions, so a parsimonious encompassing representative can be found by a search algorithm like *Autometrics*. Such a selection can be made without knowing any of the prior identification restrictions (see e.g., Hendry and Krolzig,

2005). The simultaneous representation of the LDGP does need to be identified (e.g., by the usual rank condition when only inclusion and exclusion restrictions are used), but the specific constraints do not need to be known in advance. The key insight is that the initial conditional linear statistical system is just identified, so its parsimonious version is in fact already over-identified. It is well known that the former has many equivariant just-identified simultaneous representations (see e.g., Koopmans, Rubin and Leipnik, 1950, Fisher, 1966, and Hsiao, 1983), all with equal likelihood, so the parsimonious system can also have equivariant over-identified simultaneous forms: see Hendry and Mizon (1993). These are also reductions of just-identified models, so can be found by an algorithm seeking the most parsimonious, congruent representation, although we do not explicitly discuss that generalization in this book.

Correct modeling of the system (4.1)–(4.4) necessitates handling the simultaneity between Δc_t and Δi_t in (4.1) and (4.2) and the different intercept pre- and post-1973(3) in equation (4.3). When that omniscient knowledge is available, full information maximum likelihood estimation yields:

$$\Delta c_t = -0.83 - 0.156(c-i)_{t-1} + 0.424\Delta i_t - 0.979\Delta p_t, \tag{4.7}$$
$$ \underset{(0.33)}{} \underset{(0.024)}{} \underset{(0.064)}{} \underset{(0.088)}{}$$

$$\Delta i_t = -81.4 - 0.271(i-q)_{t-1} - 0.204\Delta c_t + 0.477\Delta q_t, \tag{4.8}$$
$$ \underset{(17)}{} \underset{(0.056)}{} \underset{(0.57)}{} \underset{(0.35)}{}$$

$$\Delta p_t = -90.8 + 0.729\Delta p_{t-1} + 0.076q_{t-1} + 1.73 S_{1973(3)}, \tag{4.9}$$
$$ \underset{(3.0)}{} \underset{(0.014)}{} \underset{(0.0025)}{} \underset{(0.06)}{}$$

$$\Delta q_t = 115 - 1.41\Delta p_{t-1} - 0.094q_{t-1} - 0.28 S_{1973(3)}, \tag{4.10}$$
$$ \underset{(50)}{} \underset{(0.23)}{} \underset{(0.041)}{} \underset{(1.0)}{}$$

$$\chi^2_{nd}(8) = 4.8 \quad F_{ar}(80, 515) = 1.06 \quad F_{het}(60, 540) = 1.04,$$

where $(\widehat{\sigma}_1, \widehat{\sigma}_2, \widehat{\sigma}_3, \widehat{\sigma}_4) = (1.12, 3.24, 0.18, 3.04)$, so the parameter and residual standard deviation estimates are reasonably close to their population values. None of the system mis-specification tests on the residuals rejects, where $\chi^2_{nd}(8)$ is a test of multivariate normality with 8 degrees of freedom (developed by Doornik and Hansen, 2008), F_{ar} is an approximate F-test for vector residual autocorrelation of order 5 (see Hendry, 1974), and F_{het} tests for residual heteroskedasticity (generalizing White, 1980). The step indicator $S_{1973(3)}$ has been included in (4.10) as a test of the specification described in (4.1)–(4.4). Figure 4.2 shows the fitted and actual values, and the residuals for the estimated system.

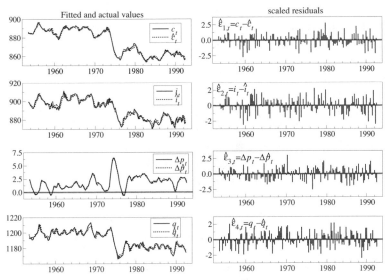

Figure 4.2
Fitted and actual values, and the residuals for the estimated system

4.3   Illustrating model selection concepts

In practice, theorizing or guessing the completely correct specification is very unikely, so we now consider how well (4.1) would be found commencing from a much larger specification that nests it. Thus, we address the topics summarized in Chapter 3 as follows. Section 3.5 considered the impact of selection, retaining only coefficients that were significant in the available sample, so we will report the extent to which that occurs below when using *Autometrics* as discussed in 3.6. We have already seen that none of the mis-specification tests (see section 3.7) rejected, and will note their behavior as diagnostic tests as we proceed. Section 3.8 introduced parsimonious encompassing as a selection criterion, and that will be reported for (4.1)

Although section 3.9 only briefly described indicator saturation (IIS), as the DGP has a location shift, but (4.1) did not, we will check that no spurious shifts are found as well as illustrate *Autometrics* for $N \geq T$. The DGP here is non-stationary, but not integrated so although that issue from section 3.10 does not arise we will test for cointegration since an investigator cannot know there are no unit roots. Section 3.11 on selecting lag length will be described for much longer lags than those in the DGP (which has $s = 1$), which will also create considerable collinearity among the autocorrelated variables, as discussed in section 3.12. Retaining the relevant economic theory is also an issue of importance as section 3.13 noted, and the benefits of doing so as against the dangers of direct imposition of a theory will be shown. This is the third setting discussed above, where a theory is rescued by including additional variables when a direct fit rejects.

Although the DGP is linear in the variables, functional form (considered in section 3.14) is rarely known for certain, so that too will be investigated by considering the alternative of a 3rd order polynomial in the principal components augmented with an exponential. Finally, to check the validity of conditioning, exogeneity as described in section 3.15, will be investigated.

4.4   Modeling the artificial data consumption function

Estimating (4.1) or (4.2) by ordinary least squares (OLS) entails simultaneity bias from the cross presence of Δi_t and Δc_t in the other equation. However, the insignificance of the former in (4.2) implies that bias will be relatively small. Indeed, estimating the levels relationship between c_t and $c_{t-1}, i_t, i_{t-1}, \Delta p_t$ by instrumental variables (IVE) using q_t, q_{t-1} and Δp_{t-1} as additional instruments delivers almost identical results to those reported in (4.11) using OLS.

4.4.1   Selection

Creating a GUM in the levels of all four variables each with 5 lags, a constant (not selected), centered seasonals (CSj, as the data are quarterly and seasonality may remain) and the step-shift dummy, makes for 28 regressors in total, estimated over 1954(2) – 1992(3):

$$c_t = 0.819c_{t-1} + 0.0384c_{t-2} - 0.138c_{t-3} + 0.201c_{t-4} - 0.133c_{t-5}$$
$$\quad\;(0.085)\qquad\quad(0.11)\qquad\quad(0.11)\qquad\quad(0.11)\qquad\quad(0.075)$$

$$+\, 0.507i_t - 0.294i_{t-1} - 0.0475i_{t-2} + 0.119i_{t-3} - 0.0433i_{t-4}$$
$$\quad(0.032)\qquad(0.059)\qquad\quad(0.063)\qquad\quad(0.063)\qquad\quad(0.065)$$

$$-\, 0.00938i_{t-5} - 0.392\Delta p_t + 0.379\Delta p_{t-1} - 0.618\Delta p_{t-2} - 0.423\Delta p_{t-3}$$
$$\quad\;(0.049)\qquad\quad(0.42)\qquad\quad(0.61)\qquad\qquad(0.6)\qquad\qquad(0.59)$$

$$+\, 0.537\Delta p_{t-4} - 0.0537\Delta p_{t-5} - 0.0109q_t - 0.0337q_{t-1} - 0.0707q_{t-2}$$
$$\quad\;(0.58)\qquad\qquad(0.32)\qquad\quad(0.032)\qquad\quad(0.052)\qquad\quad(0.057)$$

$$+ 0.0281q_{t-3} + 0.0316q_{t-4} - 0.0508q_{t-5} + 106$$
$$\quad (0.053) \qquad (0.052) \qquad\quad (0.043) \qquad\quad (75)$$

$$+ 0.235CS1_t + 0.2CS2_t + 0.143CS3_t + 2.54S_{1973(3)}$$
$$\quad (0.26) \qquad\quad (0.27) \qquad\quad (0.27) \qquad\quad (1.4)$$

$$R^2 = 0.995 \ \ \widehat{\sigma}_1 = 1.07 \ \ F_{ar}(5, 121) = 1.11 \ \ F_{arch}(4, 146) = 1.35$$
$$\chi^2_{nd}(2) = 2.19 \ \ F_{het}(50, 103) = 0.99 \ \ F_{RESET}(2, 124) = 3.5^*.$$

Automatic model selection by *Autometrics* at 1% yields a final model that is greatly simplified:

$$c_t = 0.81c_{t-1} + 0.51i_t - 0.30i_{t-1} - 0.996\Delta p_t - 19.1 \qquad\qquad (4.11)$$
$$\quad\ (0.025) \qquad (0.028) \qquad (0.035) \qquad (0.086) \qquad (8.6)$$

$$R^2 = 0.993 \ \ \widehat{\sigma}_1 = 1.08$$

$$F_{ar}(5, 144) = 0.94 \ \ F_{arch}(4, 146) = 0.86 \ \ t_{ur} = -7.51^{**} \ \ \chi^2_{nd}(2) = 1.94$$
$$F_{het}(8, 145) = 1.17 \ \ F_{RESET}(2, 147) = 0.87 \ \ F_{nl}(12, 137) = 0.98.$$

The retained variables coincide with those in the corresponding DGP equation (4.1) with recognizably similar coefficients. New misspecification test statistics—discussed more fully in section 12.1—are F_{arch} for autoregressive conditional heteroskedasticity (denoted ARCH: see Engle, 1982), F_{reset} which is the RESET test (see Ramsey, 1969) and F_{NL} which is the low-dimensional test for non-linearity from Castle and Hendry (2010a) noted in section 3.14, using squares, cubics and exponentials of the principal components of the regressors in (4.11). Again, none of the tests rejects. Also, $t_{ur} = -7.51^{**}$ is the *PcGive* unit-root t-test (see Banerjee and Hendry, 1992, and Ericsson and MacKinnon, 2002), which strongly rejects the presence of a unit root in (4.11), matching the properties of the DGP in (4.1)–(4.4). Figure 4.3 reports the fitted and actual values, residuals, residual density and residual correlogram for (4.11) in its four panels.

Selecting from lag lengths much longer than those in the DGP (described in section 3.11), as in the above GUM (which had $s = 5$) seems unproblematic despite the considerable collinearity from the autocorrelated variables (discussed in section 3.12): there are 58 correlations between the GUM regressors larger than 0.9 and another 93 greater than 0.8, but that did not preclude finding the relevant DGP equation.

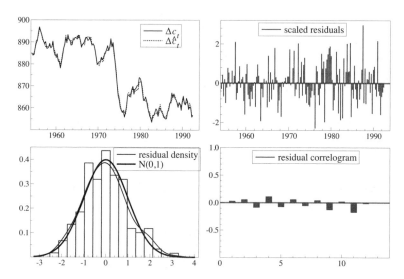

Figure 4.3
Fitted and actual values, residuals, residual density and residual correlogram
for the estimated consumption equation

The solved long-run static outcome from (4.11) is:

$$c = \underset{(0.045)}{1.10} \; i - \underset{(0.56)}{5.25} \; \Delta p_t - \underset{(40.3)}{100.5} \; ,$$

which when written as $c = i - 5.25\Delta p_t - 10.5 + 0.1\,(i - 900)$ is reasonably close to (4.5) given that the coefficient of income is slightly over-estimated (in fact by a similar magnitude to IVE).

Despite commencing from a highly over-parametrized GUM, the correct final equation is selected. The impact of selection by retaining only coefficients that are significant considered in section 3.5 is not the explanation for the over-estimate of the income coefficient here. The new mis-specification tests did not reject, nor did the re-use of the earlier ones as diagnostic tests of an appropriate selection (see section 3.7). The test of parsimonious encompassing noted in section 3.8 corresponds to testing for a valid reduction from the GUM to (4.11), used here as a selection criterion, and for (4.1) yields $F_{enc}(23, 126) = 0.98$ so also does not reject.

4.4.2 Constancy

Next, we turn to evidence of non-constancy. Estimating (4.11), or (4.1), by recursive least squares (RLS: see e.g., Doornik and Hendry, 2013b) shows some evidence of parameter non-constancy owing to the change in the simultaneity bias after the oil crisis, as seen in Figure 4.4. The first five panels record the recursively estimated coefficients of the variables noted on the figure, together with twice their estimated standard errors on either side, shown as $\pm 2\widehat{\sigma}_t$. The sixth panel reports the 1-step residuals, defined by the deviations between actual and fitted value using the recursive estimates, shown with $\pm 2\widehat{\sigma}_{1,t}$. The last two panels record constancy tests, based on Chow (1960), testing 1-step ahead and between the past and future fits (called break-point) for each time point.

Estimating either the GUM or (4.1) using IIS delivered (4.11), so no outliers or shifts were detected, matching the properties of the DGP and the probability theory prediction of $\alpha N = 0.001 \times 158 \simeq 0.16$ indicators being retained under the null.

However, most mis-specifications of (4.1) lead to induced predictive failure, partly corrected by IIS. For example, omitting Δp_t from (4.11) led to some non-constancy, as seen in Figure 4.5, but using IIS led to retaining indicators for 1974(1), 1974(2) and 1974(4) with similar magnitude coefficients, suggesting a shift had occurred in that mis-specified equation. We can use this example as the third setting discussed above for retaining a relevant economic theory (section 3.13), showing the dangers of directly imposing the theory that c_t only depends on c_{t-1}, i_t, i_{t-1}. Rather, if the GUM includes Δp_t while retaining the simpler theory, its insights are rescued by that additional variable included in (4.11), when a direct fit rejects (see the many examples in Hendry and Mizon, 2011).

More notably, estimating (4.3) without the oil dummy manifests considerable predictive failure after 1973(3), as seen in Figure 4.6. The comparison with Figure 4.7 is marked, the non-constancy compared to the model with the step-shift dummy highlighting the advantages of embedding even an excellent theory in a more general framework that allows for data properties that may be absent from the theory.

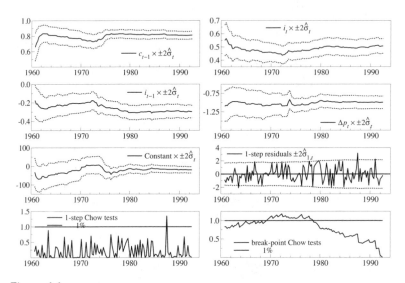

Figure 4.4
Recursive least squares graphics for the correctly specified consumption equation

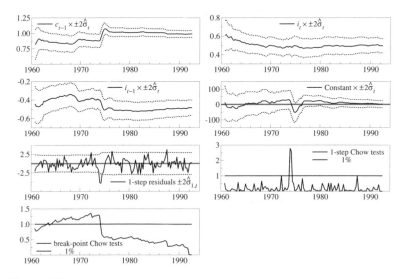

Figure 4.5
Recursive least squares graphics for the mis-specified consumption equation

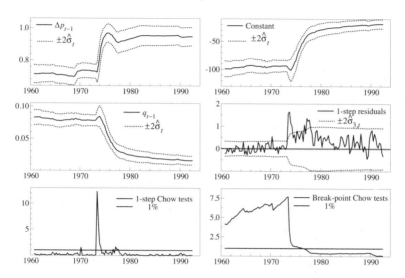

Figure 4.6
Recursive least squares graphics for the mis-specified inflation equation

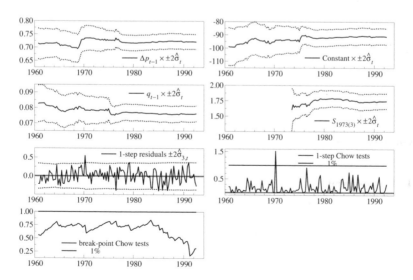

Figure 4.7
Recursive least squares graphics for the correctly specified inflation equation

4.4.3 Exogeneity

The last issue to be illustrated is checking the validity of conditioning on contemporaneous variables, the topic of exogeneity discussed in section 3.15. There is not much power to test that hypothesis for i_t but the dependence of Δp_t on $S_{1973(3)}$ does allow a powerful check. First, $S_{1973(3)}$ is highly significant in (4.9), so shifts the mean of Δp_t. Secondly, if the parameters of (4.7) depended on those of (4.9), they should shift at the same time. The simplest test of that hypothesis is to add $S_{1973(3)}$ to (4.7) and test its significance: the outcome is a t-test value of 0.63. Thirdly, in practice such a shift would not be known, but would have to be determined from the data evidence modeling Δp_t. Thus, we formulate a GUM for Δp_t involving $s = 5$ lags of all four variables (but no contemporaneous values), constant (retained) and centered seasonals, then select using IIS at 0.1%, which delivers two significant impulse indicators for 1973(3) and 1973(4). These are insignificant when added to (4.11) with $F_{SE}(2, 151) = 1.41$, so there is no evidence against treating Δp_t as exogenous in the consumption equation here.

IIS has relatively low power as a test of exogeneity in settings where location shifts persist for prolonged periods as here. A recent innovation as this book was being completed was step-indicator saturation (SIS), which uses a saturating set of increasing step functions, denoted $\{1_{\{t \leq j\}}\}$, where $j = 1, \ldots, T$ when $1_{\{t \leq j\}} = 1$ for observations up to j, and zero otherwise, rather than impulses as the basis for detecting breaks: see Castle, Doornik, Hendry and Pretis (2013). This is already available in *PcGive*, so we will also apply SIS here.

For the same GUM as just above, selection at 0.1% yielded:

$$\Delta p_t = \underset{(0.014)}{0.726\Delta p_{t-1}} + \underset{(0.0025)}{0.076q_{t-1}} - \underset{(0.063)}{1.74 \times 1_{\{t \leq 1973(2)\}}} - \underset{(3.0)}{89.6}, \tag{4.12}$$

$$R^2 = 0.980 \quad \widehat{\sigma}_3 = 0.18 \tag{4.13}$$

$$F_{reset}(2, 148) = 0.86 \quad \chi^2_{nd}(2) = 0.18 \quad F_{arch}(4, 146) = 0.55,$$

$$F_{het}(5, 148) = 0.92 \quad F_{ar}(5, 145) = 1.63 \quad F_{NL}(12, 137) = 0.98,$$

where $t_{ur} = -7.51^{**}$. As can be seen, the "obverse" shift was detected, ending in 1973(2), with almost the same magnitude, opposite-signed coefficient as $S_{1973(3)}$ in (4.9). Second, as before, adding $1_{\{t \leq 1973(2)\}}$ to (4.11) is insignificant, now with $t = -0.63$.

4.5   Summary

The comparison of the inflation equation with and without the step shift indicator highlights the dangers of under-specification in processes subject to location shifts, which seems to include most macroeconomic time series. As (4.12) illustrates, searching for such shifts can be part of the automatic discovery process, here learning about a feature that was not included in the initial analysis. Although the Oil Crisis impact on inflation is of course well known and remembered, other shifts are not (see the discussion in Hendry, 1999). Conversely, the selection of (4.11) from a much larger GUM illustrates the low costs we will find for the approach described below, even when there are more candidate variables than observations. In particular, Chapter 14 will establish the considerable advantages deriving from embedding a theory model in a much more general GUM and seleting only over the additional variables, suitable orthogonalized with respect to the theory variables. We return to illustrations based on this artificial data set in sections 18.5 and 19.6.

5 Evaluating Model Selection

Empirical models could be chosen according to many criteria, as this chapter discusses. Selection criteria can conflict, such as achieving empirical congruence may thwart theory consistency and vice versa, so we consider nine possible ways to judge the success of selection. Of these, four seem infeasible, two are widely used but seem suspect, so we focus on the remaining three practical criteria, namely a selection algorithm's ability to recover the local data-generating process (LDGP) starting from the general unrestricted model as often as when starting from the LDGP itself; whether the operating characteristics of the algorithm match their desired properties; and whether selection can almost always find a well-specified, undominated model of the LDGP. Achieving all three jointly seems feasible.

5.1 Introduction

Before deciding on what selection criteria to use for evaluating model selection, one must first specify what the search is for. Chapter 6 discusses why the LDGP is an obvious target when modeling for understanding, policy analyses, or testing theories, whereas chapter 23 considers the very different issues involved in selecting forecasting models. Here, we first summarize some desirable properties of an econometric model where the potential uses may range across all of the above, so that a model needs to be as robust as possible in six distinct senses. We require a model to be

(a) robust to model mis-specification, such that the reported parameter estimates are reliable even for extensions of the set of variables;

(b) robust to past outliers and breaks, especially location shifts, so the estimated model accurately characterizes the salient data features;

(c) robust to policy changes, so those do not alter the model in ways that vitiate its implementation;

(d) robust in both identification and interpretation;

(e) robust to the level of aggregation over space, time and variables;

(f) robust in forecasting, especially to unmodeled breaks at the forecast origin.

To obtain the first either requires all omitted effects to be orthogonal to those so far included, which is unlikely in economics, or necessitates analyzing a sufficiently general set of candidate explanatory variables to include all substantively relevant effects, based on a sound theoretical analysis of both the long-run and short-run. The choice of variables determines the form of the LDGP and the overall quality of the final model. To discover a well-specified undominated model requires allowing for empirically-determined lag reactions, and possibly non-linear (including threshold) effects. Additionally, integration and cointegration must be handled using the appropriate non-standard critical values for their decisions. That step facilitates partitioning reactions between long-run steady-state equilibria and short-run dynamics, which also helps produce a more orthogonal parametrization. Those two features, namely including all substantively relevant determinants and having a near-orthogonal formulation, are key to achieving this aspect. *Autometrics* allows both long-run theory relationships and any known dynamics or parameter signs to be embedded in its general search procedure. For the overall system to be coherent potentially requires joint modeling and estimation of equations for all the relevant variables as in Hendry, Neale and Srba (1988).

To obtain the second form of robustness requires mitigating the impacts of all past outliers and location shifts on the underlying structure. Impulse-indicator saturation (IIS) is able to achieve this jointly with the resolution of (a) by adding a complete set of indicators to the candidate regressors from the outset as discussed in chapter 15, noting *Autometrics* can handle more variables than observations. Johansen and Nielsen (2009), Doornik (2009b) and Castle et al. (2011, 2012) show that this is not only viable, but remarkably efficient. Other tests for multiple breaks can suffer from being inapplicable to the start and end of the sample period: a break in the former period can hide later breaks; and a break in the latter will have detrimental effects on the estimated model when data processes are evolving, as shown in Hendry and Mizon (2011).

To obtain the third requires first successfully implementing both (a) and (b), then testing whether the resulting model satisfies super exogeneity, such that changes in policy do not change the model itself. Structural breaks allow tests of the Lucas (1976) critique (see Hendry, 2002, for a bibliographic perspective), since a conditional model remaining constant despite data moments changing is strong evidence of super exogeneity for that model's parameters. A test based on IIS applied to the conditioning variables can ascertain whether breaks have impacted in the past on the empirical model (see Hendry and Santos, 2010, building on super exogeneity tests in Engle and Hendry, 1993). This applies especially to the assumption that conditional variables are weakly exogenous in regression models, which could still hold despite dynamic feedbacks (as in Granger, 1969: see Hendry and Mizon, 1999).

To obtain the fourth needs success on (a)–(c). Identification both entails the uniqueness of the relationships and that they correspond to the underlying reality, whereas interpretation requires that causal factors are correctly delineated (see Hendry, 1992, for an example of some of the difficulties in achieving the second). A theoretical model is not essential for identification (see Hendry, Lu and Mizon, 2009), but can be invaluable in specifying the links between relationships under analysis.

Robustness to aggregation over space (e.g., regions), time (e.g., days to quarters) and variables (e.g., over all consumers' expenditure) is impossible to achieve completely, as the greater the extent of disaggregation, the less constancy and the more complexity seems to emerge. Consequently, the best that can be obtained is to group the most homogeneous units. Thus, many macro studies use national data, aggregated to groups most germane for the associated policy analysis (e.g., GDP and inflation), and model quarterly data as a compromise where such a frequency is available.

Finally, to obtain (f) needs success on (a)–(e), and then adopting one of the robust forecasting devices proposed in Hendry (2006), as used successfully in a number of studies, such as Hendry (2004a).

5.2 Judging the success of selection algorithms

There are many grounds on which to select empirical models. Four central categories are: theoretical, empirical, aesthetic, and philosophical. Within each category, there are also many criteria, including

(a) *theory*: generality; internal consistency; clarity; invariance, identification;

(b) *empirical*: goodness-of-fit; parsimony; consistency with theory; constancy; empirical congruence (statistically well-specified); encompassing (not dominated by rival models); forecast accuracy; robustness;

(c) *aesthetic*: elegance; relevance; telling a story;

(d) *philosophical*: novelty; excess content; making money; etc.

An obvious solution to resolve the dilemma as to which should be used is to match all of these criteria. Unfortunately, in general one cannot do so as many of the criteria conflict (e.g., generality versus parsimony; elegance versus congruence, etc.), human knowledge is limited, and economies are complex, high dimensional, heterogeneous, and non-stationary, with data samples that are often small, incomplete and may be inaccurate. As noted in the chapter 3, many empirical modeling decisions are undocumented and are often not recognized as involving selection. For example, empirical models selected to match a theory are usually treated as if no selection was involved, although it would be remarkable if the very first specification investigated was the final choice. Any test followed by an action entails selection: a well-known example is testing for residual autocorrelation then using a correction after rejecting the null hypothesis of white noise—albeit this is a practice which has been warned against on many occasions (e.g., Hendry and Mizon, 1978, and Mizon, 1995). Unstructured selection is not open to analysis, nor can its empirical properties be determined, so false null rejection frequencies cannot be pre-set. Consequently, we restrict our attention to formally defined selection approaches, usually embodied in algorithms. Often these are then too complicated to be studied in detail mathematically, although many of their stages can be rigorously analyzed. Fortunately, computer algorithms allow operational studies of the available alternative selection strategies by Monte Carlo simulation when analysis becomes intractable.

When models are constructed with a specific purpose in mind, they need to be evaluated accordingly: see e.g., Granger (1999) and Granger and Pesaran (2000). Nevertheless, that evaluation process itself may need to be evaluated, in so far as many assumptions often remain implicit. As two examples, the best model selected by an information criterion could still fail to describe the evidence at all usefully if applied to an inadequate set of variables; and conventional estimated coefficient standard errors may be used in test statistics, but in fact be inappropriate because of unmodeled error autocorrelation or heteroskedasticity, leading to incorrect inferences. Thus, selection without evaluation will always remain problematic.

To resolve the dilemma of which criteria to use, we consider some practical ways to judge the success of selection algorithms. Here we address nine in the subsequent sections

1. maximizing the goodness of fit (section 5.3),

2. high probability of locating the LDGP (section 5.4),

3. improved inference about parameters of interest over the GUM (section 5.5),

4. improved forecasting over the GUM and other selection methods (section 5.6),

5. working well for realistic DGPs (section 5.7),

6. matches a theory-derived specification (section 5.8),

7. able to recover the LDGP starting from the GUM almost as often as from the LDGP itself (section 5.9),

8. operating characteristics of the algorithm match their desired properties (section 5.10),

9. generally finding a well-specified and undominated model of the LDGP (section 5.11).

We conclude in section 5.12 that the last three offer viable measures of the success of selection algorithms, and can be achieved jointly with retaining any data-consistent theory insights, an approach addressed in chapter 14.

5.3   Maximizing the goodness of fit

Many selection algorithms seek to maximize the goodness of fit, possibly penalized for model size, which seems an intuitively sensible approach given one would not wish to minimize it. When the model specification is known, maximum likelihood is a widely-used estimation principle, and for regression estimation, for example, entails minimizing the residual variance, $\widehat{\sigma}_\epsilon^2$. The general model from which *Gets* commences is estimated by maximum likelihood methods, so often correspond to obtaining the best fit from the given set of variables. However, in the context of model *selection*, maximizing the goodness of fit raises a number of serious difficulties.

First, an often rehearsed criticism of model selection is that a perfect fit can be obtained by using a polynomial of the same order as the number of observations, or by an indicator for every observation. In fact, such gross overfitting is not an issue of selection—as none is needed—but of estimation. Below, we will consider many cases where there are more candidate variables than observations, yet do not overfit.

Second, there are many measures of fit, including correlations and residual, or error, variances, both corrected for degrees of freedom and uncorrected, or penalized more or less stringently in various ways for the number of parameters fitted. Different selections usually result from each of these. In chapter 17 below, we will show that they correspond to different implicit significance levels α, and a more coherent approach is to specify α. Indeed, it will transpire that the probability of locating an LDGP is not monotonic in the critical value chosen, and can rise as α becomes more stringent. As an extreme example, if $N = 100$ and $n = 0$, so no variables matter, setting $\alpha = 0.05$ will almost invariably lead to selecting a false model (on average with 5 variables) whereas $\alpha = 0.005$ will almost always select the null LDGP, so procedures which maximize goodness of fit must be flawed in that setting.

Third, the best fitting model in a given class may not characterize the evidence at all well, and could still exhibit systematic deviations from the observations, such as residual autocorrelation or heteroskedasticity, so other criteria are clearly needed in addition.

Fourth, Lovell (1983) conducted a Monte Carlo experiment which sought to evaluate several model selection methods based on maximizing the goodness of fit (such as maximum adjusted R^2, usually denoted $\bar{R}^2$), and demonstrated just how bad it was to transfer a concept relevant to estimating a pre-specified model to selecting from a set of candidate variables. Since $\bar{R}^2$ is maximized in a regression by retaining each and every variable whose estimated coefficient has a $|t|$-value greater than unity, $\widehat{\sigma}_\epsilon^2$ is minimized and so underestimates σ_ϵ^2, leading to overfitting.

Finally, as shown in chapter 13, variance dominance (best fitting on the criterion of minimum $\widehat{\sigma}_\epsilon^2$) is necessary, but not sufficient, for encompassing, so selecting the best fitting model does not ensure being able to explain other empirical models of the same phenomenon, whereas selecting the parsimonious encompassing model will.

5.4 High probability of recovery of the LDGP

Historically, a failure to recover the LDGP has been seen as a major drawback of data-based selection. In part, this was due to weaknesses in the selection methods (e.g., Lovell, 1983), and in part to considering situations where the LDGP would not have been retained even when it was the postulated model (see, e.g., some of the experiments in Hoover and

Perez, 1999). Thus, this criterion is overly demanding, as it may be nearly impossible to retain the LDGP even when commencing from it and using conventional inference. For example, some of the estimated coefficients may have $|t| < 0.1$ at the available sample size, so would rarely be retained even when the LDGP was the GUM.

Selection cannot improve an inference problem in the LDGP, be it low levels of significance (e.g., Leeb and Pötscher, 2003), a lack of identification (see, e.g., Faust and Whiteman, 1997, and the reply in Hendry, 1997), or an inability to forecast because of repeated unanticipated location shifts (see e.g., Clements and Hendry, 2008). Phillips (2003) provides an insightful analysis of the limits of econometrics. If an LDGP would be badly estimated when it was known, selection will not work well either: but we do not deem that a problem for the algorithm *per se*. In Monte Carlo simulations, it is feasible to evaluate how well an algorithm does on this criterion when commencing from the GUM, and compare its performance with starting from the LDGP, which is considered in section 5.9 below.

5.5   Improved inference about parameters of interest

The third criterion attempts to use selection to improve inference about parameters of interest, by seeking small yet accurate uncertainty regions around their estimates. This has been criticized by Leeb and Pötscher (2003, 2005) among others. Chapter 9 discusses their analysis of a bivariate linear regression that coincides with the DGP, but where only one parameter is deemed of interest and the other is small relative to the sample size. Despite the unrealistic assumptions of such an analysis, it is a special case of selecting from a high-dimensional GUM that nests an unknown LDGP. When the two variables are intercorrelated, conventional t-tests on the estimated coefficient of the latter will only occasionally reject the null, inducing a bimodal distribution for estimates of the parameter of interest when the decision rule is to eliminate insignificant variables. Thus, intermittently significant estimates can lead to increases in uncertainty from selection.

Analyses of the properties of selection methods when the GUM is the DGP only reflect costs of inference, and ignore the costs and benefits of narrowing the range of useful specifications, and discovering crucial data features such as non-constancy. Here the DGP is specified initially, but it is not possible to consistently estimate both its parameters, precluding consistent selection. The approach in chapter 14 would embed their DGP model in a more general GUM if both variables were deemed relevant in the underlying theory, so retain them without search. If only the first variable was relevant in the theory, that would be retained, but the second orthogonalized with respect to the first (as would all other candidate variables) and selected only if significant. The distribution of the estimator of the parameter of interest would be incorrectly centered on the coefficient of the univariate LDGP, but unaffected by selection.

In addition, the sampling variances of bias-corrected estimates of the parameters of retained relevant variables tend to exceed those from directly estimating the DGP, so this second objective will not be achieved in our approach. Instead, a large increase in knowledge can be achieved both by excluding a range of potential determinants—narrowing the scope of the analysis–and discovering features not previously known.

5.6   Improved forecasting

There are many contending approaches when improved forecasting is the objective, including using the GUM, other selection methods, averages over a class of models, factor methods, robust devices, and neural nets among others. Unfortunately, in processes subject to unanticipated breaks, which seem all too common in economics, in-sample performance need not be a reliable guide to later forecasting success: see Clements and Hendry (1998, 1999). Thus, it is difficult to see how this objective could be implemented without fore-knowledge that breaks will not occur in future, or will be correctly anticipated. Absent such omniscience, then forecasting devices that are robust to location shifts can outperform relative to a dominant in-sample model: see e.g., Clements and Hendry (2006) and Hendry (2006). Consequently, it is unclear as yet how to select viable forecasting devices that will actually improve forecast accuracy in practice on a systematic basis. Chapter 23 considers some recent findings.

5.7   Working well for realistic LDGPs

There are also many possible contenders for an algorithm that succeeds for realistic LDGPs, albeit with different properties in different states of nature—although, it is unclear that anyone could specify what a realistic DGP or LDGP would be in general in empirical economics. The long list of possible methods includes, but is not restricted to, AIC (e.g., Akaike, 1973), BIC (also called SC, see Schwarz, 1978), Phillips (1994,

1995, 1996), Tibshirani (1996) and Efron, Hastie, Johnstone and Tibshirani (2004), Hoover and Perez (1999, 2004) (also see Hendry and Krolzig, 1999), Hendry and Krolzig (2001), White (2000) and Perez-Amaral et al. (2003) (also see Castle, 2005), Krolzig (2003), and Demiralp and Hoover (2003), as well as that old perennial, step-wise regression.

In important respects, different methods are designed for different problems, and will tend to work well in their own setting. The large-scale simulation study in Castle et al. (2013) of many of the above methods highlights that property. For example, if the LDGP was a stationary infinite autoregressive process, and the objective was 1-step forecasting after a large sample, AIC can be a valuable tool. However, Hannan and Quinn (1979) show that AIC does not consistently select a finite-order stationary autoregressive process as the sample size increases without bound, whereas BIC does. Both of these methods select a model using a measure of goodness of fit penalized for the number of estimated parameters. In essence, they seek to trade off omitting a relevant but small effect against estimation uncertainty as to its parameter value. Neither seems useful when there may be dozens, or even hundreds, of irrelevant candidate regressors: Campos et al. (2003) show that without further modification, BIC tends to retain every variable when the number of irrelevant variables grows close to the sample size, not quite what might be expected of an approach that penalizes additional parameters, although corrections have been proposed (e.g., Hurvich and Tsai, 1989). We will compare *Autometrics* with some of these alternatives below.

5.8   Matching a theory-derived specification

Much of the history of empirical econometrics has been driven by the desire to match theory-based models to data, from early estimates of demand curves in Moore (1925) and Schultz (1928) (see, e.g., Morgan, 1990, for a history), through Keynesian macromodels in Klein (1950) and Klein, Ball, Hazlewood and Vandome (1961) (e.g., Qin, 1993), to dynamic stochastic general equilibrium models as in Kydland and Prescott (1991) and Smets and Wouters (2003) for example. Thus, matching a theory-derived specification is the dominant paradigm in economics, and is often viewed as the only reasonable approach, because of the issues of specification, endogeneity and identification, following from Keynes (1939, 1940) and Koopmans (1947) inter alia. Although considerable technical progress in econometrics has resulted, many have questioned whether there has been much empirical value added from a "quantifying theory" approach: see inter alia, Vining (1949a, 1949b), Haavelmo (1989), Summers (1991), and the critiques of Ireland (2004) in Johansen (2006b) and Juselius and Franchi (2007).

Four fundamental problems confront any strategy of selecting an empirical model by matching it exactly to a theory-derived specification: first, progress in economic theory itself; second, how to evaluate the resulting models; third, naive corroborationism where success is judged by forcing a match; and finally, model revision following data evaluation, thereby inducing a simple to general approach. We briefly consider these in turn; Hendry (2009) has a more extensive discussion, and Boland (2014) provides a penetrating analysis.

First, no theory is complete, correct, and immutable, so forcing a theory-derived model onto data imposes a theory that is incomplete, certain to be incorrect, and will shortly be replaced, thereby rendering previous evidence useless. Such an activity has been all too common historically, and differs markedly from guiding an empirical analysis using theory insights (e.g., Bårdsen, Eitrheim, Jansen and Nymoen, 2005).

Second, it is unclear how to evaluate the success of imposing a theory on evidence, beyond appraisal of signs and magnitudes of the resulting parameter estimates (i.e., matching a subset of data moments). Partly, this is because many theories are imprecise in important respects, such as functional forms and latencies, but often about signs and magnitudes, so could be deemed successful even when seriously at odds with the data, and partly because corroboration (the next topic) is far from persuasive. Once the data are allowed more than a token role, selection issues arise (the final topic of this section), and these are often hidden as criticized in e.g., Leamer (1983). Testing the auxiliary assumptions of a theory (such as white-noise errors) need throw no light on its validity or otherwise.

Third, corroboration occurs when one formulates a theory, seeks data with the same names as the theory, imposes the theory on the data, and checks that some of the theory predictions are not refuted. Anomalies are either ignored, or left for later theory to explain, renamed puzzles to suit the fashion of the present generation of journal editors. Such an approach seems to be due to a mis-understanding of science as postulating deep theories then testing these by evidence, at which point Eddington's famous test of Einstein's theory of relativity from light bent by the sun during the 1919 solar eclipse is cited. Eddington tested two rival theories with different predictions, so was seeking refutation of one of them, and succeeded (see Eddington, 1928). Moreover, in all branches of the natural and biological sciences, many theories have come after evidence, from Newton (using Kepler's laws: see Spanos, 2007), and Charles Darwin (Beagle records and specimens, as well as later experiments at Down House), through Wilhelm Roentgen (discovery of X-rays), and Ernest Rutherford (showing that atoms are not unitary), to list but a small subset of a distinguished lineage.

Finally, how should one proceed when a test rejects a theory? Unfortunately, there is no unique answer—any aspect being wrong could have induced rejection, so patching the apparent problem need not rescue the model. Examples include location shifts inducing residual serial correlation; omitted variables inducing heteroskedasticity; functional-form mis-specification suggesting non-constancy or residual serial correlation; and so on. The process of evaluation involves a simple-to-general approach if more than one hypothesis is tested, as rejection of any one invalidates tests of all the others. Below, we consider instead embedding a theory model in a more general specification, such that it will be selected if it is a valid simplification, and otherwise can still help guide the analysis.

5.9   Recovering the LDGP starting from the GUM or the LDGP

The distinction between costs of inference and costs of search helps to clarify from what source mistakes arise during selection. Costs of inference are inevitable when tests have non-zero null rejection frequencies, and non-unit power against the relevant alternatives. Costs of search are additional, owing to commencing from a GUM that is more general than the LDGP. Only the costs of search are really due to selection, as the costs of inference would confront an investigator who began from the LDGP, but could not be certain that the specification was indeed correct, and omniscience is not realistic in empirical economics.

Perhaps surprisingly, costs of inference dominate costs of search for well structured *Gets* selection strategies (these two costs are analyzed in greater details in section 7.6 and section 7.7). This finding has already been alluded to above, since there is little efficiency loss in examining many candidate variables that transpire to be irrelevant for the given analysis. Monte Carlo simulations can examine the behavior of selection from the LDGP compared to from the GUM which nests it to see how much selection matters. Some points in the parameter space of the joint density of all the variables in the analysis must produce major differences, such as having higher correlations between irrelevant and relevant variables than between the latter and the dependent variable, so the LDGP is almost always retained when fitted whereas selection from the GUM is frequently incorrect. Such cases caution that there is no *panacea*, but a progressive research strategy that rechecks models as new observations accrue can help avoid systematic mistakes.

As the sample size, T, increases without bound for a given model size, N, with fixed parameters, the selection significance level can be allowed to decline at a suitable rate towards zero, so no Type I errors are made, yet power rises towards unity, so no Type II mistakes occur either. Thus, consistent estimation leads to consistent selection for a suitable sequence of critical values, and both costs become zero asymptotically for a fixed model.

5.10 Operating characteristics

Possible operating characteristics of any proposed method might include the requirements that

(a) the nominal null rejection frequency α matches the actual gauge g,

(b) estimated coefficients of retained variables are unbiased for the corresponding LDGP parameters,

(c) potency is close to the power of the corresponding test in the LDGP,

(d) equation standard errors are unbiasedly estimated,

(e) conditional MSEs are small,

(f) unconditional MSEs are small.

All of these attributes can be evaluated by Monte Carlo simulations, and such experiments will play an important role below. Since the algorithms are automatic, it is straightforward to simulate their behavior for any chosen combinations of DGP and GUM, and evaluate the resulting properties. A drawback of Monte Carlo studies is their limitation to the specific cases investigated when the formulation of a canonical case is unclear, although techniques, such as response surfaces, allow some generalizations: see Hendry (1984); Doornik (2006) provides a recent update. Nevertheless, general theoretical analyses would circumvent that difficulty, and although they are presented below for a number of the stages in *Gets* selection, overall distributional results have proved relatively intractable to date. The analytical derivations in Leeb and Pötscher (2003, 2005) noted above provide an invaluable baseline, but serve to highlight the likely difficulties of also incorporating the impacts of mis-specification testing, IIS, etc., into explicit distributional results.

Some operating characteristics may be mutually incompatible. For example, unconditional unbiased estimation seems infeasible after selection, and the bias corrections discussed in chapter 10 for the conditional distribution would exacerbate the unconditional bias due to potency being less than unity. Also, for irrelevant variables, both conditional and unconditional MSEs could be small, but that again seems infeasible for relevant variables. Thus, the desired operating characteristics must be relevant to the purpose of the model selection exercise, so we seek to satisfy requirements (a)–(d).

5.11   Finding a congruent undominated model of the LDGP

This is an internal criterion, checking that the algorithm could not do better for the given sample, in that no other congruent model dominates the one that is selected at the chosen significance level from the initial specification. Moreover, a computer algorithm must deliver the same answer in identical repetitions, but may also be able to do so from different GUMs and even different settings of α, as we will see. Indeed, for the consumption equation (4.1) in chapter 4, the result in (4.11) was already shown to be invariant to including T impulse indicators in the GUM, and is also found starting from 10 lags of all the variables, even with IIS.

5.12   Our choice of evaluation criteria

Our framework is one in which many features of models are not derivable from subject-matter theory, so require empirical evidence to determine what is relevant and what is not. Consequently, model uncertainty comprises much more than whether one selected the correct model from a pre-specified set of candidate variables claimed to nest the LDGP, which essentially assumes the *axiom of correct specification* for that LDGP (e.g., Leamer, 1978). Rather, much the largest component of uncertainty concerns what the LDGP is. As noted above, specifying a GUM that nests an LDGP usually entails a large candidate set of variables. Then the key aim of model selection is to reduce some of the uncertainties about the many aspects involved in that general specification, at the cost of a local increase in uncertainty as to precisely which influences should be included and which excluded around the margin of significance.

Embedding any claimed theory in a general specification that is congruent with all the available evidence offers a chance to both utilize the best available theory insights and learn from the empirical evidence, perhaps by refuting the theory. Nevertheless, the best model selection approaches cannot be expected to select the LDGP on every occasion, even when *Gets* is directly applicable and the initial GUM nests the LDGP. Conversely, no approach will work well when the LDGP is not a nested special case of the postulated model, especially in processes subject to breaks that induce multiple sources of non-stationarity. The dot-com boom and bust, rapidly followed by the credit boom, financial crisis and Great Recession, in the first decade of the 21st century, together emphasize that problem: the mantra that "nothing is correct till everything substantive is included" applies to modeling the real world. Consequently, we use the last three criteria of the list above, namely

1. ability to recover the LDGP starting from the GUM almost as often as from the LDGP itself,

2. operating characteristics of the algorithm match their desired properties,

3. generally finding a well-specified undominated model of the LDGP,

as the main bases for evaluating the performance of model selection methods, noting that for some choices at least, all three criteria could in principle be achieved together.

Now that the criteria for evaluating model selection are established, we can describe general-to-specific (*Gets*) modeling, before turning to an analysis of the "1-cut" approach, namely selecting a model from a large set of potential variables by a single decision. First, however, we must establish the nature of the LDGP that is the objective of the search, and its relationships to possible models thereof.

6 The Theory of Reduction

A well-defined sequence of reduction operations leads from the data-generating process (DGP) of the economy under analysis to the local DGP (LDGP), which is the generating process in the space of the variables under analysis. The resulting LDGP may be complex, non-linear and non-constant from aggregation, marginalization, and sequential factorization, depending on the choice of the set of variables under analysis. A good choice—one where there are no, or only small, losses of information from the reductions—is crucial if the DGP is to be viably captured by any empirical modeling exercise. In practice, the LDGP is also approximated by a further series of reductions, designed so there are again no (or small) losses of information, but now if the LDGP does not satisfy those reductions, evidence of departures can be ascertained by appropriate tests, so they need not be undertaken. The resulting (operational) LDGP is then nested within a general unrestricted model (GUM), which becomes the initial specification for the ensuing selection search.[1]

6.1 Introduction

The data generation process is the joint density of all the variables in the economy being studied—in principle the world in this era of globalization. It is impossible to theorize about, or model, an economics DGP precisely, as it is far too high dimensional, heterogeneous and non-stationary. Any analysis must reduce the problem to a manageable size, and that is achieved by deriving the entailed joint density in the space of the variables $\{x_t\}$ being modeled, namely the local DGP (LDGP).

---

[1]This chapter draws on Hendry (2009).

The theory of reduction explains the derivation of that LDGP in general terms, and is addressed in section 6.2: see (e.g.) Hendry (1987, 1995a, 2009) and Florens, Mouchart and Rolin (1990). The LDGP is the joint density $D_X(x_1 \ldots x_T | \theta, X_0)$ where X_0 is the initial information set, and the parameter $\theta \in \Theta$ may be time varying. Then $D_X(\cdot)$ acts as the DGP for $\{x_t\}$, in that knowing the LDGP, one could generate look alike data for $\{x_t\}$ which will deviate from the observed data only by unpredictable noise. Thus, one cannot do better than know $D_X(\cdot)$—and so the LDGP becomes the main target for model selection.

Empirical modeling has to discover the properties of $D_X(\cdot)$, using all available information, from an economic analysis, through the institutional and historical background, previous findings, to data and its measurement characteristics. That requires specifying a general unrestricted model which nests the LDGP, and section 6.3 formulates that stage. In practice, the LDGP is first approximated by a further series of reductions, designed so there are no (or small) losses of information, but now if the LDGP does not in fact satisfy those reductions, evidence of departures can be ascertained by appropriate tests, so that they are not undertaken. Finally, the formal reductions from the GUM to a specific model thereof are briefly described in section 6.4, although in practice that is primarily an issue of model selection. Both stages are part of empirical model discovery of the LGDP generated by the choice of $\{x_t\}$.

These various reductions are of a very different nature across the three stages. Those in section 6.2 characterizing the derivation of the LDGP from the DGP are inevitable and intrinsic, entailed by the choice of the variables $\{x_t\}$ to model. Different $\{x_t\}$ lead to different LDGPs, and a good choice of $\{x_t\}$ is essential if the resulting LDGP is to deliver useful empirical findings. Many seminar questions about empirical results often query the choice of LDGP to investigate. In particular, if $\{x_t\}$ depends substantively on other variables which alter, then θ may be too time varying to even deserve the epithet parameter.

The reductions in section 6.3 from the LDGP to the GUM are potentially open to empirical evaluation depending on the sample size relative to the total number of variables. In most of the cases we will consider, however, there will be more variables than observations, so some simplification is needed even before the GUM can be evaluated for congruence. Finally, all the reductions in section 6.4 can be evaluated by the congruence of the resulting specific model and its ability to parsimoniously encompass the feasible GUM.

6.2   From DGP to LDGP

Let $W_T^1 = (w_1, \ldots, w_T)$ be the set of all the random variables relevant to the economy under investigation over a time span $t = 1, \ldots T$,
conditional on the pre-sample outcomes W_0 and deterministic terms
$Q_T^1 = (q_1, \ldots, q_T)$ (including constants, seasonal effects, trends, and
shifts). Denote the joint distribution of $\{w_t\}$ by:

$$\mathsf{D}_W\left(W_T^1 \mid W_0, Q_T^1, \kappa_T^1\right),\tag{6.1}$$

where $\kappa_T^1 \in \mathcal{K} \subseteq \mathbb{R}^k$ are the parameters of the agents' decision rules that
led to the outcomes in (6.1). Then $\mathsf{D}_W(\cdot)$ is the unknown, and almost
certainly unknowable, DGP. We now consider the various reductions in
a relatively natural order, though many could be undertaken at alternative stages.

6.2.1   Aggregation

Almost all economic data are aggregated across one or more of com-
modities, agents, space and time. Although some finance data relate to
point-in-time individual transactions, their determinants often include
aggregates (such as GDP and inflation). Implicitly the disaggregates are
discarded, but measured aggregates may not even be that, being merely
a grossed up inference based on small samples of activity. Nevertheless,
we represent the mapping from the events underlying $\{w_t\}$ in (6.1) to a
set of aggregates plus the remaining disaggregates by $W_T^1 \rightarrow V_T^1$ where
the latter matrix is thereby a mixture of the data to be analyzed and all
other disaggregate variables that will be neglected in due course. The
aggregation transformation induces a mapping $\kappa_T^1 \rightarrow \phi_T^1 \in \Phi \subseteq \mathbb{R}^k$,
where the ϕ_T^1 parameters may be more or less constant depending on
the benefits or costs of aggregation. However, at this stage, there is no
actual reduction in the number of variables under consideration.

6.2.2   Data transformations

Most econometric models analyze data after transformations (such as
logs, growth rates, etc.), written here as $U_T^1 = g(V_T^1)$. Again, the key
impact is on $\phi_T^1 \rightarrow \rho_T^1 \in \mathcal{R} \subseteq \mathbb{R}^k$ with consequences for the constancy
of, and cross links between, the resulting parameters. At this stage we
have created:

$$\mathsf{D}_U\left(U_T^1 \mid U_0, Q_T^1, \rho_T^1\right).\tag{6.2}$$

The functional form of the resulting representation is determined by
the choice of $g(\cdot)$. Many economic variables are intrinsically positive

in levels, a property imposed in models by taking logs, which also ensures that the error standard deviation is proportional to the level and so could represent a constant feature. As discussed in Hendry (1995a, Ch. 2), aggregates are linear sums of the disaggregates, so log transforms of aggregates can be well behaved even if the behavior of the individual agents being aggregated is heterogeneous.

6.2.3   Data partition

No reduction is involved simply by specifying that $U_T^1 = (\overline{U}_T^1 : S_T^1)$, where S_T^1 denotes the $m \times T$ data set to be analyzed, and $\overline{U}_T^1$ the remaining variables that will be ignored. The impact of that choice comes from the marginalization discussed in the next subsection, so is fundamental to the success of the modeling exercise. If S_T^1 is insufficiently comprehensive, the parameters of the resulting processes are unlikely to be either constant or interpretable in light of the background subject-matter theory.

6.2.4   Marginalization

Implementing the choice of S_T^1 as the data set under analysis entails discarding all the remaining variables $\overline{U}_T^1$, which corresponds to the statistical operation of marginalizing (6.2) with respect to $\overline{U}_T^1$:

$$\mathsf{D}_U\left(\overline{U}_T^1, S_T^1 \mid U_0, Q_T^1, \rho_T^1\right) = \mathsf{D}_{\overline{U} \mid S}\left(\overline{U}_T^1 \mid S_T^1, U_0, Q_T^1, \overline{\rho}_T^1\right) \times$$
$$\mathsf{D}_S\left(S_T^1 \mid U_0, Q_T^1, \omega_T^1\right). \tag{6.3}$$

A conditional-marginal factorization as in (6.3) is always possible, as the joint probability $\mathsf{P}(a, b)$ equals the conditional $\mathsf{P}(a \mid b)$ times the marginal $\mathsf{P}(b)$. However, a viable analysis requires that there is no substantive loss of information from just retaining S_T^1. That requires the parameters induced from ρ_T^1 in (6.2) namely, $(\overline{\rho}_T^1, \omega_T^1) \in \mathcal{R} = \mathcal{R}^* \times \Omega \subseteq \mathbb{R}^k$, to satisfy a *cut* (see Barndorff-Nielsen, 1978), so their joint parameter space is the cross product of their individual spaces as shown, precluding links across those parameters. While such a condition may seem innocuous at first sight, it is not: implicitly, a cut entails Granger non-causality of all lagged values of $\{\overline{u}_t\}$ in $\mathsf{D}_S(\cdot)$, a demanding requirement (see Granger, 1969, and Hendry and Mizon, 1999). Spanos (1989) calls the marginal distribution $\mathsf{D}_S(\cdot)$ in (6.3) the Haavelmo distribution after Haavelmo (1944).

6.2.5   Sequential factorization

Letting $S_{t-1}^1 = (s_1, \ldots, s_{t-1})$, the retained marginal density from (6.3) can be sequentially factorized as (e.g., Doob, 1953):

$$\mathsf{D}_\mathsf{S}\left(S_T^1 \mid U_0, Q_T^1, \omega_T^1\right) = \prod_{t=1}^T \mathsf{D}_{\mathsf{s}_t}\left(s_t \mid S_{t-1}^1, U_0, q_t, \lambda_t\right). \tag{6.4}$$

where $\omega_T^1 \to \lambda_T^1 = (\lambda_1 \ldots \lambda_T)$. The sequential densities in (6.4) create the martingale difference process:

$$\epsilon_t = s_t - \mathsf{E}\left[s_t \mid S_{t-1}^1, U_0, q_t\right], \tag{6.5}$$

where $\mathsf{E}[\epsilon_t | S_{t-1}^1, U_0, q_t] = 0$ by construction, so $\{\epsilon_t\}$ is an innovation process against that information set.

6.2.6   Parameters of interest

The parameters of interest are the targets of the modeling exercise which are hypothesized on the basis of prior reasoning, past studies, and institutional knowledge. We denote them by $\theta \in \Theta$. All reduction choices need to be consistent with obtaining θ from the final specification. When the subject-matter theory supporting the empirical analysis is sufficiently comprehensive that S_T^1 retains all the relevant information, then $\{\lambda_t\}$ in (6.4) will provide the required information about the agents' decision parameters with $\theta = h(\omega_T^1)$.

6.2.7   First mission accomplished

The right-hand side of (6.4) completes the intrinsic reductions that must have occurred to move from the DGP in (6.1) to that LDGP for the set of variables $\{s_t\}$ under analysis. Most empirical studies are conceived of in the opposite direction, namely prior analysis suggests investigating $\{s_t\}$, and the implicit reductions are assumed to be satisfied: seminar questions of the kind "why did you omit X?" reveal that not all researchers agree with the given choice, and hence are questioning the validity of those implicit reductions. Any other variables not included in $\{s_t\}$ could be tested for relevance once a general model of (6.4) has been formulated, so the next stage is to specify a model of (6.4) that still retains the relevant information about $\{\lambda_t\}$. For example, a linearized version of (6.4) would be the basis for an empirical vector autoregression, after additional parameter constancy assumptions.

Nevertheless, it is important to be clear about the status of the LDGP, namely the joint distribution of the variables $\{s_t\}$ under analysis. Unless there are no losses from the reductions to this stage, $\mathsf{D}_{\mathsf{s}_t}(\cdot)$ may be

non-constant and provide a poor representation for the subsequent behavior of s_t. Instead of the order marginalize then sequentially factorize
used above, the opposite path can be followed equally well, and doing
so reveals that lagged values of all other variables may matter. Thus,
two marginalizations are needed, an easy one to eliminate $\overline{u}_t$, and a
more complicated one for $\overline{U}_{t-1}^1$. In the absence of Granger non-causality
of $\overline{U}_{t-1}^1$ for s_t, the resulting LDGP may be hard to model or interpret.
Moreover, the LDGP changes with the choice of variables to analyze, so
we also have in mind the objective of seeking to discover a good LDGP,
partly by including a wide range of candidate variables from the out-
set. In a time-series context, a subset of lagged $\overline{u}_{t-j}$ can be included to
check the LDGP choice, and the process of discovery should allow for
that possibility. In the next section, we assume a reasonable choice of
$\{s_t\}$ has been made, given all available theory and evidence about the
variables to be analyzed.

6.3   From LDGP to GUM

The LDGP in (6.4) needs to be approximated by a further series of reductions to become an operational target, so we now discuss these. There
are no losses when the LDGP in fact satisfies the entailed reductions.
Conversely, if it does not, mis-specification tests can help reveal invalid
reductions, so these are then not undertaken. That, of course, introduces the issue of discovering properties of the LDGP from data evidence. Moreover, reduction theory is only concerned with generic specifications that do entail information losses, so for example, considers the
shortest lag length that can be imposed without loss. However, in large
models with long lags, say, considerable simplification may still be feasible in practice, and is one aspect of the model selection process. The
specific approximations we now consider are: truncating the longest lag
length that needs considered; specifying the set of entities that are constant parameters; and closely related to that, choosing the functional
form transformations of the data series (the effects of the initial conditions U_0 are assumed to be captured by S_0).

6.3.1   Lag truncation

The potentially infinite set of lags in (6.4) can usually be reduced to a
small number, so $S_{t-1}^1 \simeq S_{t-1}^{t-r} = (s_{t-r} \ldots s_{t-1})$, where the maximum lag
length becomes r periods, with initial conditions S_0^{1-r} (long-memory
and fractionally integrated processes are considered by Granger and

Joyeux, 1980, Geweke and Porter-Hudak, 1983, Robinson, 1995, Baillie, 1996, and Doornik and Ooms, 2004, inter alia). Letting $f_{s_t}(\cdot)$ denote the resulting statistical process of the $\{s_t\}$, then that coincides with the LDGP when the reductions are without loss, so:

$$\prod_{t=1}^{T} D_{s_t}\left(s_t \mid S_{t-1}^1, U_0, q_t, \lambda_t\right) = \prod_{t=1}^{T} f_{s_t}\left(s_t \mid S_{t-1}^{t-r}, S_0^{1-r}, q_t, \psi_t\right). \tag{6.6}$$

The obvious check on the validity of such a reduction is whether longer lags matter; and as before, the key criterion is the impact on $\{\psi_t\}$ which would equal $\{\lambda_t\}$ when (6.6) was true.

6.3.2   Parameter constancy
The parameters in question are those that characterize the distribution $f_s(\cdot)$ in (6.6). Then their constancy entails that the $\{\psi_t\}$ depend on a smaller set of parameters that are constant, at least within regimes. Complete constancy requires $\psi_t = \psi_0 \ \forall t$, and while unlikely in economics, is often the assumption made, at least until there is contrary evidence. When there is no loss, $\theta = h(\psi_0)$, so all parameters of interest can then be recovered from the process on the right-hand side of (6.6). Again, the reduction is testable in part at the next stage (section 6.4) once a feasible GUM is available.

6.3.3   Normality
The distribution in (6.6) could correspond to a linear normal model when the functional forms of the data series $g(\cdot)$ are chosen appropriately to ensure that a homoskedastic process also results as in:

$$f_{s_t}\left(s_t \mid S_{t-1}^{t-r}, S_0^{1-r}, q_t, \psi_0\right) \simeq \mathsf{IN}_m\left[\sum_{i=1}^{r} \Pi_i g(s_{t-i}) + \Pi_{r+1} q_t, \Omega\right]. \tag{6.7}$$

The LDGP distribution need not be normal, but that is partly dependent on the specification of the deterministic terms $\{q_t\}$, particularly whether fat tails, outliers and location shifts are correctly modeled. The constancy of the coefficients also depends on the functional forms chosen for the data transformations, and a congruent GUM requires that $\{g(s_t)\}$ have been transformed appropriately, based on theoretical and past evidence. Again, remaining non-linearity, non-constancy and heteroskedasticity can be checked empirically, but if any one is detected, the tests for the others will be invalidated, so when it is feasible, an initial general specification that seeks to nest (6.4) is warranted. Chapter 21 considers discovering the $g(\cdot)$ empirically.

The left-hand side of (6.7) will be taken as the LDGP that can be nested by a suitable GUM, namely one that uses a class of data transformations sufficiently general to capture those leading to $\{s_t\}$, given the original level data series; that includes all variables in s_t in its formulation, and perhaps other variables that might transpire to be irrelevant; that has a lag length at least as large as r; and that includes all the required deterministic terms, and perhaps many that are not (as IIS does initially). Such a GUM manifestly needs to be simplified; but without omniscient knowledge, it is difficult to imagine how a smaller starting point could guarantee to nest $f_{s_t}(\cdot)$.

6.4   Formulating the GUM

Providing that a viable set of basic parameters is postulated (and below we allow for the possibility of many shifts), then a variant of (6.7) can act as the general unrestricted model, or GUM, for the statistical analysis. When the LDGP is nested in that GUM, so none of the reductions above led to important losses, a well-specified model which embeds the economic theory and can deliver the parameters of interest should result. When the LDGP is not nested in the GUM, so the reductions noted in the previous sub-section entail losses, it is difficult to establish what properties the final specific model will have, although at least a well-specified approximation could still be found. Because wide-sense non-stationarity of economic variables is such an important problem, and within that class location shifts are the most pernicious feature, chapter 15 considers the recent approach of impulse-indicator saturation: see Hendry et al. (2008) and Johansen and Nielsen (2009). First, however, we consider three further potential reductions: to remove stochastic trends by cointegration and differencing; remove variables that do not need modeled by contemporaneous conditioning; and obtain a more parsimonious representation by a simultaneous system.

6.4.1   Mapping to a non-integrated representation

Many economic variables appear to be integrated of at least first order, denoted I(1), so there is a mapping $s_t \to (\Delta s_{p,t} : \beta's_t) = x_t$, where there are $m - p$ cointegrating relations, $\beta's_t$, and p unit roots, $\Delta s_{p,t}$, so x_t is now I(0). Processes that are I(2) can be handled by mapping to second differences as well: see, e.g., Johansen (1995). This reduction to

I(0) transforms ψ_0 to δ_0 (say) and leads from (6.6) to:

$$\prod_{t=1}^{T} \mathsf{f}_{\mathsf{x}_t}\left(x_t \mid X_{t-1}^{t-r}, X_0^{1-r}, q_t, \delta_0\right). \tag{6.8}$$

Vector autoregressive representations (VARs) like (6.7) are often formulated for s_t rather than x_t as also occurs in the first stage of some cointegration analyses. The deterministic terms need handled with care, both to ensure they correctly represent their original roles (so, e.g., a linear trend does not get integrated to a quadratic trend), and that the representation allows similar inferences, so does not depend on nuisance parameters (e.g., the linear trend occurs in the cointegration relation rather than unrestrictedly: see e.g., Johansen, 1995, and Doornik, Hendry and Nielsen, 1998).

6.4.2 Contemporaneous conditioning

Conditioning concerns both contemporaneous variables in models and any current-dated instrumental variables (IVs), so let $x_t' = (y_t' : z_t')$, where the former are the n variables to be modeled and the latter $m - n$ are to be taken as given. Then letting $\delta_0 = (\gamma_1 : \gamma_2)$ in (6.8):

$$\mathsf{f}_{\mathsf{x}_t}\left(x_t \mid X_{t-1}^{t-r}, X_0^{1-r}, q_t, \delta_0\right) = \mathsf{f}_{\mathsf{y}_t\mid\mathsf{z}_t}\left(y_t \mid z_t, X_{t-1}^{t-r}, X_0^{1-r}, q_t, \gamma_1\right) \times$$
$$\mathsf{f}_{\mathsf{z}_t}\left(z_t \mid X_{t-1}^{t-r}, X_0^{1-r}, q_t, \gamma_2\right). \tag{6.9}$$

A viable analysis from the conditional distribution alone in (6.9) requires that $\theta = h_1(\gamma_1)$; so there will be no loss of information only if (γ_1, γ_2) satisfy a cut with $(\gamma_1, \gamma_2) \in \Gamma_1 \times \Gamma_2$, in which case, z_t is weakly exogenous for θ (see Engle et al., 1983). When (6.7) holds, both conditional and marginal distributions in (6.9) will be normal, and the resulting relationships linear. Whereas (6.7) leads to VAR-type modeling as noted, the conditional representation in (6.9) underpins approaches where the z_t are contemporaneous conditioning variables and/or instruments.

6.4.3 Simultaneity

Finally, at least for the order of reductions considered here, simultaneity can allow a more parsimonious representation of the conditional distribution by modeling in terms of By_t where B is a non-singular matrix that captures the current-dated interdependencies. If z_t does not enter the conditional distribution, Bx_t could be modeled directly relative to lagged information (e.g., Demiralp and Hoover, 2003). In both cases, since (6.9) or (6.8) (if unconditional) are identified, reductions can be

sought subject to the usual rank condition without any prior information.

All of these stages concern the formulation of the model class to be
investigated, leading to the GUM, rather than simplifying it which we
will address in chapter 7.

6.5   Measures of no information loss

To every stage of reduction above, there corresponds a measure for
when there is no loss of information despite the reduction, and many
of these are in turn related to the central concepts of econometrics, as
we now describe.

(a) Aggregation in section 6.2.1 entails no loss of information on
marginalizing with respect to the disaggregates if the aggregates
provide *sufficient statistics* for the ensuing analysis.

(b) The transformations in section 6.2.2 need have no associated reductions, but generally alter the *parametrization* of the joint data density.

(c) Data partition in section 6.2.3 determines which variables to include
and which to omit, usually on the basis of prior theoretical reasoning, past findings and data availability and accuracy: this is the most
fundamental *specification* decision, affecting the success of the ensuing empirical modeling.

(d) Marginalizing in section 6.2.4 with respect to the disaggregates is
without loss if they are *Granger non-causal* for the retained variables,
and the parameters of the marginal-conditional factorization satisfy
a *cut*.

(e) Sequential factorization in section 6.2.5 imposes no loss when the
created error process is an *innovation* relative to the history of the
retained variables.

(f) The parameters of interest in section 6.2.6 should be *invariant* and
identifiable.

At this stage, the LDGP in (6.4) has been created as a reduction of the
DGP, and is nested within it, so its properties are entailed by the reductions. Similarly, knowledge of the LDGP entails knowledge of all reductions thereof by tracing their impacts. However, the LDGP is not yet
directly testable, so the next group of reductions move from the LDGP
to an operational counterpart that can be nested by a GUM.

(g) Lag truncation in section 6.3.1 has no loss if the created error process
remains an *innovation*.

(h) Parameter *constancy* in section 6.3.2 should be over time, added variables, and across interventions on any marginal processes.

(i) Functional form mappings as in section 6.3.3 again need impose no reduction when both densities are equal (as with logs of log-normal variables).

These reductions are empirically testable when there are fewer variables than observations: (g) by residual autocorrelation; (h) by parameter non-constancy and forecast failure, added variables, and invariance tests; and (i) by tests for non-linearity relative to the given specification. Finally, there are the additional reductions that are feasible in some circumstances.

(j) Integrated data in section 6.4.1 can be reduced to I(0) by *cointegration* and differencing to sustain conventional inference and deliver a more parsimonious representation.

(k) The conditional factorization in section 6.4.2 entails no loss of information if the marginal process variables are *weakly exogenous* for the parameters of interest.

(l) Using a simultaneous representation as in section 6.4.3 may deliver a more parsimonious parametrization.

If one model entails knowledge of all others, the first is said to *encompass* them, the focus of chapter 13. Together with theory and measurement information, and the three tests from (g)–(i), we have now established the six main model evaluation criteria that will be used below: see section 7.4 in particular. Thus, we have partitioned the information set into six subsets, namely the past, present and future of the data under analysis, theory information, the measurement structure, and data used in rival explanations. These correspond to the reduction null hypotheses being homoskedastic innovation errors that are near normal; weakly exogenous conditioning variables; constant parameters; theory consistent, identified representations; data admissible formulations on accurate observations; and encompassing, all of which are addressed below.

6.6   Summary

Figure 6.1 summarizes the overall framework. Commencing from the unknown DGP, the many reductions implicitly imposed when a set of variables is chosen for analysis are described in section 6.2, leading to their LDGP. Given the choice of variables under analysis, the LDGP is the target for model selection. That is shown on the right-hand side of

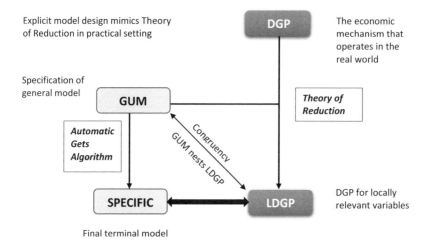

Figure 6.1
From the DGP to specific models

the diagram, and implicitly incorporates the further reductions needed to deliver an operational process from section 6.3. Next, the aim of the GUM to nest the LDGP is illustrated in the upper-middle left-hand side, where the additional stages in section 6.4 may also be implemented. Nevertheless, the object of many analyses is a theory-based model, so it is important to embed that within the GUM to be retained while selecting other features of empirical relevance, yet avoiding the unrealistic assumption that the theory is complete and correct. Importantly, the GUM should be congruent since the LDGP must be, but may be highly over-parameterized with many redundant candidate explanatory variables, indicators for outliers and breaks etc., so congruence may only be ascertainable after some initial simplification when there are more variables than observations Thus, a major simplification task remains, as shown in the lower left-hand side of the figure, a task to which we now turn.

7   General-to-specific Modeling

After noting a variety of extant approaches to automatic model selection, we consider the six main stages in formulating and implementing a *Gets* approach to model discovery. First, a careful formulation of the general unrestricted model (GUM) for the problem under analysis is essential. Second, the measure of congruence must be decided by choosing the mis-specification tests to be
used, their forms, and significance levels. Third, the desired null
rejection frequencies for selection tests must be set, together with
an information criterion to select between mutually encompassing, undominated, congruent models. Fourth, the GUM needs to
be appropriately estimated, depending on the weak exogeneity
assumptions about the conditioning variables, which then allows
congruence to be assessed. Given that is satisfactory, multiple-
path reduction searches can be commenced from the GUM, leading to a set (possibly with just one member) of terminal models.
These can then be checked for parsimonious encompassing of the
GUM. The reliability of the whole process can be investigated by
exploring sub-sample outcomes, and simulating the entire selection approach.

7.1   Background

Many strategies for automatic model selection have been proposed, and
these can be classified into four general categories. Methods in the first
category start from an empty model, adding variables until some termination criterion is satisfied. These can be called expanding or specific-
to-general model selection methods, such as step-wise regression. Termination is usually based on a measure of penalized fit or marginal significance. In the simplest form of forward selection, the next most significant omitted regressor is added to the model, and the expansion stops

when no further significant variable can be found. Step-wise regression extends this process by removing insignificant variables from the model. In certain states of nature, such as independent white-noise regressors, such a method works quite well. However, it can fail badly when allowing for the complex interdependencies that are encountered in many data sets. More recent examples of expanding searches include RETINA (Perez-Amaral et al., 2003) and the Lasso (Efron et al., 2004: a shrinkage estimator where the penalty is based on the L_1 norm of the estimated coefficients), which could also be used as a model selection device. Many manual empirical modeling exercises are specific-to-general as well, in that a (usually theory-based) initial specification is estimated and evaluated, with revisions being made to patch any obvious mis-specifications. The drawbacks of that strategy are manifold, as discussed in e.g., Anderson (1962), Hendry (1995a) and Campos et al. (2005a).

The second category starts at the opposite end, namely from the most general feasible model comprising all the variables. Then variables are deleted until a termination criterion is reached. One example would be running step-wise regression backwards, first including all variables then eliminating insignificant terms one at a time. Methods in this category are contracting: we reserve the general-to-specific (*Gets*) label for the multi-path search algorithms discussed in the next section. When sufficient data are available, contracting methods can check if the initial model matches the underlying statistical assumptions, so an upper bound can be placed on the amount of information lost from simplification. Moreover, each simplified model is nested in the initial model, so can be evaluated by parsimonious encompassing, and is part of the reason why automated *Gets* outperforms other methods.

A third category contains hybrid methods, which combine expanding and contracting searches. This includes an extended *Gets* algorithm that can handle more variables than observations (see Doornik, 2009b). That state may seem infeasible at first sight, but can be tackled by expanding searches.

The final category contains unordered searches. For example, when selecting using an information criterion, it may be necessary to estimate all models, in which case there is no natural ordering of the search. Another example is averaging over all models or a subset thereof, as can arise in portfolio modeling and when forecasting.

All automated methods require the formulation of an initial general information set. Expanding methods need a well defined set of candidate variables from which to select. Contracting methods use the same information set as the initial model. The applied modeler must formulate this information set, based on subject matter considerations, institutional knowledge, experience, data availability and quality, and existing findings. If the initially chosen information set is inadequate, the resulting empirical study (even using *Gets*) involves unordered searches. This is not a criticism of selection, because there are two distinct activities. One involves collecting the relevant information, evaluating current knowledge, and thinking of possible improvements; the other concerns what to do with the information once it is available, and selection algorithms deal with the second phase. In practice there may be interactions and even iterations between these two stages. The quality of the information set is of paramount importance: any method will find a model, which could be the empty model, but the result may be valueless if the information set is poor. If one seeks to discover the properties of an LDGP suggested by economic theory, then a large information set seems likely to be required given the non-stationarity and complexity of economic data processes.

7.2 A brief history of *Gets*

There are five main strands in the development of general-to-specific methods. First, statistical analyses of model selection procedures involving sequential simplification. Second, developments leading to a general formalization of the theory of reduction and its various stages. Third, the development of multi-path searches, evaluated by simulation experiments. Campos, Ericsson and Hendry (2005b) summarize these developments in 2 volumes of readings, so here we only briefly comment on some of the more salient innovations. Fourth, the extension of *Gets* to more variables than observations, necessitating both block expanding and contracting searches. Finally, the approach discussed in this book of embedding theory models in general specifications with other candidate variables orthogonalized. We now consider these five strands in turn.

First, Anderson (1962) provided a formal *Gets* analysis for sequential simplification to determine the order of a polynomial. He showed that specific-to-general was non-optimal in contrast to the optimality of *Gets*, and extended that implication in Anderson (1971) to an autoregressive process. Both of those were ordered testing problems, in that commencing from (say) an rth order polynomial or autoregression, lower orders $s < r$ were sought. Mizon (1977) generalized Anderson's approach for sequential simplification of some non-ordered hypotheses. Davidson et al. (1978) sought a general encompassing empirical model to explain the *gestalt* of evidence about UK consumers' expenditure, which nevertheless was as parsimonious as the evidence would sustain. Hendry (1979, 1980) re-analyzed specific-to-general and *Gets* for estimating dynamic equations and showed that the former failed badly both in theory and practice, whereas the latter appeared to deliver useful results.

Second, a general theory of reductions in Bayesian experiments was proposed by Florens and Mouchart (1980), reported later as Florens et al. (1990). Hendry and Richard (1982) developed a similar framework for empirical modeling by *Gets*, viewing econometric concepts as corresponding to valid reductions. Their approach was reinforced in Engle et al. (1983) where weak, strong and super exogeneity were all formalized in terms of reductions on joint densities. Mizon and Richard (1986) formalized encompassing, and Hendry (1987) presented an overview of all the stages involved in model reduction (updated in Hendry, 1995a, 2009, and chapter 6).

Third, Lovell (1983) investigated data mining in econometrics, presenting simulation evidence that a number of model selection approaches rarely recovered the DGP in his experiments. Gilbert (1986) discussed data mining as ignoring conflicting evidence, such as rival models that cannot be encompassed by the claimed finding. Campos and Ericsson (1999) and Spanos (2000) discuss less pejorative senses of data mining, and Spanos (1999) provides a general analysis of econometric modeling with observational data. Hoover and Perez (1999) proposed a multi-path search to implement *Gets*, and obtained dramatic improvements in their Monte Carlo simulations using a modification of Lovell's design (these experiments are denoted HPj below, where $j \in [0, 9]$ denotes the number of their experiment). This led Hendry and Krolzig (1999) to implement the *PcGets* automatic model selection algorithm based on the theory of reduction, a precursor to *Autometrics*. They investigated the performance of *PcGets* in a range of calibration experiments.

Fourth, the extension of *Gets* to more candidate variables than observations is considered in part III; and embedding theory models in chapter 14.

We now consider the six main stages in formulating and implementing a *Gets* approach.

7.3   Specification of the GUM

The first, and crucial, stage is to formulate the general unrestricted model (GUM) for the problem under analysis. The GUM should be based on the best subject-matter theory, institutional knowledge, historical contingencies, data availability and measurement information, seeking to ensure that the resulting model encompasses previous evidence. This is by far the most difficult aspect of any empirical study and usually takes the most time. Numerous detailed issues need to be addressed, and there may be various preliminary data descriptions such as graphical analyses. Functional form transformations, parametrizations, exogeneity, possible breaks, lag lengths and integrability for time series, etc. all need to be considered. One of the aims of automatic selection is to facilitate such initial formulations for the GUM: a poor initial framework is unlikely to lead to a good final model choice. The consistency properties of *Gets* have been established in Campos et al. (2003) for the setting where the DGP is nested in the GUM, and while such is unlikely to occur in empirical practice, the GUM should at least be designed as a good approximation to the LDGP (see Hendry, 1995a, and Bontemps and Mizon, 2003). The results in White (1990) establish that a consistent selection can result using *Gets* in a progressive research strategy with rigorous mis-specification testing. More prosaically, five considerations merit note.

1. The larger the number of variables in the GUM, the more likely some are irrelevant, and hence there is an increased probability of retaining more adventitious effects. Although that effect can be offset by using $\alpha = 1/N$ (or a similar value), the alternative cost is reduced potency to retain relevant variables that have smaller non-centralities.

2. Conversely, the smaller the number of variables in the GUM, the more likely relevant variables have been omitted, so the GUM does not nest the LDGP. When the data series being modeled are highly inter-correlated and not time invariant, omitting a variable whose distribution changes has a deleterious impact on the resulting model, generally inducing non-constant parameters, which would be inconsistently estimated even if constant.

3. Consequently, prior theoretical analysis remains invaluable: guidance on relevant variables, their exogeneity status, appropriate functional forms, indicator variables for outliers, timings and forms of breaks, information about maximum lag lengths, etc. can all help improve the quality of the final model by restricting the initial GUM

without sacrificing nesting of the LDGP. Within a *Gets* approach, a central role still remains for subject-matter theory in facilitating valid prior simplifications, both generically, and in their specific role in chapter 14.

4. Comprehensive coverage of previous empirical evidence can help ensure encompassing of previous studies, and thereby improve the chances of nesting the LDGP. This goes beyond the usual literature review that merely notes what has been studied, to incorporate the relevant variables from those studies in the GUM.

5. A relatively orthogonal parametrization of the N candidate regressors can facilitate locating a unique representation of the information set being analyzed. The less the orthogonality between variables, the more confusion there must be over the final selection with many nearly equivalent equations being undominated, congruent and parsimoniously encompassing the GUM.

Autometrics can also help with many of these decisions, by exploring which variables matter, what lag lengths are relevant; which functional forms do best; when and how structural breaks occur; what exogeneity status contemporaneous variables have; and handling $N > T$. We present several examples below to illustrate its approach.

7.4   Checking congruence

Next, one must decide on the measure of congruence, which entails choosing the set of q mis-specification tests (e.g., residual autocorrelation; heteroskedasticity, etc.), their forms (e.g., s^{th}-order; squares only), and significance levels (generically denoted η below). Section 6.5 discussed how these tests related to the various reduction stages. Chapter 12 considers the mis-specification tests used in *Autometrics* and both the impact of selection on their properties and of diagnostic testing on the selection process. A well-specified representation is important to ensure that selection decisions are based on valid inferences. Misspecification tests are used precisely once to test the GUM; if any misspecification test rejects at a tight significance level, it would seem prudent to recommence the analysis with a re-specified GUM, although it can happen that the same test is not significant in the final model. Otherwise, their re-use as diagnostic tests is simply as a constraint on the reduction paths, ensuring that only congruent models are considered. Thus, apparent repeated use of the tests at most marginally affects their behavior as there are some finite-sample effects from eliminating irrelevant variables (see section 12.2). Again a number of practical considerations can be noted.

(a) The choice of the congruence null hypotheses to be tested will depend on data type (time series, cross section, panel, discrete, financial etc.) but for the given form, should be comprehensive. The theory of reduction reviewed in chapter 6 highlights the partition into six information sets, corresponding to the past, present and future of the data under analysis, theory information, the measurement structure, and data used in rival explanations. In turn that leads to the nulls being homoskedastic innovation errors that are near normal; weakly exogenous conditioning variables; constant parameters; theory consistent, identified representations; data admissible formulations on accurate observations; and encompassing. Thus, a basic set of mis-specification statistics would test for heteroskedasticity, autocorrelation, and non-normality; failures of the relevant weak, strong or super exogeneity; non-constancy; invalid over-identifying restrictions; measurement errors; and non-encompassing.

(b) There is a wide range of test types which can be used, especially Wald, likelihood ratio, and Lagrange multiplier, often with different properties even when the DGP is assumed known. Econometric analysis of the selected tests is essential, and there is a vast literature on such tests, but it can be helpful to simulate their properties using Monte Carlo to check that they are appropriate for the data under study.

(c) Next, although the null hypotheses of congruence are easily specified, there are huge numbers of potentially relevant alternatives, determined by different choices of the parameters of the tests. There is a temptation to try testing against many alternatives, such as (say) every order of residual autocorrelation from 1 through s, but unless the null rejection frequency is carefully controlled, simulation will reveal that well-specified models are often rejected by chance. Thus, a small set of pertinent tests seems advisable, and generally five are used in *Autometrics*.

(d) In part, the problem noted in (c) of excess rejection can be offset by a tighter significance level, but again the cost is lower power to reject when there is indeed a mis-specification. The choice of critical values of tests is not innocuous, and merits careful thought in advance of the analysis.

(e) Finally, it is always worth checking the accuracy of the assumed test distributions for the relevant data. Calibration of test sizes and powers is relatively easy by simulation, generating artificial data from the final model and reselecting to examine the closeness of the match to the reference distribution.

7.5   Formulating the selection criteria

Next, the significance levels for selection tests (generically denoted α below) at the desired null rejection frequencies will need to be set, as will the information criterion (e.g., BIC) for selection between mutually encompassing undominated congruent terminal models. Careful thought is required to appraise the relative costs of retaining irrelevant, or losing relevant, variables. Knowledge of the likely number, n, and importance of the relevant effects under analysis can be beneficial here, although the absolute and relative numbers of candidate variables N and data points T, and the objectives of the analysis, also matter. The selection criterion for breaking ties and the chosen strategy should both be set relative to the nature of the problem. Gauge, or retention of irrelevant variables, and potency, keeping relevant, are analyzed in the next two sections.

7.6   Selection under the null

Table 7.1 records the probabilities of all null rejections when t-testing for N irrelevant regressors at significance level α, or critical value c_α in a well-specified, constant, orthogonal regression. As the DGP is the null model, all mistakes are attributable to costs of search. While no economic DGP is likely to be empty, a similar analysis applies to finding significant irrelevant variables in models where a theory is correctly retained as in chapter 14.

The probabilities in the second column of table 7.1 correspond to the terms from the expansion of $(1 - \alpha)^N$. The bottom row shows α^N is the probability of all N coefficients being significant. Then $N\alpha^{N-1}(1 - \alpha)$ is the probability of $N - 1$ being significant, etc., and in the top row, $(1 - \alpha)^N$ is the probability of none being significant. The average number of null variables retained is, therefore:

$$k = \sum_{i=0}^{N} i \frac{N!}{i!\,(N-i)!} \alpha^i (1 - \alpha)^{N-i} = N\alpha. \tag{7.1}$$

Table 7.1
Rejection probabilities under the null

event	probability	no. rejected
$P\left(\lvert t_i\rvert < c_\alpha, \forall i = 1, \dots N\right)$	$(1-\alpha)^N$	0
$P\left(\lvert t_i\rvert \geq c_\alpha \mid \lvert t_j\rvert < c_\alpha, \forall j \neq i\right)$	$N\alpha(1-\alpha)^{N-1}$	1
$P\left(\lvert t_i\rvert \geq c_\alpha, \lvert t_k\rvert \geq c_\alpha \mid \lvert t_j\rvert < c_\alpha, \forall j \neq i, k\right)$	$\frac{1}{2}N(N-1)\alpha^2(1-\alpha)^{N-2}$	2
$\vdots$	$\vdots$	$\vdots$
$P\left(\lvert t_i\rvert < c_\alpha \mid \lvert t_j\rvert \geq c_\alpha, \forall i \neq j\right)$	$N\alpha^{(N-1)}(1-\alpha)$	$N-1$
$P\left(\lvert t_i\rvert \geq c_\alpha, \forall i = 1, \dots N\right)$	α^N	N

For $N = 40$ when $\alpha = 0.01$, (7.1) yields $k = 0.4$, which entails eliminating on average all 40 variables 3 times out of 5, and 39 twice out of five, despite initially being uncertain about the potential relevance of the 40 regressors. Consequently, few irrelevant variables are retained adventitiously, although the so-called size of the procedure is $1 - (1 - \alpha)^N = 1 - (1 - 0.01)^{40} = 0.34$, which does not sensibly represent the role and purpose of selection. Interpreting 0.34 as the proportion of times the DGP is not retained under the null is in fact consistent with $k = 0.4$, and the high size reflects how large N is: despite $N = 40$, the correct result is obtained almost 2/3rds of the time (i.e., the probability in the first row of table 7.1), and the final selection is incorrect by one variable in 40 only 1/3rd of the time. Here the gauge is k/N which equals α on average in this simple setting as there were no relevant variables, and no mis-specification testing was undertaken.

Chapter 8 considers selection when $N = 1000$ at $\alpha = 0.001$, so although a huge number of candidate variables is being tested for significance, $k = 1$. On average, 999 irrelevant variables will be correctly eliminated, greatly increasing knowledge as to what does not matter, although the overal size of approximately 0.63 suggests a very poor procedure.

When the distributions of tests are close to the normal, with what were called thin tails in Denis Sargan (2001), critical values increase slowly in the tails with decreases in α. Table 7.2 records these changes, rounded.

For example, even at 0.25%, $c_{0.0025} = 3.0$, just requiring a t-value of 3.0, rather than the famous 2.0, to reject the null. Yet, if 0.25% is applied to (7.1), $m = 100 \times 0.0025 = 0.25$ so only one irrelevant variable out of 100 would be retained once every four trials, with none retained on average

Table 7.2
Significance levels and corresponding critical values under the null for t_{150}

α	0.05	0.01	0.005	0.0025	0.001
c_α	1.98	2.61	2.85	3.075	3.35

on the remaining three trials. While critical values of 2 are conventional for the t-statistics, moving to values around 3 (at $\alpha = 0.0025$) would entail almost never retaining irrelevant variables even after starting with $N = 100$ candidates. Of course, such an analysis places a premium on having approximate normality. Indeed, bias corrections discussed later also require approximate normality, making that feature doubly important. We address this issue below with IIS.

7.7 Keeping relevant variables

The second crucial aspect is retaining the variables from the GUM that matter in the LDGP. Here, the results are not so encouraging for small non-centralities, denoted ψ. Let ξ denote a test statistic with a central normal distribution when the null hypothesis H_0 is true:

$$\xi \underset{H_0}{\sim} N[0,1],$$
(7.2)

where the notation $\underset{H_0}{\sim}$ denotes that the distribution takes the form shown only when H_0 is true. When H_0 is true, we can choose a significance level α and an associated critical value c_α such that on H_0:

$$P(\xi \geq c_\alpha \mid H_0) = \alpha.$$
(7.3)

When H_0 is false:

$$\xi \sim N[\psi, 1],$$
(7.4)

where $\psi \neq 0$, so switches from a mean-zero, or central, normal distribution to a non-central normal distribution with mean ψ. The larger is ψ in absolute value, the more likely $\xi \geq c_\alpha$ leading to the null hypothesis being rejected.

The approximate powers when a null hypothesis about a normally-distributed coefficient estimate is only tested once are recorded in table 7.3 for various ψ and α. Mistakes here are the failure to reject false null hypotheses, and so correspond to costs of inference. The comparison of the high probabilities of non-retention of all relevant variables in

Table 7.3
Rejection probabilities of a t_{100}-test for one and four variables under the alternative with non-centrality ψ

ψ	$\alpha = 0.05$		$\alpha = 0.01$	
	$P(|t| \geq c_\alpha)$	$[P(|t| \geq c_\alpha)]^4$	$P(|t| \geq c_\alpha)$	$[P(|t| \geq c_\alpha)]^4$
1	0.16	0.001	0.06	0.000
2	0.50	0.063	0.26	0.005
3	0.84	0.498	0.64	0.168
4	0.98	0.902	0.91	0.686
6	1.00	1.000	1.00	0.997

table 7.3 with the ease of eliminating most irrelevant in table 7.1 shows that costs of inference dominate costs of search.

Thus, for $\alpha = 0.05$ ($c_\alpha \approx 2$), there is only a 50–50 chance of retaining a variable when its population non-centrality is 2, roughly corresponding to $E[t^2] = 4$, and only a 6% chance of keeping 4 variables with such non-centralities. However, rejection frequencies rise rapidly with increases in ψ so by $\psi = 4$, four such regressors will all be retained more than 90% of the time at $\alpha = 5\%$ and about 70% of the time when $\alpha = 1\%$.

Together, the results in sections 7.6 and 7.7 emphasize the key trade off between retaining irrelevant variables by chance, or omitting relevant because of low significance. The value of α or c_α needs to be carefully chosen to reflect the costs of these mistakes in the context of the modeling exercise. Pertinent considerations will include the magnitudes of N and T, the likely number of relevant variables, n, and the purpose of the final model for testing theory, forecasting or policy, where different choices of α can be justified. However, on some measures of costs, such as MSEs, omitting variables with small non-centralities can be less expensive than retaining them.

7.8 Repeated testing

A further issue that is sometimes raised as a criticism of model selection is that repeated testing distorts selection: see e.g., Hendry, Leamer and Poirier (1990). However, three cases need to be distinguished, as they have distinctly different implications. First, imagine you suddenly experience a severe abdominal pain and are rushed to hospital for treatment. Doctors have first to diagnose the cause, as there are many organs near the site of your pain: stomach, liver, kidney, appendix, etc., and treatment clearly depends on which is affected. In such a setting, more tests *increase* the probability of a correct diagnosis, each test being designed to preclude or reveal a problem with a specific organ. This is the opposite of what some critics envisage.

However, critics are correct in the second setting, namely testing under the null. If r independent tests, denoted τ_j, are conducted at a relatively small significance level η corresponding to the critical value c_η, when the null is true then:

$$P(|\tau_j| < c_\eta \mid j = 1, \ldots, r) = (1 - \eta)^r \simeq 1 - r\eta. \tag{7.5}$$

Thus, more tests now increase the probability of an overall false null rejection: indeed, when $\eta = 0.05$ and $r = 10$ (say) a congruent specification would be rejected 50% of the time, which is a serious mistake. Consequently, (7.5) suggests setting a significance level η of 1% or tighter, and restricting $r \leq 5$ so an overall false null rejection rate of 5% is obtained. The key difference between these two cases is that between alternative and null: in the first case, the null was blatantly falsified by the pain. Had you turned up at the hospital without any symptoms and requested 10 tests, it is quite likely one would have rejected, and suggested you had a health problem—this is a well-known cost of blanket medical screening.

The third and final setting is repeated application of diagnostic tests during path searches. Here their role is not to test for congruence, which has been established for the GUM, but to check for invalid reductions that are then not followed. Thus, the rejection probabilities are essentially unaltered, however often the tests are recalculated: see chapter 12 for the evidence. We conclude that there is no generic answer as to whether repeated testing distorts selection: it could do, but need not.

7.9   Estimating the GUM

Given the formulation of the GUM and the choice of the mis-specification tests for congruence, the next step is to estimate the GUM appropriately by least squares, OLS, or instrumental variables, IV, depending on the weak exogeneity assumptions. Providing the sample size is sufficiently large relative to the number of variables, one can check using the mis-specification tests that the GUM captures the essential characteristics of the data so is congruent, perhaps with outlier adjustments—see chapter 15 for impulse-indicator saturation.

This completes the characterization of the approach, using OLS or IV estimators although in principle, any maximum likelihood method could be implemented, with the set of tests selected computed as likelihood ratios. If a congruent model results, reduction can proceed; if not, re-thinking seems advisable.

7.10   Instrumental variables

Gets can also be used to select the relevant instrumental variables for IV estimation, and check for the problem of weak instruments, where the available instrumental variables are so poorly correlated with the endogenous variables, that for practical purposes, the estimation uncertainty is close to unbounded. A large literature exists on this problem: see e.g., Staiger and Stock (1997), Zivot, Startz and Nelson (1998), Wang and Zivot (1998), Phillips (1989), Stock and Wright (2000), and Mavroeidis (2004) (compare Hall, Rudebusch and Wilcox, 1996). The issue is intrinsic to the available information in the data, and is not a problem created by model selection procedures.

The first step is to test for the relevance of the instruments, and failure to reject no relation warns of seriously weak instruments. Zivot et al. (1998) suggest that such testing of the significance of the first-stage regression is better performed using Lagrange multiplier or Likelihood ratio than Wald statistics. Conversely, failing to eliminate irrelevant instruments could generate spurious identification, and so mislead estimation. Thus, there is a narrow path between these two difficulties, one that would also be present when theory-based model identification depended on the significance of an irrelevant regressor, or be rejected by the insignificance of a relevant one.

However, even if conventional instruments are weak, when IIS captures major location shifts or outliers, indicators that enter some, but do not enter other, equations can provide powerful identifying information, as it is now known that they are correlated with the endogenous variables, strengthening the instrument set. In particular, such an outcome is close to establishing super exogeneity, as the manifest shift in one equation has not affected another.

Hendry (2011c) showed that IVs that matter for some endogenous variables can be added with minimal impact to the estimates of another over-identified equation if they are irrelevant in that equation, so significant added instruments reject the hypothesis that the second equation is correctly specified. Castle, Doornik, Hendry and Nymoen (2013) use a version of this approach to test the invariance of new Keynesian Phillips curves (NKPCs), and establish that under the null of no unmodeled breaks in an NKPC, such data-based indicator-instruments should not be significant if added to the "structural" equation.

7.11   Path searches

Multiple-path reduction searches can be commenced from a feasible GUM, exploring each deletion. The multi-path search procedure is invaluable for avoiding path-dependent selections (e.g., Pagan, 1987), and builds on the pioneering study in Hoover and Perez (1999): see Hendry and Krolzig (2003). The validity of each reduction can be diagnostically checked to ensure the congruence of the resulting model, or an evaluation postponed till a model is selected, possibly with backtracking if a rejection has occurred. If all reductions and diagnostic tests are acceptable, and all retained variables in the model are significant, or further reductions induce mis-specifications, that model becomes a *terminal* selection, and the next path search commences from the GUM. Section 11.2 discusses the tree search algorithm used in *Autometrics*.

7.12   Parsimonious encompassing of the GUM

When all paths have been explored and all distinct terminal models have been found, they are tested against the GUM to find the undominated encompassing contenders. If a unique choice of *final* model does not emerge, so the search converges to a set of mutually encompassing and undominated contenders, all the selected models are reported. When there are multiple terminal candidate models, their union can be formed and become a new starting point for another application of the search. When the set of terminal candidate models has converged, an information criterion can be used to select one, such as the smallest Schwarz criterion, SC or BIC, but a modeler may have reasons to prefer another terminal model. This iterative aspect was introduced by Hendry and Krolzig (1999), and used in both *PcGets* and *Autometrics*, although the details differ, including the choice of encompassing test—see chapter 13. Alternatively, the set of terminal models could be retained for thick modeling (e.g., Granger and Jeon, 2004) or for averaging (e.g., Hendry and Reade, 2008).

7.13   Additional features

We consider four additional aspects of *Gets* selection. First, transformations of the original measures of the variables; second, imposing sign restrictions on estimated coefficients; third, the practice known as hold back, where a sub-sample is not used in the initial selection but retained to test it; and fourth, assessing the reliability of the model selected from the GUM.

7.13.1   Transformations of the variables

Gets selection is based on simplifying the GUM, but the parametrization of a GUM is not unique. For example, linear regressions are equivariant under linear transformations so have many equivalent representations. Consequently, a search that eliminates insignificant regressors will remove different variables depending on the combinations entered. Campos and Ericsson (1999) emphasize that this non-uniqueness can be used to advantage: if (say) x_t and x_{t-1} entered with equal magnitudes, opposite signs, then using x_t and Δx_t could lead to a more parsimonious representation by retaining only Δx_t. More generally, transformations that make the candidate regressor set more nearly orthogonal can facilitate search, subject to the caveat that the transformations do not combine relevant with irrelevant variables and thereby enforce the latter to enter: as an illustration where that occurs, see Boughton (1992) and Hendry and Starr (1993). Below, we return to the issue of transformations in the context of cointegration and differencing reductions to remove stochastic trends (unit roots), and non-linear functions.

7.13.2   Sign restrictions

It is also feasible to impose sign restrictions on estimated coefficients when there is strong prior information. At present, *Autometrics* only offers such restrictions on the long-run relationship implicit in a dynamic model, or any variables in static models. In principle, search could be constrained to a set of signs on any coefficients. Such restrictions have to be non-rejected in the GUM, otherwise a dominated model will be selected because invalid signs are being imposed, and the selection need not be the best model feasible for such restrictions, since the sign of any estimated coefficient can be changed by deleting a more significant variable (e.g., Visco, 1988). Since a variable can be formed by any linear combination of other variables—as linear regressions are equivariant under linear transformations—it is impossible to explore the effect of every possible linear transformation to find the least worst combinations that maintain the desired signs.

Thus, prior theoretical reasoning plays several major roles other than determining the LDGP as the target of the search by the choice of variables to analyze. The theory model can be embedded within the search procedure as the retained outcome, but augmented by variables that were not derived in the theory. The signs of the overall effects of the theory variables can be imposed if unequivocal and not rejected. Moreover, IIS could remove outliers and location shifts conjointly with selecting variables, to avoid rejecting the theory from mis-specification, or because such unmodeled effects swamped its insights.

7.13.3   Hold-back, or over-lapping, sub-samples

The significance of every variable in the final model can be assessed in (possibly over-lapping) sub-samples to check the reliability of the selection. Hendry and Krolzig (2004b) show that the sub-sample reliability assessment is dominated by choosing an appropriately smaller significance level for the full sample. This matches the findings in Lynch and Vital-Ahuja (1998), who show that "selecting variables that are significant on all three splits (the two sub-samples and overall)" delivers no gain over simply using a smaller nominal size. The Lynch and Vital-Ahuja (1998) argument applies widely to approaches that hold back observations, and to (e.g.) Hoover and Perez (1999, 2004), who retain variables at the selection stage only if they are significant in two overlapping sub-samples. However, the efficiency loss seems to be relatively small, so a sub-sample selection procedure is not too pernicious in a constant-parameter world. RETINA, for example, places great weight on sub-sample behavior when selecting relevant variables (see Perez-Amaral et al., 2003, 2005). A different difficulty when examining only sub-samples is parameter non-constancy, where using a rule that significance is required in all sub-samples could lead to substantive mis-interpretations of the evidence following a break. *Gets* should always include a test for parameter constancy, which certainly compares sub-samples, but does not do so to select which variables to retain.

Hold-back fails to distinguish between a coefficient estimate being insignificant in some of the sub-samples because it is irrelevant overall or because information varies. Finally, using sub-samples makes it difficult to handle non-linearities, dynamics and non-constancies jointly, all of which can be tackled by the general approach here.

7.13.4   Assessing the reliability of the selection

It is feasible to re-simulate the entire selection process to check its reliability. Given the final model and the assumptions about the status of its variables, simulated data for the dependent variables can be generated from its selected conditional representation (for examples, see Castle, 2008, and Doornik, 2009b). Then the original GUM for that information set can be used as a starting point for a further selection reduction on the simulated data. Repeating this exercise many times, the distributions of the final model estimates and tests can be obtained, to evaluate (e.g.) the probability of finding each of the variables in the final model, and hence its reliability. This is a conditional reliability assessment, keeping the regressor variables fixed, and indeed is what Hoover and Perez (1999) undertook in simulating *Gets* to investigate its properties. As such, it is not a general bootstrap exercise: for example, there may well be lagged feedbacks between the dependent variables and weakly exogenous regressors, which are irrelevant for selecting conditional models, whereas a valid bootstrap requires that such regressors are also regenerated in each replication. If the latter is desired, the techniques in Hendry and Richard (1989), Lu, Mizon and Monfardini (2008) and Bontemps, Florens and Richard (2008) could be adapted to this setting.

7.14   Summarizing *Gets* model selection

How costly is it to search across many alternative variables? Certainly, in finite samples, selection tests have non-zero rejection frequencies under the null, but as we have seen, Type I errors need not accumulate: chapter 8 investigates selecting a model in one decision so there is no repeated testing at all. The pre-testing literature implies that selection leads to biased coefficients as measured in their unconditional distribution, so suggests that search has high costs (see inter alia, Bock et al., 1973, Judge and Bock, 1978, and Judge, Griffiths, Hill, Lütkepohl and Lee, 1985, for a textbook discussion). However, unconditional distributions are not as relevant as conditional distributions for most uses of selected models, and the latter can be bias corrected in our framework, as discussed in chapter 10. Moreover, claims that repeated testing vitiates model selection are far too pessimistic: a small null-rejection frequency can be achieved at some cost in lower power. If there were 100 null candidate variables evaluated at 1% significance, one variable would on average be retained by chance, with 99 correctly eliminated, yet $t_{100}(1\%) \approx 2.6$, so there is only a small power loss for low non-centralities. If there were even 1000 irrelevant candidate variables, so an appropriate significance level would be 0.1%, then $t_{1000}(0.1\%) \approx 3.4$ which will lose rather more power, yet on average eliminate 999 irrelevant candidate variables about which there must have been previous doubt, leading to a vast increase in knowledge. Of course, these calculations rely on approximate normality, an issue we address in chapter 15. Finally, as one cannot be sure of congruence ex ante, mis-specification testing is essential, and its impact is considered in chapter 12. We conclude that it is not very costly to search, and present evidence to that effect throughout the remainder of this book. Part II now considers the selection process integral to model discovery.

II

Model Selection Theory and Performance

8 Selecting a Model in One Decision

We now consider the special case in which a congruent, constant regression model in mutually orthogonal, valid conditioning variables can be successfully selected in one decision using the criteria discussed in chapter 5. This establishes a baseline, which demonstrates that the false null retention rate can be controlled, and that repeated testing is not an intrinsic aspect of model selection, even if there are 10^{300} possible models, as occurs here when $N = 1000$. Goodness-of-fit estimates, mean squared errors, and the consistency of the selection are all discussed. However, the estimates from the selected model do not have the same properties as if the DGP equation had been estimated directly, so chapter 10 develops bias corrections, after chapter 9 considers the 2-variable case in more detail.

8.1 Why *Gets* model selection can succeed

When all the regressors are mutually orthogonal, valid conditioning variables in a constant parameter, correctly-specified equation, it is easy to explain why *Gets* model selection can be successful. Consider the perfectly orthogonal regression:

$$y_t = \sum_{i=1}^{N} \beta_i z_{i,t} + \epsilon_t, \tag{8.1}$$

where $E[z_{i,t}\epsilon_s] = 0\ \forall i, t, s$ and $\sum_{i=1}^{T} z_{i,t}z_{j,t} = \lambda_i \delta_{i,j}\ \forall i, j$, when $\delta_{i,j} = 1$ if $i = j$ and 0 if $i \neq j$, $\epsilon_t \sim IN[0, \sigma_\epsilon^2]$ and $T \gg N$. It is not known how many β_i are non-zero ($n \leq N$), nor which regressors are relevant (and which irrelevant). After unrestricted least-squares estimation of (8.1), square the N sample t-statistics testing $H_0: \beta_j = 0$ (so signs are irrelevant), then order the t^2-statistics:

$$t^2_{(1)} \geq t^2_{(2)} \geq \cdots \geq t^2_{(N)}. \tag{8.2}$$

The cut-off number, $\tilde{n}$, between retained and excluded variables for significance level c_α is given by:

$$t^2_{(\tilde{n})} \geq c^2_\alpha > t^2_{(\tilde{n}+1)}. \tag{8.3}$$

Variables with the $\tilde{n}$ largest t^2 values for their estimated coefficients are retained, and all other variables are eliminated. Only one decision is needed to implement (8.3), even for $N = 1000$ or larger. Thus, repeated testing manifestly does not occur in this model selection process. Using the 1-cut decision rule for (8.1), it is straightforward to maintain the false null retention rate at α, which can be (say) just one irrelevant variable by setting $\alpha \leq 1/N$, $\forall N$, so the criterion of section 5.10 is met, since that key operating characteristic of the algorithm matches its desired property. Sections 8.2 and 8.5 respectively consider estimation of σ^2_ϵ and MSEs. For small N, much tighter choices of α are, of course, feasible than $1/N$.

If the DGP was the initial specification, but it was not known which variables mattered, after estimation all regressors with $t^2_i \geq c^2_\alpha$ would be retained, and no irrelevant variables. In general, the former will coincide with those in (8.3), so the criterion of section 5.11—finding a well-specified, undominated model of the LDGP—is met. If the GUM is larger than the DGP but nests it, αN irrelevant variables will be retained by chance sampling (unity when $\alpha = 1/N$), so the selected model commencing from the GUM will differ on average from the selected model starting from the DGP just by retaining one additional irrelevant variable. Thus, given a small α, there is little loss of efficiency from testing even large numbers of candidate variables that happen to be irrelevant, so the criterion of section 5.9—the ability to recover the LDGP starting from the GUM almost as often as when starting from the LDGP—is also met within about one variable despite commencing with $(N - n)$ irrelevant regressors.

8.2 Goodness of fit estimates

It is well known that the OLS estimate $\widehat{\sigma}^2_\epsilon$ of σ^2_ϵ from the GUM (8.1) based on the residual sum of squares divided by the degrees of freedom:

$$\widehat{\sigma}^2_\epsilon = \frac{1}{T - N} \sum_{t=1}^{T} \widehat{\epsilon}^2_t,$$

(i.e., without selection) will be unbiased. The impact of selection on the resulting estimate $\tilde{\sigma}_\epsilon^2$ (say) of σ_ϵ^2:

$$\tilde{\sigma}_\epsilon^2 = \frac{1}{T - \tilde{n}} \sum_{t=1}^{T} \tilde{\epsilon}_t^2,$$

depends on the value chosen for c_α^2: $\tilde{\beta}_{(\tilde{n}+1)} = \ldots = \tilde{\beta}_{(N)} = 0$, while the remainder are estimated by OLS. Three cases that span the range are:

(a) $c_\alpha^2 = 1$. Adding an irrelevant variable to a regression will, on average, produce a $t^2 = 1$, compensated by the degree of freedom adjustment, so removing only those regressors with smaller *ex post* t^2 values than unity must produce a downward biased estimate of σ_ϵ^2.

(b) Precisely all the irrelevant variables are eliminated and all relevant variables are retained. This is the LDGP estimate $\bar{\sigma}_\epsilon^2$ of σ_ϵ^2, which will again be unbiased.

(c) c_α^2 is so large that almost no variables are retained. Now the estimate $\tilde{\sigma}_\epsilon^2$ of σ_ϵ^2 will be upward biased as all irrelevant variables are removed but so are some of the relevant, thereby worsening the fit relative to (b).

Consequently, selection may induce over or underfitting. Overfitting is not an intrinsic property of data-based selection, but is dependent on the stringency of selection, all the non-centrality parameters of the t-tests of the relevant variables, and the numbers of irrelevant variables.

From (8.3), $\tilde{n}$ variables were retained with $t^2 \geq c_\alpha^2$. Let $\tilde{n}_1$ of these be relevant, so $n - \tilde{n}_1$ relevant variables are missed, and $\tilde{n} - \tilde{n}_1$ irrelevant variables are retained. Then the residual sum of squares is inflated by the sum of the squared omitted relevant variables, and reduced by the spurious significance of the retained irrelevant regressors with $t^2 \geq c_\alpha^2$. However, the baseline $\hat{\sigma}_\epsilon^2$ of σ_ϵ^2 from (8.1) provides an unbiased reference value. If the final model fits much better, so $\tilde{\sigma}_\epsilon^2 \ll \hat{\sigma}_\epsilon^2$, some overfitting has almost certainly occurred and so $\tilde{\sigma}_\epsilon^2$ will be a downward biased estimate; if the final model fits much worse, yet is not rejected on a parsimonious encompassing tests against (8.1), then c_α^2 may be too stringent.

8.3   Consistency of the 1-cut selection

The setting is one in which N, n and all the $\{\beta_i\}$ in (8.1) are fixed, whereas $T \to \infty$. The information matrix $(\mathbf{Z}'\mathbf{Z})$ of the regressors should also increase without bound, where $z_t = (z_{1,t} \ldots z_{N,t})'$ and

$Z = (z_1 \ldots z_T)'$ so $(Z'Z) \to \infty$ whereas $T^{-1}(Z'Z) \to D$ a finite, positive-definite matrix. Let $\beta = (\beta_1 \ldots \beta_N)'$, $y = (y_1 \ldots y_T)'$ and $\epsilon = (\epsilon_1 \ldots \epsilon_T)'$, then under the assumptions of (8.1):

$$\widehat{\beta} - \beta = (Z'Z)^{-1} Z'\epsilon \xrightarrow{P} 0 \tag{8.4}$$

and:

$$\sqrt{T}\left(\widehat{\beta} - \beta\right) = \left(T^{-1}Z'Z\right)^{-1} \frac{Z'\epsilon}{\sqrt{T}} \xrightarrow{D} N\left[0, \sigma_\epsilon^2 D^{-1}\right]. \tag{8.5}$$

From (8.4), if the variables are organized such that the first n are non-zero, denoted β_1, and the remaining $(N - n)$ are zero, denoted β_2, then $\beta' = (\beta_1' : \beta_2') = (\beta_1' : 0')$ and $\widehat{\beta}$ converges to those population values, so is consistently estimated.

Let $(Z'Z)^{-1} = \{c^{(i,j)}\}$ and $D^{-1} = \{d^{(i,j)}\}$, then in (8.2):

$$T^{-1}t_{(j)}^2 = \frac{\widehat{\beta}_{(j)}^2}{T\widehat{\sigma}_\epsilon^2 c^{(j,j)}} \xrightarrow{P} \frac{\beta_{(j)}^2}{\sigma_\epsilon^2 d^{(j,j)}} = \begin{cases} 0 & \text{if } \beta_{(j)} = 0 \\ \neq 0 & \text{if } \beta_{(j)} \neq 0 \end{cases}. \tag{8.6}$$

Despite the apparently clear-cut distinction in (8.6) between relevant and irrelevant variables, $t_{(j)}^2$ has a distribution around its probability limit, so even for $\beta_{(j)} = 0$ will take values consistent with a Student-t^2 distribution with the associated probabilities. Consequently, α should also tend to zero at an appropriate rate as T increases to ensure a consistent selection: for example, $\alpha \propto T^{-\delta}$ for $\delta \in [-0.9, -0.8]$ (see Hannan and Quinn, 1979, Pötscher, 1991, and Campos et al., 2003). Then relevant variables are retained with probability unity, and irrelevant never retained. While a consistent selection is not of fundamental importance—as AIC is not consistent, for example, but can be optimal for some settings and criteria—it is a useful benchmark.

8.4 Monte Carlo simulation for $N = 1000$

We now illustrate the above theory by simulating selection of $n = 10$ relevant regressors from $N = 1000$ variables. The DGP is given by:

$$y_t = \beta_1 z_{1,t} + \cdots + \beta_{10} z_{10,t} + \epsilon_t, \tag{8.7}$$

$$z_t \sim IN_{1000}[0, \Omega], \tag{8.8}$$

$$\epsilon_t \sim IN[0, 1], \tag{8.9}$$

Table 8.1
Coefficients β_i and their non-centralities ψ_i for 1-cut DGP, with corresponding theoretical retention probabilities

DGP coefficients and non-centralities									
$i = 1$	2	3	4	5	6	7	8	9	10
β_i 0.06	0.08	0.09	0.11	0.13	0.14	0.16	0.17	0.19	0.21
ψ_i 2	2.5	3	3.5	4	4.5	5	5.5	6	6.5

Theoretical retention probabilities									
z_1	z_2	z_3	z_4	z_5	z_6	z_7	z_8	z_9	z_{10}
$P_{0.01}$ 0.28	0.47	0.66	0.82	0.92	0.97	0.99	1.00	1.00	1.00
$P_{0.001}$ 0.10	0.21	0.38	0.55	0.76	0.89	0.96	0.99	1.00	1.00

where $z_t' = (z_{1,t}, \cdots, z_{1000,t})$. We set $\Omega = I_{1000}$ for simplicity, keeping the regressors fixed between experiments, and use $T = 2000$ observations. Consequently, the regressors are only orthogonal in expectation. The DGP coefficients and their non-centralities, ψ, are reported in table 8.1, together with the theoretical powers of t-tests on the individual coefficients when the DGP is known.

The GUM contains all 1000 regressors and a constant term:

$$y_t = \beta_0 + \beta_1 z_{1,t} + \cdots + \beta_{1000} z_{1000,t} + u_t, \quad t = 1, \ldots, 2000. \tag{8.10}$$

The DGP has the first $n = 10$ variables relevant, so 991 variables are irrelevant in the GUM (including the intercept).

Selection is undertaken by ordering the t^2s as in (8.2), retaining (discarding) all variables with t^2-statistics above (below) the critical value as in (8.3), so selection is made in one decision. We report the outcomes for $\alpha = 1\%$ and 0.1% using $M = 1000$ replications. As discussed in chapter 1, because the size of a test statistic has a definition which is only precise for a similar test, and the word is anyway ambiguous in many settings (such as sample size), we use the term *gauge* to denote the empirical null retention frequency on selection tests. Similarly, retaining relevant variables by rejecting their null no longer corresponds to the conventional notion of power, so we use the term *potency* to denote the average non-null retention frequency using such tests. In DGP (8.7), $\beta_1 = \cdots = \beta_n \neq 0$ (with $n = 10$) and $\beta_0 = \beta_{n+1} = \cdots = \beta_N = 0$. After selection, we have estimated coefficients $\tilde{\beta}$: $\tilde{n}$ of these are non-zero (retained), while the remaining $N - \tilde{n}$ have been set to zero (so their associated variables are discarded). The non-zero $\tilde{\beta}$ are estimated by OLS from an equation with the retained variables only.

Table 8.2
Potency and gauge for 1-cut selection with 1000 variables

α	Gauge	Potency
1%	1.00%	80%
0.1%	0.10%	68%

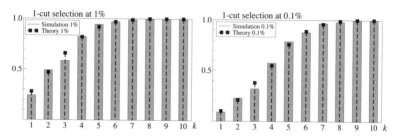

Figure 8.1
Retention rates $\widetilde{p}_k$ of relevant variables $z_k, k = 1, \ldots, 10$ using 1-cut rule with $\alpha = 1\%$ (left) and $\alpha = 0.1\%$ (right). $N = 1000, T = 2000, M = 1000$.

Using subscript i to denote the replication, and $1_{(\cdot)}$ for the indicator function, we define:

$$\text{retention rate } \widetilde{p}_k = \frac{1}{M} \sum_{i=1}^{M} 1_{(\widehat{\beta}_{k,i} \neq 0)}, \quad k = 1, \ldots, N,$$

$$\text{potency} = \frac{1}{n} \sum_{k=1}^{n} \widetilde{p}_k,$$

$$\text{gauge} = \frac{1}{N - n + 1} \left(\widetilde{p}_0 + \sum_{k=n+1}^{N} \widetilde{p}_k \right).$$

The gauges and potencies resulting from the simulation are recorded in table 8.2. The gauges are not significantly different from their nominal sizes α, so the selection is not oversized despite $N = 1000$. Also, the potencies do not deviate relative to the average powers of 0.81 and 0.69 based on table 8.1. Thus, there is a close match between theory and evidence even when selecting 10 relevant regressors from 1000 variables. Figure 8.1 shows that the retention rates for individual relevant variables are close to those expected from the theory.

8.5 Simulating MSE for $N = 1000$

In addition to the gauges and potencies recorded above to illustrate the theory, we calculate the mean-squared error (MSE) after model selection from the simulation of $n = 10$ relevant regressors from $N = 1000$ variables. The DGP in (8.7)–(8.9) and the GUM from (8.10) are as before. Let $\widehat{\beta}_{k,i}$ denote the OLS estimate of the coefficient on $z_{k,t}$ in the GUM for replication i. Let $\widetilde{\beta}_{k,i}$ be the OLS estimate after model selection, so $\widetilde{\beta}_{k,i} = 0$ when $z_{k,t}$ was not selected in the final model. We calculate the mean squared error in the GUM:

$$\text{MSE}_k = \frac{1}{M} \sum_{i=1}^{M} \left(\widehat{\beta}_{k,i} - \beta_k \right)^2,$$

as well as after selection:

$$\text{UMSE}_k \;=\; \frac{1}{M} \sum_{i=1}^{M} \left(\widetilde{\beta}_{k,i} - \beta_k \right)^2,$$

$$\text{CMSE}_k \;=\; \frac{\sum_{i=1}^{M} \left[\left(\widetilde{\beta}_{k,i} - \beta_k \right)^2 \cdot 1_{(\widetilde{\beta}_{k,i} \neq 0)} \right]}{\sum_{i=1}^{M} 1_{(\widetilde{\beta}_{k,i} \neq 0)}}, \quad (\beta_k^2 \text{ if } \sum_{i=1}^{M} 1_{(\widetilde{\beta}_{k,i} \neq 0)} = 0).$$

The unconditional mean-squared error (denoted UMSE) substitutes zeros when a variable is not selected, whereas the conditional mean-squared error (CMSE) is computed over the retained variables only.

The CMSEs are always below the UMSEs for the relevant variables in figure 8.2, with the exception of β_{10}. A line at 0.0005 is the anticipated UMSE for any estimated coefficient in the GUM, or the relevant coefficients in the DGP. As can be seen, the CMSEs are relatively close to that value except for small population non-centralities, and as expected, the UMSEs are somewhat larger.

8.6 Non-orthogonal regressors

In non-orthogonal problems, path search is required to establish genuine relevance, as the t^2 statistics in the GUM need not reflect the importance of the corresponding variable in the DGP. As different regressors are eliminated, t^2 values can change markedly, so many simplification paths need to be explored, which gives the impression of repeated testing. Path search should also not be confused with selecting the best

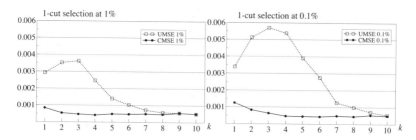

Figure 8.2
MSE of coefficients on relevant variables $z_k, k = 1, \ldots, 10$ using 1-cut rule with $\alpha = 1\%$ (left) and $\alpha = 0.1\%$ (right). $N = 1000, T = 2000, M = 1000$.

fitting model from the $2^{1000} \approx 10^{301}$ possible models when $N = 1000$. As discussed in more detail below, *Autometrics* uses a tree-path search to detect and eliminate statistically insignificant variables. Such an algorithm does not become stuck in a single-path sequence where a relevant variable is inadvertently eliminated, retaining other variables as proxies (e.g., as in step-wise regression). At any stage, a variable removal is only accepted if the new model is a valid reduction of the GUM, so the new model must parsimoniously encompass the GUM at the chosen significance level (see Doornik, 2008). A path terminates when no variable meets the reduction criterion.

Goodness-of-fit, penalized or otherwise, is not directly used to select models, and no attempt is made to prove that a given set of variables matters although the choice of c_α obviously affects R^2 and $\tilde{n}$ (and its closeness to n) through retention by the decision rule that $t^2_{(\tilde{n})} \geq c^2_\alpha$. Generalization to instrumental variables estimators is straightforward (see Hendry and Krolzig, 2005), and likelihood estimation in general is also feasible (Doornik, 2009a), as discussed below.

8.7 Orthogonality and congruence

Under the null of no relevant variables, regression models can be orthogonalized without loss. Reconsider (8.1), but now with regressors that are not orthogonal:

$$y_t = \sum_{i=1}^{N} \beta_i z_{i,t} + \epsilon_t \quad \text{where} \quad \epsilon_t \sim \mathsf{IN}[0, \sigma_\epsilon^2], \tag{8.11}$$

where $E[z_{i,t}z_{j,t}] = \omega_{i,j} \neq 0$, but $\boldsymbol{\beta} = \mathbf{0}$ with $T \gg N$. Let $z_t \sim D_n[\boldsymbol{\mu}, \boldsymbol{\Omega}_z]$ then $\boldsymbol{\Omega}_z = H\boldsymbol{\Lambda}H'$ where $H'H = I_n$, $\boldsymbol{\Lambda}$ a diagonal matrix, and $x_t = H'z_t$ so that $x_t \sim D_n[H'\boldsymbol{\mu}, \boldsymbol{\Lambda}]$, which returns us to the orthogonal case.

However, as noted above, when $\boldsymbol{\beta} \neq \mathbf{0}$, a transformation like H can mix relevant and irrelevant variables, making the latter matter through their presence in functions of the former. A solution discussed in Castle et al. (2013) is to form principal components of the set of initially unselected variables, then retaining those already found, reselect to see if any combinations matter.

Congruence is essential for conventional inference procedures and to ensure that the gauge equals the nominal null rejection frequency α. Transformations in dynamic models can also induce residual autocorrelation when relevant and irrelevant variables are tied together. As problems with residuals do not entail that the corresponding feature occurs in the DGP or LDGP errors, it can be hazardous to rely on heteroskedastic and autocorrelation consistent standard errors (HACSEs: see e.g., White, 1980, and Andrews, 1991) to correct such anomalies, as shown in Castle and Hendry (2014a). Thus, commencing from an untransformed GUM can be useful unless collinearity is very high.

9 The 2-variable DGP

One of the few settings where analytical distributions are available is 1-cut selection in a 2-variable, constant parameter, linear regression model that coincides with the DGP. Leeb and Pötscher (2003, 2005) derive the distributions of post model-selection estimators, their associated confidence intervals, and estimator biases, and establish that asymptotic derivations do not hold uniformly for local alternatives. Consequently, finite-sample behavior could differ markedly from the asymptotic distribution. We review their main results, consider some implications of their analyses, and discuss what they might entail in the realistic setting when the GUM is more general than the LDGP, as the latter is unknown, so model discovery remains an issue.

9.1 Introduction

Leeb and Pötscher (2003, 2005) analyze selection in a 2-variable, constant parameter, linear regression model $y_t = \beta_1 x_{1,t} + \beta_2 x_{2,t} + \epsilon_t$ that coincides with the DGP. They derive the distributions of the post model-selection estimators, their associated confidence intervals, and estimator biases. They are critical of consistency proofs as sufficient justification, since the asymptotic derivations do not hold uniformly over all $\beta \in \mathbb{R}^2$, and hence finite-sample behavior could differ markedly from the asymptotic results. Indeed, in some cases, biases and inaccuracies of confidence intervals worsen as T increases. They claim an *impossibility result*: any estimate of the distribution of post model-selection estimators is doomed due to this non-uniformity defect. Since Leeb and Pötscher (2003, 2005) are analyzing the 1-cut approach for a 2-variable DGP, their results are of importance. However, as the GUM coincides with the DGP when both parameters of the regressor variables are non-zero, it may be less of a surprise that selection cannot improve over direct estimation. We review their main results, consider some implications, and note what they entail when the GUM is more general than the LDGP.

9.2 Formulation

Their basic model is:

$$y_t = \beta_1 x_{1,t} + \beta_2 x_{2,t} + \epsilon_t, \tag{9.1}$$

where $\epsilon_t \sim \text{IN}[0, \sigma_\epsilon^2]$, and σ_ϵ^2 is known. Let:

$$\sigma_\epsilon^2 (T^{-1} X'X)^{-1} \xrightarrow{P} \begin{pmatrix} \sigma_{11} & \sigma_{12} \\ \sigma_{12} & \sigma_{22} \end{pmatrix} = \Sigma \tag{9.2}$$

be a finite positive definite matrix, then $\rho = \sigma_{12}/\sqrt{\sigma_{11}\sigma_{22}}$ is the correlation between the OLS estimators of β_1 and β_2 in (9.1). The parameter of interest is deemed to be β_1, and as the general model coincides with the DGP, selection merely entails whether or not to include $x_{2,t}$ in the final model. Their focus is on whether inference about β_1 is improved or worsened by attempting to select the presence or absence of $x_{2,t}$.

The unrestricted regression coincides with (9.1), denoted M_U, and the restricted, denoted M_R, with:

$$M_R : y_t = \beta_1 x_{1,t} + v_t. \tag{9.3}$$

When $\beta_2 \neq 0$, (9.3) should really be written as:

$$M_R : y_t = (\beta_1 + \pi\beta_2) x_{1,t} + v_t, \tag{9.4}$$

where:

$$x_{2,t} = \pi x_{1,t} + w_{2,t}, \tag{9.5}$$

and, as $E[w_{2,t} x_{1,t}] = 0$:

$$\pi = \frac{E[x_{2,t} x_{1,t}]}{E[x_{1,t}^2]} = \frac{\sigma_{12}}{\sigma_{11}} = \rho \frac{\sqrt{\sigma_{22}}}{\sqrt{\sigma_{11}}}.$$

Let $\hat{}$ denote an estimator in M_U and $\tilde{}$ in M_R so that the contending estimated models are:

$$\widehat{M}_U : y_t = \widehat{\beta}_1 x_{1,t} + \widehat{\beta}_2 x_{2,t} + \widehat{\epsilon}_t,$$

$$\widetilde{M}_R : y_t = \widetilde{\beta}_1 x_{1,t} + \widetilde{v}_t.$$

The DGP is denoted M_0 and has the property that:

$$M_0 = \begin{cases} M_U & \text{if } \beta_2 \neq 0, \\ M_R & \text{if } \beta_2 = 0, \end{cases}$$

so M_0 depends on the unknown parameter β_2. Then, the post model-selection decision rule is:

$$\overline{M} = M_U \quad \text{if} \quad \left| \frac{\sqrt{T}\widehat{\beta}_2}{\sigma_{22}} \right| > c_\alpha,$$

$$\overline{M} = M_R \quad \text{otherwise,} \tag{9.6}$$

so the post model-selection estimator is:

$$\overline{\beta}_1 = \widetilde{\beta}_1 1_{(\overline{M}=M_R)} + \widehat{\beta}_1 1_{(\overline{M}=M_U)}, \tag{9.7}$$

where $1_{(.)}$ is the indicator function.

The finite-sample distribution of $\overline{\beta}_1$ depends on:

$$P_{T,\beta_1,\beta_2}(\overline{\beta}_1 \leq s) = P_{T,\beta_1,\beta_2}(\widetilde{\beta}_1 \leq s \mid \widehat{M} = M_R) P_{T,\beta_1,\beta_2}(\widehat{M} = M_R)$$

$$+ P_{T,\beta_1,\beta_2}(\widehat{\beta}_1 \leq s \mid \widehat{M} = M_U) P_{T,\beta_1,\beta_2}(\widehat{M} = M_U). \tag{9.8}$$

Analytical derivations of (9.8) are obtained by Leeb and Pötscher (2003, 2005). We first consider the implications they draw from such results for a fixed hypothesis where $\beta_2 \neq 0$, then $\beta_2 = 0$, and finally a local alternative, which is the case of interest to them.

9.3   A fixed non-zero alternative

When $\beta_2 \neq 0$, under suitable assumptions on information accrual so Σ in (9.2) is a finite positive definite matrix, then, first for a fixed, finite choice of c_α:

$$P_{T,\beta_1,\beta_2}\left(\left| \frac{\sqrt{T}\widehat{\beta}_2}{\sqrt{\sigma_{22}}} \right| > c_\alpha \right) \overset{T \to \infty}{\to} 1, \tag{9.9}$$

as:

$$\sqrt{T}\left(\widehat{\beta}_2 - \beta_2 \right) \overset{D}{\to} N[0, \sigma_{22}]$$

using (9.2). For sufficiently large T:

$$P_{T,\beta_1,\beta_2}\left(\left| \frac{\sqrt{T}\widehat{\beta}_2}{\sqrt{\sigma_{22}}} \right| > c_\alpha \right) \overset{T \to \infty}{\to} P_{T,\beta_1,\beta_2}\left(\left| \frac{\sqrt{T}\beta_2}{\sqrt{\sigma_{22}}} \right| > c_\alpha \right) \to 1.$$

Hence:

$$P_{T,\beta_1,\beta_2}\left(\widehat{M}=M_R\right)\to 0 \text{ and } P_{T,\beta_1,\beta_2}\left(\widehat{M}=M_U\right)\to 1. \tag{9.10}$$

Moreover, (9.9) can hold even letting c_α diverge at a suitable rate as $T\to\infty$, akin to selecting by BIC. Such consistency results for linear regression were discussed in chapter 8.

9.4   A fixed zero alternative

When $\beta_2=0$, provided c_α diverges at a suitable rate as $T\to\infty$, denoted $c_{\alpha,T}=c_\alpha f(T)$, then:

$$P_{T,\beta_1,\beta_2}\left(\left|\frac{\sqrt{T}\widehat{\beta}_2}{\sqrt{\sigma_{22}}}\right|>c_{\alpha,T}\right)=P_{T,\beta_1,\beta_2}\left(\left|\frac{\sqrt{T}\widehat{\beta}_2}{f(T)\sqrt{\sigma_{22}}}\right|>c_\alpha\right)$$

$$\overset{T\to\infty}{\to} P_{T,\beta_1,\beta_2}\left(0>c_\alpha\right)=0, \tag{9.11}$$

and again a consistent selection results, this time from (9.11) as:

$$P_{T,\beta_1,\beta_2}\left(\widehat{M}=M_R\right)\to 1 \text{ and } P_{T,\beta_1,\beta_2}\left(\widehat{M}=M_U\right)\to 0. \tag{9.12}$$

Such results are valuable, but Leeb and Pötscher (2003, 2005) question their relevance in finite samples, and instead analyze a local alternative, that is, where β_2 is small relative to the available sample.

9.5   A local alternative

Consider instead the local alternative $\beta_2=\gamma/\sqrt{T}$ still for:

$$y_t=\beta_1 x_{1,t}+\beta_2 x_{2,t}+\epsilon_t. \tag{9.13}$$

Now, unlike (9.10) and (9.12), both probabilities converge to non-unit, non-zero values. The selection test statistic for retaining or dropping $x_{2,t}$ is correlated with $\widehat{\beta}_1$, so the conditional density is not normal.

9.6   Interpreting non-uniform convergence

Although linear models are equivariant under linear, and hence orthogonalizing, transforms, Leeb and Pötscher (2003, 2005) preclude such transformations here as β_1 is the parameter of interest. Second, β_2 is determined by a local alternative to capture a small non-centrality parameter relative to the sample size, but the correlation ρ between the two regressors is a fixed non-zero number at all sample sizes. Thus, the incorrect decision to omit $x_{2,t}$ from (9.13) when $\beta_2 \neq 0$, contaminates the estimate of β_1, as seen from (9.4), an effect that is absent when $\rho = 0$. Third, $x_{2,t}$ is only retained when $\widehat{\beta}_2$ is significant, and hence a bimodal distribution is likely to occur for it, similar to what occurs when $\beta_2 = 0$ as only estimates that are large negative or large positive values are then retained. In turn, Leeb and Pötscher (2003, 2005) show that outcome can induce bimodality in the distribution of $\widehat{\beta}_1$ when $\rho \neq 0$. Fourth, reliable and useful confidence intervals cannot be constructed in this setting for either estimator.

However, given (9.13), the parameter β_2 is effectively non-constant. If γ is used instead, one can re-write (9.13) as:

$$y_t = \beta_1 x_{1,t} + \gamma \frac{x_{2,t}}{\sqrt{T}} + \epsilon_t = \beta_1 x_{1,t} + \gamma x_{2,t}^* + \epsilon_t, \tag{9.14}$$

in which case:

$$\text{plim } T^{-1} \sum_{t=1}^{T} \begin{pmatrix} x_{1,t}^2 & x_{1,t} x_{2,t}^* \\ x_{1,t} x_{2,t}^* & \left(x_{2,t}^* \right)^2 \end{pmatrix} = \begin{pmatrix} \sigma_{11} & 0 \\ 0 & 0 \end{pmatrix}. \tag{9.15}$$

Consequently, in terms of $x_{1,t}$, $x_{2,t}^*$, the second-moment matrix is asymptotically singular, so one cannot consistently estimate γ in (9.14). This difficulty seems to lie at the heart of the non-uniform selection problem: it is unsurprising that consistent selection fails when consistent estimation is infeasible. In correspondence, Søren Johansen has noted that selection is consistent for the DGP when β_2 is larger than $1/\sqrt{T}$, or when it is smaller than $1/T$ (so vanishes), but not between, yet the interval between these disappears as $T \to \infty$. Consequently, selection is feasible over much of the parameter space, but not all.

Such analytical results match the operational characteristics of *Gets* methods. When the non-centrality parameter of a relevant hypothesis test is small, the null will seldom be rejected, and so the associated variable will rarely be retained. The resulting conditional distribution is non-symmetric bimodal in Monte Carlo simulations, and the unconditional distribution is trimodal, with much of the mass at zero for non-centrality parameters less than 2 in absolute value. High correlations with other retained variables then distort their parameter estimates both conditionally and unconditionally from (9.4). Such problems must persist in more general settings, so the key issue is their relative importance compared to model mis-specification by using an under-parametrized model, or failing to discover major features that were previously unsuspected.

9.7   An alternative interpretation

The above analysis concerns inference in the DGP, not search for a LDGP when many features are unknown. The best that can occur if the initial specification is correct is to retain the GUM, which is then the DGP. When uncertainty concerns only one parameter like β_2, selection is advantageous if $\beta_2 = 0$, irrelevant if β_2 has a large enough non-centrality, and disadvantageous otherwise. More generally, there are four possibilities when there is doubt about the relevance of $x_{1,t}$ as well: retain both; just $x_{1,t}$; just $x_{2,t}$; neither. Linear transformations of the initial specification further magnify that number.

When many aspects of the LDGP's specification are in doubt, as is almost always the case for some candidate variables, and most lag reactions, functional forms and the timing and types of breaks, selection can greatly narrow the range of contending possibilities. The specification in (9.1) not only assumes that the correct set of regressors and their transformations are known for certain, but that the error process is also known to satisfy optimal assumptions of serial independence, homoskedasticity, and independence from the regressors when the parameter of interest is β_1, that both parameters are known to be constant over the whole sample (and asymptotically), and that the regressors are weakly exogenous for β_1 and β_2. All of these assumptions require to be investigated in practice in every social science: thus selection remains inevitable and unavoidable. The main aim of empirical model discovery is to reduce the uncertainties just noted, by eliminating some possible effects that transpire not to be important in the observed sample. The omnipresent cost is a local increase in uncertainty, captured by the above analysis for small non-centralities, but also applying to decisions in the interval around the critical value.

The practical alternative to overspecification, with its attendant need to simplify an initial GUM, is not correctly specifying the LDGP, so commencing with a mis-specified model. The corresponding costs of underspecification can be very large, with inconsistent and non-constant estimates, as well as distorted inference from inducing non IID residuals. Understanding, testing theories, forecasting and policy analysis all perform badly in such a state.

At least one of the costs of selection, namely the bias induced in the conditional distribution by only retaining significant estimates, can be addressed, and we consider that next. Chapters 11, 12 and 13 will respectively evaluate the additional costs of path search, diagnostic testing, and encompassing checks, some of which may in fact be negative.

10 Bias Correcting Selection Effects

We develop approximate bias corrections for the conditional distributions of the estimated parameters of retained variables after model selection, such that approximately unbiased estimates of their coefficients are delivered. Such corrections also drive estimated coefficients of irrelevant variables towards the origin, substantially reducing their mean squared errors (MSEs). We illustrate the theory by simulating selection from $N = 1000$ variables, to examine the impacts of our approach on estimated coefficient MSEs for both relevant and irrelevant variables in their conditional and unconditional distributions.

10.1 Background

The estimates from the selected model do not have the same properties as if the LDGP equation had just been estimated. Sampling entails that some relevant variables will by chance have $t^2 < c_\alpha^2$ in the given sample, so will not be selected. Moreover, conditional estimates will be biased away from the origin as variables are retained only when their $t^2 \geq c_\alpha^2$. Approximately $\alpha(N-n)$ irrelevant variables will by chance have $t^2 \geq c_\alpha^2$ so be adventitiously significant. Fortunately, in our framework, approximate bias correction is relatively straightforward (see Hendry and Krolzig, 2005), which not only delivers approximately unbiased estimates of the coefficients of the relevant variables, but also drives coefficients on irrelevant variables towards the origin, substantially reducing their MSEs in both conditional and unconditional distributions. Section 10.2 derives the formulae for approximate bias correction after selection, section 10.3 evaluates the impact of these bias corrections on the MSEs of the estimated coefficients, and section 10.4 discusses the interpretation of the results.

10.2   Bias correction after selection

Consider the univariate regression over $t = 1, \ldots, T$:

$$y_t = \beta x_t + \epsilon_t, \; \epsilon_t \sim \mathsf{IN}\left[0, \sigma_\epsilon^2\right],$$

where β is constant, x_t is fixed in repeated sample, and $\mathsf{E}[x_t \epsilon_s] = 0 \; \forall t, s$. Let $\sigma_{\widehat\beta}^2 = \mathsf{E}[\widehat\sigma_{\widehat\beta}^2]$ be the population standard error for the OLS estimator $\widehat\beta$ at T. To simplify the derivations, approximate the t-test on the estimated parameter by:

$$t_{\widehat\beta} = \frac{\widehat\beta}{\widehat\sigma_{\widehat\beta}} \approx \frac{\widehat\beta}{\sigma_{\widehat\beta}} \sim \mathsf{N}\left[\frac{\beta}{\sigma_{\widehat\beta}}, 1\right] = \mathsf{N}[\psi, 1],$$

where $\psi = \beta / \sigma_{\widehat\beta}$ is the non-centrality parameter of the t-test. Let $\phi(x)$ and $\Phi(x)$ denote the standard normal density and its integral:

$$\phi(w) = \frac{1}{\sqrt{2\pi}} \exp\left(-\frac{1}{2} w^2\right),$$

$$\Phi(w) = \frac{1}{\sqrt{2\pi}} \int_{-\infty}^{w} \exp\left(-\frac{1}{2} x^2\right) dx.$$

The expectation of the truncated t-value for a post-selection estimator $\widetilde\beta$, where $|t_{\widetilde\beta}| > c_\alpha$ determines retention of x_t, is (see, e.g., Johnson and Kotz, 1970, ch. 13):

$$\psi^* = \mathsf{E}\left[t_{\widetilde\beta} \;\middle|\; |t_{\widetilde\beta}| > c_\alpha; \psi\right]$$

$$= \psi + \frac{\phi(c_\alpha - \psi) - \phi(-c_\alpha - \psi)}{1 - \Phi(c_\alpha - \psi) + \Phi(-c_\alpha - \psi)}$$

$$= \psi + r(\psi, c_\alpha). \tag{10.1}$$

Consequently, when (say) $\psi > 0$:

$$\mathsf{E}\left[\widetilde\beta \mid \widetilde\beta \geq \sigma_{\widehat\beta} c_\alpha\right] = \beta + \sigma_{\widehat\beta} r(\psi, c_\alpha) = \beta\left(1 + \psi^{-1} r(\psi, c_\alpha)\right), \tag{10.2}$$

so an unbiased estimator after selection is:

$$\bar\beta = \widetilde\beta\left(\frac{\psi}{\psi + r(\psi, c_\alpha)}\right). \tag{10.3}$$

Implementing the bias correction in (10.3) requires an estimate $\widetilde\psi$ of ψ based on estimating ψ^* from the observed $t_{\widetilde\beta}$ and solving iteratively for ψ from (10.1):

$$\psi = \psi^* - r(\psi, c_\alpha). \tag{10.4}$$

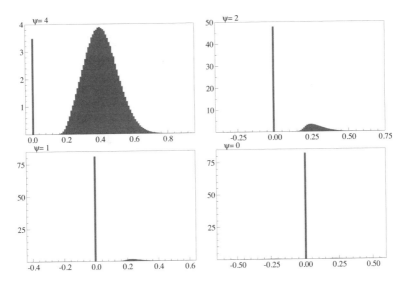

Figure 10.1
Unconditional distributions after 1-cut selection.

As a first step, replace $r(\psi, c_\alpha)$ in (10.4) by $r(t_{\widetilde{\beta}}, c_\alpha)$, and ψ^* by $t_{\widetilde{\beta}}$ so:

$$\overline{t}_{\widetilde{\beta}} = t_{\widetilde{\beta}} - r\left(t_{\widetilde{\beta}}, c_\alpha\right). \tag{10.5}$$

This gives a 1-step bias correction:

$$\overline{\beta} = \widetilde{\beta}\left(\frac{\overline{t}_{\widetilde{\beta}}}{t_{\widetilde{\beta}}}\right). \tag{10.6}$$

Next, let:

$$\overline{\overline{t}}_{\widetilde{\beta}} = t_{\widetilde{\beta}} - r\left(\overline{t}_{\widetilde{\beta}}, c_\alpha\right), \tag{10.7}$$

then the two-step bias-corrected parameter estimate is:

$$\overline{\overline{\beta}} = \widetilde{\beta}\left(\frac{\overline{\overline{t}}_{\widetilde{\beta}}}{t_{\widetilde{\beta}}}\right). \tag{10.8}$$

Hendry and Krolzig (2005) show that most, but not all, of the selection bias is corrected for relevant retained variables by (10.8), at the cost of a small increase in their conditional MSEs.

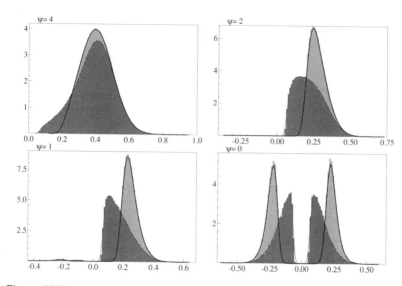

Figure 10.2
Impact of bias corrections on conditional distributions after 1-cut selection.
Light: conditional distribution, dark: conditional distribution after bias correction.

Figure 10.1 shows the unconditional distributions in a Monte Carlo, using three relevant variables with non-centralities of 4, 2 and 1 respectively, and one irrelevant variable. Here we used a small version of the 1-cut DGP of section 8.4: $N = 4, T = 100, M = 10^6$, together with 1-cut selection at $\alpha = 0.05$. As figure 10.1 shows, the number of cases in which a variable is dropped increases as the non-centrality falls. The retention rates for $\psi = 4, 2, 1, 0$ are 97%, 49%, 16%, 5.0% respectively, with the last also equalling the gauge (because it is the only irrelevant variable).

Figure 10.2 illustrates the impact of bias correction on the conditional distribution. In all four cases, the conditional distributions after two-step bias correction (dark gray) are shifted towards the origin relative to the uncorrected distributions (light gray). The conditional distribution for the irrelevant variable has only about 5% of the mass in its unconditional distribution, so after bias correction, $(1 - \alpha)$% of the estimates are precisely zero, and the remainder close to zero as shown.

When the conditional distributions of estimates are the focus of interest, reflecting the outcomes in the model that is selected, such bias corrections remove the so-called pre-test bias. Conversely, such corrections exacerbate the downward bias in the unconditional estimates of the relevant coefficients, so must also increase their unconditional MSEs somewhat. Against that cost, as section 10.3 will show and matching figure 10.2, bias correction considerably reduces the MSEs of any retained irrelevant variables, giving a substantive benefit in both their unconditional and conditional distributions.

10.3 Impact of bias correction on MSE

In 1-cut selection, all variables are significant at c_α by design. However, with automated *Gets*, this is not necessarily the case: irrelevant variables may be retained because of diagnostic checking (i.e., when a variable is insignificant, but deletion would make a diagnostic test significant), or because of encompassing (a variable can be individually insignificant, but not jointly with all variables deleted at that stage). This is one reason gauge differs from size. As retained variables that are less than the critical value are in a sense irrelevant, and the bias-correction formula is nonlinear at the critical value, we only adjust significant retained variables, setting insignificant variables to zero after correction. Although it is not known whether insignificant values are for relevant or irrelevant variables, bias correction reduces MSEs for the irrelevant variables because it heavily down weights chance significance. Intuitively, when a variable is irrelevant, but its estimated coefficient is significant by chance, the t-value will have a high probability of being close to the critical value, and a low probability of being far outside. Thus, the bias correction will be large on average: that also applies to correcting the estimated coefficient of a relevant variable when its t-value is close to the critical value.

The MSEs from the simulations in section 8.4 for the bias-corrected relevant coefficient estimates in their conditional distributions are shown in figure 10.3. Here, the impacts of bias corrections are quite small: when non-centralities are high, few relevant variables' coefficients will be downweighted.

Table 10.1 shows the effects of the 1-step bias correction (10.6) and the 2-step bias correction (10.8) on MSEs of the small 1-cut experiment of the previous section. There are substantial reductions in the MSEs in the conditional distributions of about 50% for the irrelevant variable. This reduction applies as well to the UMSEs.

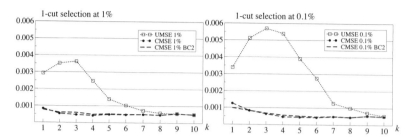

Figure 10.3

Impact of bias correction on CMSE_k for relevant variables at $\alpha = 1\%$ (left) and $\alpha = 0.1\%$ (right). BC2 refers to the two-step bias correction.

Table 10.1

Effect of bias correction on CMSE and UMSE after 1-cut selection at 5%, $T = 100, M = 10^6$

	ψ	Unconditional **MSE** after selection			
		Uncorrected	BC 1-step	BC 2-step	**MSE in GUM**
β_1	4	0.0143	0.0174	0.0193	0.0106
β_2	2	0.0257	0.0252	0.0258	0.0106
β_3	1	0.0128	0.0110	0.0105	0.0106
β_4	0	0.0029	0.0017	0.0013	0.0106

	ψ	Conditional **MSE** after selection		
		Uncorrected	BC 1-step	BC 2-step
β_1	4	0.0093	0.0120	0.0139
β_2	2	0.0108	0.0088	0.0100
β_3	1	0.0270	0.0167	0.0132
β_4	0	0.0587	0.0382	0.0282

10.4   Interpreting the outcomes

As well as bias-correcting the conditional coefficient estimates for selecting only significant outcomes, the t-statistics could also be corrected using $\tilde{t}_{\tilde{\beta}}$ in (10.7). As yet, the distribution of that statistic is not known, but a useful check on which variables are most likely to be relevant is if the correction does not shift the t-value below c_α. For relevant variables, the bias that is being corrected is that due to selecting only significant outcomes. When relevant variables are omitted by chance and are correlated with retained variables, the latter's coefficient estimates will be biased from the omission, and that bias may or may not be corrected in part by the present procedure, depending on the unknown omitted variables' biases being towards the origin or not. Also, the formulae assume a near normal distribution for the t-statistics used to select variables, so section 15.6 considers a fat-tailed distribution (where the errors are drawn from t_3).

Despite selecting from a large set of potential variables, nearly unbiased estimates of coefficients and equation standard errors can be obtained with little loss of efficiency from testing irrelevant variables, but suffering some loss from not retaining relevant variables at large values of c_α. As the normal distribution has thin tails, the power loss from tighter significance levels is rarely substantial, but could be for fat-tailed error processes at tighter α, an issue also examined in section 15.6.

To record more detail about selection outcomes and make comparisons with *Autometrics*, the next chapter considers experiments with the much smaller number of candidate regressors, $N = 10$, rather than $N = 1000$ considered earlier.

11 Comparisons of 1-cut Selection with *Autometrics*

Having established that the properties of bias-corrected 1-cut selections match our three criteria, having appropriate gauge and potency, with near unbiased estimates, and relatively small MSEs, we now evaluate the comparative properties of *Autometrics*. First, the tree-search algorithm of *Autometrics* is described and its operational procedures outlined. The framework remains the same as in chapter 8, namely a congruent, constant regression model in mutually orthogonal, valid conditioning variables, but unlike 1-cut, *Autometrics* does not use, nor need, to exploit orthogonality. We wish to evaluate whether despite exploring many paths, there is any deterioration in the selection quality: in several important respects, *Autometrics* matches 1-cut even when the latter is applicable.

11.1 Introduction

The history of general-to-specific or *Gets* modeling was outlined in chapter 7.2. Starting from a general statistical model (GUM) which captures the essential characteristics of the data (congruence) to sustain valid inference, statistically insignificant variables are eliminated to reduce its complexity. A key aim of the generality of the initial model was also to support a progressive research strategy of increasing understanding over time. The two main improvements in the Hoover and Perez (1999) algorithm of commencing from the GUM and searching a number of paths lowered the retention rate of irrelevant variables and raised the retention rate of relevant. The *PcGets* approach in Hendry and Krolzig (1999) commenced from all feasible initial reductions, checked the validity of each reduction by diagnostic tests to ensure the congruence of the final model, and tested that the final selection parsimoniously encompassed the GUM and hence also encompassed rival contenders based on the same information. Their experiments demonstrated further improvements, with the gauge close to the nominal size, and no major loss of potency relative to the theoretical power of an equivalent single test of the false null hypothesis, as well as an accurately estimated equation standard error. Hendry and Krolzig (2005) added the ability to bias correct the estimates as just described.

Autometrics builds on *PcGets* with important improvements, which we now describe in section 11.2. Section 11.3 outlines the tree-search approach in *Autometrics* before section 11.4 considers the impact of sequential search versus 1-cut. Section 11.5 explains the Monte Carlo simulation experiments used for comparing 1-cut with *Autometrics* in a setting where the former is valid. Finally, section 11.6 and section 11.7 respectively report the findings for their comparative gauges and potencies, then conditional and unconditional MSEs relative to the baseline of 1-cut.

11.2   *Autometrics*

The operation of *Autometrics* is described more fully in Doornik (2009a) and Doornik and Hendry (2013b). Here we focus on the ingredients helpful to understanding its implementation of the stages in this part of the book, albeit that several of those are still to be explained. However, some knowledge of its baseline functioning will prove useful. We return in chapter 19 to describe how *Autometrics* handles the general setting of more candidate variables than observations.

Four main ingredients define a *Gets* selection approach. First, the model class (linear or non-linear, system or single equation, simultaneous or conditional etc.), the corresponding estimation criterion (such as least squares, instrumental variables, or maximum likelihood), and the associated type of data (such as discrete or time series etc.). Secondly, the form of search algorithm, whether single or multiple path (as in backward selection as compared to Hoover and Perez, 1999, or Hendry and Krolzig, 1999), a tree search (as in Doornik, 2009a), or comparison of every possible model (as when selecting by information criteria like AIC, Akaike, 1973, or BIC, Schwarz, 1978). Thirdly, the evaluation checks or diagnostic tests conducted on the GUM (in all *Gets* approaches, but rarely in other model selection methods), on intermediate models (as in *PcGets*) and on the final choice (again, included in *Gets* approaches that seek congruent selections). Finally, the criteria for determining the termination decision, usually corresponding to a nominal significance level for false null retention, or its equivalent in a penalty function in information criteria. In *PcGets* and *Autometrics*, parsimonious encompassing of the GUM is also checked to ensure the entire sequence of reductions did not cumulatively lead to a poor model choice, as explained more fully in chapter 13.

Prior to its multi-path search, *PcGets* used a general pre-search test to eliminate highly insignificant groups of variables, which served to improve its speed at a potential risk of eliminating individual variables that mattered. During path searches, sub-paths were not explored, and the same terminal model could be found down several routes. Also, diagnostic tests were calculated at every simplification to avoid non-congruent selections and sustain valid inference during simplifications, but at the cost of more time-consuming calculations, and the possibility of missing parsimonious selections where a gap had to be jumped across an invalid intermediate model to find a valid simplification. Finally, there were many possible settings for the nominal significance levels of various decisions, and while these were set consistently for the packaged choices of *Liberal* (roughly 5%) and *Conservative* (roughly 1%) strategies, it was relatively easy for non-expert users to make incoherent choices.

Autometrics separates all four choices noted above: estimation criterion, the search algorithm, the evaluation checks, and the termination decision. Although we mainly focus on least squares here, the estimation criterion is implemented in a general likelihood framework, so many different classes of model can be handled, including those designed for discrete and financial data, as well as time-series, cross-section, and panels.

Autometrics both examines the whole search space as shown in section 11.3, and discards irrelevant routes in a systematic way: when a terminal model is found, because the tree is uniquely ordered, there is no need to enter branches that yield the same model. *Autometrics* also usually functions without pre-search, except for lag length where the natural ordering from longest to shortest allows a structured testing sequence (as an extension of e.g., Anderson, 1971: also see Mizon, 1977). *Autometrics* also improves in terms of computational efficiency by avoiding repeated estimation and diagnostic testing, and remembering terminal models already located, as the following section describes. Next, diagnostic tests are only evaluated when a terminal model is reached.

If any test fails, the algorithm back-tracks along the tree until an earlier valid model is found. This approach still ensures a congruent final selection, but avoids relatively costly diagnostic testing as well as diagnostic failures that might temporarily block a reduction path. Because of this step, insignificant variables may sometimes be retained in a final model: such variables could be either irrelevant, and acting as proxies for the non-congruence, or relevant, but poorly determined in the given sample. To correctly calibrate the operational properties of the algorithm (section 5.10), the gauge reflects the former by being defined as the null retention frequency, and the potency the latter, as the retention frequency of relevant variables.

A more general problem is when any mis-specification tests fail for the GUM: this might reflect an invalid specification or a chance significance of that test or tests. Model selection could work when commencing from an invalid GUM, in that some representations will still be better than others, but a lack of congruence invalidates a fundamental assumption of *Gets*. In practice, *Autometrics* tries to find a diagnostically valid model along the way. Chapter 12 discusses the role of diagnostic testing in *Autometrics*.

11.3   Tree search

The tree-search approach in *Autometrics* is illustrated in figure 11.1 for a four-variable GUM, where all four variables, denoted A, B, C, and D, are insignificant: paths with all remaining variables significant would not be explored. The first path to be searched is that corresponding to eliminating A, which thereby is taken as the least significant of the four variables in the GUM. Next, B is eliminated, then C leading to retaining just D, which would also be deleted if it was still insignificant. Such a single-path search corresponds to what backward selection algorithms would perform.

However, unless all variables are mutually orthogonal, the order of elimination can matter. Consequently, *Autometrics* also examines all the other non-redundant paths, so from BCD, drops C next, and then from BD eliminates D, but does not need to go further as D is already known to be insignificant; and finally from BCD, eliminates D, but only needs to check BC then does not need to go further. As can be seen from the figure, that completes the branch commenced by deleting A, so returning to the start, a new set of branches formed by first dropping B can be

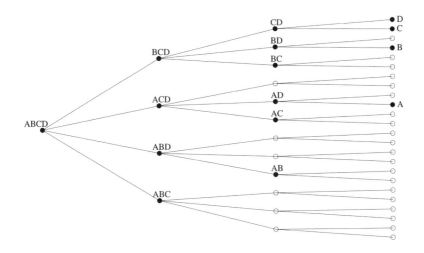

Figure 11.1
Tree search diagram

followed, and so on, each time leaving fewer models to explore. Nevertheless, the maximum total number of models to be checked could be $2^4 = 16$ including the GUM and null. However, *Autometrics* implements three strategies to skip nodes as follows.

Pruning   If a deletion fails, or results in another failure (such as on back-testing, which is a joint test of variables removed so far on that path, or on diagnostic testing), such a node is recorded as invalid at a p-value determined by p_a. The subsequent sub-branches can therefore be pruned.

Bunching   Blocks of variables along any given search path can be deleted together. If that block deletion fails, then the algorithm back-tracks until the remaining bunch can be deleted. This aspect is controlled by a p-value denoted p_b.

Chopping   When a bunch is highly insignificant, it is chopped from the tree search when the sub-branch is processed, to save on computation, which decision is governed by a p-value denoted $p_c = p_b$ which is set equal to p_b as shown.

The reduction procedure is then re-run to refine the choices and check for any substantive omissions.

11.4   The impact of sequential search

The 1-cut procedure in chapter 8 differs from the many forms of sequential search procedure primarily because the latter re-estimate the model after each deletion. In 1-cut, the GUM is estimated, the resulting t^2-statistics are ranked in increasing order, and all those above c_α^2 are retained with the rest eliminated. In sequential search, including backward elimination, multi-path simplifications and tree search, the remaining variable with the smallest t^2 is eliminated, and the model is re-estimated to decide which variable is next for elimination, if any remains. When variables are intercorrelated, each deletion alters the correlations that remain, sometimes markedly with substantial collinearity, so re-estimation is essential to reveal the hidden t^2-values. The order of elimination then matters, which is why single path searches can be misleading.

Even in orthogonal designs, there is an important difference between 1-cut and sequential search as follows. The probability that the observed t^2-statistic on an irrelevant variable in the GUM is less than unity is approximately 0.68. For N variables with n relevant, the probability that no t^2 is less than unity is $(0.32)^{(N-n)}$ which is negligible for $(N - n) \geq 5$. Deleting a variable with a $t^2 < 1$ reduces the estimated equation standard error, $\widehat{\sigma}$, a key component in calculating the t^2s on the remaining variables, thereby raising these. Since variables with the smallest t^2s are eliminated first, $\widehat{\sigma}$ tends to fall till $\min \widehat{\sigma}$ is reached when all remaining $t^2 \geq 1$. Search usually requires $c_\alpha^2 > 1$, so continues till all insignificant variables are deleted according to $t^2 < c_\alpha^2$. Over the interval $1 \leq t^2 < c_\alpha^2$, $\widehat{\sigma}$ increases, reducing the t^2s on the remaining variables. There is also a small impact from the increasing degrees of freedom as variables are eliminated. Alternatively expressed, 1-cut uses the $\widehat{\sigma}$ from the GUM for all decisions, so when the design is orthogonal, does not need to re-estimate models to determine t^2s. When the GUM can be estimated, that strategy could be adopted for sequential search algorithms.

Otherwise, the net effect of these tendencies is unclear, in that the final $\widehat{\sigma}$ could be upward or downward biased depending on the choice of c_α^2, the sample size, and the configuration of the t^2, but is likely to alter the behavior of *Autometrics* relative to 1-cut, an issue we now investigate by simulating their comparative performance.

Table 11.1
Non-centralities for simulation experiments (11.1)–(11.3).

n	1	2	3	4	5	6	7	8	9	10
$\psi_1 = \ldots = \psi_n$	21.6	15.3	12.5	10.8	9.7	8.8	8.2	7.7	7.2	6.9

11.5 Monte Carlo experiments for $N = 10$

The experimental design is one of those used by Castle et al. (2013), and consists of 10 separate DGPs, indexed by $n = 1, ..., 10$:

$$y_t = \beta_0 + \beta_1 z_{1,t} + \cdots + \beta_n z_{n,t} + \epsilon_t, \tag{11.1}$$

$$z_t \sim \text{IN}_{10}[0, I_{10}], \tag{11.2}$$

$$\epsilon_t \sim \text{IN}\left[0, \left(0.4 \times n^{0.5}\right)^2\right], \quad n = 1, \ldots, 10, \; t = 1, \ldots, T, \tag{11.3}$$

where $z'_t = (z_{1,t}, \cdots, z_{10,t})$. The z_t are fixed across replications. Equations (11.1)–(11.3) specify 10 different DGPs, each having n relevant variables with $\beta_1 = \cdots = \beta_n = 1$ and $10 - n$ irrelevant variables ($\beta_{n+1} = \cdots = \beta_{10} = 0$). Throughout, they set $\beta_0 = 5$ and use $T = 75$. Table 11.1 reports the non-centralities, ψ, of the t-tests on the relevant regressors, where all ψ are the same within each experiment, but vary between.

The GUM is the same for all 10 DGPs:

$$y_t = \beta_0 + \beta_1 z_{1,t} + \cdots + \beta_{10} z_{10,t} + u_t.$$

Consequently, the GUM coincides with the DGP when $n = 10$.

11.6 Gauge and potency

We first investigate how the general search algorithm in *Autometrics* performs relative to the 1-cut selection rule in terms of the three criteria in section 5.12 above (ability to recover LDGP, operating characteristics, finding a well-specified and undominated model). Their comparative gauges are recorded in figure 11.2 where *Autometrics* selects without diagnostic tracking to match 1-cut. In default mode, *Autometrics* has diagnostic tracking switched on, and the impact of this is considered in chapter 12. *Autometrics* is slightly over-gauged at looser significance levels like 10%, but is close to 1-cut at 1%, and quite similar at 5%, which is an appropriate level for $N = 10$ and $T = 75$. As all regressors are relevant at $n = 10$, there is then no measure of gauge.

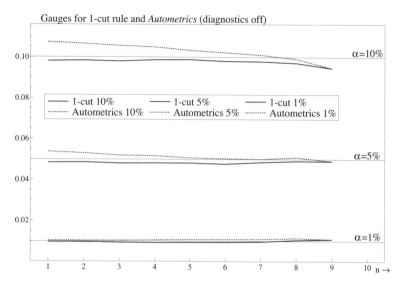

Figure 11.2
Gauges for 1-cut rule (solid lines) and *Autometrics* without diagnostic track-
ing (dotted lines) for $\alpha = 0.01, 0.05, 0.1$. The horizontal axis represents the
$n = 1, \ldots, 10$ DGPs, each with n relevant variables. $T = 75, M = 10\,000$.

The potency ratio is unity for all significance levels, so is not shown.
Thus, these two aspects are similar. In 1-cut, the t^2-tests implicitly need
to be *ranked* from largest to smallest as in (8.2) (although in practice, each
t^2 just needs to be checked against c_α^2), whereas path search in *Autometrics* seeks to *order* the correct t^2-statistics, taking account of the impact of
eliminating other variables. Thus, the addition of path search does not
greatly affect the false null retention rates, nor change the retention of
relevant variables compared to a single decision rule, when the latter is
valid, consistent with the earlier discussion about repeated testing. Nevertheless, the next section shows that there are differences between the
selection procedures in MSEs for both relevant and irrelevant variables.
   In general, overfitting is more likely to occur at looser significance
levels like 10%, since retaining several irrelevant variables which are
significant by chance will downward bias the estimated equation standard error, and increase the probability of others seeming significant.
Thus, a relatively tight significance level such as 1% is more likely to
deliver the same magnitude of gauge, as seen in figure 11.2. The costs
are a somewhat lower potency for coefficients with relatively small non-
centralities, but the normal distribution has thin tails, so decreasing α

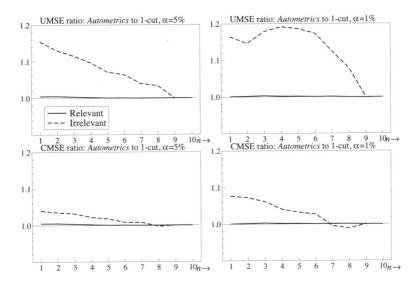

Figure 11.3
Ratios of MSEs for *Autometrics* to 1-cut rule as n changes

from 5% through 1% to 0.1% only raises the critical value c_α from 2 through 2.6 to 3.3.

11.7   Mean squared errors

Figure 11.3 records the ratios of MSEs of *Autometrics* selection to the 1-cut rule for both unconditional and conditional distributions, with no diagnostic tests and no bias correction, for $M = 10\,000$. The top row of the four panel graph shows UMSE ratios, and the bottom row the CMSE ratios, whereas the columns record the outcomes at $\alpha = 0.05$ (left) and $\alpha = 0.01$ (right).

The lines labelled *Relevant* report the ratios of average MSE s over all relevant variables for a given n. Analogously, the lines labelled *Irrelevant* are based on the average MSEs of the irrelevant variables for each DGP (none when $n = 10$). Both unconditionally and conditionally, the ratios are close to unity for the relevant variables, but there is some advantage to selection using 1-cut for the irrelevant variables, where the ratios are uniformly greater than unity. The benefits to 1-cut selection are largest when there are many irrelevant variables. Conditionally, *Autometrics* manages to outperform the 1-cut rule in a few cases. Thus, there is little loss from using the path-search algorithm even when 1-cut is applicable, and *Autometrics* will dominate in non-orthogonal problems when 1-cut is inappropriate.

11.8   Integrated data

Autometrics conducts inferences using normal I(0) critical values. The issue of normality is addressed in chapter 15, and here we merely note that most selection tests remain valid when applied in I(1) processes, as shown in Sims et al. (1990). Only tests for a unit root imposition, reducing the data to I(0), need non-standard critical values. That is unlikely to occur as part of the general selection procedure, as the t-test for the significance of a unit root will strongly reject.

However, when there are irrelevant I(1) variables that do not combine to I(0), critical values need to be higher. In estimation, that can always be avoided by including z_t and z_{t-1}, but during selection, one of the two may be deleted leaving just a single I(1) variable. In that case, over retention will occur unless a tighter significance level is used.

12   Impact of Diagnostic Tests

Chapter 7 considered the main mis-specification tests in *Gets* model selection using an information taxonomy of past, present and future data, theory and measurement information and rival models. The first seeks a homoskedastic innovation error $\{\epsilon_t\}$; the second weak exogeneity of conditioning variables for the parameters of interest θ (say); the third, constant, invariant parameters, θ; the fourth theory consistent, identifiable structures; the fifth data-admissible formulations on accurate observations; and the sixth, encompassing rival models. We now address the specific mis-specification tests used in *Autometrics* to determine congruence, and consider their operating characteristics when applied to the DGP, the GUM and the finally selected model. We also examine the impact of their repeated use as diagnostic checks to ensure that reductions maintain congruence.

12.1   Model evaluation criteria

The default settings for mis-specification tests in *Autometrics* are the same as those in *PcGive* (Doornik and Hendry, 2013b). They have the form of $F_j(k, T - l)$, denoting an approximate F-test against the alternative hypothesis j. These correspond to the discussion in section 7.4, so for time-series data comprise: k^{th}-order serial correlation (F_{ar}: see Godfrey, 1978); k^{th}-order autoregressive conditional heteroskedasticity (F_{arch}: ARCH, see Engle, 1982); heteroskedasticity (F_{het}: see White, 1980); parameter constancy over k periods (F_{Chow}: see Chow, 1960); and a chi-square test for normality ($\chi^2_{nd}(2)$: see Doornik and Hansen, 2008). The first two are omitted for cross-section data. These make up the standard battery of tests reported by *PcGive*: for more information see Doornik and Hendry (2013b). Parsimonious encompassing of the feasible GUM is checked during selection as discussed in chapter 13 (see Hendry and Richard, 1989, Govaerts et al., 1994, and Doornik, 2008).

After estimation, functional-form mis-specification can be evaluated by the RESET test (F_{reset}: see Ramsey, 1969), as could non-linearity by a low-dimension portmanteau test (F_{NL}: see Castle and Hendry, 2010a, and chapter 21), the validity of any over-identifying instrumental variables (F_{IV}: see Sargan, 1964), and super exogeneity (F_{SE}: see Hendry and Santos, 2010, and chapter 22).

Section 12.2 first examines the impact of selection on mis-specification tests against two baselines. The first is the infeasible application to the DGP, the usual setting in econometric theory for deriving the properties of a test statistic. The second is their application to a feasible GUM, where congruence will initially be tested when the GUM is estimable from the available data. Then section 12.3 simulates the performance of *Autometrics* with diagnostic tracking, as against without, to evaluate the costs of testing congruence. Section 12.4 describes the impact of diagnostic tracking on MSEs. Finally, section 12.5 considers the consequences when modeling integrated data in levels rather than after I(0) reductions.

12.2 Selection effects on mis-specification tests

The following tests are used as the default set for mis-specification testing in *Autometrics*:

Test	Distribution	In JEDC DGP
AR(p)	$F(p, T - k - p)$	$F(2, 93)$
ARCH(p)	$F(p, T - 2p)$	$F(1, 98)$
Normality	$\chi^2(2)$	$\chi^2(2)$
Heteroskedasticity	$F(s, T - s - 1)$	$F(10, 89)$
Chow	$F(T - \tau, \tau - k)$	$F(29, 66)$

Here T is the sample size of the regression, k the number of regressors (counting the intercept if included), s the number of regressors in the auxiliary regression (regressors and their non-redundant squares, excluding the intercept). The JEDC DGP (using $\rho = 0$: see section 17.2.2) has $T = 100$, no intercept and 5 regressors, so $k = 5$ and $s = 10$: see Krolzig and Hendry (2001). The GUM has $k = 21$ and $s = 40$. The Chow test is at 70%, so for a break on or after observation $\tau = 71$.

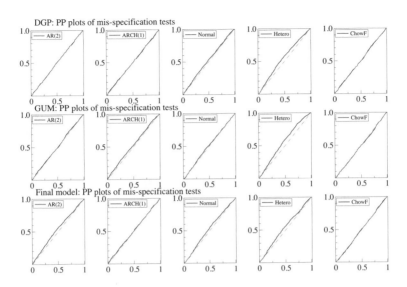

Figure 12.1
Calibrating mis-specification test null rejection frequencies, $T = 100, M = 1000$.

Figure 12.1 shows a calibration of the simulated cumulative null rejection frequencies against their reference distributions (these are probability versions of QQ plots: instead of quantiles, the inverse quantiles are used on the axes) for the five mis-specification tests that are used from 1000 replications.

The top row shows the PP plots for the estimated DGP; the second row for the estimated GUM; and the third row for the selected model using $\alpha = 5\%$. That selection may differ across replications and is often different from the DGP, both by omitting relevant variables and retaining irrelevant adventitiously. The columns show the outcomes for the five tests in the table. Almost all the plots are close to straight lines at $45°$, even for the selected model where the tests are used to decide if a terminal candidate can be accepted (if congruent) or back-tracking is needed to find a larger model that does pass the tests (if significant).

It can be seen that repeated testing is not occurring: the overall distributions of the final model are not much different from those in the GUM. The congruence decision is taken for the GUM, and conditional on that, no substantive changes should occur.

Thus, the five mis-specification tests are reasonably well calibrated against their reference distributions in the DGP, GUM and selected model. Nevertheless, this is precisely the setting in which conducting

Table 12.1
Effect of model selection on distribution of diagnostic tests at nominal significance level η: rejection frequencies in the right tail. $M = 100\,000$, $T = 100$

	10%	5%	2.5%	1%	0.5%
GUM					
AR(2)	0.0948	0.0467	0.0229	0.0090	0.0047
ARCH(1)	0.0763	0.0337	0.0158	0.0070	0.0039
Normal	0.0948	0.0506	0.0282	0.0136	0.0081
Hetero	0.0913	0.0500	0.0293	0.0143	0.0080
ChowF	0.0981	0.0497	0.0256	0.0101	0.0050
Selected model $\alpha = 5\%$, $\eta = 1\%$					
AR(2)	0.0798	0.0350	0.0153	0.0011	0.0008
ARCH(1)	0.0775	0.0351	0.0153	0.0016	0.0012
Normal	0.0919	0.0482	0.0239	0.0042	0.0034
Hetero	0.0940	0.0529	0.0283	0.0015	0.0012
ChowF	0.0972	0.0483	0.0236	0.0034	0.0024
Selected model $\alpha = 1\%$, $\eta = 1\%$					
AR(2)	0.0897	0.0419	0.0181	0.0009	0.0007
ARCH(1)	0.0770	0.0353	0.0158	0.0011	0.0009
Normal	0.0899	0.0469	0.0232	0.0033	0.0027
Hetero	0.0979	0.0550	0.0285	0.0010	0.0008
ChowF	0.0958	0.0478	0.0232	0.0028	0.0021
Selected model $\alpha = 5\%$, $\eta = 5\%$					
AR(2)	0.0718	0.0091	0.0059	0.0012	0.0009
ARCH(1)	0.0677	0.0091	0.0057	0.0018	0.0013
Normal	0.0826	0.0176	0.0124	0.0044	0.0036
Hetero	0.0790	0.0072	0.0052	0.0016	0.0012
ChowF	0.0946	0.0220	0.0155	0.0037	0.0025

five tests matters as discussed in section 7.8. Assume that each test is performed at a nominal significance level of η. Rejections of congruence will occur with probability of approximately $1 - (1 - \eta)^5$, so that small values of η, such as $\eta = 0.01$, should be used to control the overall rejection frequency at about 0.05 (say), declining with sample size to maintain a consistent selection.

Figure 12.1 does not provide much detail for small values of η, so we also ran the experiments with $M = 10^5$. Table 12.1 records the empirical rejection frequencies. The first block is for the GUM, where the rejec-

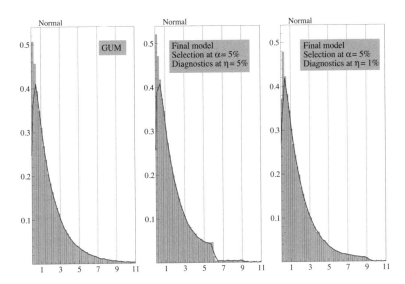

Figure 12.2
Distribution of normality test, before and after selection. $T = 100, M = 10^5$.

tion frequencies match their corresponding nominal values well. The second block is for the final model that is selected by *Autometrics*, with selection at nominal significance of 5% and the diagnostic test significance at the default of $\eta = 1\%$. Now the tails collapse at 1%: *Autometrics* is designed not to accept a non-congruent models, using the specified η, and is largely succesful at doing so. The final two blocks in the table confirm that this effect is governed by η, and not by α.

Figure 12.2 shows the impact of diagnostic tracking in *Autometrics* for the normality test (the only test in the battery of five with a distribution independent of the number of selected variables). The first graph is the distribution in the GUM. The second and third show the impact of selection: the tail collapses at the 5% critical value, and again at 1%. This is caused by non-congruent GUMs, when *Autometrics* proceeds with a smaller η, trying to restore the initial value of η if possible. An alternative would be to reject such draws (mimicking what should happen in practice, namely a reassessment of the GUM).

Diagnostic checking of reduction steps may also affect the properties of the selection algorithm, so we now consider that issue.

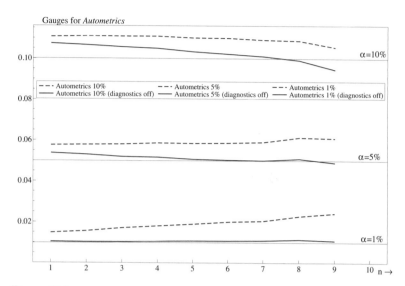

Figure 12.3
Gauges for *Autometrics* with diagnostic tracking at $\eta = 0.01$ (dashed lines) and
without (solid lines) for $\alpha = 0.01, 0.05, 0.1$. The horizontal axis represents the
$n = 1, \ldots, 10$ DGPs, each with n relevant variables (and a further $10 - n$ irrelevant
in the GUM).

12.3   Simulating *Autometrics* with diagnostic tracking

Figure 12.3 compares the gauges for *Autometrics* with diagnostic tracking switched on versus off for the experimental design from Castle
et al. (2013) as described in section 11.5, when the GUM is a congruent representation of the LDGP. The sample size remains 75, and we use
$M = 10\,000$. The gauge is close to, but slightly higher than, the nominal
significance level when the diagnostic tests are checked to ensure a congruent reduction. With diagnostic tracking switched off, as we showed,
the gauge is essentially equal to the nominal significance level. The difference seems due to irrelevant variables proxying part of a chance de-
parture from the null of one of the five mis-specification tests, or the
parsimonious encompassing check, and then being retained despite insignificance.

   Figure 12.3 suggests that *Autometrics* is over-gauged by about 1 percentage point, which is the significance level of each individual diagnostic check. However, to place the magnitude of over-gauging in perspective, figure 12.4 records the outcomes on the [0,1] scale relative to

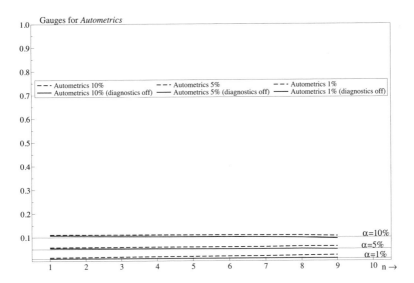

Figure 12.4
Gauges for *Autometrics* with diagnostic tracking at $\eta = 0.01$ (dashed lines) and without (solid lines) for $\alpha = 0.01, 0.05, 0.1$. The horizontal axis represents the $n = 1, \ldots, 10$ DGPs, each with n relevant variables (and $10 - n$ irrelevant).

the maximum potency. As can be seen, the impact on gauge is a relatively small price to pay under the null for avoiding non-congruent selections. Moreover, calculation of gauge could be based on significant retained irrelevant variables only (e.g., Hoover and Perez, 1999, compute their measure of size this way), whereas the above measure computes gauge over all retained irrelevant variables. As discussed in chapter 10, bias correction of insignificant retained variables sets their coefficients to zero, so they would not enter the bias-corrected final representation. Thus, gauge calculated only for significant retained variables would more closely match α.

12.4   Impact of diagnostic tracking on MSE

Figure 12.5 records the ratios of the UMSEs with diagnostic tests switched off to on in the top panel, and the same for the CMSEs in the bottom panel, averaging within relevant and irrelevant variables for the experiments in section 11.5. Switching the diagnostics off generally improves the UMSE s, but worsens the results conditionally, with the impact coming through the irrelevant variables. Switching the diagnostics off leads to fewer irrelevant regressors being retained overall,

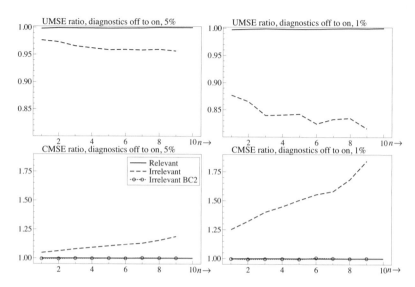

Figure 12.5
Ratios of MSEs with diagnostic tests off to on for unconditional and conditional distributions. BC2 is the two-step bias correction.

improving the UMSEs, but those irrelevant variables that are retained are now more significant than with the diagnostics on, so increase the CMSEs. This effect is entirely mitigated by the bias correction: the CMSE ratio using the two-step bias correction (labeled BC2 in the graph) is indistiguishable from unity. The impact of diagnostic tracking is largest at tight significance levels: at 10% the ratios are so close to unity they are not plotted. There is almost no effect on the UMSEs or CMSEs for relevant variables, which remain close to unity in all panels.

12.5   Integrated data

Most diagnostic tests remain valid in integrated data series as shown by Wooldridge (1999). Specifically, tests based on residuals (such as F_{ar}, F_{arch}, and χ^2_{nd}) have their anticipated distributions, a finding confirmed by Caceres (2007). Caceres also shows that powers of I(1) variables make heteroskedasticity, and some non-linearity, tests converge to different distributions (including F_{het}, F_{reset} and F_{NL}), so care is required in interpreting their findings when applied to I(1) data before cointegration and differencing.

13 Role of Encompassing

Encompassing seeks to reconcile competing empirical models, all of which claim to explain some economic phenomena. If distinct competing models exist, all but one must either be incomplete or incorrect—and all may be false. By testing whether one model can account for the results found by the other models, investigators can learn how well their model performs relative to those, as well as reduce the class of admissible models. Some features of the LDGP may not be included, so different empirical models capture different sets of salient features. All empirical models are encompassed by the LDGP, in that knowledge of that LDGP allows one to account for all the findings reported, even when some models are not nested with respect to others. It is natural to seek models which encompass the LDGP, and that motivates our selection strategy: specify a GUM which nests the LDGP, then simplify it to a model that is as parsimonious as feasible while still encompassing the GUM.

13.1 Introduction

Given any two distinct empirical models M_1 and M_2 of a variable y, encompassing is a way of testing whether a rival model (M_2 say) captures features of the LDGP of y, denoted M_0, not already embodied in the investigator's model, M_1. If M_2 does not offer any new insights about the LDGP beyond M_1, it is said that M_1 *encompasses* M_2, denoted by $M_1 \mathcal{E} M_2$. In turn, M_1 could also be encompassed by M_2, in which case the two models are not distinguishable on the available evidence, so may be isomorphic.

Encompassing tests are based on two implications of the encompassing principle. First, if M_1 encompasses M_2, then M_1 ought to be able to explain the predictions of M_2. Alternatively, as the encompassed model does not capture all the features of the LDGP which are captured by the encompassing model, M_1 ought to be able to predict some mis-specifications of M_2. Both types of prediction are of interest (see the review in Hendry and Richard, 1989, and the papers in Hendry et al., 2008). Here we focus on the former as part of a model selection strategy.

13.1.1 Variance dominance

Let M_1 and M_2 have innovation error processes denoted by $\{\epsilon_t\}$ and $\{\nu_t\}$ with constant, finite variances σ_ϵ^2 and σ_ν^2. Then M_1 variance dominates M_2 (denoted by $M_1 > M_2$) if M_1 has the smaller variance: $\sigma_\epsilon^2 < \sigma_\nu^2$. An LDGP must variance dominate all models thereof in the popula-tion. To see this, let Z_t denote the available valid information, and let $\epsilon_t = y_t - E[y_t|Z_t]$. Then, as the conditional expectation for an unchanged distribution has minimum mean-square error (but see e.g., Hendry and Mizon, 2014), $\sigma_\epsilon^2 \le \sigma_\xi^2$ where $\xi_t = y_t - f[y_t|Z_t]$ for all choices of $f[\cdot]$.

A nesting model M_n for a class of models $\{M_i\}$, denoted by $M_i \subseteq M_n$, must population-variance dominate in its class, a result which favors general over simple empirical models in large samples. Let $M_i(\psi_i)$ have κ_i parameters in ψ_i, then M_1 is parsimoniously undominated in the class of models $\{M_i\}$ if $\forall i$, $\kappa_1 \le \kappa_i$ and no $M_i > M_1$.

13.2   Parsimonious encompassing

Parsimonious encompassing is a relationship where a smaller model ex-plains the results of a larger model within which it is nested, and con-sequently is suited to checking reductions from a GUM. This is denoted $\mathcal{E}_p$, and is defined by $M_1\mathcal{E}_pM_2$ if $M_1 \subseteq M_2$ and $M_1\mathcal{E}M_2$. $\mathcal{E}_p$ satisfies the three conditions for a partial ordering (see Hendry, 1995a, Ch. 14) as it is

1. reflexive, since $M_1\mathcal{E}_pM_1$;

2. asymmetric, since $M_1\mathcal{E}_pM_2$ entails M_2 does not parsimoniously en-compass M_1 when the models are distinct; and

3. transitive, since $M_1\mathcal{E}_pM_2$ and $M_2\mathcal{E}_pM_3$ (say), then $M_1\mathcal{E}_pM_3$.

Thus, parsimonious encompassing helps implement a progressive re-search strategy, namely model building where knowledge gradually ac-cumulates. It is natural to seek models which encompass the LDGP, an aspect formalized by Bontemps and Mizon (2003), and that motivates our selection strategy: specify a GUM which nests the LDGP, then simplify it to a model that is as parsimonious as feasible while still encompassing the GUM.

13.2.1   Testing parsimonious encompassing

When the models under analysis are all reductions of the GUM which nests them, the most direct test of parsimonious encompassing is an F-test of the simplifications against that GUM. Govaerts et al. (1994) investigate a number of encompassing tests, and show the advantages of the parsimonious encompassing F-test.

13.3   Encompassing the GUM

Monte Carlo experiments are used to study the impact of encompassing on automatic model selection algorithms: in *Autometrics* this is called back-testing. Four model selection methods will be compared to help elucidate the role of parsimonious encompassing: although step-wise regression will be examined in more detail later, it is insightful to contrast the *Autometrics* outcomes with both an expanding search and a method that only explores a single path. The four model selection methods are:

1. *Autometrics* at its default settings, except that pre-search, mis-specification tests and diagnostic tracking are all switched off to concentrate on the role of encompassing.[1] The significance level p -value for the reduction is set to α. *Autometrics* derives other control parameters from α. Most importantly, back-testing will also be undertaken at α.

2. *Autometrics* is set as in 1., but now without checking whether simplifications encompass the GUM, so back-testing is also switched off.

3. Step-wise regression, starting from the empty model. Thus, the omitted variable that would be most significant at each stage is added to the model. If at any stage, variables in the model become insignificant, the most insignificant is deleted, so in each iteration up to one regressor can enter, and one can leave. This process is repeated until all variables in the model are significant at α, and all omitted variables would be individually insignificant if added.

4. Backward elimination, starting from the GUM. All regressors are added to the initial model, then regressors are deleted one at a time

---

[1]The lag pre-search is switched off to avoid another layer of complexity. In general, this pre-search is helpful when it corresponds to a modeler's preference for shorter lag lengths, but can be too strict when only the lagged dependent variable matters.

Table 13.1
Simulated effects of λ on experiment HP8(λ). $M = 100\,000$, $T = 139$

	$\lambda = 50$	$\lambda = 10$	$\lambda = 1$	$\lambda = 0.1$
$t(\beta_1)$	12.7	12.7	12.4	12.7
$t(\beta_2)$	-1.2	-5.9	-58.8	-588
$t(\beta_3)$	0.9	4.1	12.1	12.7
R^2	0.54	0.60	0.97	0.9997

DGP:
$$y_t = 0.75y_{t-1} - 0.046x_{3,t} + 0.0345x_{3,t-1} + 0.073\lambda u_t, \quad u_t \sim \text{IN}[0,1].$$
Model:
$$y_t = \beta_0 + \beta_1 y_{t-1} + \beta_2 x_{3,t} + \beta_3 x_{3,t-1} + \epsilon_t.$$

starting from the least significant. This is continued until all regressors have a p-value of α or less. Like step-wise regression, backward elimination only explores a single path, but in the opposite direction.

The DGP is a modified version of model 8 from Hoover and Perez (1999), denoted HP8, and described in section 17.2.1. Here, we add an additional parameter λ to create HP8(λ):

$$y_{8,t} = 0.75y_{8,t-1} - 0.046x_{3,t} + 0.0345x_{3,t-1} + 0.073\lambda u_t, \quad u_t \sim \text{IN}[0,1],$$

using a sample size of $T = 139$. Hoover and Perez set $\lambda = 1$, but the λ parameter creates more variation in the significance of the estimated coefficients on $x_{3,t}$. This is shown in table 13.1, which records the simulated t-values for this sample size, always using the actual $x_{3,t}$ variable in the DGP and model. When $\lambda = 50$, the x_3 variable and its lag are insignificant, so even when starting from the DGP, one should only expect to retain either of them about 30% of the time. This is a cost of inference rather than search.

The experiment starts model selection from GUM (13.1): the 3 variables that matter and an additional 37 that are irrelevant.

$$y_t = \gamma_0^F + \sum_{j=1}^{4} \alpha_j y_{t-j} + \sum_{i=1}^{18} \sum_{j=0}^{1} \gamma_{i,j} x_{i,t-j} + u_t \text{ where } u_t \sim \text{IN}\left[0, \sigma_u^2\right]. \quad (13.1)$$

The irrelevant variables consist of $y_{t-2}, y_{t-3}, y_{t-4}$ and the remaining 17 regressors from the macro-economic database, both current-dated and their first lag. An intercept is always forced into the model. The results reported in this chapter use $M = 10\,000$ Monte Carlo replications throughout.

Table 13.2
Experiment HP8 with $T = 139$ for four automatic model selection methods: 1. is *Autometrics* with encompassing but without pre-search and diagnostics; 2. is *Autometrics* with neither encompassing nor pre-search nor diagnostics

	1. *Autometrics* encompassing		2. *Autometrics* no encompassing		3. Step-wise regression		4. Backward elimination	
α	Gauge	Potency	Gauge	Potency	Gauge	Potency	Gauge	Potency
$\lambda = 50$								
0.1	0.093	0.434	0.055	0.394	0.073	0.422	0.192	0.524
0.05	0.056	0.406	0.021	0.360	0.039	0.389	0.106	0.455
0.01	0.014	0.354	0.002	0.337	0.009	0.348	0.021	0.366
$\lambda = 10$								
0.1	0.097	0.942	0.061	0.902	0.079	0.891	0.197	0.933
0.05	0.058	0.937	0.031	0.832	0.046	0.817	0.110	0.923
0.01	0.017	0.904	0.018	0.623	0.022	0.696	0.029	0.902
$\lambda = 1$								
0.1	0.093	1.000	0.048	1.000	0.094	0.793	0.184	1.000
0.05	0.057	1.000	0.020	1.000	0.061	0.693	0.100	1.000
0.01	0.014	1.000	0.002	0.999	0.032	0.533	0.020	1.000

Table 13.2 shows the results of this experiment for a range of λs and three reduction significance levels α. The gauge is the fraction of irrelevant variables in the final model, regardless of significance. In this case, there are 37 irrelevant variables, so a gauge of 0.05 means that on average, the final model contains 1.85 variables that should not be there. The potency records the fraction of relevant variables that are in the final model. A potency of 0.9 means that 2.7 correct variables are in the final model (on average). The DGP has a gauge of zero and potency of unity if no inferences are conducted, whereas the GUM has both equal to unity. Consequently, potency is not gauge adjusted, and can be high merely because the gauge is much larger than the nominal significance level (as occurs in table 13.2 with backward elimination).

The results of table 13.2, visually presented in the gauge-potency plots of figure 13.1, show that backward elimination (labelled '4' in the graphs) is considerably over-gauged at all values of α. This is not surprising because backward elimination follows only one path, so once a search gets stuck in a wrong path, other variables tend to be spuriously significant.

Next, step-wise regression can be very poor: when $\lambda = 0.1$, all other methods have potency at 100%, while step-wise is less than 40%. In

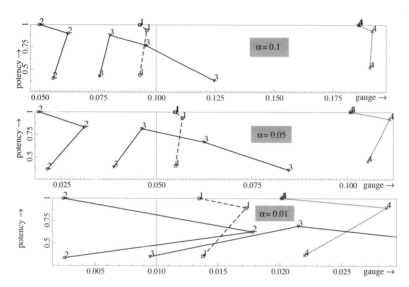

Figure 13.1
HP8: $\alpha = 0.1$ (top panel), $\alpha = 0.05$ (middle panel), $\alpha = 0.01$ (bottom panel), all with gauge (fraction of irrelevant variables) on the horizontal, and potency (fraction of relevant variables) on the vertical axis. Each line connects the different values of λ, ranging from $\lambda = 50$ at the bottom to $\lambda = 0.1$ at the top (left-right for step-wise). There are 4 model selection algorithms: 1=*Autometrics* without pre-search and diagnostics, 2=*Autometrics* without pre-search, diagnostics and encompassing, 3=step-wise, 4=backward elimination. All points correspond to table 13.2.

that case, it finds neither y_{t-1} nor $x_{3,t-1}$, adding other terms instead. Thus, step-wise is erratic and unreliable. The second method, *Autometrics* without encompassing (labelled '2' in the graphs), loses both gauge and potency. The final model is too small, because although it searches quite comprehensively, lack of quality control makes it too aggressive.

Autometrics with encompassing (method '1'), on the other hand, is well behaved: the gauge is close to the nominal rejection frequency α. Thus, search tightens the final specification and adds path independence, roughly, moving from the lines labelled '4' to those labelled '2' in figure 13.1, while encompassing then provides the statistical control, moving from '2' to '1'. Adding encompassing to the single path of backward elimination would make it even more over-gauged, because it can only lead to earlier termination of the reduction. Thus, encompassing is beneficial only for a search procedure where gauge is close to the nominal size.

13.4   Iteration and encompassing

The initial GUM is the GUM specified by the modeler. When search is applied repeatedly, there are several possible "GUM"s:[2]

Initial GUM   This is the most general model, using the full initial information set.

GUM_1   After one pass of the search, the union of the terminal candidate models forms a new "GUM", denoted GUM_1, which is the starting point for another search within the reduced space, leading to GUM_2, smaller than or the same as GUM_1, continuing until GUM_i is the same as GUM_{i-1}.

Final GUM   When successive searches do not change the GUM, the iterative procedure terminates with one or more final models. The final GUM is the union of these.

As the search continues, there are three possible approaches to encompassing. The first is to always test encompassing of the initial GUM. The second is to use GUM_0 throughout, which is the default in *Autometrics*. The third is to always use the most recent GUM, i.e., GUM_{i-1}, which was the default in *PcGets*.

Using the initial GUM (or GUM_0 after pre-search) for back-testing in each iteration means that all encompassing tests are against an identical alternative. Iterated encompassing tests, where intermediate GUMs are used (i.e., the union of final models from the previous round), increase the complexity of the algorithm, and it is also possible that apparently invalid reductions appear. A further drawback is that the status of an intermediate "GUM" is unclear, so is not necessarily a good basis for encompassing tests: some of the constituent models may be large and not of much interest.

Table 13.3 compares back-testing with respect to the initial GUM (shown in columns 3 and 4, which are the same as the first method in table 13.2) to back-testing with respect to the intermediate GUM. The latter increases the gauge, moving it further away from the target, while not having much effect on the potency.

---

[2]More so when there is a pre-search prior to the main multi-path search, which in *Autometrics* by default consists of a lag reduction only, attempting to remove highly insignificant lags (e.g., all regressors at lag 5). The GUM after pre-search would be denoted GUM_0; without pre-search, GUM_0 and the initial GUM are identical.

Table 13.3
Experiment HP8 with $M = 10000$ and $T = 139$ for *Autometrics* using two encompassing (back-testing) methods (pre-search and diagnostics switched off)

α	Encompassing GUM_0		Encompassing intermediate GUM	
	Gauge	Potency	Gauge	Potency
$\lambda = 50$				
0.1	0.093	0.434	0.138	0.477
0.05	0.056	0.406	0.078	0.422
0.01	0.014	0.354	0.015	0.357
$\lambda = 10$				
0.1	0.097	0.942	0.135	0.950
0.05	0.058	0.937	0.084	0.944
0.01	0.017	0.904	0.022	0.909
$\lambda = 1$				
0.1	0.093	1.000	0.130	1.000
0.05	0.057	1.000	0.076	1.000
0.01	0.014	1.000	0.014	1.000

The calibration experiments in Doornik (2009a) also found that back-testing with respect to the intermediate GUM somewhat increased the incidence of irrelevant variables without any commensurate gains in detecting relevant variables.

Together, these experiments suggest that it is the encompassing principle (i.e., back-testing) that keeps the reduction on track, rather than which particular encompassing method is used for the next iteration. Overall, parsimonious encompassing of the initial GUM maintains the gauge near α without much loss of potency.

14 Retaining a Theory Model During Selection

Economic theories are often fitted directly to data to avoid any issues of model selection. This is an excellent strategy when the theory is complete and correct, but less successful otherwise. We consider embedding a theory model that specifies the set of n relevant exogenous variables, x_t, within a larger set of $n+k$ candidate variables, (x_t, w_t), but only select over the w_t. When the theory model is complete and correct, so the w_t are in fact irrelevant, by orthogonalizing them with respect to the x_t, selection over the orthogonalized components can be undertaken without affecting the theory parameters' estimator distributions. This strategy keeps the theory-parameter estimates when the theory is correct, yet protects against the theory being underspecified when some w_t are relevant.[1]

14.1 Introduction

The Royal Society of London was founded in 1660 as a "Colledge for the Promoting of Physico-Mathematicall Experimentall Learning", to bridge the gap between theory and evidence that had started with the views and approaches of Plato against those of Aristotle, and had continued to Galileo versus William Gilbert (see Goldstein, 2010). As noted in Hendry (2011b), such a gap persists to this day in economics: but need no longer as this chapter explains.

Economic theories are often fitted directly to data to avoid possible model selection biases. This is an excellent strategy when the theory is complete and correct, but less successful otherwise (see Spanos, 1995, for a discussion of testing theories on non-experimental data). Here we

---

[1]This chapter is based on Hendry and Johansen (2014).

show that by embedding a theory model that specifies the correct set of n relevant exogenous variables, x_t, within a larger set of $n + k$ candidate variables, (x_t, w_t), selection over the second set by their statistical significance can be undertaken without affecting the theory parameters' estimator distributions. We mainly consider regression models to illustrate the analysis, but similar principles apply in more complicated settings.

The two key features are

(a) not selecting over the theory variables, so they are always retained;

(b) orthogonalizing them with respect to the other candidate variables.

Then under the null that the theory is complete and correct, identical estimator distributions must result after selection, despite checking the theory against a potentially very large number of alternatives. Conversely, when the theory is incomplete, or possibly incorrect, but the GUM nests the DGP, the selected model will be a far better approximation to that DGP. Such a procedure can formally nest so-called "theory-driven" and "data-driven" approaches, which Spanos (2011) shows to be inadequate on their own.

Section 14.2 shows that the distributions of the estimated coefficients of retained x_t are unaffected by model selection when the candidate variables w_t are orthogonalized with respect to x_t, for $(k + n) \ll T$, so the general model is estimable. Section 14.3 discusses possible decision rules for rejecting a theory model. The analysis also applies to a valid theory with endogenous variables, and can be used to assess the validity of the instrumental variables. Section 14.4 briefly considers embedding rival theories. After investigating the general case where there are more variables than observations in chapter 19, section 19.7 returns to establish that even when $(k + n) > T$, provided $n \ll T$, the results developed here for selection when retaining a valid theory still apply.

14.2   Selection when retaining a valid theory

Consider a theory model which correctly matches the DGP specified over $t = 1, \ldots, T$ as:

$$y_t = \beta' x_t + \epsilon_t, \tag{14.1}$$

where $\epsilon_t \sim \mathsf{IID}[0, \sigma_\epsilon^2]$, and $\{\epsilon_t\}$ is independent of the n strongly exogenous variables $\{x_1, \ldots, x_T\}$, assumed to satisfy:

$$T^{-1} \sum_{t=1}^{T} x_t x_t' \xrightarrow{\mathrm{P}} \Sigma_{xx},$$

which is positive definite, and:

$$T^{1/2} \left(\widehat{\beta} - \beta_0 \right) = \left(T^{-1} \sum_{t=1}^{T} x_t x_t' \right)^{-1} T^{-1/2} \sum_{t=1}^{T} x_t \epsilon_t$$

$$\xrightarrow{D} \mathsf{N}_n \left[0, \sigma_\epsilon^2 \Sigma_{xx}^{-1} \right], \tag{14.2}$$

where β_0 denotes the constant population parameter.

Although believing the theory, an investigator may nevertheless be willing to contemplate the possibility that an additional set of k exogenous variables w_t also influences y_t, so postulates the more general model:

$$y_t = \beta' x_t + \gamma' w_t + \epsilon_t, \tag{14.3}$$

where $\gamma_0 = 0$ under the null that the theory model (14.1) is correct and complete. The w_t could be variables known to be exogenous, functions of those, lags of the x_t or other lagged variables in time series, and indicators for outliers or breaks. We assume the same assumptions for $\{\epsilon_t, x_t, w_t\}$ as above.

Since the investigator regards the theory in (14.1) as correct and complete, the analysis must ensure that the x_t are always retained, so are not selected over. However, retaining the variables is distinct from imposing the theory on the data, or restricting its parameter estimates, though that could also be implemented. The issue we address is the possible additional cost of searching over the candidate variables w_t in (14.3) when retaining the x_t, rather than directly estimating (14.1) for $(k + n) \ll T$.

Using a variant of the theorem in Frisch and Waugh (1933), x_t and w_t can be orthogonalized by first computing:

$$\widehat{\Gamma} = \left(\sum_{t=1}^{T} w_t x_t' \right) \left(\sum_{t=1}^{T} x_t x_t' \right)^{-1}$$

and defining the residuals $\widehat{u}_t$ by:

$$w_t = \widehat{\Gamma} x_t + \widehat{u}_t, \tag{14.4}$$

so that:

$$\sum_{t=1}^{T} x_t \widehat{u}_t' = 0. \tag{14.5}$$

Using (14.4) in (14.3):

$$y_t = \beta' x_t + \gamma' w_t + \epsilon_t$$
$$= \beta' x_t + \gamma' \left(\widehat{\Gamma} x_t + \widehat{u}_t \right) + \epsilon_t$$
$$= \beta'_+ x_t + \gamma' \widehat{u}_t + \epsilon_t, \tag{14.6}$$

where $\beta_+ = \beta + \widehat{\Gamma}' \gamma$. The population value of β_+ is still β_0 because $\gamma_0 = 0$. Consequently, as (14.1) is the DGP, by orthogonality from (14.5):

$$T^{1/2} \left(\begin{array}{c} \widetilde{\beta}_+ - \beta_0 \\ \widetilde{\gamma} \end{array} \right)$$

$$= \left(\begin{array}{cc} T^{-1} \sum_{t=1}^{T} x_t x_t' & T^{-1} \sum_{t=1}^{T} x_t \widehat{u}_t' \\ T^{-1} \sum_{t=1}^{T} \widehat{u}_t x_t' & T^{-1} \sum_{t=1}^{T} \widehat{u}_t \widehat{u}_t' \end{array} \right)^{-1} \left(\begin{array}{c} T^{-1/2} \sum_{t=1}^{T} x_t \epsilon_t \\ T^{-1/2} \sum_{t=1}^{T} \widehat{u}_t \epsilon_t \end{array} \right)$$

$$= \left(\begin{array}{c} \left(T^{-1} \sum_{t=1}^{T} x_t x_t' \right)^{-1} T^{-1/2} \sum_{t=1}^{T} x_t \epsilon_t \\ \left(T^{-1} \sum_{t=1}^{T} \widehat{u}_t \widehat{u}_t' \right)^{-1} T^{-1/2} \sum_{t=1}^{T} \widehat{u}_t \epsilon_t \end{array} \right)$$

$$\overset{D}{\to} \mathsf{N}_{n+k} \left[\left(\begin{array}{c} 0 \\ 0 \end{array} \right), \sigma_\epsilon^2 \left(\begin{array}{cc} \Sigma_{xx}^{-1} & 0 \\ 0 & \Sigma_{ww|x}^{-1} \end{array} \right) \right]. \tag{14.7}$$

The estimator $\widetilde{\beta}_+$ in (14.7) is identical to $\widehat{\beta}$ in (14.2), independently of the inclusion or exclusion of any or all of the $\widehat{u}_t$. Even after selection over the $\widehat{u}_t$ at significance level α, and corresponding critical value c_α, say, by sequential t-tests on each $\widetilde{\gamma}_i$, the theory-parameter estimator is unaffected by retaining significant $\widehat{u}_t$. For a gaussian distribution and fixed regressors, the estimator $\widetilde{\beta}_+ = \widehat{\beta}$ is statistically independent of the test statistics used to select. Thus, in terms of not affecting the distribution of the valid theory model's parameter estimates, this approach to selection is costless.

A variant could also orthogonalize the $\{\widehat{u}_t\}$: as they are assumed irrelevant, no issue of interpretability arises. Then 1-cut could be used for selection. However, a decision has to be made as to whether or not the theory model is indeed correct and complete, to which issue we now turn.

14.3   Decision rules for rejecting a theory model

The possible costs of selection are

(a) the chance retention by selection of some $\widehat{u}_{i,t}$, which may mislead on the validity of the theory model; and

(b) their impact on the *estimated* distribution of $\widehat{\beta}$, through mis-estimation of σ_ϵ^2 in (14.7).

Against these, possible benefits are that

(c) the theory-model is tested against a wide range of alternatives; and

(d) when the theory is incomplete, the selected model will be less mis-specified.

We consider these in turn.

For (a), if all $\widehat{u}_{i,t}$ are irrelevant, then on average αk of the $\widehat{u}_{i,t}$ will be retained by chance, with estimated coefficients $\widetilde{\gamma}_i$, where:

$$|t_{\gamma_i=0}| = \frac{|\widetilde{\gamma}_i|}{\mathsf{SE}\left[\widetilde{\gamma}_i\right]} \geq c_\alpha. \tag{14.8}$$

Setting $\alpha = \min\left[1/k, 1/T, 1\%\right]$ is an appealing rule. When $T = 100$ and $k = T/4 = 25$, say, then because $k\alpha = 0.25$, the probability of retaining more than one irrelevant variable is:

$$p_1 = 1 - \sum_{i=0}^{1} \frac{(0.25)^i}{i!} e^{-0.25} \simeq 2.6\%.$$

Moreover, under normality and letting $h > 2/c_\alpha$ then:

$$\Pr\left(|t_{\gamma_i=0}| \geq hc_\alpha \mid H_0\right) \leq \frac{1}{\sqrt{2\pi}} \exp\left(-\frac{h^2}{2}c_\alpha^2\right),$$

which is 0.01% at $h = 1.5$ and $c_{0.01} = 2.65$. Thus, it is unlikely any $|t_{\gamma_i=0}|$ will be larger than $1.5c_\alpha$. Problem (a) can be resolved by rejecting a theory when more than one of the $\widehat{u}_{i,t}$ are retained, or when one is more significant than $1.5c_\alpha$. Estimates of γ_i can be approximately bias corrected if desired after their chance retention, as in section 10.2.

Addressing (b), an unbiased estimated error variance under the null that $\gamma_0 = 0$, so that (14.2) is correctly estimated, is:

$$\bar{\sigma}_\epsilon^2 = (T - n)^{-1} \sum_{t=1}^{T} \left(y_t - \widetilde{\beta}_+' x_t\right)^2, \tag{14.9}$$

although under the alternative, (14.9) will be an overestimate.

The converse to (a) is (c), as the theory-model is tested simultaneously against all w_t, evaluating the theory against a wide range of alternatives at little cost; and if incomplete as in (d), selection will reduce mis-specification relative to direct estimation, as we now discuss.

14.3.1   Retaining an incomplete or invalid theory

Under the alternative $\gamma_0 \neq \mathbf{0}$, directly estimating (14.1) will result in biased outcomes. However, when (14.3) nests the DGP, from (14.6) the coefficient of x_t is $\beta_0 + \widetilde{\boldsymbol{\Gamma}}' \gamma_0$, which will also be estimated if (14.1) is directly fitted to the data. When (14.3) nests the DGP, selection can improve the final model relative to (14.1), as in Castle et al. (2011). While retaining x_t when selecting from (14.6) will then deliver an incorrect estimate of β_0, some of the $\widehat{u}_{i,t}$ will also be retained, this time correctly, so an estimate of β_0 can be derived from $\widetilde{\beta} + \widehat{\boldsymbol{\Gamma}}' \widetilde{\gamma}$, $\widetilde{\gamma}$ and $\widehat{\boldsymbol{\Gamma}}$.

If the theory is completely incorrect in that $\beta_0 = \mathbf{0}$, the estimated coefficient $\widehat{\beta} + \widehat{\boldsymbol{\Gamma}}' \widehat{\gamma}$ of x_t in (14.6) will generally not be zero, so it may be worth also selecting without orthogonalization when $\widetilde{\beta}_+$ does not conform to theory expectations.

14.4   Rival theories

Often there co-exist rival theories of economic phenomena. Thus, it is conceivable that two investigators might use the above approach to embed their own theory models in a range of alternatives and each conclude by not rejecting their favored specifications, given the tight significance level used to privilege each retained model. The issue now becomes one of choice between these, so encompassing tests can be used at more conventional significance levels such as 1%, in which case neither, either, or both could be rejected against their nesting GUM. Alternatively, automatic selection could be used starting from that GUM to ascertain which variables best characterize the data. In this setting, neither theory can be privileged by being fixed without selection.

14.5   Implications

The approach in this chapter provides economists with the ability to retain a theory model while also evaluating it against a wide range of possible candidate variables (or functions thereof), without affecting the parameter estimators' distributions, yet at the same time discover what matters empirically when that theory is not a complete description of the LDGP. As noted above, an investigator can then know in advance the answer to all the likely seminar questions of the impacts of including other variables that may be deemed relevant. Moreover, by jointly investigating all of the k additional variables in a congruent model, inferences as to their irrelevance will be validly based. Despite checking the potential relevance of many candidate variables, a stringent critical value ensures there is little chance of retaining irrelevant variables (which anyway would be heavily downweighted by bias correction), and no chance of omitting any of the retained variables. The approach therefore creates a win-win situation: the same outcome as imposing a theory-based specification without selection when that theory is correct and complete, and an improved model of the LDGP when the theory is incomplete.

15   Detecting Outliers and Breaks Using IIS

The last of our six stages concerns detecting outliers and breaks. Impulse-indicator saturation (IIS: see Hendry et al., 2008, and Johansen and Nielsen, 2009) is analyzed under the null of no outliers, but with the aim of detecting and removing outliers and location shifts when they are present. The procedure creates an indicator for every observation, entered (in the simplest case) in blocks of $T/2$, noting that indicators are mutually orthogonal. First, add half the indicators, select as usual, record the outcome, then drop that set of indicators; next add the other half, selecting again. These first two steps correspond to dummying out $T/2$ observations for estimation. Now combine the significant indicators and select as usual. Overall, αT indicators will be retained on average by chance. Setting $\alpha \leq r/T$ (when r is small, e.g., unity) then maintains the average false null retention at r outliers, equivalent to losing r observations, which is a small efficiency loss when testing for breaks at T points. The theory generalizes to more, and unequal, splits, as well as to dynamic models, and is related to robust estimation. IIS also introduces selection when $N \geq T$ in its simplest setting.

15.1   Introduction

Economic data are prone to contamination from various sources. Measurement errors are pandemic, but sometimes can be sufficiently large to distort an empirical analysis. In model selection, normality plays several roles, but is particularly important for valid inference during path searches (see chapter 8) and for post-selection bias corrections (chapter 10). Consequently, there are substantive advantages to having a general approach that is relatively robust to distortions from data contamination and outliers in the residuals. Impulse-indicator saturation

(IIS) was proposed by Hendry et al. (2008) with the aim of detecting and removing outliers when they are present. The procedure in section 15.2 creates an impulse indicator for every observation, entered (in the simplest case) in blocks of $T/2$, called split half, noting that indicators are mutually orthogonal. First, add half the indicators, select as usual, record the outcome, then drop that set of indicators; now add the other half, selecting again, with the significant outcomes recorded. Each of these first two steps corresponds to dummying out the relevant block of $T/2$ observations for estimation on the remainder. Now combine the significant indicators and select as usual by *Autometrics*.

The idea for IIS arose accidentally from Hendry (1999) when seeking to locate what caused the problems many investigators had experienced in modeling US food demand in the 1930s and 1940s. Hendry (1999) introduced zero-one dummies for 1931–36, 1938, 1941–46, almost saturating the period, selecting major outliers for 1931–1933 and war-time rationing. Adding these led to a model that seemed to be constant over the whole period, which he tested by the Chow (1960) test for parameter constancy on the post-war data. However, Salkever (1976) showed that the Chow (1960) test can be implemented by testing the significance of impulse indicators over the relevant period. Consequently, impulse indicators had been implicitly added for the sample from 1953 onwards. In effect, as many impulse indicators had been used as observations, entered in two large blocks (see the follow up discussion in Hendry, 2009).

Like much of the related robust estimation literature, we first analyze the IIS procedure under the null of no outliers, initially in a simple IID setting where the large-sample distributions can be derived despite intrinsically having more candidate regressors than observations. The post-selection mean estimator is shown to be unbiased, and its variance is obtained in section 15.3, dependent on the selection significance level α and the form of the IID distribution. Overall, αT indicators will be retained on average by chance under the null. Setting $\alpha \leq r/T$ (when r is small, e.g., unity) then maintains the average false null retention at r outliers, equivalent to losing r observations, which is a small efficiency loss for testing the potential relevance of T indicator variables.

The generalization by Johansen and Nielsen (2009) to dynamic models is discussed in section 15.4. Section 15.5 describes how IIS is implemented in *Autometrics*, section 15.6 applies IIS to a fat-tailed distribution, and section 15.7 calculates the non-null rejection frequency for a single outlier. The simplest example of detecting a location shift in section 15.8 is followed by a simulation illustration in section 15.9. IIS draws on the

developments in automatic *Gets* to search multiple paths to find any outliers, which in turn greatly extends its capability.

Several advances discussed below depend on IIS either directly as in
chapter 20 on detecting multiple location shifts, and chapter 22 on testing for super exogeneity by applying IIS to detect breaks in marginal
models then testing the relevance of those in conditional equations. Indirectly, as in chapter 19, IIS led to ways of handling excess numbers
of variables, $N > T$, in general, based on a mixture of reduction and
expansion steps, and in chapter 21, IIS is crucial when selecting non-
linear models to avoid confusing outliers with non-linearities. Finally,
in chapter 23, IIS can help select forecasting models in the face of location shifts, or as in Castle et al. (2013) when testing the invariance of
models involving expectations. In each case, information is discovered
during the empirical analyses that cannot have been known in advance.
Consequently, this chapter describes a pivotal setting for much of the
remainder of the book.

15.2   Theory of impulse-indicator saturation

Following the analysis in Hendry et al. (2008), let an observed random
variable y_i be independently identically distributed as $y_i \sim \mathsf{IID}\left[\mu, \sigma_\varepsilon^2\right]$
for $i = 1, \ldots, T$, where $\mu \in \mathbb{R}$, $\sigma_\varepsilon^2 \in \mathbb{R}_+$ are the parameters of interest.
Define a saturating set of T indicators $I_{i,t} = 1_{\{i=t\}}$, one for every obser-
vation. First add half the indicators (assuming for simplicity that T is
even), select as usual, and record the significant outcomes. Now drop
that subset of indicators and add the other half, selecting the significant
outliers again. Finally, combine any significant indicators and select as
usual to retain the set that is significant overall.

Figure 15.1 illustrates IIS on artificial data $y_i \sim \mathsf{IN}[10, 1]$ for $T = 100$
to show precisely how the split-sample version works under the null.
The three rows correspond to the three stages: the first half of the indicators, second half, then combined. The three columns respectively report
the indicators entered, the indicators finally retained in that model, and
the resulting fitted and actual values for the selected model. Here, one
indicator is retained in the first half at $\alpha = 0.01$, none in the second half,
and the combination retains that one indicator, matching $\alpha T = 1$. Thus,
despite including T irrelevant indicators, just one is selected. Because
impulse indicators are mutually orthogonal within each block, 1-cut selection could be used.

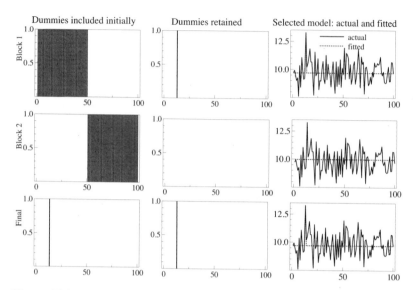

Figure 15.1
Impulse-indicator saturation stages in a split-half approach

Using the split-sample algorithm in Hendry et al. (2008), IIS takes the following form when the indicators enter ordered as $I_{1,t}, \ldots, I_{T,t}$.

1. Partition the indicators into $k = 2$ blocks, $\mathcal{B}_1 = \{I_{1,t}, \ldots, I_{T/2,t}\}$ and $\mathcal{B}_2 = \{I_{T/2+1,t}, \ldots, I_{T,t}\}$;
2. Estimate the parameters in the two sub-samples of $T/2$;
3. Run model selection on each block to obtain $\widehat{\mathcal{B}}_1$ and $\widehat{\mathcal{B}}_2$ as the significant sets;
4. Form the union $S = \widehat{\mathcal{B}}_1 \cup \widehat{\mathcal{B}}_2$;
5. Rerun model selection on S.

As the indicators are orthogonal, there is no need for cross-blocks where different sets of indicators are mixed and re-selected. The distribution under the null is presented below for the equal-split case, but generalizes to more, and unequal, splits.

The first step of adding half the indicators, $\mathcal{B}_1$, for $j = 1, \ldots, T/2$, together with the intercept yields for $i = 1, \ldots, T$:

$$y_i = \mu + \sum_{j=1}^{T/2} \delta_j I_{j,t} + \varepsilon_i. \tag{15.1}$$

Hence, (15.1) contains $T/2$ parameters for $T/2$ indicators for the first $T/2$ observations, as well as the mean and variance (alternative divisions of the sample are considered by Hendry et al., 2008). Then, using a subscript (1) to denote first-half estimates:

$$\widehat{\mu}_{(1)} = \frac{1}{T/2} \sum_{i=T/2+1}^{T} y_i, \tag{15.2}$$

$$s^2_{(1)} = \frac{1}{T/2 - 1} \sum_{i=T/2+1}^{T} (y_i - \widehat{\mu}_{(1)})^2 \tag{15.3}$$

$$\delta_i = y_i - \widehat{\mu}_{(1)}, \quad i = 1, \ldots, T/2, \tag{15.4}$$

so that:

$$\widehat{\varepsilon}_i = 0, \quad i = 1, \ldots, T/2$$
$$\widehat{\varepsilon}_i = y_i - \widehat{\mu}_{(1)}, \quad i = T/2 + 1, \ldots, T.$$

Because the estimates of μ and σ^2 are the usual ones for the remaining sample:

$$\mathsf{E}\left[\widehat{\mu}_{(1)}\right] = \mu \text{ and } \mathsf{V}\left[\widehat{\mu}_{(1)}\right] = (T/2)^{-1}\sigma^2_\varepsilon,$$

and:

$$\mathsf{E}\left[s^2_{(1)}\right] = \sigma^2_\varepsilon.$$

Consequently, both sub-sample estimators are unbiased at this stage.

Next, using a *Gets* approach, a parsimonious model is selected from (15.1), always retaining the intercept, such that all retained indicators are significant at the desired level by eliminating any indicator where $|t_{(1),\widehat{\delta}_i}| < c_\alpha$ for significance level c_α. The terminal model is stored.

Now re-commence from the equivalent of (15.1), but entering only the other half of the indicators namely $(1, I_{j,t}, j = T/2 + 1, \ldots, T)$, repeat the process to estimate μ and σ^2 by $\widehat{\mu}_{(2)}$ and $s^2_{(2)}$, then again apply *Gets*, eliminating indicators where $|t_{(2),\widehat{\delta}_i}| < c_\alpha$ and storing the resulting parsimonious selection. Lastly, formulate a model where all significant selected indicators from the two terminal models are combined, and reselect from that for the final model. This demonstrates that despite saturating by indicators, a feasible algorithm exists for checking for outliers or shifts at every observation.

The final estimates are:

$$\widetilde{\mu} = \frac{\sum_{i=1}^{T_1} y_i \mathbf{1}_{\{|t_{1,\widehat{\delta}_i}| < c_\alpha\}} + \sum_{i=T_1+1}^{T} y_i \mathbf{1}_{\{|t_{2,\widehat{\delta}_i}| < c_\alpha\}}}{\sum_{i=1}^{T_1} \mathbf{1}_{\{|t_{1,\widehat{\delta}_i}| < c_\alpha\}} + \sum_{i=T_1+1}^{N} \mathbf{1}_{\{|t_{2,\widehat{\delta}_i}| < c_\alpha\}}}, \tag{15.5}$$

and:

$$\tilde{\sigma}_{\varepsilon}^2 = \frac{\sum_{i=1}^{T_1}(y_i - \hat{\mu}_1)^2 1_{\{|t_{1,\hat{\delta}_i}|<c_\alpha\}} + \sum_{i=T_1+1}^{T}(y_i - \hat{\mu}_2)^2 1_{\{|t_{2,\hat{\delta}_i}|<c_\alpha\}}}{\sum_{i=1}^{T_1} 1_{\{|t_{1,\hat{\delta}_i}|<c_\alpha\}} + \sum_{i=T_1+1}^{T} 1_{\{|t_{2,\hat{\delta}_i}|<c_\alpha\}} - 1}. \tag{15.6}$$

We next describe the large-sample properties of the estimators (15.5) and (15.6).

15.3   Sampling distributions

Hendry et al. (2008) prove that:

$$T^{1/2}\left(\tilde{\mu} - \mu\right) \xrightarrow{D} N\left[0, \sigma_{\varepsilon}^2 \sigma_{\mu}^2\right], \tag{15.7}$$

where:

$$\sigma_{\mu}^2 = \frac{1}{P(c_\alpha)}\left(1 + 4c_\alpha f(c_\alpha) - \frac{2c_\alpha f(c_\alpha)}{P(c_\alpha)} - \frac{4c_\alpha^2 f(c_\alpha)^2}{P(c_\alpha)}\right), \tag{15.8}$$

when the errors are distributed as $f(\cdot)$ and for $\hat{u}_i = y_i - \hat{\mu} - \hat{\delta}_i$:

$$P(c_\alpha) = P\left(|\hat{u}| \leq c_\alpha \sigma_\varepsilon\right) = \int_{-c_\alpha}^{c_\alpha} f(u)du \tag{15.9}$$

measures the impact of truncating the residuals. Thus, despite checking T candidate indicators, large-sample normality is retained as shown in (15.7), correctly centered, and the variance of the limiting distribution can be obtained explicitly as in (15.8). Also the estimated error variance converges:

$$\tilde{\sigma}_{\varepsilon}^2 \xrightarrow{P} \frac{\int_{-c_\alpha}^{c_\alpha} \varepsilon^2 f(\varepsilon)d\varepsilon}{\int_{-c_\alpha}^{c_\alpha} f(\varepsilon)d\varepsilon} = V(\varepsilon \mid |\varepsilon| < c_\alpha). \tag{15.10}$$

Moreover, αT indicators will be selected on average under the null when the significance level α corresponds to the correct point of $f(\varepsilon)$. For near normality, setting $\alpha = 1/T$ would lead to just one adventitiously significant indicator being retained on average. This corresponds to losing one observation—which is an efficiency of $(1 - T^{-1})$ despite testing T candidate variables for their relevance. That outcome is confirmed by inspecting (15.8). The last three terms cancel in substantial part, so the increment over σ_ϵ^2—when no indicators are tested—is less than $2c_\alpha f(c_\alpha)$, and for small α, $f(c_\alpha)$ will be small, hence the inflation in σ_μ^2 over unity will be small. Selection of the largest outliers will induce a downward bias in $\widetilde{\sigma}_\epsilon^2$ for σ_ϵ^2 under the null, and although that could be corrected using (15.10), such a correction would not be useful under the alternative of multiple outliers or breaks.

We conclude that the costs of implementing IIS are small under the null, albeit that it is not then needed, at least in this simple setting. The main reason for using such a procedure is when there are outliers, which could induce non-normality and might distort both inference during selection and in the bias-correction formulae in chapter 10. More importantly, having established that it has low cost under the null, the IIS procedure can be used in general, and as we address in chapter 20, can be used to detect multiple outliers and structural breaks when it is needed.

15.4 Dynamic generalizations

Johansen and Nielsen (2009) have extended the above theorems to both stationary and unit-root autoregressions, but using different proof techniques based on empirical processes. They show that if $f(\cdot)$ is symmetric, then for the correctly specified regression model when x_t is always retained:

$$y_t = \beta' x_t + \epsilon_t \text{ where } \epsilon_t \sim \text{IN}\left[0, \sigma_\epsilon^2\right].$$

The large-sample distribution is given by:

$$T^{1/2}(\widetilde{\beta} - \beta) \xrightarrow{D} N_n\left[0, \sigma_\epsilon^2 \Sigma^{-1} \phi\right],$$

where the efficiency under the null of the IIS estimator $\widetilde{\beta}$ with respect to the OLS estimator $\widehat{\beta}$ is:

$$\text{eff}\left(\widehat{\beta}, \widetilde{\beta}\right) = \left(\text{AV}\left[\widetilde{\beta}\right]\right)^{-1} \text{AV}\left[\widehat{\beta}\right] = \phi^{-1},$$

which only depends on $f(\cdot)$, c_α and the selection of the sets $\mathcal{B}_1$ and $\mathcal{B}_2$. The left-hand panel of figure 15.2 taken from their paper shows efficiency as a function of c_α, and the right-hand panel as a function of the tail probability $p = P(|\epsilon_t| > \sigma_\epsilon c_\alpha)$.

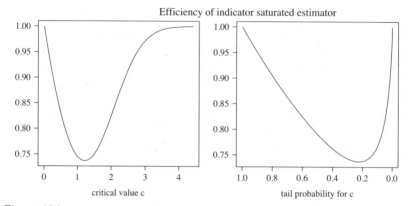

Figure 15.2
Efficiency of the IIS estimator

Table 15.1
Gauge and potency for selection averaged across all $n = 1, \ldots, 10$ experiments
with and without IIS using *Autometrics* with no diagnostic testing

	$\alpha = 1\%$		$\alpha = 0.1\%$	
	no IIS	IIS	no IIS	IIS
average gauge% (variables)	1.06	1.46	0.10	0.10
average gauge% (vars & dummies)	—	1.48	—	0.09
average potency%	99.99	99.98	99.90	99.86

15.5   Impulse-indicator saturation in *Autometrics*

Rather than just implement the split-half method that underlies the
above theory of IIS under the null, *Autometrics* uses its more sophisti-
cated general selection algorithm for $N > T$, described in chapter 19.
Although the indicators are orthogonal, *Autometrics* does not explicitly
exploit this, and usually tries several block divisions. This approach
simplifies the algorithmic structure and allows selection over variables
jointly with IIS.

   Using the same experimental design as section 11.5 to investigate
any loss of efficiency of *Autometrics* with IIS under the null of no outliers and breaks, we record the gauge and potency averaged across all
$n = 1, \ldots, 10$ experiments in table 15.1, where no diagnostic testing is
undertaken. With no IIS, the gauge is close to the nominal significance
level: see figure 12.3. With indicator saturation, at our recommended

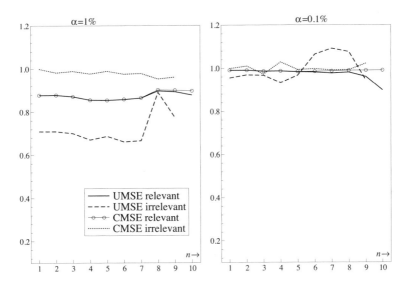

Figure 15.3
Ratios of MSEs without IIS to with.

tight significance levels, selection has the appropriate properties. The gauge is slightly too large at a 1% nominal significance level (when 0.75 dummies are retained on average), but slightly too small at the 0.1% significance level (low probability of retaining any dummies). The average potencies are all close to unity reflecting the high non-centralities of the relevant variables.

Figure 15.3 records ratios of the unconditional and conditional MSEs without IIS to with, so ratios greater than unity show a benefit. Under the null, applying IIS at tight significance levels, the costs are small, although the MSEs of the irrelevant variables in particular are larger than without IIS at 1%. Correlations between dummies and retained irrelevant variables could increase the weight of the retained irrelevant variables leading to an increase in MSE. At very tight significance levels (0.1%), so few dummies are retained that IIS has little impact on the MSE, although in some cases, it could even improve the MSE under the null that none are significant.

15.6   IIS in a fat-tailed distribution

IIS is designed to detect outliers and location shifts, but we first assess its impact for a fat-tailed distribution, focusing on the Student-t distribu-

Table 15.2

Gauge and potency for t_3-distribution. Average across all $n = 1, \ldots, 10$ experiments with and without IIS and diagnostics

	$\alpha = 1\%$			$\alpha = 0.1\%$		
IIS	no	no	yes	no	no	yes
diagnostic tracking	yes	no	no	yes	no	no
average gauge% (variables)	8.05	1.19	1.52	6.39	0.31	0.14
avg gauge% (vars & dummies)	–	–	5.25	–	–	0.17
average potency%	96.26	95.58	98.78	92.42	91.01	90.80

tion with 3 degrees of freedom. The design of the experiment is identical to (11.1) and (11.2), but (11.3) becomes:

$$\epsilon_t \sim \left(0.4 \times n^{0.5}\right) \times t_3, \quad n = 1, \ldots, 10. \tag{15.11}$$

Autometrics checks normality in its batch of diagnostic tests. If it rejects, the p-value of the test is reduced, but the program tries to return to the original p-value at a later stage in selection, and may retain irrelevant variables which help to ensure the diagnostic test is passed.

Table 15.2 records the average gauge (both counting and excluding retention of indicators) and potency across all of the $n = 1, \ldots, 10$ experiments using t_3, with diagnostic testing, without, and with, IIS.

If diagnostic testing is applied, and the DGP is incorrectly assumed to be normal, the gauge is higher than the nominal significance level, and is much higher at tight significance levels (6.4% for $\alpha = 0.1\%$). Omitting diagnostic testing improves the gauge, but it is still too large. While the critical values used in the selection algorithm will be incorrect for a t_3-distribution, this does not have a substantial impact on the gauge as the regressors are normally distributed here. Applying IIS reduces the gauge relative to no IIS and diagnostic testing, but the definition of gauge is ambiguous. Retained dummies are counted as irrelevant variables since they do not enter the DGP, and therefore contribute to gauge, but the fat-tailed distribution implies that some of these are indeed extreme observations, so could be considered as contributing to potency. Thus, there is no objective measure of the success of IIS in the form of potency and gauge. Instead, we also calculate the average retention probability of the retained irrelevant variables not counting dummies. The gauge is substantially reduced in all cases, but is still larger than the nominal significance level, even for a 0.1% significance level.

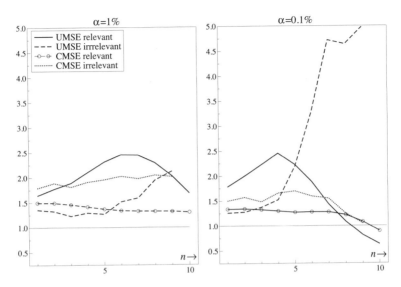

Figure 15.4
Ratios of MSEs without IIS to IIS for a t_3-distribution with no diagnostic testing.

Figure 15.4 records the ratios of MSEs without IIS to with for t_3. The benefit of IIS is observed by smaller MSEs for the coefficient estimates of the retained regressors at significance levels of 1% or 0.1%. Although the gauge is larger than for selection without IIS and no diagnostic testing, the coefficient estimates for the retained variables are much closer to their DGP values as the dummies account for the fat-tails, bringing the distribution conditional on the dummies closer to a normal distribution.

Figure 15.5 shows the CMSE ratios of without IIS to IIS, comparing with and without bias correction. The ratios with bias correction are closer to unity, indicating that the correction has a larger impact without IIS.

To check the impact of IIS, figure 15.6 compares the conditional distributions for $\widetilde{\beta}_1, \ldots, \widetilde{\beta}_{10}$ where $n = 5$, such that $\beta_1, \ldots, \beta_5 = 1$ and also 5 irrelevant variables: $\beta_6, \ldots, \beta_{10} = 0$. The IIS distributions are superimposed on the conditional distributions. The distributions are similar for relevant variables, although those with IIS have slightly thinner tails. The long tails for the non-saturated conditional distributions of the coefficient estimates for the irrelevant variables relative to the saturated outcomes are evident. Thus, if irrelevant variables are retained, indicator saturation in the presence of fat-tails will imply the reported coefficient estimates are smaller than would otherwise be reported and bias

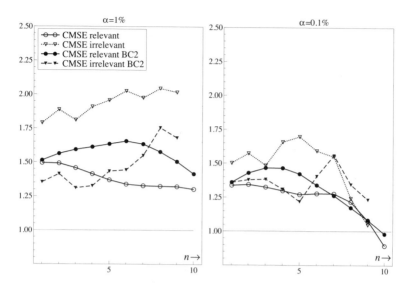

Figure 15.5
Ratios of MSEs without IIS to IIS for a t_3-distribution with no diagnostic testing.
BC2 is the two-step bias correction.

correction will down weight even further, providing insurance against
highly significant but irrelevant variables.

15.7 Potency for a single outlier

From Hendry and Santos (2005), let the DGP for a single outlier at time
τ be:

$$y_i = \lambda 1_{\{i=\tau\}} + \varepsilon_i, \tag{15.12}$$

where $\varepsilon_i \sim \mathsf{IN}\left[0, \sigma_\varepsilon^2\right]$ and $\lambda \neq 0$. Then at observations $i \neq \tau$, $\widehat{\lambda}_i = \varepsilon_i$,
whereas for $i = \tau$:

$$\widehat{\lambda}_\tau = \lambda + \varepsilon_\tau \text{ with } \mathsf{V}[\widehat{\lambda}_\tau] = \sigma_\varepsilon^2.$$

Estimated indicator coefficients are tested for significance at level α using:

$$t_{\lambda=0}\left(\psi_\lambda\right) = \frac{\widehat{\lambda}_i}{\widehat{\sigma}_\varepsilon} = \frac{\lambda 1_{\{i=\tau\}} + \varepsilon_i}{\widehat{\sigma}_\varepsilon},$$

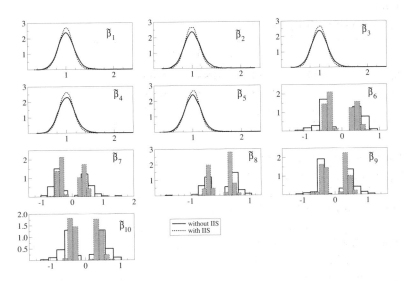

Figure 15.6
Conditional distributions of estimates with IIS (dotted lines and light shading) and without IIS (solid lines and no shading) for the $n = 5$ experiment with a t_3 error distribution at $\alpha = 1\%$, $M = 10\,000$.

so the probability of rejecting the coefficient null at $i = \tau$ in (15.12) depends on the non-centrality:

$$E\left[t_{\lambda=0}\left(\psi_\lambda\right)\right] = E\left[\frac{\lambda + \varepsilon_\tau}{\widehat{\sigma}_\varepsilon}\right] \simeq \frac{\lambda}{\sigma_\varepsilon} = \psi_\lambda. \tag{15.13}$$

To compute the non-null rejection frequency when $H_1 : \lambda \neq 0$, we approximate $t_{\lambda=0}^2$ by a chi-squared with 1 degree of freedom (e.g., Hendry, 1995a):

$$t_{\lambda=0}^2\left(\psi_\lambda^2\right) \sim \chi_1^2\left(\psi_\lambda^2\right), \tag{15.14}$$

where:

$$\chi_1^2\left(\psi_\lambda^2\right) \simeq h\chi_m^2\left(0\right) \tag{15.15}$$

with:

$$h = \frac{1 + 2\psi_\lambda^2}{1 + \psi_\lambda^2} \quad \text{and} \quad m = \frac{1 + \psi_\lambda^2}{h}, \tag{15.16}$$

such that the power function of the $t_{\lambda=0}^2\left(\psi_\lambda^2\right)$ test is approximately:

$$P\left[t_{\lambda=0}^2(\psi_\lambda^2) > c_\alpha \mid H_1\right] \simeq P\left[\chi_1^2(\psi_\lambda^2) > c_\alpha \mid H_1\right] \simeq P\left[\chi_m^2(0) > \frac{c_\alpha}{h}\right]. \tag{15.17}$$

Table 15.3
Approximate outlier potency

c_α	$\psi_\lambda = 1$	$\psi_\lambda = 2$	$\psi_\lambda = 3$	$\psi_\lambda = 4$
$c_{0.05}$	0.17	0.50	0.86	0.99
$c_{0.025}$	0.11	0.39	0.79	0.98
$c_{0.01}$	0.09	0.27	0.66	0.94

For non-integer values of m, a weighted average of the neighboring integer values can be used.

Table 15.3 records the resulting approximate outlier rejection frequencies for $\psi_\lambda = 1, 2, 3, 4$ based on (15.13) and $\alpha = 0.05, 0.025, 0.01$.

Potency is low at $\psi_\lambda = 1$, even at $\alpha = 0.05$, albeit that is close to the exact t-distribution power of 0.16, but rises rapidly as ψ_λ increases to 4. Since (15.17) is the probability of retaining a relevant impulse, then approximately $100P[t^2_{\lambda=0}(\psi^2_\lambda) > c_\alpha | H_1]\%$ of the time, such an indicator will be retained. For example, at $\alpha = 0.01$, appropriate when $T = 100$, then 2/3rds of the time an impulse of $3\sigma_\varepsilon$ will be found to be significant. Larger outliers will be found most of the time.

15.8   Location shift example

Next, we consider a location shift of magnitude λ over the last k observations, given by:

$$y_i = \lambda 1_{\{i \geq T-k+1\}} + \varepsilon_i, \tag{15.18}$$

where, as before, $\varepsilon_i \sim \mathsf{IN}[0, \sigma^2_\varepsilon]$ and $\lambda \neq 0$. Then for observations $i < T - k + 1$:

$$\widehat{\lambda}_i = \varepsilon_i,$$

whereas from (15.18) for $i \geq T - k + 1$:

$$\widehat{\lambda}_i = \lambda + \varepsilon_i.$$

The optimal test in this setting would be a t-test for a location shift at $T - k + 1$ onwards in (15.18) when a single dummy variable $\{1_{\{i > T-k\}}\}$ is added. Let ι_k denote a k-long vector of ones, then:

$$y = d\lambda + \varepsilon,$$

where $d' = \left(0'_{T-k} : \iota'_k\right)$ with $(d'd)^{-1} = 1/k$, and so:

$$\widehat{\lambda} = (d'd)^{-1}d'y = \lambda + \frac{1}{k}\sum_{i=T+k-1}^{T}\varepsilon_i \sim \mathsf{N}\left[\lambda, \frac{1}{k}\sigma_\varepsilon^2\right],$$

hence:

$$\frac{\sqrt{k}\left(\widehat{\lambda} - \lambda\right)}{\sigma_\varepsilon} \sim \mathsf{N}[0, 1],$$

where the non-centrality is:

$$\frac{k\lambda^2}{\sigma_\varepsilon^2} = k\psi_\lambda^2. \tag{15.19}$$

This would be a powerful test, but requires knowledge of the location shift timing, that it is the only shift, and that it is the same shift throughout.

More usually, an investigator would use a variant of a Chow (1960) test, equivalent to adding k impulse indicators (see Salkever, 1976), so corresponding to sub-sample impulse-indicator saturation (over $T-k+1$ to T), but without selection. Now:

$$y = D\lambda + \varepsilon,$$

where $D = (0_{T-k} : I_k)$ with $(D'D)^{-1} = I_k$, and $\lambda = \lambda\iota_k$, so:

$$\widehat{\lambda} = (D'D)^{-1}D'y = \lambda + \varepsilon_2 \sim \mathsf{N}_k\left[\lambda, \sigma_\varepsilon^2 I_k\right]$$

leading to:

$$\frac{\left(\widehat{\lambda} - \lambda\right)'\left(\widehat{\lambda} - \lambda\right)}{\widehat{\sigma}_\varepsilon^2} \sim \chi_k^2(0), \tag{15.20}$$

so the non-centrality is $k\psi_\lambda^2$ as in (15.19). The power can be calculated directly from (15.20) approximating $\chi_k^2\left(k\psi_\lambda^2\right)$ by a central chi-squared where $\chi_k^2\left(k\psi_\lambda^2\right) \simeq h\chi_m^2(0)$, with:

$$h = \frac{1 + 2\psi_\lambda^2}{1 + \psi_\lambda^2} \quad \text{and} \quad m = \frac{k\left(1 + \psi_\lambda^2\right)}{h}. \tag{15.21}$$

When c_α is the critical value for a $\chi_k^2(0)$, the approximate power is:

$$\mathsf{P}\left[\chi_k^2\left(k\psi_\lambda^2\right) > c_\alpha \mid \mathsf{H}_1\right] \simeq \mathsf{P}\left[\chi_m^2(0) > h^{-1}c_\alpha\right]. \tag{15.22}$$

Table 15.4
Approximate $\chi^2_k\left(k\psi^2_\lambda\right)$ location-shift potency

c_α	$\psi_\lambda = 1$	$\psi_\lambda = 2$	$\psi_\lambda = 3$	$\psi_\lambda = 4$
$c_{0.05} = 31.4$	0.78	0.99	1.00	1.00
$c_{0.025} = 34.2$	0.68	0.99	1.00	1.00
$c_{0.01} = 37.5$	0.56	0.99	1.00	1.00

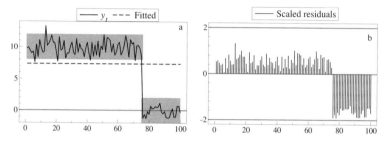

Figure 15.7
No apparent outliers despite a location shift

When $k = 20$, and as before, $T = 100$, table 15.4 records the approximate location-shift potency. Thus, a location shifts of 2 error standard deviations or larger for the last 20 observations would almost always lead to a test reject outcome.

Here, the objective is somewhat different, as IIS is also concerned with the proportion of location shifts detected. When a break is concentrated in one block of the sample, tests like Chow (1960) do well, and the split-sample procedure performs reasonably. Multiple breaks are more problematic for both of those, and such a setting is considered in chapter 20.

However, there is an important difference between outlier detection procedures based on residuals, and IIS that we now illustrate for a location shift, with $\psi_\lambda = 10$, occurring at $0.75T = 75$ in (15.18) as figure 15.7 panel a shows. When only the sample mean is estimated, there are no outliers, as is apparent in panel b: all the residuals satisfy $\widehat{\varepsilon}_t \in [-2, 2]\widehat{\sigma}_\varepsilon$, so step-wise regression would have zero potency in such a case.

That location shift in (15.18) can be used to show how IIS behaves when the null is false, as recorded in figure 15.8. Initially, many indicators are retained, as there is a considerable discrepancy between the first- and second-half means (in this case, the skewness component of the normality test also causes retention of many dummies). When those

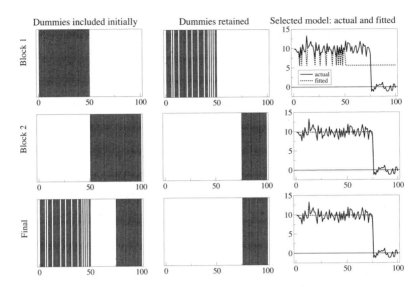

Figure 15.8
Impulse-indicator saturation stages for a location shift

impulse indicators are dropped and the second half entered, all those for the period after the location shift are now retained as the comparison is with the homogeneous first half. Finally, the combined set is entered, and despite the large number of dummies, selection reverts to just those for the break period. The importance of selecting from the combined set is also clear in this example: under the null of no outliers or breaks, it may be thought that any indicator which is significant on a sub-sample would remain so overall, but for many alternatives, sub-sample significance can be transient, being due to an unmodeled feature that occurs elsewhere in the data set.

When location shifts are smaller, so ψ_λ^2 is lower, some outliers may be missed, raising the estimated error standard deviation, and inhibiting detection of others, so potency tends to rise very rapidly as ψ_λ^2 increases. Retention of irrelevant indicators can also occur, and operates in the opposite direction. Overall, however, outliers are not equivalent to structural breaks, and IIS works well despite the initial model apparently having no outliers when just a mean is estimated.

Table 15.5
Experimental design

DGP:

$D_1: y_{1,t} = \lambda (I_{T-19} + \cdots + I_T) + u_t, \qquad u_t \sim N[0,1]$
$D_2: y_{2,t} = \lambda (I_1 + \ldots + I_{20}) + u_t, \qquad u_t \sim N[0,1]$
$D_3: y_{3,t} = \lambda (I_1 + I_6 + I_{11} + \cdots) + u_t, \qquad u_t \sim N[0,1]$

GUM:

retained constant and T indicators, $T = 100$

Table 15.6
Gauge and potency for IIS experiments at $\alpha = 1\%$ using split-sample algorithm

	D_1: break at end		D_3: evenly spread	
	$\lambda = 3$	$\lambda = 4$	$\lambda = 3$	$\lambda = 4$
Gauge %	0.3	0.4	0.5	2.8
Potency %	49.6	86.0	5.4	10.1
DGP found %	0.1	14.0	0.0	0.0
time (min.)	144	174	7	22

15.9   Impulse-indicator saturation simulations

The experiments take the form of three variants of location shifts of
length 20, at the start, end, and scattered through the sample. The DGPs
are shown in table 15.5, where $I_j = 1_{\{j=t\}}$ and λ determines the magnitude of the location shift.

15.9.1   Sample-split simulations

Selection is first undertaken using the sample-split approach in the theory presented above. Selection is at $\alpha = 1\%$, with $M = 1000$ replications.
The outcomes were closely similar for D_1 and D_2, so we only report the
former together with D_3 in table 15.6. As can be seen, the gauge is higher
and the potency lower for D_3 than D_1, suggesting that a more general
procedure may be useful than just split-half indicators. That is an excellent choice for concentrated breaks, but not when multiple location
shifts are scattered through a sample, so we now consider the more general algorithm.

Table 15.7
Gauge and potency for IIS experiments at $\alpha = 1\%$ using *Autometrics*

	D_1: break at end		D_3: evenly spread	
	$\lambda = 3$	$\lambda = 4$	$\lambda = 3$	$\lambda = 4$
Gauge %	0.4	0.7	0.3	1.1
Potency %	54.8	86.3	24.1	65.9

15.9.2 Block-search algorithm in *Autometrics*

The split-sample algorithm for IIS is implicitly optimized for breaks at the start or end of the data sample. A more generally applicable algorithm is needed, but the cross-block algorithm for $N > T$ proposed in Hendry and Krolzig (2005) does not learn as it proceeds, and struggles when N is considerably larger than T. The *Autometrics* algorithm has both expansion and reduction phases as it tries to learn about the model, roughly 2/3 general-to-specific, and 1/3 specific-to-general. In practice, this improves on previous algorithms, but makes many heuristic decisions, so there may be better algorithms, and does not search the whole model space, so may miss complex interactions. Nevertheless, as the simulation results below show, the new algorithm performs quite well in practice.

The potency is considerably higher for D_3 than before, with an improvement in gauge, yet equal performance on D_1 as table 15.7 shows. Even with 20 one-off location shifts in 100 observations, which is an extreme of multiple breaks, 2/3rds are removed at $\psi_\lambda = 4$, noting that the individual impulse detection probability from table 15.3 at 1% is 0.94 when $\psi_\lambda = 4$. This is the approach that we will apply in chapter 20 for multiple breaks, and in chapter 21 for removing outliers in non-linear models. Castle *et al.* (2013) consider a generalization of IIS to step-indicator saturation (SIS) which should have higher power to detect location shifts, as illustrated in chapter 4.

16   Re-modeling UK Real Consumers' Expenditure

Many features of viable empirical models cannot be derived from economic theory, institutional knowledge, or past findings alone, and need to be based on current empirical evidence. Important aspects that have to be data-based include the complete set of explanatory variables, all their functional forms and the lag reactions to these, as well as any structural breaks. Specification of the general model is mainly up to the investigator, but can be supplemented by mis-specification information, as well as by commencing from a more general embedding model and selecting automatically. We consider the specific application of modeling aggregate real consumers' expenditure in the UK, using *Autometrics* applied to the data in Davidson et al. (1978), and discuss the considerations involved.[1]

16.1   Introduction

Many correct decisions are needed for successful modeling of any variable or group of variables. The key choices concern specifying the:

(a) dependence on all the determining variables;

(b) how their effects vary with changes in outside factors;

(c) whether the dependence is linear or non-linear;

(d) how the short-run, long-run, and seasonal responses may differ;

(e) ways in which the relationship being modeled may evolve over time;

(f) the exogeneity status of all contemporaneous variables;

(g) whether the level of aggregation matters: national or regional; by income levels; by categories of transactions;

---

[1]This chapter draws heavily on Hendry (2010).

(h) non-stationarities involved, as mis-specifying these may entail dele-
    terious effects, including non-constant relationships;

(i) how well the data are measured; their timeliness; and the possibility
     of major intermittent revisions.

In the case of real consumers' expenditure in the UK, these general
considerations become:

(a) income; prices; interest rates; inflation; taxes; wealth; demography;

(b) such outside factors may include new legislation; wars and policy
    regime changes; technical and financial innovations;

(c) linear or log-linear are perhaps the main choices here;

(d) the long-run concerns cointegration; the short-run requires deter-
    mining the lag lengths and the forms of dynamic reactions, as well
    as seasonal responses;

(e) evolution of the relationship over time is likely as overall wealth has
    changed greatly;

(f) the weak exogeneity status of the contemporaneous variables needs
    to be checked if they are to be valid conditioning or instrumental
    variables;

(g) here we consider only the UK national aggregates;

(h) the crucial non-stationarities are stochastic trends and location shifts,
    and both require careful handling;

(i) the data on nominal consumers' expenditure should be quite well
    measured, but that level of accuracy may not hold for all other deter-
    mining variables, especially prices, and indeed, major revisions have
    occurred.

Against that background, we now consider modeling aggregate real
consumers' expenditure over the sample used by Davidson et al. (1978),
known by the acronym DHSY (pronounced "daisy") to investigate what
changes, if any, result from using an automatic selection algorithm relative to their careful manual analysis. Section 16.2 reports the replication
of DHSY's findings; section 16.3 discusses the selection based on *Autometrics*; and section 16.4 notes some additional tests of the new model,
namely whether it encompasses DHSY, whether there is any remaining
evidence of non-linearity, and whether conditioning was valid.

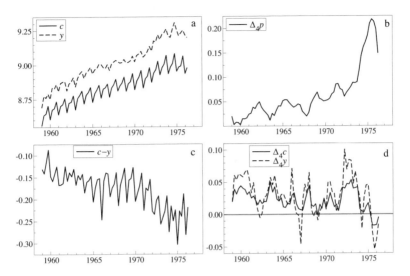

Figure 16.1
UK real aggregate consumers' expenditure, income and price data

16.2   Replicating DHSY

The data are quarterly observations, not seasonally adjusted, for the UK over the period 1959(1) to 1976(2). The variables are defined as follows (lower case denotes logs):

c constant-price aggregate consumers' expenditure;

p price index of nominal aggregate consumers' expenditure;

y constant-price total disposable income;

past values of these three variables.

Figure 16.1 shows the main time series and three auxiliary graphs, revealing considerable changes over the period. Panel (a) records the levels of c and y, with the former being markedly more seasonal than the latter, due to holidays and festivals (and far from smoothing quarterly). Panel (b) shows the major changes in annual inflation ($\Delta_4 p_t$) over the DHSY sample, reaching a peak of more than 20% in 1975: one of their concerns was to explain the falling ratio of consumers' expenditure to disposable income at a time of high inflation. Panel (c) records that drop, from an implicit gross savings rate of 10% in 1959 to one of more than 25% at the end. Panel (d) shows the annual changes in consumers' expenditure and disposable income ($\Delta_4 c_t$, and $\Delta_4 y_t$), where annual smoothing is more apparent: their respective sample standard deviations are 0.016 and 0.031, so the latter is nearly twice the former.

First, we replicate by *PcGive* the final model DHSY reported as (45)[**]:

$$\Delta_4 c_t = \underset{(0.029)}{0.48}\, \Delta_4 y_t - \underset{(0.039)}{0.23}\, \Delta_1 \Delta_4 y_t - \underset{(0.022)}{0.12}\, \Delta_4 p_t - \underset{(0.010)}{0.30}\, \Delta_1 \Delta_4 p_t$$

$$+ \underset{(0.0022)}{0.0065 \Delta_4 D_t} - \underset{(0.012)}{0.094}\, (c - y)_{t-4} \tag{16.1}$$

$$\widehat{\sigma} = 0.0061 \quad (R^*)^2 = 0.86 \quad F_M(6, 61) = 62.0^{**} \quad F_{ar}(5, 57) = 0.26$$

$$F_{arch}(4, 60) = 2.05 \quad F_{reset}(2, 60) = 0.39 \quad F_{het}(12, 55) = 0.72$$

$$\chi^2_{nd}(2) = 0.18 \quad F_{Chow}(2, 62) = 0.90 \quad T = 68 : 1959(1) - 1975(4).$$

In (16.1), $(R^*)^2$ is the squared multiple correlation when a constant is added, $F_M(6, 61)$ is the associated test of the null, and $\widehat{\sigma}$ is the residual standard deviation, with coefficient standard errors shown in parentheses. The diagnostic tests are defined in section 12.1. It is more than 35 years since that equation was first reported, but the only reason why (16.1) has slightly different estimates from DHSY (45)[**] is that here we started in 1959(1) rather than 1959(2).

The DHSY model was an early example of an "error-correction mechanism", following the pioneering developments in Phillips (1954) and Sargan (1964). The long-run steady-state solution of (16.1) when the annual growth rates of c and y are equal to g_y is:

$$e = 5.8 g_y + c - y + 1.3 \Delta_4 p, \tag{16.2}$$

which explains the falling ratio $c - y$ by the inflation rate, later attributed to inflation eroding liquid assets in Hendry and von Ungern-Sternberg (1981). The dummy variable D_t takes the value unity in 1968(1) for a budget warning of impending purchase tax (sales tax) rises, with -1 in 1968(2) when those occurred and lowered expenditure, then unity in 1973(1) and -1 in 1973(2) following the introduction of Value Added Tax (VAT) on 1 April 1973 at a rate of 10%. The Chow test is for constancy over 1976(1)–1976(2). We comment on the mis-specification tests in section 16.4.

16.3   Selection based on *Autometrics*

Given the sample size of 1959(1)–1975(4) after lags are created, so $T = 68$ (which determines the number of impulse indicators included in the set of candidate regressors) and the number of other potential regressors (2 contemporaneous variables, 5 lags times 2 variables, plus 2 lags for annual inflation, $\Delta_4 D_t$, intercept and centered seasonal dummies, denoted S_i), $\alpha = 0.025$ was used, and all deterministic variables always retained. For the initial formulation in levels, selection with IIS yielded:

$$c_t = \underset{(0.04)}{0.25} y_t + \underset{(0.04)}{0.21} y_{t-1} - \underset{(0.05)}{0.23} y_{t-5} - \underset{(0.09)}{0.41} \Delta_4 p_t$$

$$+ \underset{(0.10)}{0.24} \Delta_4 p_{t-1} + \underset{(0.06)}{0.74} c_{t-4} + \underset{(0.12)}{0.22} + \underset{(0.002)}{0.008} \Delta_4 D_t$$

$$- \underset{(0.007)}{0.016} S_1 - \underset{(0.003)}{0.010} S_2 - \underset{(0.003)}{0.006} S_3 \tag{16.3}$$

$$\hat{\sigma} = 0.0059 \quad R^2 = 0.998 \quad F_M(10, 57) = 2874^{**} \quad F_{ar}(5, 52) = 0.69$$

$$F_{arch}(4, 60) = 2.12 \quad F_{het}(17, 50) = 1.32 \quad F_{reset}(2, 55) = 6.48^{**}$$

$$\chi^2_{nd}(2) = 0.33 \quad F_{Chow}(4, 57) = 0.20 \quad t_{ur} = -4.62^* \quad T : 1959(1) - 1975(4).$$

All diagnostic tests are insignificant other than RESET, and the *PcGive* unit-root test rejects the null of no cointegration ($t_{ur} = -4.62^*$: see Banerjee and Hendry, 1992, and Ericsson and MacKinnon, 2002) with the long-run solution:

$$e = c - 0.90y + 0.66\Delta_4 p - 0.85. \tag{16.4}$$

No additional outliers were detected in (16.3) when $\Delta_4 D_t$ was included. However, when $\Delta_4 D_t$ was not included in the candidate set, none of its components was found by IIS (even though they are highly significant when combined), and again, no further outliers were detected. There are 8 indicators in the unrestricted form of $\Delta_4 D_t$, and individually none of these is significant even if added to (16.1) when $\Delta_4 D_t$ is excluded, nor are they jointly significant ($F(8, 55) = 1.32$, $p = 0.25$). Thus, there is a lack of power to detect the impact of tax changes treated in isolation. As D_t was based on institutional and historical information, a substantive role remains for the economist in modeling, even with all the powerful tools now available.

Also, the centered seasonals are significant, consistent with later research on longer samples of c and with the need for some mechanism to maintain the strong seasonal pattern (e.g., Osborn, 1988, 1991, and Birchenhall, Bladen-Hovell, Chui, Osborn and Smith, 1989). The constancy test on the last two observations does not reject, although previous repeated forecast failure had led DHSY to seek a more constant model.

Transforming to fourth differences (i.e., annual changes), after modifying the equilibrium-correction term from (16.4) to the theoretically preferred form $c - y$ that DHSY used, *Autometrics* selected over 1959(1)–1975(4) (at 2.5%, again including IIS, retaining all the other variables):

$$\Delta_4 c_t = \underset{(0.028)}{0.47} \Delta_4 y_t - \underset{(0.034)}{0.21} \Delta_1 \Delta_4 y_t - \underset{(0.026)}{0.16} \Delta_4 p_t - \underset{(0.09)}{0.21} \Delta_1 \Delta_4 p_t$$

$$- \underset{(0.034)}{0.13} \left(c - y \right)_{t-4} - \underset{(0.003)}{0.009} S_1 - \underset{(0.002)}{0.006} S_2 - \underset{(0.002)}{0.003} S_3$$

$$+ \underset{(0.006)}{0.015} I_{62(2)} + \underset{(0.006)}{0.014} I_{72(1)} - \underset{(0.005)}{0.004} + \underset{(0.002)}{0.007} \Delta_4 D_t \tag{16.5}$$

$$\hat{\sigma} = 0.0053 \ \ R^2 = 0.90 \ \ F_M(11, 56) = 46.7^{**} \ \ F_{ar}(5, 51) = 1.11$$

$$F_{arch}(4, 60) = 0.47 \ \ F_{reset}(2, 54) = 0.94$$

$$\chi^2_{nd}(2) = 1.20 \ \ F_{het}(15, 50) = 0.64 \ \ F_{Chow}(2, 56) = 0.36.$$

This time, two indicators are selected, and now the implied long-run solution is:

$$e = (c - y) + 1.2\Delta_4 p - 4g_y + 0.03 + \text{seasonals.} \tag{16.6}$$

No mis-specification test rejects. Figure 16.2 records the fitted and actual values for $\Delta_4 c_t$, the residuals from the estimated model (16.5), and the residual density and correlogram.

The derived long-run income elasticity is close to unity in (16.4), matching most economic theories of consumption, and the unit-root test rejected the absence of cointegration. However, that long-run implication is modified by the presence of $\Delta_4 p$, which is probably best interpreted as a correction to the income measure (as in Hendry and von Ungern-Sternberg, 1981), which the UK Central Statistical Office overestimated by including nominal interest earnings, whereas consumers realized that the real value of their liquid assets was being eroded by the high inflation, so implicitly calculated income using real interest rates. Thus, despite inflation entering with apparently the opposite sign to the predictions of the simple theory that expenditure is brought forward as inflation rises, the sign has a reasonable interpretation: imposing the opposite sign would be strongly rejected here.

The low impact income elasticity of less than a half is consistent with some smoothing, and as the long-run is unity, entails considerable short-run saving. This is corrected by the equilibrium correction term $(c - y)_{t-4}$ (or that adjusted for inflation), so implies that savings rise with

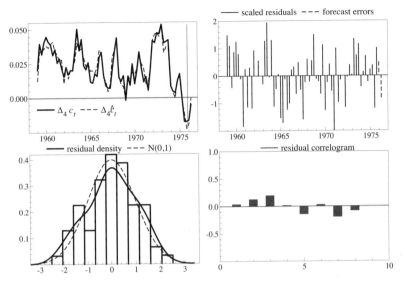

Figure 16.2
Fitted and actual values, residuals and graphical statistics for $\Delta_4 c_t$

income growth, but eventually expenditure converges back to proportionality with income, matching cross-country evidence (e.g., Ando and Modigliani, 1963).

16.4 Tests of DHSY

In this section, we consider four sets of tests additional to those undertaken by DHSY. The first of these was already carried out above, namely the mis-specification tests for (16.1), none of which rejected. Although most of those tests were developed after their study, less stringent design criteria, such as no residual autocorrelation, were nevertheless used.

The second is whether there is any evidence of non-linearity in their selected model based on the low-dimension, portmanteau test for non-linearity in Castle and Hendry (2010a). That test, denoted F_{NL}, uses squares, cubics and exponential functions of the principal components of the linear variables to circumvent problems of high-dimensionality and collinearity, as well as not being restricted to quadratic departures from linearity. For k linear variables, the test has $3k$ non-linear terms. Castle and Hendry (2011b) discuss the interaction between outliers and non-linearity, although here we have taken account of the former, so the test should not merely reflect outliers. Applied to (16.1), $F_{NL}(15, 47) = 0.89$, so does not reject.

Thirdly, (16.5) nests (16.1) so the interesting question is whether (16.1) parsimoniously encompasses (16.5). That can be tested by the significance of excluding the additional variables in (16.5), which strongly rejects ($F_{enc}(6, 56) = 4.72^{**}$).

Finally, are y_t and $\Delta_4 p_t$ valid conditioning variables? Section 22.9 tests the hypothesis that y_t and $\Delta_4 p_t$ are super exogenous for the parameters of (16.5), following a description of the IIS-based super-exogeneity test.

17 Comparisons of *Autometrics* with Other Approaches

There are many possible methods of model selection, most of which can be implemented in an automatic algorithm. General contenders include single path approaches such as forward and backward selection, mixed variants like step-wise, multi-path search methods including Hoover and Perez (1999) and *PcGets*, information criteria (AIC, BIC etc.), Lasso, and RETINA, as well as a number of selection algorithms specifically designed for a forecasting context (such as PIC: see e.g., Phillips, 1995, 1996, and Phillips and Ploberger, 1996). Here we only consider the former group of methods in relation to *Autometrics*, partly to evaluate improvements over time in the conventional selection aspects of its performance. Three key findings are that *Autometrics* does indeed deliver substantive improvements in many settings; that performance is not necessarily adversely affected by having more variables than observations; and that although other approaches sometimes outperform, they are not reliable and can also deliver very poor results, whereas *Autometrics* tends to perform similarly to commencing from the LDGP using the same significance level.

17.1 Introduction

Many approaches to automatic model selection have been proposed in the literature, and here we compare *Autometrics* with a number of these. First, section 17.2 documents the main simulation experiments on which the various methods will be compared. Then section 17.3 investigates improvements in the *Gets* approaches, commencing with Hoover and Perez (1999) and Hendry and Krolzig (2001), re-analyzing simulations for four of the first authors' experiments. Next, section 17.4 compares the most-commonly used algorithm of step-wise regression in variants of the same experiments. Section 17.5 considers information criteria like AIC and BIC, as well as relating those approaches to consistent model selection, and section 17.6 contrasts Lasso, implemented as an automatic model selection algorithm. The experiments mainly compare the variable-selection aspects of the various approaches, rather than their ability to facilitate empirical model discovery, as most methods cannot handle all the aspects involved, and even when they do allow $N > T$, do so by single-variable expanding searches, which are ineffective for negative correlations, and especially for multiple structural breaks.

The performance of *PcGets* in a wide range of states of nature has been documented by Hendry and Krolzig (2001, 2003), and readers are referred to their publications for details, so we will only present a few comparisons with *PcGets* below.

17.2   Monte Carlo designs

As noted in chapter 9, there are few general analytical results in model selection theory. Consequently, simulations of computer-selection algorithms play a major role in evaluating the operational performance of alternative strategies. The main drawbacks of Monte Carlo experiments in general are the limitations of the findings to the specific cases investigated, as the canonical case is rarely clear, and the imprecision of only conducting a limited number of replications. When simulating automatic methods, less obvious additional drawbacks are:

1. the approach cannot look at the data first, so misses data anomalies, albeit those are partly fixed by outlier removal, but conversely avoids accusations of data snooping;

2. additional rules are needed for how to proceed when the GUM is rejected *ab initio*, namely discard the given experiment and redraw a new sample, or drop the rejecting test and continue;

3. if diagnostic tests reject *en route*, the algorithm must be pre-programmed to one of:

    (a) tighten the significance level;

    (b) stop the search along that path; or

    (c) drop the rejecting test;

4. need for a tiebreaker: if multiple terminal models are found, a final model must be selected, as only one model can be used in the automatic comparison of different approaches.

Table 17.1
Selected Hoover–Perez DGPs

HP2	$y_t = 0.75y_{t-1} + 85.99\varepsilon_t$
HP7	$y_t = 0.75y_{t-1} + 1.33x_{11,t} - 0.9975x_{11,t-1} + 6.44\varepsilon_t$
HP8	$y_t = 0.75y_{t-1} - 0.046x_{3,t} + 0.0345x_{3,t-1} + 0.073\varepsilon_t$
HP8(λ)	$y_t = 0.75y_{t-1} - 0.046x_{3,t} + 0.0345x_{3,t-1} + 0.073\lambda\varepsilon_t$
HP9	$y_t = 0.75y_{t-1} - 0.023x_{3,t} + 0.01725x_{3,t-1}$
	$\quad +0.67x_{11,t} - 0.5025x_{11,t-1} + 3.25\varepsilon_t$

The apparent operational performance is clearly altered by which decision is made in each of these cases. For example, Hoover and Perez (1999) discarded simulations where the GUM was rejected, whereas Krolzig and Hendry (2001) did not. In simulating *Autometrics*, even if the GUM fails one or more mis-specification tests, the search path still commences but using a tighter significance level, so all draws are retained. Paths are followed without testing for mis-specifications, backtracking to an earlier unrejected selection if the terminal fails. Insignificant variables can be retained if their deletion induces a significant diagnostic, and for irrelevant variables, their retention adds to the calculated gauge (and to potency for relevant): again this differs from (e.g.) Hoover and Perez (1999).

Two groups of experiments undertaken by various researchers, and rerun below, are briefly described in sub-sections 17.2.1 and 17.2.2.

17.2.1   HP: US macroeconomic data experiments

Hoover and Perez (1999) reran a variant of the experiments in Lovell (1983), using eighteen actual US macroeconomic time series for the fixed regressors. These are mapped to stationarity by taking first or second differences (without taking logarithms) and displayed in figure 17.1. The data are quarterly, and the sample used in the experiments is 1960(3) to 1995(1), so $T = 139$. Table 17.1 reports the data generating processes that are used in this book. The numbering of the variables is that used by Hoover and Perez (1999), with $x_{3,t}$ referring to government purchases of goods and services, and $x_{11,t}$ to M1.[1] In all cases $\varepsilon_t \sim \text{IN}[0, 1]$.

Table 17.2 lists some properties of the Hoover–Perez DGPs when estimating the simulated DGP with an additional constant in the model,

---

[1]In their table 3, the coefficient on x_3 of model 8 should be 0.0345 (computed as 0.75×0.046), using $0.073 \approx (\sqrt{7})/4$ instead of $\sqrt{(7/4)}$.

Table 17.2
Small sample properties of some HP experiments, $T = 139$ and $M = 100\,000$

	T	n	R^2	t-values
HP2	139	1	0.53	12.7
HP7	139	3	0.81	12.4, 15.2, −8.2
HP8	139	3	0.97	12.7, −58.8, 12.1
HP9	139	5	0.81	12.4, −0.7, 0.5, 15.2, −8.2

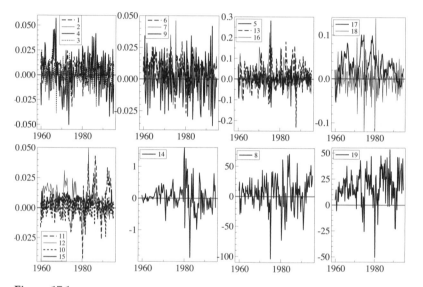

Figure 17.1
Graphs of Hoover–Perez time series in cognate blocks

$T = 139$ and $M = 100\,000$. Properties for HP8(λ) for several values of λ were given in table 13.1.

As can be seen from figure 17.1, many of the regressors are highly heteroskedastic, and the impact of that on the ARCH test was described in Hendry and Krolzig (2003). The standard GUM has $N = 40$ free variables:

$$y_t = \gamma_0^F + \sum_{j=1}^{4} \alpha_j y_{t-j} + \sum_{i=1}^{18} \sum_{j=0}^{1} \gamma_{i,j} x_{i,t-j} + u_t \text{ where } u_t \sim \text{IN}\left[0, \sigma_u^2\right]. \quad (17.1)$$

The superscript F in γ_0^F indicates that the intercept is not selected over (always retained, or forced) in the model: all selections have an intercept and it is not a candidate for removal, so forms no part of gauge or potency.[2] Between one and five variables are relevant in (17.1) (denoted n), so there are up to 39 irrelevant regressors (m), making $N = n + m$ candidate variables in total.

17.2.2 JEDC: artificial data experiments

In the JEDC experiments (Krolzig and Hendry, 2001), artificial data is generated according to:

$$\begin{aligned} y_t &= \textstyle\sum_{i=1}^{5} \beta_i x_{i,t} + \epsilon_t, \text{ where } \epsilon_t \sim \text{IN}[0,1], \\ x_t &\sim \text{IN}_{10}[0, C_x], \end{aligned} \tag{17.2}$$

where $x'_t = (x_{1,t}, ..., x_{10,t})$ and the elements $c_{i,j}$ of the correlation matrix C_x are specified as $c_{i,i} = 1$ and:

$$c_{i,j} = \rho^{|i-j|}.$$

Finally, we specify the coefficients as:

$$\beta_1 = 8/\sqrt{T}, \beta_2 = 6/\sqrt{T}, \beta_3 = 4/\sqrt{T}, \beta_4 = 3/\sqrt{T}, \beta_5 = 2/\sqrt{T}.$$

Krolzig and Hendry (2001) used this DGP with $\rho = 0$, i.e. independent standard normal regressors, and t-values of $8, 6, 4, 3, 2$ respectively.

The GUM has a forced intercept and $N = 21$ free variables:

$$y_t = \gamma_0^F + \gamma_1 y_{t-1} + \sum_{i=1}^{10} \sum_{j=0}^{1} \gamma_{i,j} x_{i,t-j} + u_t \text{ where } u_t \sim \text{IN}[0, \sigma_u^2]. \tag{17.3}$$

So there are $n = 5$ relevant and $m = 16$ irrelevant regressors.

The JEDC experiments with $\rho = 0$ were used to calibrate *PcGets* and help check the operational characteristics of the mis-specification tests, similar to figure 12.2, as well as guiding choices for *Autometrics*.

Hendry and Krolzig (2005, section 5.1) use another method to introduce correlated regressors to the DGP, which we shall label the JEDC-EJ experiment:

$$\begin{aligned} y_t &= \textstyle\sum_{i=1}^{5} \beta_i x_{i,t} + \epsilon_t, \text{ where } \epsilon_t \sim \text{IN}[0,1], \\ x_t &= \rho x_{t-1} + v_t, \text{ where } v_t \sim \text{IN}_{10}[0, (1-\rho^2)I_{10}]. \end{aligned} \tag{17.4}$$

The GUM remains that given by (17.3).

---

[2]This means it is labeled as 'U' in *PcGive*.

Table 17.3

Comparisons of Hoover–Perez, *PcGets* and *Autometrics*, all without pre-search

	Hoover–Perez				*PcGets*				*Autometrics*			
	HP2	HP7	HP8	HP9	HP2	HP7	HP8	HP9	HP2	HP7	HP8	HP9
1% nominal significance level												
Gauge%	5.7	3.0	0.9	3.2	2.4	2.4	–	2.5	1.5	1.5	1.5	1.5
Potency%	100	94.0	99.9	57.3	100	99.9	–	61.9	100	99.7	100	60.6
DGP found	0.8	24.6	78.0	0.8	60.2	59.0	–	0.0	68.6	69.6	69.0	0.0
5% nominal significance level												
Gauge%	10.7	8.2	3.7	8.5	10.7	10.2	–	10.4	5.6	5.7	5.8	5.8
Potency%	100	96.7	100	60.4	100	99.9	–	66.2	100	99.9	100	62.8
DGP found	0.0	4.0	31.6	1.2	8.4	4.0	–	0.0	16.3	18.4	17.9	0.3
10% nominal significance level												
Gauge%	16.2	14.2	10.6	14.1	–	–	–	–	9.2	9.6	9.3	9.5
Potency%	100	96.9	100	62.5	–	–	–	–	100	99.9	100	64.1
DGP found	0.0	0.2	7.6	0.4	–	–	–	–	3.3	2.7	3.1	0.2

17.3   Re-analyzing the Hoover–Perez experiments

To compare the three multi-path approaches on a par, we run *PcGets* and *Autometrics* without pre-searches (the Hoover–Perez algorithm does not include a pre-search). The results are recorded in table 17.3, with the *PcGets* and Hoover–Perez results taken from Doornik (2009a, table 6). The gauge reported for the Hoover–Perez algorithm only counts significant variables, and the tie-breaker in their experiments was the best-fitting model. Gauge for *PcGets* and *Autometrics* is calculated for all retained irrelevant variables, and BIC was used as the tie-breaker between mutually encompassing terminal models. We initially consider the three conventional levels of significance $\alpha = 0.01$, 0.05, and 0.10, for the four experiments denoted HP2, HP7, HP8, and HP9. Gauge and potency are reported as a percentage for convenience, and "DGP found" denotes the percentage of experiments in which the DGP was found exactly.

Gauge is well controlled in *Autometrics*, being relatively constant, and close to the chosen nominal significance level α, and usually nearer α than the other two algorithms. At 5%, for example, with approximately 40 irrelevant variables, about 2 will be retained adventitiously on average, and for a gauge of 5.8%, 2.3 will. So in both cases, about 38 out of 40 irrelevant variables will be correctly eliminated on average.

Table 17.4
Comparisons of *PcGets* and *Autometrics* with pre-search

	PcGets default		*Autometrics* default				*Autometrics* tight		
	HP2	HP7	HP2	HP7	HP8	HP9	HP2	HP7	HP8
1% nominal significance level									
Gauge%	0.9	1.0	1.2	1.6	1.6	1.6	0.9	1.0	0.9
Potency%	100	99.8	100	99.0	100	60.2	100	99.1	100
DGP found%	81.0	80.8	73.5	68.0	68.5	0.0	79.0	80.0	79.5
5% nominal significance level									
Gauge%	5.5	5.4	5.1	5.9	5.9	6.1	3.8	4.1	4.0
Potency%	100	99.8	100	99.7	100	62.6	100	99.6	100
DGP found%	34.5	34.7	28.2	17.0	17.9	0.3	39.4	38.9	38.7

Despite usually having the smallest gauge, potency in *Autometrics* also generally exceeds Hoover–Perez and is close to *PcGets*: potency is not gauge corrected. Potency is generally high because most of the relevant variables have large non-centralities, except in HP9, where the two additional regressors have small non-centralities. Finally, because there are many irrelevant variables, the DGP is found more often at tighter significance levels, though sometimes not at all when a relevant variable is insignificant on conventional criteria, as in HP9.

17.3.1   HP experiments with pre-search

Table 17.4 reports the results of using pre-search for comparison both with *PcGets* and with the findings in table 17.3. "Tight" denotes a more stringent search (labeled "quick" in Doornik, 2009a), closer to that implicit in the additional pre-search of *PcGets*.

Allowing pre-search, generally for *PcGets* and for lags in *Autometrics*, improves the closeness of *PcGets*'s gauges to the nominal significance levels at both 1% and 5%. Doing so also increases the probability of finding the DGP, since the relevant variables are almost always retained (with potencies close to 100%). Thus, at a 1% nominal significance level in HP2, HP7 and HP8, *Autometrics* would correctly eliminate more than 39 of 40 irrelevant variables on average, and locate the DGP more than 65% of the time.

Summarizing these experiments, *Autometrics* generally performs at least as well as its predecessors. Since it can handle $N > T$, we now consider comparisons with other algorithms that can also do so.

17.4   Comparing with step-wise regression

A forward-selection procedure simply:

1. orders the regressors from the most to the least correlated with y;
2. adds the most highly correlated regressor;
3. reorders the remainder;
4. continues until all significant variables are found.

Such an approach can operate for any number of candidate variables, perhaps modified by stopping well before $n \approx T$.

Several problems confront its successful application in general. First, the initial ordering by simple correlations can prevent relevant regressors from entering. An important example in economics is when x_1 and x_2 are negatively correlated but both feature positively in the model, or are positively correlated but enter the model with opposite signs (as in a difference or a differential). However, individually they will not rank highly on the initial correlation ordering. Secondly, the ordering may be biased at an early stage by the omission of relevant factors: this plagues all simple-to-general approaches, when x_1 only becomes significant once the addition of x_2 improves the fit sufficiently. Thirdly, the smallest initial models are unlikely to be congruent, so the apparent inferences may be unjustified. For example, residual heteroskedasticity may upward bias the computed coefficient standard error, incorrectly making the estimated coefficient appear insignificant. Finally, partial correlations matter in a multivariate setting, and these may be very different from the simple correlations on which decisions are being based in forward search.

Step-wise regression augments the forward search by possibly eliminating variables already entered if they have since become insignificant. One can of course alternatively run the step-wise procedure backwards, so all variables are entered initially, and the least significant are then eliminated in turn. This single-path variant of *Gets* is feasible when $N \ll T$, will maintain pairs of variables when necessary, and its starting point should be statistically better behaved, but congruence still needs tested. However, only one path is searched, which can induce path dependence, as when collinearity leads to a variable that is relevant in the LDGP being eliminated early by chance, so cannot be recovered later. Moreover, adding insignificant regressors will change the path, and that may change the finally selected model.

Table 17.5
Comparisons of step-wise regression and *Autometrics*

	Step-wise		Autometrics	
	HP7	HP8	HP7	HP8
1% nominal significance				
Gauge%	0.9	3.1	1.6	1.6
Potency%	100	53.3	99.0	100
DGP found%	71.6	22.0	68.0	68.5
DGP nested%	100	30.0	97.1	100
5% nominal significance				
Gauge%	3.8	6.1	5.9	5.9
Potency%	100	69.3	99.7	100
DGP found%	26.8	13.5	17.0	17.9
DGP nested%	99.9	53.9	99.2	100
0.1% nominal significance				
Gauge%	0.1	1.9	0.9	0.3
Potency%	99.9	40.5	97.1	100
DGP found%	95.1	10.5	85.0	92.9
DGP nested%	99.8	10.8	91.4	100

17.4.1 Step-wise regression comparisons

As before, we illustrate the differences between the approaches using some of the Hoover–Perez experiments with $\alpha = 0.01,\ 0.05$, when $T = 139$, with 3 relevant and 37 irrelevant variables. Table 17.5 records those results. In addition to the percentage of cases in which the DGP is found exactly, we also report the percentage of times in which the DGP is contained in the final model, so all the relevant variables are retained. The bottom panel of table 17.5 shows the impact of setting $\alpha = 0.001$, so a much tighter significance level is demanded.

The gauge in step-wise regression is erratic, and the potency more so, yet these are not offsetting, in that a higher gauge need not improve potency. In HP8, even at 5%, step-wise regression only retains the highly significant relevant variables 70% of the time, probably because the regressors have opposite signs and are positively correlated. Nevertheless, for these settings, step-wise regression can find the DGP most often, though again unreliably.

The results for $\alpha = 0.001$ may be a surprise: there is a much *higher* probability of locating the DGP at the *tighter* criterion, primarily because the gauge is smaller, so fewer irrelevant variables are retained, and there is only a small fall in potency given the high significance of the relevant variables. The point of such an illustration is to emphasize the importance of the choice of the nominal significance level: here tighter is better, and while that most certainly need not always be the case, careful thought should be given to setting the significance level. Moreover, seeking the best-fitting model is not a good strategy, as the tighter significance level must lead to a worse fit, yet finds the DGP more often. It also shows that success in finding the DGP is of limited use as an evaluation citerion. Section 19.4 returns to compare step-wise and *Autometrics* on the Hoover–Perez experiments with $N > T$.

17.5   Information criteria

Information criteria like AIC (see Akaike, 1973), or BIC (see Schwarz, 1978) were originally developed for selection in stationary and ergodic autoregressions, but are widely used as selection algorithms, in particular for choosing lag length but sometimes more generally. For example, BIC selects k from N regressors in:

$$y_t = \sum_{i=1}^{N} \beta_i z_{i,t} + u_t, \tag{17.5}$$

to minimize the penalty-adjusted log-likelihood:

$$BIC_k = \ln \widetilde{\sigma}_k^2 + \frac{k \ln T}{T},$$

where:

$$\widetilde{\sigma}_k^2 = \frac{1}{T} \sum_{t=1}^{T} \left(y_t - \sum_{i=1}^{k} \widetilde{\beta}_i z_{i,t} \right)^2 = \frac{1}{T} \sum_{t=1}^{T} \widetilde{u}_t^2. \tag{17.6}$$

Such an approach requires a search over all $k \in (0, N)$ so entails estimating 2^N models. When $N = 40$, then $2^{40} = 10^{12}$ possible models need considered, which is barely feasible, but for $N = 100$, that becomes $2^{100} = 10^{30}$, which is infeasible.

AIC and HQ (Hannan and Quinn, 1979) penalize the log-likelihood by less stringent functions $f(k, T)$ than BIC, for k parameters and sample

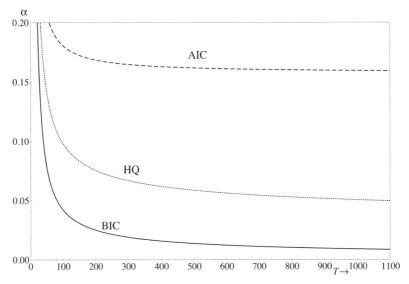

Figure 17.2
Significance levels of AIC, BIC and HQ selection rules for $N = 10$

size T. Hannan and Quinn (1979) show that $2k \log(\log(T))/T$ is the minimum rate of penalty increase to ensure a consistent selection. Both BIC and HQ are consistent in that a LDGP$\subseteq$model is selected with $p \to 1$ as $T \to \infty$ relative to k. Although AIC does not deliver a consistent selection as $T \to \infty$, it is asymptotically efficient for selecting a forecasting model when the LDGP is a stationary autoregression of infinite lag length (e.g., Sober, 2003 argues that AIC is the best choice for prediction). Thus, its penalty reflects a trade-off between the forecasting costs of estimating an additional small parameter and of omitting that lag from the model.

Despite apparently adopting a different framework, information criteria operate in a similar way to other approaches, since the level of penalty at which a marginal variable is retained is easily translated into the implicit significance level of the associated test (e.g., Campos et al., 2003). Figure 17.2 shows those corresponding significance levels for $N = 10$. The wide range of possible significance levels reveals that imposing the asymptotic restriction of a consistent selection would not greatly constrain the selection strategy in small samples. AIC has an even looser significance level, relevant for selecting a forecasting model with the smallest mean square forecast error (MSFE) for a stationary process as in chapter 23.

There are a number of drawbacks to selecting a model by any information criterion, and here we focus on BIC. First, the adequacy of the initial general model specification is not checked: the choice may be the best on the given criterion, yet be a poor characterization of the data evidence. This is particularly important in processes that are non-stationary because they lack time invariance, where a failure to model breaks delivers a non-constant representation. The proof of consistent selection requires that the model with all N variables from which a selection is to be made nests the LDGP, and the set characterizing the former may still need to be discovered when the LDGP experiences breaks and has non-linearities.

Secondly, BIC is not invariant to the addition of irrelevant variables: pre-search alters the penalty entering BIC calculations and thereby changes the probability of locating the LDGP, sometimes markedly. Campos et al. (2003) show that when $T = 140$, with $N = 40$ and an intercept, then after ordering the variables by their significance, $BIC_{41} < BIC_{40}$ whenever $\widehat{t}^2_{(41)} \geq 3.63$, or $|t_{(41)}| \geq 1.9$. Thus, to select no variables when the null is true requires that:

$$\widehat{t}^2_{(k)} \leq (T - k)(T^{1/T} - 1) \; \forall k \leq N$$

and hence needs every $|\widehat{t}_{(i)}| < 1.9$, which occurs with probability:

$$P\left(|t_{(i)}| < 1.9, \; \forall i = 1, \ldots, 40\right) = (1 - 0.0595)^{40} = 0.09. \tag{17.7}$$

Consequently, BIC would retain some null variables 91% of the time. If the twenty least significant variables were eliminated, and no account taken of doing so, namely those where $|\widehat{t}_{(i)}| < 0.5$, say, then the new criterion is $|\widehat{t}_{(i)}| < 2.2$, so that $P(|t_{(i)}| < 2.2) = 0.3$. Thus, BIC still keeps irrelevant variables 70% of time, but the outcome is much improved. Such arbitrary elimination explains why BIC does well in Hansen (1999).

Thirdly, the trade-off between the probability of retaining irrelevant *versus* losing relevant variables remains: the BIC penalty corresponds to an implicit significance level as figure 17.3 illustrates. The diagram also highlights another key difficulty of selecting by information criteria: despite their apparent derivation as penalizing non-parsimonious models, the selection becomes increasingly loose as $N \to T$ such that almost every variable would be retained. There are corrections proposed in the literature, as in Hurvich and Tsai (1989) who derive:

$$AIC^c = \ln \widehat{\sigma}^2_k + \frac{2k}{T} + \frac{2k(k+1)}{T(T-k-1)}. \tag{17.8}$$

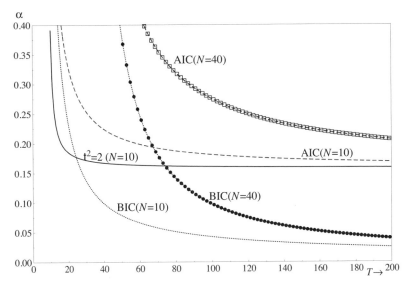

Figure 17.3
Implicit significance levels of AIC, BIC and $t^2 = 2$

As $N \to T$, models with $k \approx N$ are strongly selected against by (17.8), nevertheless, that behavior suggests a fundamental difficulty with the approach outside its original framework.

Finally, it is unclear how to use information criteria when $N > T$, which arises both with general non-linear approximations and long lags, as well as with IIS in *Autometrics*.

17.6 Lasso

Write a linear regression model in conventional matrix notation:

$$\widehat{\epsilon} = y - X\widehat{\beta},$$

where y and ϵ are $T \times 1$, β is $N \times 1$ when $N < T$ and X is $T \times N$. Then the Lasso (e.g., Tibshirani, 1996) minimizes the residual sum of squares (RSS) subject to the sum of the absolute values of the coefficients being less than a constant τ:

$$\min \widehat{\epsilon}'\widehat{\epsilon} \text{ subject to } \sum_{i=1}^{N} |\widehat{\beta}_i| \le \tau. \tag{17.9}$$

The solution can be found by a forward-selection type algorithm, see Efron et al. (2004).

Estimating β as in (17.9) has two effects. The first is shrinkage, as some estimated coefficients are forced towards zero relative to their unrestricted counterparts. The second is selection, so some coefficients are set to zero, and only regressors with non-zero coefficients are kept, perhaps using their OLS estimates instead. The Lasso is like forward selection:

1. find the next regressor most correlated with y;
2. partial out its influence from y and the remaining xs;
3. repeat.

Computationally, the Lasso solution can be found through a modification of the closely related least angle regression (e.g., Efron et al., 2004), which is a less greedy version of forward selection, taking many small steps:

1. find the regressor most correlated with y, say x_1;
2. only take a step up to the point that the next most correlated regressor has equal correlation, say x_2;
3. increase both β_1 and β_2 until the third in line has equal correlation with current residuals;
4. repeat.

Inference is slightly more problematic, as there are no standard errors, but either a bootstrap procedure can be used or a sandwich-type calculated from the penalized log-likelihood. The degree of shrinkage can be set by AIC, BIC, C_p (see Mallows, 1973) or generalized cross-validation (e.g., Stone, 1974, and Efron and Gong, 1983). The degrees of freedom for the chosen information criterion can be approximated by $\widehat{k}$, the number of non-zero coefficients retained.

17.6.1 Comparing Lasso and *Autometrics* on the HP experiments

We next compare Lasso and *Autometrics* on the same Hoover–Perez experiments HP2, HP7, HP8 and HP9 as used for step-wise regression above. The selection criterion for Lasso was BIC, initially unrestricted, then with the true model size, n, assumed known. Table 17.6 reports the simulation results.

As can be seen, the gauge in Lasso is very erratic, and often unacceptably large, and despite that, its potency can be lower. Overall, such performance is sufficiently poor that step-wise would in fact dominate Lasso.

Enforcing the true model size n helps Lasso's selection performance somewhat as table 17.6 records. Even so, despite knowing the true

Table 17.6
Comparisons of Lasso selection and *Autometrics*

	HP2	HP7	HP8	HP9	HP2	HP7	HP8	HP9
	Lasso selection: BIC				*Autometrics, $\alpha = 0.05$*			
Gauge%	2.2	19.5	35.1	18.6	5.1	5.9	5.9	6.1
Potency%	100	94.4	86.3	65.6	100	99.7	100	62.6
DGP found%	53.1	0.1	0.0	0.0	28.2	17.0	17.9	0.3
DGP nested%	100	83.2	68.1	7.4	100	99.2	100	1.3
	Lasso selection: true n				*Autometrics, $\alpha = 0.01$*			
Gauge%	0.0	2.7	3.3	7.9	1.2	1.6	1.6	1.6
Potency%	100	66.8	59.3	44.5	100	99.0	100	60.2
DGP found%	100	0.5	0.0	0.0	73.5	68.0	68.5	0.0
DGP nested%	100	0.5	0.0	0.0	100	97.1	100	0.4
	Lasso selection: true n				*Autometrics true n, $\alpha = 5\%$*			
Gauge%	0.0	2.7	3.3	7.9	0.0	0.1	0.0	5.4
Potency%	100	66.8	59.3	44.5	100	98.8	100	62.5
DGP found%	100	0.5	0.0	0.0	100	96.4	100	0.8
DGP nested%	100	0.5	0.0	0.0	100	96.4	100	0.8

model size n, Lasso still has an erratic gauge and relatively poor potency, other than in HP2, where there is a single highly significant relevant variable, which when found allows all other regressors to be eliminated using the knowledge that $n = 1$.

As a final comparison, we also endow *Autometrics* with knowledge of the true model size, n, as reported in table 17.6. The performance of *Autometrics* is markedly improved, and outperforms Lasso in each of the four experiments.

17.6.2 Step-wise regression and Lasso on the JEDC experiments

To check whether the form of the Hoover–Perez experiments was singularly inimical to Lasso, we evaluated its performance on the JEDC-EJ experiments for two values of ρ, defining the serial correlation in the regressors, see (17.4). As step-wise regression was not simulated in section 17.4 above, we also record its behavior. Table 17.7 records the outcomes at two values of the autocorrelation parameter ρ, where we have attempted to match the gauge of Lasso by also re-setting the nominal significance level in *Autometrics*. In this case, step-wise regression was

Table 17.7

Comparisons of step-wise regression, Lasso selection and *Autometrics* for different DGP values of the autocorrelation parameter ρ

	$\rho=0.2$	$\rho=0.8$	$\rho=0.2$	$\rho=0.8$	$\rho=0.2$	$\rho=0.8$	$\rho=0.2$	$\rho=0.8$
	Step-wise		Lasso		*Autometrics*			
	BIC	BIC	BIC	BIC	5%	5%	11%	15%
Gauge%	4.5	5.7	11.3	16.5	5.3	6.3	11.1	15.2
Potency%	82.5	70.6	85.8	76.9	85.2	76.5	89.5	81.0
DGP found%	16.4	7.0	7.3	0.9	20.9	13.1	14.5	7.2
DGP nested%	31.5	11.5	46.1	27.7	38.1	21.4	53.4	30.8
Final rej. 5%	8.6	7.4	10.7	13.2	1.9	3.6	0.2	0.1
	Step-wise		Lasso		*Autometrics*			
	true n	true n	true n	true n	5%	10%		
Gauge%	4.8	8.1	5.5	10.0	5.3	10.9		
Potency%	84.6	74.0	82.5	67.8	85.2	79.2		
DGP found%	33.9	12.3	26.3	3.8	20.9	9.7		
DGP nested%	33.9	12.3	26.3	3.8	38.1	26.9		
Final rej. 5%	10.0	9.0	21.4	40.6	1.9	0.5		

run to completion, but the actual model from the step-wise search path was selected by BIC, which is more similar to the approach used for Lasso.

Lasso still has a large gauge with little commensurate increase in potency. The new final row of the table denoted "Final rej. at 5%" shows the percentage of experiments in which the final selected model of each method is rejected against the union of that final model and the DGP, tested at 5%: both step-wise regression and Lasso choices are dominated much more often.

Next, we repeat the comparisons under the assumption that the true model size is known, as reported in the second panel of table 17.7. There is little obvious improvement: as before step-wise regression and Lasso final choices are dominated much more often than *Autometrics*.

Figure 17.4 provides a more complete graphical portrayal of the outcomes as the degree of collinearity in the experiments is varied by changing $\rho \in (-1, 1)$, this time using the JEDC DGP (17.2). Panel a shows that gauge is fairly well controlled for both step-wise and *Autometrics* over the entire range of possible correlation values, whereas

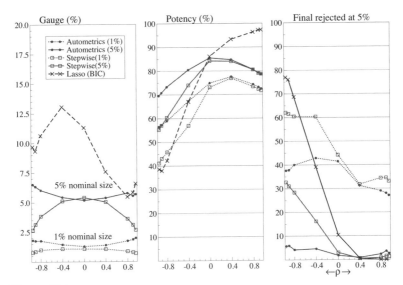

Figure 17.4
Correlation range experiments JEDC(ρ)

it is not for Lasso. The potency (panel b) of Lasso also varies greatly from 40% to nearly 100%, and step-wise is generally dominated by *Autometrics* at each significance level. However, the most telling panel is c, which shows the frequency with which a direct test would reject the selected model against the union of the selected model and the DGP, which exceeds 70% for Lasso, and with step-wise regression dominated by *Autometrics*, revealing the poor quality of their selected models when there are negative correlations between candidate variables.

17.7 Comparisons with RETINA

RETINA is the acronym from RElevant Transformation of the Inputs Network Approach: see Perez-Amaral et al. (2003, 2005). Its main aim is to investigate non-linear relations, so a class of non-linear functions is automatically generated, and an expanding search used to locate the model. The criterion is based on the best parsimonious out-of-sample performance evaluated on a combination of sub-samples, using a tri-partite split of the whole sample, like a generalized cross-validation approach. As with other expanding searches, RETINA could in principle handle $N > T$.

The RETINA algorithm, as of late 2008, took the following form, given a set of linear candidate variables, $x_{i,j}, i = 1, \ldots, T; j = 1, \ldots, M$:

1. Level 1 transforms; $x_{i,h}^{\alpha} x_{i,j}^{\beta}$ for $\alpha, \beta = -1, 0, 1$ to generate a total candidate set denoted $\{w_{i,k}\}, k = 1, \ldots, N$;

2. Divide the overall sample into 3 disjoint sub-samples and rank the candidates $w_{i,k}$ based on their correlations, $|\hat{\rho}_k|$ with y;

3. Include $w_{i,s}$ if $R_s^2 \leq \lambda_p$ in the model $w_{i,s} = \beta_0 + \sum_{k=1}^{s-1} \beta_k w_{i,k} + \epsilon_i$ for $s = 1, \ldots, N$. A grid search over λ_p is used to control collinearity;

4. Cross-validate using mean-square prediction error (MSPE) to find the local best model;

5. The search strategy tries to find a parsimonious model using AIC;

6. The steps are repeated over the six combinations of sub-samples.

17.7.1 Monte Carlo evidence

The aim of this section is to evaluate the comparative gauges and potencies of RETINA and *PcGets*, building on the comparisons in Castle (2005). The DGP is:

$$y_t = \sum_{i=1}^{J} \beta_i x_{i,t} + \epsilon_t, \quad \epsilon_t \sim \text{IN}[0, 1], \tag{17.10}$$

$$x_t = 10\iota + v_t, \quad v_t \sim \text{IN}_2[0, I_2], \tag{17.11}$$

for $t = 1, \ldots, T$ where $J = 1$ or $J = 2$ and ι is a 2×1 vector of ones. Substantial collinearity is generated between the linear and non-linear functions by the large intercept in (17.11), leading to very small eigenvalues in the second-moment matrix. Consequently, to ensure power is not negligible, large β_j are required for significant non-central t-values.

The GUM is specified as an example of a RETINA formulation:

$$y_t = \gamma_1 x_{1,t} + \gamma_2 x_{2,t} + \gamma_3 x_{1,t}^2 + \gamma_4 x_{2,t}^2 + \gamma_5 \left(\frac{1}{x_1}\right)_t + \gamma_6 \left(\frac{1}{x_2}\right)_t$$
$$+ \gamma_7 \left(\frac{1}{x_1^2}\right)_t + \gamma_8 \left(\frac{1}{x_2^2}\right)_t + \gamma_9 (x_1 x_2)_t + \gamma_{10} \left(\frac{1}{x_1 x_2}\right)_t$$
$$+ \gamma_{11} \left(\frac{x_1}{x_2}\right)_t + \gamma_{12} \left(\frac{x_2}{x_1}\right)_t + \gamma_{13} + \varepsilon_t.$$

We focus on just two experiments here. First, when $J = 1$, $\beta_1 = 1100$, corresponding to $t_{\beta_1} \approx 4$ in the GUM; and secondly, when $J = 2$, $\beta_1 = 800$, $\beta_2 = 1600$, corresponding to $t_{\beta_1} \approx 3$, and $t_{\beta_2} \approx 6$ in the GUM.

Table 17.8
Comparisons of RETINA, *PcGets* and *Autometrics*: ddm indicates that double demeaning is used

	RETINA	PcGets		Autometrics	
		Lib.	Cons.	5%	1%
Gauge%					
$J = 1, \beta_1 = 0.4$	10.0	25.4	14.2	8.9	7.1
$J = 1, \beta_1 = 1100$	0.3	15.3	4.4	4.6	1.1
$J = 2, \beta_1 = 800, \beta_2 = 1600$	66.6	16.5	6.8	4.7	1.4
$J = 1, \beta_1 = 0.4$,ddm				5.3	1.5
$J = 1, \beta_1 = 1100$, ddm	2.6	5.2	1.2	5.3	1.3
Potency%					
$J = 1, \beta_1 = 0.4$	6.6	33.1	19.0	61.1	58.7
$J = 1, \beta_1 = 1100$	100	98.0	98.4	99.6	99.6
$J = 2, \beta_1 = 800, \beta_2 = 1600$	98.7	97.0	97.0	99.6	99.7
$J = 1, \beta_1 = 0.4$, ddm				97.8	97.6
$J = 1, \beta_1 = 1100$, ddm	81.2	97.0	87.0	100	100

Thus, there are 12 variables and an intercept (which is free), where in fact either one or two of the linear terms matter, and all the non-linear terms are irrelevant. The *PcGets* and RETINA results are taken from Castle (2005, table 9).

Table 17.8 reports the gauges and the potency at $T = 100$ using $M = 1000$ replications when $J = 1, 2$, as well as a much smaller coefficient $\beta_1 = 0.4$. First we compare RETINA and *PcGets*. The *Liberal* (roughly 5%) and *Conservative* (roughly 1%) selection criteria were preset in *PcGets*. When $J = 1, \beta_1 = 1100$, the potency is high, although the gauges exceed the nominal significance level. Overall, RETINA performs well in this setting of a single highly-significant variable, and is close to the *Conservative* outcomes in *PcGets*. However, there is a major change when there are two relevant variables in the model, $J = 2, \beta_1 = 800, \beta_2 = 1600$. Now RETINA performs badly, retaining six of the irrelevant variables 100% of the time. The gauge of *PcGets* is tto high when $\beta_1 = 0.4$, which corresponds to a non-centrality of 4 in the DGP, but much lower in the GUM.

Autometrics outperforms both other algorithms. For the experiments with large coefficients, the gauges are close to the nominal levels, and potency almost perfect. When $\beta_1 = 0.4$, the gauge is too large, but better than RETINA and *PcGets*, while detecting substantially more relevant variables. Doornik (2009a, table 8) gives a similar example where *Autometrics* outperforms *PcGets*.

The bad performance appears to be due to the collinearity, despite the check in RETINA, and possibly confounding the pre-search of *PcGets*. Good performance can be re-established by orthogonalizing, which here simply requires double de-meaning all the variables, as in:

$$\tilde{x}_1^2 = (x_{1,t} - \bar{x}_1)^2 - \overline{(x_{1,t} - \bar{x}_1)^2}$$

where $\tilde{x}$ is the de-meaned variable and $\bar{x}$ is the mean of x. This operational procedure is easy to implement, and makes RETINA less prone to erratic outcomes, see table 17.8. However, by being a single-variable expanding search, negative correlations between variables remain problematic, as for many of the other algorithms considered in this chapter. Double de-meaning markedly improves the gauge for *PcGets* with little impact on potency.

Autometrics does not need the double demeaning to obtain a well-behaved gauge. It does have a positive impact on potency, though, which remains better than RETINA and *PcGets*. Chapter 21 considers in more detail selecting non-linear models within a *Gets* approach using *Autometrics*.

18 Model Selection in Underspecified Settings

Despite seeking to commence an empirical study from a general initial specification that nests the LDGP for the set of variables under analysis, the GUM may be an underspecification. Moreover, the selection of the variables to analyze could lead to a poor representation of the economic data generation process. In this setting, model selection, rather than just fitting a prior specification, may help. Impulse-indicator saturation can correct nonconstancies induced by location shifts in omitted variables that alter the intercepts of models. Since IIS is a robust estimation method, it can mitigate some of the adverse effects of induced location shifts when models are mis-specified. The chapter provides an analysis of a simple setting, a Monte Carlo study thereof, and an artificial data example to illustrate.[1]

18.1 Introduction

The costs of underspecification of a model relative to the DGP are well analyzed in the econometrics literature in terms of omitted-variables biases: if any relevant variables omitted from a model are correlated with any that are included, the estimated coefficients of the latter will be biased for the corresponding DGP parameters. Apart from the three golden-rule exhortations to think of the correct answer before starting, or as the analysis proceeds, or stumble over it before completion (e.g., Hendry, 1987), there is little useful advice on how to solve that problem. Orthogonalizing included variables relative to excluded would suffice to avoid the bias, though not the resulting poorer fit and possible insignificance of the relevant variables that were included, but since it is not

---

[1]This chapter draws on Castle and Hendry (2014a).

known what has been omitted, it is unclear how such a strategy could be implemented, especially when unknown omitted variables shift.

DGPs in economics are too complicated to be a reasonable baseline for judging how well a selection method will work in practice. A more feasible alternative is to seek a good approximation to the LDGP, although "omitted variables" transpires to be an ambiguous notion as we consider in section 18.2. Then section 18.3 looks at the role of model selection in mitigating some of the consequences of underspecification in static models, followed in section 18.4 by an analysis of a dynamic DGP, illustrated in section 18.5 using the artificial data set from chapter 4. Castle and Hendry (2011a) discuss model selection in the four settings of over-, exact-, under-, and mixed specifications where a subset of relevant variables is included, but some are omitted and irrelevant variables are included in the GUM. They show that model selection has low costs when an exact specification is correctly postulated, and is preferable to estimating a prior specification otherwise.

18.2   Analyzing underspecification

There are two distinct forms of underspecification. The first is that just alluded to, where a model is underspecified relative to its target LDGP, where the LDGP is a well-specified process that could be usefully modeled. For example, a variable x_t is known to matter and is included in the data set under analysis, but its lag, x_{t-1}, is not included in the specific model being estimated, although x_{t-1} is in fact relevant. The second is where the LDGP is non-constant and uninterpretable due to the omission of a key determinant in the DGP of the behavior of the variables under consideration, because the implicit marginalization in deriving the LDGP eliminated one or more causal, changing processes of considerable relevance. For example, in a small macroeconomic model of money, inflation, income and interest rates, if the exchange rate was not considered, but was important and also experienced several large devaluations or revaluations, its omission would induce non-constancies in the estimated model.

Textbook treatments rarely distinguish between these two types of omitted variables bias, but the solutions to these two problems are very different. The first can be solved simply by commencing from a GUM that does nest the associated LDGP. In section 2.5, we addressed the ways in which we sought to expand the set of candidate variables, to include longer lags to ensure a viable sequential factorization, impulse indicators to remove outliers and location shifts, and non-linear functions of the basic variables to capture departures from linearity. Since the costs of search are low, these extensions can help avoid underspecification of a model relative to the target LDGP when the latter is well behaved. The cost of retaining adventitious effects is of order $1/T$, whereas omitting an important variable is an order one mistake, so these costs can be far from symmetric.

The second can only be fully resolved by including the variables omitted from the DGP to create a constant, interpretable LDGP for which a congruent nesting GUM can be specified. A forward search of testing for potential omissions *seriatim* to find what is omitted is sometimes used, but makes it difficult to control the null rejection frequency of the procedure. Thus, if a possible set of candidate variables is known, it would be better to include them all and use *Gets*.That suggestion raises the general issue of the impact of model selection when either the initial GUM is underspecified for the LDGP, or the LDGP itself is a poor representation of the DGP for the variables under consideration.

18.3   Model selection for mitigating underspecification

The usual analysis of omitted variables bias takes the DGP as fixed, and considers the impact of estimating a given mis-specified model thereof: the impact of selecting the model from a larger candidate set is not considered. Of course, if that candidate set included all the relevant variables, the problem of underspecification would vanish. Thus, the first setting has to be one where the LDGP is not nested by the GUM, but a model is selected from the data evidence. Castle et al. (2011) provide examples of this case, when the LDGP is a constant, stationary autoregressive-distributed lag with a longer lag length (2 periods) than considered by an investigator who uses zero or one lag. They show that estimation of the mis-specified representation (denoted an LDGP*) is generally dominated by selecting from the underspecified GUM, as measured by unconditional parameter estimator root mean squared errors (RMSEs), so search costs are actually negative in that case. When the DGP has many relevant, but not highly significant, variables, selecting from the underspecified GUM can even dominate directly estimating the DGP itself, despite the unconditional RMSEs being calculated relative to the parameters of that DGP. The estimated DGP, however, continues to dominate the LDGP*.

Castle and Hendry (2014a) show that when a variable is omitted because its relevance is unknown, or the variable is unobserved so cannot be included, model selection can again be beneficial relative to estimating a pre-specified equation. Location shifts in any omitted variables alter the intercepts of estimated static models, but leave estimated slope parameters unaltered, even when correlated with included variables. However, location shifts in *included* variables also induce changes in estimated slopes when there are correlated omitted variables, irrespective of the latter's generation processes being constant or not. They show that IIS helps mitigate the adverse impacts of such induced location shifts.

Although it is a relatively simple example to keep the mathematics tractable, the following analysis of omitting a non-constant variable from a static regression highlights several of the key considerations. We first analytically derive the impact of omitting a variable that experiences a location shift, then consider the impact of selection using IIS to remove the break effects. Section 18.4 extends the analysis to underspecification in a dynamic DGP.

18.3.1   An underspecified static model with a break
Let:

$$x_t = \lambda^{(1)} 1_{\{t < T_1\}} + \lambda^{(2)} 1_{\{t \geq T_1\}} + v_t. \tag{18.1}$$

When the DGP is:

$$y_t = \beta_0 + \beta_1 x_t + \beta_2 z_t + \varepsilon_t \tag{18.2}$$

and (18.1) operates, but the relevance of x_t is unknown, then a step shift would occur as the reduced LDGP in the space of y_t, z_t is:

$$y_t = \left(\beta_0 + \beta_1 \lambda^{(1)}\right) + \beta_1 \left(\lambda^{(2)} - \lambda^{(1)}\right) 1_{\{t \geq T_1\}} + \beta_2 z_t + \varepsilon_t + \beta_1 v_t. \tag{18.3}$$

The composite error, $\varepsilon_t + \beta_1 v_t$, in (18.3) is IID and if the location shift were to be correctly modeled, the coefficient of z_t would remain the DGP parameter β_2, so the costs of omission would be the lack of knowledge that x_t was relevant, a slightly worse fit, and a possibly inexplicable location shift. The simulation evidence in section 20.2, especially table 20.2, shows that almost all the indicators for breaks of $(\lambda^{(2)} - \lambda^{(1)}) \geq 4/\sqrt{(\sigma_\varepsilon^2 + \beta_1^2 \sigma_v^2)}$ would be retained most of the time.

On the other hand, when the model is simply:

$$y_t = \gamma_0 + \gamma_1 z_t + u_t, \tag{18.4}$$

then γ_0 would not be constant, the residual variance could be greatly increased by the unmodeled location shift, and the estimate of γ_1 could be badly determined. Most forms of mis-specification checks would detect such a violation of congruence, either by recursive estimation and constancy tests, or residual autocorrelation, non-normality or heteroskedasticity tests. However, it is unclear what actions an investigator might take in the light of such rejections: there is no unique generalization path, and the fact that several tests reject warns that none can be easily interpreted as due to a violation of its erstwhile null hypothesis.

One likely route with time series is to generalize (18.4) by including lags:

$$y_t = \rho_0 + \rho_1 y_{t-1} + \rho_2 z_t + \rho_3 z_{t-1} + e_t. \tag{18.5}$$

Then from (18.1), as:

$$\Delta x_t = \left(\lambda^{(2)} - \lambda^{(1)} \right) 1_{\{t=T_1\}} + \Delta v_t,$$

it follows that:

$$\begin{aligned} \Delta y_t &= \beta_1 \Delta x_t + \beta_2 \Delta z_t + \Delta \varepsilon_t \\ &= \beta_1 \left(\lambda^{(2)} - \lambda^{(1)} \right) 1_{\{t=T_1\}} + \beta_2 \Delta z_t + \Delta \left(\varepsilon_t + \beta_1 v_t \right), \end{aligned}$$

leading to:

$$y_t = y_{t-1} + \beta_1 \left(\lambda^{(2)} - \lambda^{(1)} \right) 1_{\{t=T_1\}} + \beta_2 z_t - \beta_2 z_{t-1} + \Delta \left(\varepsilon_t + \beta_1 v_t \right), \tag{18.6}$$

which has a near unit root and a large outlier at the break date with (possibly) some negative residual autocorrelation. Correcting the outlier, (18.5) would look like (18.6). Notice that (18.6) is not the LDGP, which remains (18.3) on marginalizing (18.2) with respect to x_t, and has the error variance:

$$\sigma_u^2 = \sigma_\varepsilon^2 + \beta_1^2 \sigma_v^2,$$

whereas (18.6) does not have a white-noise error and has:

$$\sigma_{\Delta u}^2 = 2 \left(\sigma_\varepsilon^2 + \beta_1^2 \sigma_v^2 \right).$$

Autometrics would allow for both longer lags and IIS when approximating (18.3). In principle, when the GUM nests (18.3), one might expect IIS to pick up the step shift, and deliver a constant model with $\beta_2 z_t$ as the key regressor, which would be a huge improvement over (18.4).

Indeed for large shifts, that is the outcome. However, as approximating the location shift by individual indicators leads to a large reduction in the degrees of freedom, the more parsimonious, but non-congruent, form in (18.6) could be found instead, so IIS would merely remove the observation at T_1 (although whether the effects of doing so are beneficial or not is unclear). The next section explains this occurrence in a dynamic DGP.

18.4   Underspecification in a dynamic DGP

Now the DGP for y_t is dynamic:

$$y_t = \beta_0 + \beta_1 x_t + \beta_2 z_t + \beta_3 y_{t-1} + u_t$$

or using the lag operator L:

$$(1 - \beta_3 L)\, y_t = \beta_0 + \beta_1 x_t + \beta_2 z_t + u_t \tag{18.7}$$

and x_t is generated by the autoregressive process:

$$(1 - \psi L)\, x_t = \lambda^{(1)} + \left(\lambda^{(2)} - \lambda^{(1)}\right) 1_{\{t \geq T_1\}} + v_t. \tag{18.8}$$

When (18.8) holds, then the LDGP for y_t is much more complicated, as pre-multiplying (18.7) by $(1 - \psi L)$, then:

$$
\begin{aligned}
(1 - \psi L)(1 - \beta_3 L)\, y_t &= (1 - \psi)\beta_0 + \beta_1 (1 - \psi L)\, x_t + \beta_2 (1 - \psi L)\, z_t \\
&\quad + (1 - \psi L)\, u_t \\
&= (1 - \psi)\beta_0 + \beta_1 \left(\lambda^{(1)} + \left(\lambda^{(2)} - \lambda^{(1)}\right) 1_{\{t \geq T_1\}} + v_t\right) \\
&\quad + \beta_2 (1 - \psi L)\, z_t + (1 - \psi L)\, u_t \\
&= \left((1 - \psi)\beta_0 + \beta_1 \lambda^{(1)}\right) + \beta_1 \left(\lambda^{(2)} - \lambda^{(1)}\right) 1_{\{t \geq T_1\}} \\
&\quad + \beta_2 (1 - \psi L)\, z_t + (1 - \psi L)\, u_t + \beta_1 v_t.
\end{aligned}
$$

Consequently in levels:

$$
\begin{aligned}
y_t &= \left((1 - \psi)\beta_0 + \beta_1 \lambda^{(1)}\right) + \beta_1 \left(\lambda^{(2)} - \lambda^{(1)}\right) 1_{\{t \geq T_1\}} + \beta_2 z_t - \beta_2 \psi z_{t-1} \\
&\quad + (\psi + \beta_3)\, y_{t-1} - \psi \beta_3 y_{t-2} + \left(u_t - \psi u_{t-1} + \beta_1 v_t\right). \tag{18.9}
\end{aligned}
$$

The adjustment path generated by (18.9) commences with a jump in y_{T_1} of $\beta_1(\lambda^{(2)} - \lambda^{(1)})$, then a further $\beta_1(\lambda^{(2)} - \lambda^{(1)})$ is added plus the carry over of $(\psi + \beta_3)$ from y_{T_1}, and so on, converging to the new equilibrium mean μ:

$$\mu = \frac{(1 - \psi)\beta_0 + \beta_1\lambda^{(2)}}{(1 - \psi)(1 - \beta_3)}.$$

Thus, unlike the static model, for a sufficiently large shift, IIS would pick up a sequence of changing indicators, which would end when μ is reached. Because the lagged values of y reflect the shift, it is quite probable that a differenced variant is selected instead, namely:

$$\Delta y_t = \beta_1\left(\lambda^{(2)} - \lambda^{(1)}\right)1_{\{t=T_1\}} + \beta_2\Delta z_t - \beta_2\psi\Delta z_{t-1} + \left(\psi + \beta_3\right)\Delta y_{t-1}$$
$$- \psi\beta_3\Delta y_{t-2} + w_t,$$

where $w_t = \Delta\left(u_t - \psi u_{t-1} + \beta_1 v_t\right)$ or in levels:

$$y_t = \beta_1\left(\lambda^{(2)} - \lambda^{(1)}\right)1_{\{t=T_1\}} + \beta_2 z_t - \beta_2\left(1 + \psi\right)z_{t-1} + \beta_2\psi z_{t-2}$$
$$+ \left(1 + \psi + \beta_3\right)y_{t-1} - \left(\psi + \beta_3 + \psi\beta_3\right)y_{t-2} + \psi\beta_3 y_{t-3} + w_t,$$

again inducing a near unit root with a large outlier at the break date, where the negative moving-average error would bias the estimated coefficients away from an exact unit root. In this setting, IIS may just remove a few observations at, and just after, T_1, so interpretation becomes difficult. Nevertheless, the residual variance of (18.9) after IIS will be considerably smaller than without, and constancy will be improved. The next section illustrates this analysis for the *PcGive* artificial data described in chapter 4 and also used in section 19.6.

18.5   A dynamic artificial-data example

Leaving inflation out of the initial GUM of the *PcGive* artificial data set considered in chapter 4 yields for 1955(3) – 1992(3):

$$c_t = \underset{(11.7)}{2.1} + \underset{(0.03)}{0.98c_{t-1}} + \underset{(0.04)}{0.50i_t} - \underset{(0.04)}{0.48i_{t-1}} \tag{18.10}$$

$$R^2 = 0.988 \ \ \widehat{\sigma} = 1.51 \ \ \chi^2_{nd}(2) = 6.58^* \ \ F_{ar}(5, 140) = 7.40^{**}$$
$$F_{arch}(4, 141) = 6.58^{**} \ \ F_{reset}(2, 143) = 2.80 \ \ F_{het}(6, 151) = 1.09.$$

The omission of the shifting variable, Δp_t, leads to the fitted model being essentially in first differences, and suggests the absence of any long run. Moreover, several mis-specification tests reject, and the entailed solution in first differences suggests that c only responds 2/3rds to i (although the DGP has a 1-1 response).

Refitting in first differences yields the parsimonious but incorrect representation:

$$\Delta c_t = 0.23\Delta c_{t-1} + 0.50\Delta i_t \tag{18.11}$$
$$\quad\quad\quad (0.05) \quad\quad\quad (0.03)$$

$$\widehat{\sigma} = 1.42 \quad \chi^2_{nd}(2) = 1.86 \quad F_{ar}(5,142) = 3.19^{**}$$
$$F_{arch}(4,141) = 2.25 \quad F_{reset}(2,145) = 0.15 \quad F_{het}(5,143) = 2.46^{*}.$$

18.5.1 Model selection with IIS

Selecting from a GUM having 10 lags on both variables, with IIS at $\alpha = 0.005$ yields:

$$c_t = 1.06c_{t-1} - 0.18c_{t-5} + 0.09c_{t-8} + 0.50i_t - 0.47i_{t-1}$$
$$\quad\quad (0.03) \quad\quad\quad (0.03) \quad\quad\quad (0.02) \quad\quad\quad (0.03) \quad\quad (0.04)$$

$$- 4.651_{1974(1)} - \quad 3.98 \ 1_{1974(2)} \tag{18.12}$$
$$\quad (1.29) \quad\quad\quad\quad (1.31)$$

$$\widehat{\sigma} = 1.28 \quad \chi^2_{nd}(2) = 0.02 \quad F_{ar}(5,137) = 1.09$$
$$F_{arch}(4,141) = 0.48 \quad F_{reset}(2,141) = 0.27 \quad F_{het}(20,126) = 0.63.$$

As in chapter 4, indicators at the artificial "oil-crisis" dates 1974(1) and 1974(2) and longer lags of c proxy the omission of Δp_t. That is a distinct advantage of *Autometrics* over conventional modeling even when the basic set is substantively incomplete—picking up the effects of an omitted variable that shifts is beneficial relative to having a non-constant model. The break is only partly modeled by the dummy, and the rest by a near unit root (a typical outcome empirically), which helps in forecasting but misleads in policy reactions and latencies. However, no diagnostics are now significant, and the fit is closer to that of the DGP. The solved static long-run equation for c on i has a coefficient of 0.98, albeit that a unit root cannot be rejected.

Overall, therefore, selection remains helpful even when the GUM is underspecified for the LDGP, or the latter is a poor representation of the economic process: a flexible approximation can get closer than a fixed one. Nevertheless, it is far better to formulate an initial LDGP that is a good representation of the DGP, and nest that in a GUM which can capture all the salient features of the data.

III

Extensions of Automatic Model Selection

19 More Variables than Observations

We now move to also using *Autometrics* as a new way of thinking about a range of problems previously deemed almost intractable. In this part, we consider five major areas. First, the approach of impulse-indicator saturation leads in this chapter to ways of handling excess numbers of variables, $N > T$, based on a mixture of reduction and expansion steps, with an empirical illustration. Secondly, IIS also allows the investigation of multiple breaks, addressed in chapter 20. Third, chapter 21 considers selecting non-linear models, which raise some new issues, and also often involve more candidate variables than observations. In turn, applying IIS to detect breaks in models of marginal processes, then testing the relevance of the retained indicators in conditional equations leads to a new test for super exogeneity, described in chapter 22. Finally, chapter 23 discusses selecting forecasting models. Throughout, we use automatic model selection as a new instrument, which changes how to think about existing problems, and suggests novel solutions.

19.1 Introduction

There are many ways of selecting models even when commencing with more candidate variables, N, than observations, T. Indeed, some are venerable, although not always seen in that context. For example, principal components and related factor analytic methods can be applied to summarize evidence when $N > T$. Likewise, forward selection methods can handle $N > T$ as they commence from a null model and add variables, but the evidence above suggests step-wise, Lasso etc., can be defective in some settings.

Gets aims to start from the GUM, but this is not estimable when there are more variables than observations. Nevertheless, we wish to retain as many as possible of the good properties of *Gets* model selection. Impulse-indicator saturation suggests a possible route, namely to undertake block searches, earlier proposed by Hendry and Krolzig (2005). Their procedure had the form:

1. Partition the N candidate variables into $K \geq 2$ blocks;

2. apply *Gets* to every $K(K-1)/2$ combination of blocks;

3. take the union M of the surviving variables in each terminal model as a new 'GUM';

4. repeat as necessary till $M \ll T$ and a conventional search can be undertaken.

To illustrate with $K = 3$ blocks, denoted A, B and C:

$$
\begin{array}{lll}
A \cup B & \text{model selection} \rightarrow & G_1 \\
A \cup C & \text{model selection} \rightarrow & G_2 \\
B \cup C & \text{model selection} \rightarrow & \underline{G_3} \\
& G_1 \cup G_2 \cup G_3 & \text{model selection} \rightarrow \quad S
\end{array}
$$

While feasible, that approach does not learn as it proceeds, so if some variables from block A are retained in G_1, that is not used when examining $A \cup C$. More seriously, if a substantive variable is missed from any block, there is no recovery procedure, checking later for such occurrences. Thus, we will consider a mixed approach, involving both contracting and expanding searches, again in blocks.

19.2 *Autometrics* expansion and reduction steps

To formalize the expansion and reduction procedure when the GUM cannot be estimated directly, we use the following notation:

$\overline{B}$ is the initial set of all $N > T$ regressors;

S_i is the set of regressors selected at the end of iteration i;

$\overline{B} \backslash S_i$ are regressors not selected at the start of iteration $i + 1$;

$\mathcal{B}_1^0, ..., \mathcal{B}_{B^0}^0$ is a block partition of $\mathcal{B}^0 = \overline{B} \backslash S_i$;

O_i are the candidate omitted regressors in iteration i.

Thus at the start of any search iteration, a set of variables has been selected for inclusion, and the remainder omitted, but neither decision is permanent, and may change as the iterations proceed.

An expansion step now searches for potentially significant, but as yet omitted, variables:

1. run B^0 reductions $\mathcal{B}^0_1 \cup \mathcal{S}_i, ..., \mathcal{B}^0_{B^0} \cup \mathcal{S}_i$ keeping $\mathcal{S}_i$ fixed;
2. let $\mathcal{B}^1$ be the selected regressors from all $\mathcal{B}^0_k, k = 1, ..., B^0$;
3. stop if dim$\mathcal{B}^1$ is small enough, else:
4. restart using B^1 blocks for $\mathcal{B}^1$ (if necessary shrinking the p-value used for selection);
5. on convergence, after J steps say, $O_i = \mathcal{B}^J$.

Having found the set of potential variables, a reduction step finds the next candidate model:

6. find $\mathcal{S}_{i+1}$ from model selection on $\mathcal{S}_i \cup O_i$.

19.2.1 *Autometrics* block-search algorithm

Thus, the algorithm begins by setting $i = 0$, $\mathcal{S}_{-1} = \varnothing$, stage=A. There are four stages, defined as follows:

1. Stage A starts from an empty model, and is run only once;
2. Stage B is run until convergence, using α for the expansion step;
3. Stage C is run only once, using 2α for the expansion step;
4. Stage D starts with 4α for the expansion step, using α thereafter;
5. When stage D converges, the block search terminates.

Then the expansion and reduction steps operate as follows:

Step 1	an expansion step finds O_i;
Step 2	a reduction step finds $\mathcal{S}_i$, then:
	if stage=A, set stage=B, go to Continuation;
	if stage=C, set stage=D, go to Continuation;
Convergence	if $\mathcal{S}_0 \cup \cdots \cup \mathcal{S}_{i-1} = \mathcal{S}_0 \cup \cdots \cup \mathcal{S}_i$ then:
	a. if the stage is B, increment the stage to C;
	b. else terminate the block search.
Continuation	increment i and return to Step 1.

19.3   Simulation evaluation of alternative block modes

To evaluate the performance of the different possible block modes, a small Monte Carlo was undertaken. Table 19.1 records the various block-search modes, numbered 0 to 5, in relation to the stages A–D described above.

Table 19.1
Block modes in *Autometrics*

block-search mode	0	1	2	3	4	5
stratified by lag	A–D	A–D	A, C	A–D	A–D	A–D
random ordering	—	—	B, D	—	—	—
cross blocks	—	—	—	C	C, D	B–D
diagnostic testing	—	B–D	B–D	B, D	B	B–D

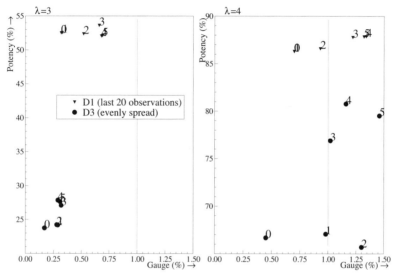

Figure 19.1
Potencies (%) and gauges (%) for experiments D_1 and D_3 of block-search modes 0–5 as defined in table 19.1. GUM with IIS at $\alpha = 1\%$, $M = 1000$

The variables are blocked according to the order in which they enter the GUM,[1] except that lags of the same variable are kept together (this is what is meant by "stratified by lag"). In one case, mode 2, random ordering is used in stages B and D. Cross blocks indicates that all cross-blocks are used, with a block size of $k/2$ to keep the magnitude of any two combined blocks the same. The last line in table 19.1 indicates in which stages diagnostic testing is used.

The IIS experiments simulate D_1 and D_3 from section 15.9, but this time to evaluate the relative potency and gauge of the alternative modes (shown in Fig. 19.1), and their speed (shown in Fig. 19.2), against the

---

[1]As a consequence, a different ordering may result in different outcomes.

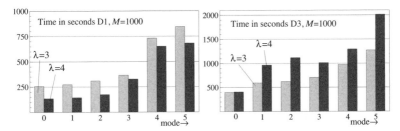

Figure 19.2
Speeds of block-search modes 0 – 5 for GUM with IIS. Dark bars have $\lambda = 4$, light bars have $\lambda = 3$.

default of mode 1. The size of the break, in terms of residual standard errors, is denoted by λ. DGP D_1 has the break in the last twenty observations for $T = 100$, whereas D_2 has the breaks evenly spread (like a seasonal component). The GUM includes all impulses, and selection is at $\alpha = 0.01$.

The results can be summarized as follows:

(a) D_1: modes 2, 3, 4, 5 have (approximately) the same potency as 0 and 1, but worse gauge;

(b) D_3: mode 2 has the same potency as 0 and 1, but worse, or the same, gauge;

(c) D_3: modes 3, 4 have better potency than mode 1 for roughly the same gauge;

(d) D_3: modes 3, 4, and 5 are much slower than 0, 1 and 2.

Consequently, mode 1 is set as the default, although mode 3 could be an alternative.

19.4   Hoover–Perez experiments with $N > T$

We now compare *Autometrics* and step-wise regression when $N > T$, as forward selection is equally applicable however many variables there are relative to observations. To do so, we reconsider two Hoover–Perez DGPs (HP7 and HP8, see section 17.2.1) with $T = 139$ and 3 relevant variables, but create 10 additional irrelevant white-noise candidate regressors, and add all regressors with lag length four to the GUM. As a consequence, the GUM has 141 irrelevant variables, compared to 37 before. Automatic selection is run using *Autometrics*, first at the conventional significance of $\alpha = 0.01$, then $\alpha = 0.001$.

Table 19.2
Comparisons of step-wise and *Autometrics* when $N > T$

	HP7big	HP8big	HP7big	HP8big
		Step-wise	*Autometrics*	
1% nominal significance				
Gauge%	0.9	1.7	1.3	1.2
Potency%	99.9	50.9	96.8	100.0
DGP found%	32.2	10.0	43.3	47.2
DGP nested%	99.8	26.3	90.5	100
0.1% nominal significance				
Gauge%	0.1	0.7	0.3	0.1
Potency%	99.7	40.3	97.0	100.0
DGP found%	87.4	9.0	82.6	90.4
DGP nested%	99.6	10.5	91.2	100

Table 19.2 records the outcome at $\alpha = 0.01$. In comparison to table 17.5, there is almost no impact of the 104 additional irrelevant variables on gauge, a small fall in potency, but of course, a drop in the percentage of times the DGP is found.

The main reason for the fall in the last of these measures is the inappropriate value for $\alpha = 0.01$, which would entail about 1.4 adventitiously-significant variables being retained per replication. Using $\alpha = 0.001$, and maintaining $T = 139$, with 3 relevant and 141 irrelevant variables yields the outcomes in the second panel of table 19.2.

We see the same effect as in section 17.4.1: there is a large increase in the probability of locating the DGP relative to $\alpha = 0.01$, as the gauges are much smaller—so few of the 141 irrelevant variables are retained—yet the potencies are still fairly high. There is also a huge difference on HP8 between step-wise regression, where the DGP is found 9% of the time, and *Autometrics*, where it is found more than 90%.

Thus, despite a highly over-parametrized general model with 144 variables, of which only 3 matter, yet just 139 observations, *Autometrics* has approximately the correct gauge at $\alpha = 0.001$, and finds the DGP between 80% and 90% of the time.

19.5   Small samples with $N > T$

A question of practical importance in many contexts is whether model selection when $N > T$ still operates successfully if the sample size is

Table 19.3
Simulating $N > T$ for $T = 20$ and $N = 40$

	Average number retained		Fraction with none retained		Fraction with one retained	
α	5%	1%	5%	1%	5%	1%
Monte Carlo	2.03	0.38	0.09	0.71	0.31	0.22
Theory	2.00	0.40	0.13	0.67	0.27	0.27

small. While the following Monte Carlo simulation is simple, its evidence shows no specific additional effect when T is small, here being 20 when $N = 40$. We consider a GUM with N candidates $x_{i,t}$ for $i = 1, \ldots, 40$, all of which are IID, when the number of DGP regressors is in fact zero. The aim is to investigate whether there is an extra danger of garbage in, garbage out when selecting in small samples due to a greater chance of high correlations.

In fact, as table 19.3 shows, the simulations for $N = 40 > T = 20$ match selection theory based on $T > N$, where the average number of variables retained should be $N\alpha$, and the probability that no or one variable is retained should be $(1 - \alpha)^N$ and $N\alpha(1 - \alpha)^{N-1}$ respectively. These are shown in the line called Theory.

The close match of theory based on $T > N$ and the simulation where $N > T$ does not support an excess retention of irrelevant variables despite $N = 2T$. Notice that the conventional measure of the overall false null rejection frequency (size) ceases to make sense when $N > T$, but could still be calculated as $1 - (1 - \alpha)^N = 1 - (1 - 0.01)^{40} = 0.33$, and simply reveals that 33% of the time, at least one of the 40 variables will be retained by chance. This is similar to the above calculation that the average number of irrelevant variables retained is $N\alpha = 0.40$.

19.6   Modeling $N > T$ in practice

To illustrate the performance of *Autometrics* when $N > T$ in a setting that can be checked easily, we apply it to the artificial DGP discussed in chapter 4. There, only four variables matter, and just one lag, with $T = 159$. There is no direct location shift in the equation determining c_t, as that is mediated by Δp_t.

To make the problem match $N > T$, we have also created 20 artificial IID variables to add to the candidate set, making 24 basic variables in total, and will use a lag length of 20, including an intercept and current-dated regressors, so $N = 504$, although $T = 139$. Setting $\alpha = 0.001$, then $\alpha N = 0.503$, so on average one adventitiously-significant irrelevant variable will be retained just over half the time. The probability that no irrelevant variables will be retained despite the plethora of candidates is approximately 60%, about 30% of the time one will, and 8% of the time two will, with a negligible probability of retaining more than two irrelevant variables. This example illustrates the Monte Carlo finding in the previous section that such results hold despite $T \ll N$.

$$c_t = \underset{(0.024)}{0.83}c_{t-1} + \underset{(0.029)}{0.49}i_t - \underset{(0.033)}{0.33}i_{t-1} - \underset{(0.09)}{0.97}\Delta p_t$$

$$\widehat{\sigma} = 1.12 \quad F_{ar}(5, 130) = 0.89 \quad F_{arch}(4, 131) = 0.85$$

$$\chi^2_{nd}(2) = 0.51 \quad F_{het}(8, 130) = 0.84 \quad F_{reset}(2, 133) = 3.31^*.$$

Indeed, here *Autometrics* finds the exact DGP equation starting from almost any overspecified candidate set, with up to 20 lags, and without or with also undertaking IIS (there are no substantial outliers or breaks in the conditional model although there are in the DGP). Including IIS, $N = 643$, so a very large excess of variables over observations has to be confronted, yet *Autometrics* again delivers the DGP. The probability of retaining no irrelevant variables was just 0.526, so the outcome that none were retained was slightly lucky; that the relevant variables were retained follows from their large non-centralities.

19.7   Retaining a theory when $k + n \geq T$

The analytic approach in Johansen and Nielsen (2009) and to understanding impulse-indicator saturation (IIS) also applies for $k = T$ IID mutually-orthogonal candidate regressors under the null. Add the first $k/2$ of the variables and select at significance level $\alpha = 1/T = 1/k$. Record which are significant, then drop them. Now add the second block of $k/2$, again selecting at significance level $\alpha = 1/k$, and record which are significant in that subset. Finally, combine the recorded variables from the two stages (if any), and select again at significance level $\alpha = 1/k$. At both sub-steps, on average $\alpha k/2 = 1/2$ a variable will be retained by chance, so on average $\alpha k = 1$ will be retained from the combined stage. Under the null, one degree of freedom is lost on average. The combination of expanding and contracting block searches implemented in (e.g.) *Autometrics* can be used.

If the model also has n theory-relevant variables that are to be re-tained without selection, so $k + n = N > T$, orthogonalize the theory-relevant variables with respect to the other candidates as in section 14.2, but in blocks: under the null, doing so has no impact on the coefficients of the relevant variables, or the estimates. When $N > T$, divide the k variables into sub-blocks of smaller than $T/4$ (say), setting $\alpha = 1/N$ over-all. The selected model retains the desired sub-set of n theory-based variables at every stage, and only selects over the putative irrelevant variables at a stringent significance level.

20 Impulse-indicator Saturation for Multiple Breaks

Chapter 15 considered the theory and practice of IIS, to show that the cost of applying that approach under the null of no outliers or breaks was low at reasonably tight significance levels. A pilot Monte Carlo illustrated its ability to detect outliers and breaks. Chapter 19 discussed the algorithm in *Autometrics* for implementing IIS together with selecting variables. Since the objective of IIS is to detect and help model breaks, in this chapter, we extend the range of experiments from D_1–D_3 considered earlier. A variety of breaks is examined, from a single start or end of sample location shift, through blocks of five 4-period shifts to 20 location shifts spread across a sample of $T = 100$. When there is more than a single break, a failure to detect one increases the residual variance and so lowers the probability of detecting any others. Consequently, potency is low for small shifts, but rises quickly with the break magnitude, even in dynamic models.[1]

20.1 Impulse-indicator saturation experiments

Having established that testing T indicators need not induce a large efficiency loss when they are irrelevant, we now apply IIS to detect outliers and locations shifts when they do in fact occur. The generality of IIS allows it to detect many shifts, and we consider up to 20 breaks in 100 observations, only one, and several intermediate settings. Moreover, the shifts can be right at the start or end of the sample, as there is no need to reserve a percentage as with (say) Bai and Perron (1998), and Castle et al. (2012) show that because of this ability, IIS can avoid other breaks being camouflaged by large events in the reserved sub-samples.

---

[1]This chapter draws on research originally reported in Castle et al. (2012).

We first undertake experiments to investigate breaks in the means of location-scale models in section 20.2. Then section 20.3 considers breaks in the means of stationary autoregressions. Next, section 20.4 simulates IIS in unit-root models, then section 20.5 generalizes to autoregressions with additional regressors, including both stationary and unit-root DGPs. Success at detecting multiple breaks lays the foundations for selecting non-linear models when there are breaks or outliers in chapter 21, the application of IIS to testing super exogeneity in chapter 22, and detecting breaks near the forecast origin in chapter 23.

20.2 IIS for breaks in the mean of a location-scale model

In the first set of experiments, we examine the detectability of various forms of location shift in the simplest setting, but for a range of magnitudes, forms and timing of breaks. The DGPs considered all have $T = 100$ with 20 shifted observations, using $M = 1000$ replications to investigate

DGP:Bc a single break in the mean (starting at $T = 81$);

DGP:B20 20 breaks in the mean (starting at $T = 1$, evenly spread);

DGP:MBc multiple breaks in the mean (five breaks of length four, evenly spread);

DGP:Bct as DGP:Bc, but with a trend in both the DGP and GUM;

DGP:MBct as DGP:MBc, but with a trend in both the DGP and GUM;

DGP:Tc a break in the trend (trending from $T = 81$, with no trend before);

DGP:BL a break in the mean in a stationary autoregression with a zero mean;

DGP:BLc a break in the mean in a stationary autoregression with a non-zero mean.

Table 20.1 gives the DGPs and the GUMs from which the *Autometrics* algorithm was started. In all GUMs, the intercept was either free, so possible eliminated by selection and counted in gauge or potency, or retained, so forced into the model and not a candidate for removal (and not counted).

Table 20.2 reports the results for DGP:Bc and DGP:B20 when $\delta = 0$ (i.e. no intercept in the DGP) for $\gamma = 1, \ldots, \gamma = 5$. It is much easier to detect a single break of length 20 than twenty breaks of one period when γ is small, but the potencies rapidly rise towards unity in both cases as

Table 20.1
DGPs and GUMs for IIS experiments

DGP	Model, $y_t =$
DGP:Bc	$\delta + \gamma \left(I_{81} + \cdots + I_{100}\right) + u_t,$
DGP:B20	$\delta + \gamma \left(I_1 + I_6 + I_{11} + \cdots + I_{96}\right) + u_t,$
DGP:MBc	$\delta + \gamma \left(I_1 + I_2 + I_3 + I_4 + I_{24} + \cdots + I_{27} + I_{49} + \cdots \right.$ $\left. + I_{52} + I_{74} + \cdots + I_{77} + I_{97} + \cdots + I_{100}\right) + u_t,$
DGP:Bct	$\delta + \gamma \left(I_{81} + \cdots + I_{100}\right) + 0.02t + u_t,$
DGP:MBct	$\delta + \gamma \left(I_1 + I_2 + I_3 + I_4 + I_{24} + \cdots + I_{27} + I_{49} + \cdots \right.$ $\left. + I_{52} + I_{74} + \cdots + I_{77} + I_{97} + \cdots + I_{100}\right) + 0.02t + u_t,$
DGP:Tc	$\delta + \gamma \left(\frac{1}{20}I_{81} + \frac{2}{20}I_{82} + \cdots + \frac{20}{20}I_{100}\right) + u_t.$
DGP:BL	$\gamma \left(I_{81} + \cdots + I_{100}\right) + 0.5y_{t-1} + u_t, \ y_0 = 0,$
DGP:BLc	$1 + \gamma \left(I_{81} + \cdots + I_{100}\right) + 0.5y_{t-1} + u_t, \quad y_0 = 0,$

GUM	Model, y_t on
GUM:Ic	1, T dummies: DGP:Bc, DGP:B20, DGP:MBc, DGP:Tc;
GUM:Ict	1, T dummies, trend: DGP:Bct, DGP:MBct;
GUM:ILc	1, T dummies, y_{t-1}: DGP:BL, DGP:BLc.

Notes DGP:	$u_t \sim \mathsf{IN}[0,1]; \quad \delta = 0,1$ as noted in the text
Notes GUM:	intercept free or forced as noted in the text

Table 20.2
Autometrics IIS in location-scale DGPs with breaks at the end and multiple breaks, $\delta = 0$, constant free, $\alpha = 1\%$

	$\gamma = 0$	$\gamma = 1$	$\gamma = 2$	$\gamma = 3$	$\gamma = 4$	$\gamma = 5$
DGP:Bc						
Gauge%	1.5	1.1	0.9	0.3	0.8	1.0
Potency%	—	6.0	31.0	58.3	89.5	99.2
DGP:B20						
Gauge%	1.5	1.2	1.0	0.9	1.0	1.0
Potency%	—	4.5	11.8	32.4	73.8	94.5

γ increases to 5. While 20 shifts in a sample of 100 is unlikely in practice, the ability to find them in such a contaminated case is encouraging. Since the distorting influence of such outliers increases with their magnitude, a 90% success rate despite no information on the spread, shows that serious mis-measurement can be tackled.

Table 20.3

Autometrics and step-wise selection for IIS in location-scale (and trend) DGPs with breaks at the end and multiple breaks, $\delta = 1$. All estimated models have a constant term

	$\gamma = 3$	$\gamma = 4$	$\gamma = 5$	$\gamma = 3$	$\gamma = 4$	$\gamma = 5$
Autometrics, **constant retained**, $\alpha = 1\%$						
		DGP:Bc			DGP:Bct	
Gauge%	0.4	0.7	1.1	1.9	1.0	1.1
Potency%	54.8	86.3	99.1	41.5	76.4	97.5
		DGP:MBc			DGP:MBct	
Gauge%	0.5	0.8	1.0	0.5	0.7	1.0
Potency%	35.0	72.5	91.9	38.2	75.4	96.0
Step-wise regression, constant retained, $\alpha = 1\%$						
		DGP:Bc			DGP:Bct	
Gauge%	0.1	0.1	0.1	0.7	0.4	0.2
Potency%	9.3	12.2	13.7	6.9	6.4	5.8
		DGP:MBc			DGP:MBct	
Gauge%	0.1	0.1	0.1	0.1	0.0	0.2
Potency%	10.0	13.0	14.2	13.7	15.6	18.5

Table 20.3 reports the results for DGPs that have an intercept ($\delta = 1$) or an intercept and trend, together with a break at the end (DGP:Bc, DGP:Bct) or five breaks of four periods (DGP:MBc, DGP:MBct). The trend makes it harder to detect the single break, masking its start, but overall the potency of *Autometrics* is high. Step-wise regression fails to detect more than 20% of the breaks in all these experiments.

20.3   IIS for shifts in the mean of a stationary autoregression

Table 20.4 reports the simulation results for DGP:BL and DGP:BLc. *Autometrics* selects the wrong model for DGP:BLc when the constant is free, namely a unit-root model without a constant, but with some additional dummies. However, when the constant is always retained, the results revert back to those found in cases with zero means.

Table 20.4
Autometrics results for IIS in stationary autoregressive DGPs with breaks at the end

	DGP:BL			DGP:BLc		
	$\gamma = 5$	$\gamma = 8$	$\gamma = 10$	$\gamma = 5$	$\gamma = 8$	$\gamma = 10$
Autometrics, **constant free**, $\alpha = 1\%$						
Gauge%	1.3	1.2	1.1	1.5	1.6	1.6
Potency%	44.4	83.5	92.7	13.5	16.7	18.2
Autometrics, **constant retained**, $\alpha = 1\%$						
Gauge%	1.3	1.2	1.2	1.3	1.2	1.2
Potency%	47.8	85.9	94.3	48.8	86.7	94.4

The results illustrate that the treatment of the constant can matter greatly for *Autometrics*:

(a) Constant is free: when the constant is free, it is not selected. This is fine for DGP:BL, but not for DGP:BLc. In most cases, the model selected for DGP:BLc has one (or two) dummies at the start of the break, and a unit root, which is a good approximation to the data process but far from the DGP.

(b) Constant is always retained: when a constant enters all models, *Autometrics* has high potency to detect the correct model for both DGPs.

Consequently, we strongly recommend always retaining constants in dynamic models, as they will be close to zero if not required, but help avoid unit-root approximations to location shifts if needed (e.g., Perron, 1989, and Hendry and Neale, 1991).

20.4   IIS in unit-root models

An impulse in a unit-root model entails a step shift in the level of the series, so is the most realistic alternative in this setting. Thus, we consider the experiments listed in table 20.5.

DGUM has Δy_t as the dependent variable, while the regressors include y_{t-1}, so is an equivariant transformation of the model. However, as shown by Campos and Ericsson (1999), although such transforms leave the model error unchanged, and estimates of either can be recovered from the other, they can affect selection based on the significance of coefficient estimates. After model selection, the final model is

Table 20.5
DGPs and GUMs for IIS experiments with unit roots

DGP	Model, $y_t =$
DGP:IUc	$0.2 + \gamma I_{81} + y_{t-1} + u_t,$
DGP:BUc	$0.2 + \gamma (I_{81} + \cdots + I_{100}) + y_{t-1} + u_t,$
DGP:MIUc	$0.2 + \gamma (I_1 + I_{24} + I_{49} + I_{74} + I_{97}) + y_{t-1} + u_t,$
DGP:MBUc	$0.2 + \gamma (I_1 + \cdots + I_4 + I_{24} + \cdots + I_{27} + I_{49} + \cdots$
	$\quad + I_{52} + I_{74} + \cdots + I_{77} + I_{97} + \cdots + I_{100}) + y_{t-1} + u_t,$

GUM	Model
GUM:ILct	y_t on 1, T dummies, y_{t-1}, and trend, $t = 1, \ldots, 100$;
DGUM:ILct	Δy_t on 1, T dummies, y_{t-1}, and trend, $t = 1, \ldots, 100$.

Notes DGP:	$u_t \sim \text{IN}[0,1],\ y_{-100} = 0,\ t = -99, \ldots, 0, 1, \ldots, 100.$

Table 20.6
Autometrics results for IIS: unit-root DGP with breaks at end and multiple breaks

	GUM			DGUM		
	$\gamma = 3$	$\gamma = 4$	$\gamma = 5$	$\gamma = 3$	$\gamma = 4$	$\gamma = 5$
Autometrics, **constant retained**, $\alpha = 1\%$						
	DGP:IUc			DGP:IUc		
Gauge%	1.8	1.9	1.8	1.6	1.6	1.6
Potency%	85.1	96.7	99.8	83.5	95.6	99.7
	DGP:BUc			DGP:BUc		
Gauge%	1.5	1.5	1.5	1.0	1.1	1.3
Potency%	21.4	38.0	53.7	24.1	60.6	90.8
	DGP:MIUc			DGP:MIUc		
Gauge%	1.6	1.8	1.9	1.4	1.4	1.4
Potency%	68.6	92.1	99.1	66.5	90.0	98.6
	DGP:MBUc			DGP:MBUc		
Gauge%	1.0	2.6	3.4	0.7	0.9	1.0
Potency%	39.1	71.8	88.0	37.8	70.5	93.6

re-estimated with y_t as the dependent variable and adding y_{t-1} as a regressor if necessary.

Table 20.6 shows that gauge remains well controlled at the nominal significance level, and potency to detect the breaks is reasonably high, but rises slowly with their magnitude. Also, the transformation to DGUM varies between moderately and strongly beneficial, because it allows y_{t-1} to be eliminated more often than with the levels.

20.5   IIS in autoregressions with regressors

In the following experiments, the regressors in the DGP, denoted X, are specified as in (20.1) where β is varied across experiments, but ρ is kept fixed at 0.9 with $x_{i,0} = 0$, and $\beta^* = (T[1 - \rho])^{-1/2}\beta$, so the parameters are scaled for both the sample size and the magnitude of the autoregression to maintain a relatively constant non-centrality parameter:

$$x_t'\beta = \sum_{i=1}^{4} \beta^* (x_{i,t} - x_{i,t-1}), \tag{20.1}$$

where:

$$
\begin{aligned}
x_{i,t} &= \rho x_{i,t-1} + v_{i,t}, \quad i = 1, \dots, 10; \\
v_{i,t} &\sim \text{IN}\left[0, (1 - \rho)^2\right]; \\
\beta &= \{2.4, 3.2, 4.0\}.
\end{aligned}
$$

Similarly, the xs are generated with mean zero and unit variance. The regressors added to the GUM are as follows:

$$X = \sum_{i=1}^{10} (\gamma_i x_{i,t} + \delta_i x_{i,t-1}),$$

so there are 8 relevant regressors as in (20.1), namely four at lag zero and four at lag one, plus 12 irrelevant variables.

The experimental designs for the various DGPs and the initial GUMs are given in table 20.7, where two DGPs have no breaks for comparison. Although $S_{81} = (I_{81} + \cdots + I_{100})$, rewriting the DGP in terms of S_s affects counting for gauge and potency.

The gauge for *Autometrics* in DGP:Ucx, GUM:Lcxt is about 10% when $\rho = 0.9$, see table 20.8, because the trend is almost always included in the final model, even though it is not in the DGP. In that case, the constant may be deleted, which suggests that a GUM with retained constant and free trend would be better.

When there are breaks, as occurs all too often in practice, gauge is reasonably well controlled and potency is moderate to high, especially for the unit-root case, as table 20.9 shows.

Table 20.7

IIS experiments for autoregressions with regressors

DGP:Lcx	$y_t = 2 + 0.5y_{t-1} + x_t'\beta + u_t,$
	$y_0 = 0, t = 1, \ldots, 100,$
GUM:Lcx	y_t on 1, y_{t-1}, X, $t = 1, \ldots, 100.$
DGP:BLcx	$y_t = 2 + \gamma\, (I_{81} + \cdots + I_{100}) + 0.5y_{t-1} + x_t'\beta + u_t,$
	$y_0 = 0, t = 1, \ldots, 100,$
GUM:ILcx	y_t on 1, T dummies, y_{t-1}, X.
DGP:BLcx	$y_t = 2 + \gamma S_{81} + 0.5y_{t-1} + x_t'\beta + u_t,$
	$y_0 = 0, t = 1, \ldots, 100,$
GUM:SLcx	y_t on 1, T dummies, $T - 1$ levels, y_{t-1}, X.
DGP:Ucx	$y_t = 0.2 + y_{t-1} + x_t'\beta + u_t,$
	$y_{-100} = 0, t = -99, \ldots, 0, 1, \ldots, 100,$
GUM:Lcx	y_t on 1, y_{t-1}.
GUM:Lcxt	y_t on 1, y_{t-1}, and trend.
DGP:BUcx	$y_t = 0.2 + \gamma\, (I_{81} + \cdots + I_{100}) + y_{t-1} + x_t'\beta + u_t,$
	$y_{-100} = 0, t = -99, \ldots, 0, 1, \ldots, 100,$
GUM:ILcxt	y_t on 1, T dummies, trend, y_{t-1}, X.

Table 20.8

Autometrics results for stationary and unit-root autoregressive DGPs without breaks

	$\rho = 0$			$\rho = 0.9$		
	$\beta = 2.4$	$\beta = 3.2$	$\beta = 4.0$	$\beta = 2.4$	$\beta = 3.2$	$\beta = 4.0$
Autometrics, **constant retained**, $\alpha = 1\%$						
	DGP:Lcx, GUM:Lcx			DGP:Lcx, GUM:Lcx		
Gauge%	2.4	2.7	2.2	3.9	4.1	3.4
Potency%	41.0	61.8	81.0	34.5	55.8	78.2
	DGP:Ucx, GUM:Lcx			DGP:Ucx, GUM:Lcx		
Gauge%	2.7	2.5	1.9	2.5	2.8	2.0
Potency%	43.4	66.3	85.2	33.2	56.2	78.5
	DGP:Ucx, GUM:Lcxt			DGP:Ucx, GUM:Lcxt		
Gauge%	5.5	5.6	4.8	11.2	12.3	11.3
Potency%	42.1	63.7	83.0	34.1	53.3	71.8

Table 20.9
Autometrics results for stationary and unit-root autoregressive DGPs with breaks

	$\rho = 0$		
	$\beta = 2.4$	$\beta = 3.2$	$\beta = 4.0$
Autometrics, **constant retained**, $\alpha = 1\%$			
	DGP:BLcx, GUM:ILcx, $\gamma = 10$		
Gauge%	2.9	2.9	2.5
Potency%	57.7	59.0	61.3
	DGP:BLcx, GUM:SLcx, $\gamma = 10$		
Gauge%	3.9	4.0	3.7
Potency%	42.1	57.3	73.0
	DGP:BUcx, GUM:ILcxt, $\gamma = 5$		
Gauge%	2.2	2.4	2.4
Potency%	35.3	38.4	42.2
	DGP:BUcx,GUM:SLcxt, $\gamma = 5$		
Gauge%	3.0	3.1	3.3
Potency%	46.5	64.7	80.7

Overall, we conclude that IIS works well for detecting outliers and breaks, and can be used jointly with selecting variables, even in dynamic models. Chapter 15 established both the null rejection frequency for IIS, and the low cost of applying it when the null was true. Here we have shown its capability to detect multiple breaks when they occur. Thus, we now consider the application of IIS when selecting non-linear models to avoid spurious retention of non-linear functions which merely fit to outlying data points, and will later use IIS to test the key hypothesis of super exogeneity.

21   Selecting Non-linear Models

The selection of a non-linear model often begins from a previous linear model and adds non-linear terms. Such an approach is specific-to-general in two respects. First, between studies, advances are bound to be generalizations as new knowledge accumulates, which is in part why scientific progress is so difficult. Second, however, one should not just extend the best earlier model, which was implicitly selected to accommodate all omitted effects, but commence with an identified and congruent general non-linear approximation which enters all the linear terms unrestrictedly and includes a complete set of impulse indicators so that non-linearities do not mis-represent breaks or outliers. As a prior step, a test for non-linearity can check whether any extension is needed. We then use squares, cubics, and exponentials of the principal components of the variables to approximate a range of possible non-linearities. Once a selection has been made therefrom, if non-linear terms remain, any proposed theory-based functions (such as logistic or squashing) can be entered to check if they further simplify the approximation. Such an approach avoids the issue of lack of identification under the null and directly tests that the postulated functions are valid reductions.[1]

21.1   Introduction

There are five issues specific to selecting non-linear models that have not arisen so far in our discussion. First and foremost is the infinite range of possible forms that non-linearity can take, so some restriction is essential even to commence a selection, or discover some features of models

---

[1]This chapter draws on research originally reported in Castle and Hendry (2011b).

beyond linearity. We propose using the squares, cubics and exponentials of the principal components of the unrestricted linear regressor set to approximate a range of possible non-linearities. Such functions can accommodate large numbers of potential non-linear terms, including more than the sample size had they been entered unrestrictedly. These could also be used as a pre-test, which if it does not reject, shows that no further extension is needed and a linear specification is adopted; and if it does reject, then there is *prima facie* evidence of some form of non-linearity needing modeled.

Second, by specifying a general non-linear approximation that is always identified, a multi-path search procedure can seek a more parsimonious, congruent, non-linear model. There will often be many more non-linear terms than the sample size, but that aspect has been addressed in chapter 19 above by expanding and contracting searches. For example, the number of potential regressors for up to a cubic polynomial in K linear variables, denoted M_K, is:

$$M_K = K(K+1)(K+5)/6$$

leading to an explosion in the number of terms as K increases:

K	1	2	3	4	5	10	15	20	30	40
M_K	3	9	19	30	55	285	679	1539	5455	12300

An additional exponential adds K more terms to M_K. The separate, but related, problem of excess retention of non-linear functions due to an over-parameterized GUM is controlled by implementing a super-conservative strategy for the non-linear functions, where selection is undertaken at stringent significance levels to control the null rejection frequency.

Third, some non-linear functions can generate extreme outcomes, and the resulting fat tails can be problematic as the assumption of normality is in-built into our model selection procedure's critical values and its bias-correction routines. Equally seriously, non-linear functions can also align with outliers or contaminated data at a couple of points in the sample space, leading to such functions being retained too often. Impulse-indicator saturation removes the impact of extreme observations in both regressors and regressand to ensure near normality for inference, so is integral to our approach. Although IIS adds greatly to the number of variables, chapter 15 showed that there was little efficiency loss under the null, and in the present context, a potentially large gain by avoiding spurious non-linear terms that capture unmodeled outliers, and so jeopardize forecasts and policy.

Next, including both the linear and non-linear transformations of a variable can generate substantial collinearity, similar to slowly-varying regressors (see Phillips, 2007, for the related issue in the time-series context). We propose transforming the non-linear functions to deviations about their means, as discussed in section 17.7 for RETINA, to reduce this problem prior to undertaking model selection.

Finally, encompassing tests of specific non-linear in parameters forms against the selected model can be carried out after selection to improve parsimony and test their validity. Examples include logistic or squashing functions, transitions, or threshold variables, such as in smooth transition autoregressive models (STAR: see Teräsvirta, 1994) The proposed order of modeling also helps to avoid any potential identification problems that might arise when starting with non-linear-in-parameter models (e.g., Granger and Teräsvirta, 1993).

Joint resolution of all five of these issues is essential for a successful algorithm, and removing any step can be deleterious.

21.2   The non-linear formulation

As there are an infinite number of potential functional forms that the LDGP may take, specifying a GUM that nests the unknown LDGP is problematic. We assume the LDGP is given by:

$$y_t = f\left(z_{1,t}, \ldots, z_{k,t}; \theta\right) + \epsilon_t \text{ where } \epsilon_t \sim \mathsf{IN}\left[0, \sigma_\epsilon^2\right], \tag{21.1}$$

for $t = 1, \ldots, T$, with $\theta \in \Theta$. Three key concerns are the specification of the functional form, $f\left(\cdot\right)$, the identification of θ, and the selection of the potentially relevant variables, $z_t' = (z_{1,t}, \ldots z_{k,t})$ from an available set of candidates $(z_{1,t}, \ldots z_{K,t})$ where $K \geq k$. The formulation must allow for the possibility that a variable only enters non-linearly.

Thus, for $\phi \in \Phi$ and a specification of $g(\cdot)$, the initial GUM becomes:

$$y_t = g\left(z_{1,t}, \ldots, z_{K,t}; \phi\right) + v_t \text{ where } v_t \sim \mathsf{IN}\left[0, \sigma_v^2\right]. \tag{21.2}$$

Theory often has little definitive to say regarding the functional-form specification, so an approximating class is required from the infinite possibilities of non-linear functions. Many non-linear models, including smooth-transition regressions, regime-switching models, neural networks and non-linear equations, can be approximated by Taylor expansions, so polynomials form a flexible approximating class for a range of possible LDGPs.

21.3 Non-linear functions

A wide range of non-linear functions has been considered to approximate (21.1) including orthogonal polynomials like Hermites, Fourier series, asymptotic series and confluent hypergeometric functions. RETINA (see section 17.7) uses the following transformations:

$$\sum_{j=1}^{K}\sum_{l=1}^{K}\beta_{j,l}z_{j,i}^{\lambda_1}z_{l,i}^{\lambda_2} \quad \text{for } \lambda_1, \lambda_2 = -1, 0, 1,$$

but we exclude inverses and squared inverses due to their sufficiently high correlations with levels. Instead, we include cubic functions as these are sign preserving flexible transformations, and exponentials which can capture an ogive shape.

Polynomials are often used because of Weierstrass's approximation theorem whereby any continuous function on a closed and bounded interval can be approximated as closely as one wishes by a polynomial. A Taylor-series expansion of $g(\cdot)$ in (21.2) leads to (e.g., Priestley, 1981):

$$g\left(z_{1,t}, \ldots, z_{K,t}; \boldsymbol{\phi}\right) = \phi_0 + \sum_{j=1}^{K}\phi_{1,j}z_{j,t} + \sum_{j=1}^{K}\sum_{i=1}^{j}\phi_{2,j,i}z_{j,t}z_{i,t}$$

$$+ \sum_{j=1}^{K}\sum_{l=1}^{j}\sum_{i=1}^{l}\phi_{3,j,l,i}z_{j,t}z_{l,t}z_{i,t} + \cdots. \tag{21.3}$$

While (21.3) helps motivate the use of polynomial functions, the number of parameters increases rapidly with both the order and K, which will be exacerbated when other candidate variables and indicators are added. Moreover, the goodness of the approximation is unknown a priori in any given application, although it can be evaluated by testing against added higher-order terms. Despite the number of variables in (21.3) increasing rapidly, the inclusion of more variables than observations does not make it infeasible for an automatic algorithm, enabling greater flexibility when examining non-linear models as the number of potential regressors is already likely to be large.

21.4 The non-linear algorithm

The proposed approach is to specify a GUM that nests the LDGP in (21.1), to ensure the initial formulation is congruent, leading to the

GUM:

$$y_t = \phi_0 + \sum_{j=1}^{K} \phi_{1,j} z_{j,t} + \sum_{j=1}^{K} \sum_{i=1}^{j} \phi_{2,j,i} z_{j,t} z_{i,t} + \sum_{j=1}^{K} \sum_{l=1}^{j} \sum_{i=1}^{l} \phi_{3,j,l,i} z_{j,t} z_{l,t} z_{i,t}$$

$$+ \sum_{j=1}^{K} \phi_{4,j} \exp\left(-|z|_{j,t}\right) + \sum_{j=1}^{T} \delta_j 1_{\{j=t\}} + u_t, \tag{21.4}$$

where $1_{\{j=t\}}$ is an indicator for the ith observation. There are (M_K+K+T) candidate terms in the GUM in (21.4). However, in a time-series context, up to $s \geq 0$ lags will also be needed, increasing the dimensionality of the GUM in (21.4) to approximately $(s + 1)(M_{K+1} + K) + T$, which will often be unmanageably large.

To simplify the task, first calculate the K principal components, w_t, say, from the K potential linear regressors, z_t. As $w_t = Hz_t$ where H is the matrix of eigenvectors of the second moments of $(z_1, \ldots, z_T)$, each $w_{j,t}$ is a linear combination of all the $z_{i,t}$. Thus, terms like $w_{j,t}^2$ implicitly involve all the squares and cross products of all the $z_{i,t}$, and $w_{j,t}^3$ adds cubes and up to triple products. Consequently, the resulting $3K$ terms (including the exponential) can often approximate (21.4) in a much lower-dimensional representation, here allowing for s lags on all terms:

$$y_t = \gamma_0 + \sum_{i=0}^{s} \sum_{j=1}^{K} \gamma_{1,i,j} z_{j,t-i} + \sum_{i=0}^{s} \sum_{j=1}^{K} \gamma_{2,i,j} w_{j,t-i}^2$$

$$+ \sum_{i=0}^{s} \sum_{j=1}^{K} \gamma_{3,i,j} w_{j,t-i}^3 + \sum_{i=0}^{s} \sum_{j=1}^{K} \gamma_{4,i,j} w_{j,t-i} \exp\left(-|w_{j,t-i}|\right)$$

$$+ \sum_{i=1}^{s} \lambda_i y_{t-i} + \sum_{j=1}^{T} \delta_j 1_{\{j=t\}} + u_t. \tag{21.5}$$

Even with such a dimensionality reduction, there are $(4K + 1)(s + 1) + T$ candidate terms in (21.5).

21.5   A test-based strategy

The first stage of a test-based algorithm retains the linear variables and selects the T^* significant indicators by IIS:

$$y_t = \sum_{j=1}^{K} \beta_j z_{j,t} + \sum_{j=1}^{T^*} \delta_j 1_{\{j=t\}} + v_t. \tag{21.6}$$

The second stage then applies a test for non-linearity, such as that in Castle and Hendry (2010a), to see if it is viable to retain (21.6), equivalent to a block reduction of all the non-linear terms in (21.4). If the test does not reject, the GUM is taken to be (21.6) and the usual selection algorithm in *Autometrics* is applied to select the relevant regressors. If the test rejects, non-linearity is established, and section 21.6 considers the resulting problems that need resolved for a viable approach. Nevertheless, this strategy is manifestly simple to general, and important linear effects may have been missed at the first stage because of confounding with unmodeled non-linearities.

21.6 Problems in directly selecting non-linear models

A number of problems arise when selecting from a GUM like (21.4) that consists of a large set of polynomial regressors. These problems include collinearity, non-normality and excess retention of irrelevant regressors. Moreover, there may be good grounds for anticipating a specific non-linear function as a simplification of the general polynomial, and that possibility must be accommodated. Solutions to all of these problems are proposed, confirming the feasibility of the non-linear model selection strategy.

21.6.1 Collinearity

A linear model is equivariant under linear transformations, and so could be defined by various isomorphic representations, which nevertheless deliver different inter-correlations. Since collinearity is not invariant under linear transformations, it is a property of the parametrization of the model and not the variables *per se*. Non-linear transformations can have substantial collinearity between the linear and non-linear functions as well as within the latter. Adding an irrelevant variable x_t^2 to a linear model of y_t on x_t can increase collinearity dramatically from zero between x_t and x_t^2 when $E[x_t] = 0$, to almost perfect collinearity when $E[x_t]$ is large. As discussed in chapter 17, double de-meaning the generated polynomial functions prior to formulating the GUM can resolve this issue, but will not remove all collinearity between higher-order polynomials. Orthogonalization by a Choleski decomposition (e.g., Rushton, 1951) could cross-link relevant and irrelevant variables, although that risk remains for an approach like (21.5).

21.6.2 Non-normality

Normality is a central assumption for model selection when conventional critical values are used, so null rejection frequencies would be incorrect for non-normality. Normality tends to be more important for selection (when many decisions are made) than inference in the LDGP. In non-linear models, normality becomes an even more essential requirement. Problems arise when extreme observations result in fat-tailed distributions, as there is an increased probability that non-linear functions may align with extreme observations, effectively acting as indicators, and therefore being retained too often. This can be illustrated by considering a simple case in which an outlier is represented by an indicator variable, $1_{\{t=s\}}$, which takes the value 1 for observation s and 0 otherwise.

Consider a regression between two unconnected variables:

$$y_t = \beta x_t + \delta 1_{\{t=s\}} + u_t, \tag{21.7}$$

$$x_t = \gamma 1_{\{t=s\}} + v_t, \tag{21.8}$$

where $\beta = 0$. If the indicator is omitted from the model, so $y_t = \beta x_t + u_t$ is estimated, $\widehat{\beta}$ is:

$$
\begin{aligned}
\widehat{\beta} = \frac{\sum x_t y_t}{\sum x_t^2} &= \frac{\delta\gamma \sum 1_{\{t=s\}}^2 + \sum (\delta v_t + \gamma u_t) 1_{\{t=s\}} + \sum v_t u_t}{\gamma^2 \sum 1_{\{t=s\}}^2 + 2\gamma \sum v_t 1_{\{t=s\}} + \sum v_t^2}, \\[2mm]
&= \frac{\delta\gamma + (\delta v_s + \gamma u_s) + \sum v_t u_t}{\gamma^2 + 2\gamma v_s + \sum v_t^2},
\end{aligned}
\tag{21.9}
$$

as $\sum 1_{\{t=s\}}^2 = 1$. Also:

$$\mathsf{V}\left[\widehat{\beta}\right] = \frac{\widehat{\sigma}_u^2}{\sum x_t^2} \tag{21.10}$$

and:

$$t_{\widehat{\beta}} = \frac{\widehat{\beta}\sqrt{\sum x_t^2}}{\widehat{\sigma}_u} = \frac{\sum x_t y_t}{\widehat{\sigma}_u \sqrt{\sum x_t^2}}. \tag{21.11}$$

Hence, if we approximate by $v_s = u_s = 0$, $\widehat{\sigma}_u = 1$, $\gamma/\widehat{\sigma}_v = 1$ and $\sum v_t u_t \approx 0$, then:

$$t_{\widehat{\beta}}^2 = \frac{\delta^2 \gamma^2}{\gamma^2 + T}. \tag{21.12}$$

To illustrate this phenomenon, suppose $\delta = 6$, $\gamma = 5$, and $N = 100$. Then:

$$t_{\hat{\beta}}^2 = \frac{6^2 \times 5^2}{5^2 + 100} = 7.2. \tag{21.13}$$

Thus, a single outlier needs to be quite large for this effect to matter, but is plausible when considering non-linear transformations.

21.6.3   Impulse-indicator saturation

One concern with non-linearity is that it is difficult to distinguish between extreme observations that are outliers and extreme observations that are due to the non-linearity in the data. Not removing outliers has the dangers just seen of spurious non-linearity. Conversely, methods that remove extreme observations could be in danger of removing the underlying non-linearity that should be modeled. IIS, discussed in chapter 15, enables any outliers to be modeled, rather than removed, ensuring that the selection process will not be biased in favor of non-linear functions that are proxying outliers, nor against genuine non-linearity when the indicators will be eliminated as the non-linear terms operate for all T.

21.6.4   Super-conservative strategy

Irrelevant non-linear functions are likely to be detrimental to both modeling and forecasting, so non-linear functions should only be retained if there is definite evidence of non-linearity. Given a preference for linear models unless there is strong evidence for non-linearity, and the possible excess retention of irrelevant functions due to the large number of non-linear functions tested, stringent critical values are needed compared to linear models. All the terms in the linear GUM could be retained together with any selected indicators while the non-linear functions are selected at a tight significance level, then a free selection made over those that were retained together with the variables from the GUM at a looser level. That last step would check if any indicators were now irrelevant as well as whether some linear terms were unnecessary. The critical values used should depend on the number of functions included in the model and the sample size, although as with all significance levels, the choice also depends on the preferences of the investigator.

21.6.5   Parsimonious encompassing

Finally, specific non-linear forms, including logistic, transition, or threshold functions (like STAR), may be suggested a priori as an appropriate formulation. These are non-linear-in-parameters and hence difficult to include in a selection process. Moreover, potential identification problems arise by starting with such functions when the null of linearity holds (e.g., Granger and Teräsvirta, 1993). The proposed order of modeling here avoids that last problem, as linearity has been rejected by this stage. The orthogonal polynomial approximation is also easy to include in the selection approach despite the large number of candidate variables.

For example, using a third-order Taylor expansion, one can approximate a logistic smooth transition model (LSTR: see e.g., Teräsvirta, 1994) in a variable s_t given by:

$$y_t = \beta' z_t + \theta' z_t \left[1 + \exp\left(\gamma\{s_t - c\}/\widehat{\sigma}_s\right)\right]^{-1} + v_t,$$

where γ determines the rapidity of the transition from 0 to 1 as a function of the transition variable, s_t with standard deviation $\widehat{\sigma}_s$, and c determines the transition point, by:

$$y_t \simeq \beta' z_t + (\theta' z_t) \left[\frac{1}{2} + \frac{w_t}{4} - \frac{w_t^3}{48}\right] + v_t, \tag{21.14}$$

where $w_t = \gamma(s_t - c)/\widehat{\sigma}_s$. Then (21.14) can be estimated as:

$$y_t \simeq \delta_1' z_t + \delta_2' z_t s_t + \delta_3' z_t s_t^2 + \delta_4' z_t s_t^3 + v_t. \tag{21.15}$$

When z_t is a scalar:

$$\delta_1 = \beta + \frac{\theta}{2} - \frac{\theta\gamma c}{4\widehat{\sigma}_s} + \frac{\theta\gamma^3 c^3}{48\widehat{\sigma}_s^3},$$

$$\delta_2 = \frac{\theta\gamma}{4\widehat{\sigma}_s} - \frac{3\theta\gamma^3 c^2}{48\widehat{\sigma}_s^3},$$

$$\delta_3 = \frac{3\theta\gamma^3 c}{48\widehat{\sigma}_s^3},$$

$$\delta_4 = -\frac{\theta\gamma^3}{48\widehat{\sigma}_s^3}.$$

Thus, (21.15) could be used to select the relevant elements without non-linear estimation or potential lack of identification even if there is no transition effect, together with non-linear terms in z_t if desired.

Nevertheless, polynomial-based terminal models may not be in the desired class. Encompassing tests of specific non-linear functions against the selected model can be carried out after selection to test their validity and improve parsimony if that is accepted. If they are indeed the correct specification of non-linearity, or even just a better approximation, then adding them to the terminal model should lead to: (a) their being significant; and (b) the polynomial terms becoming insignificant. Both are needed to validate the complete simplification, so an indirect advantage of the approach here is to reveal when the specific non-linear functions matter, but need augmented by other non-linearities.

To achieve a successful algorithm, it is essential to jointly implement all five developments: double de-meaning transformations to reduce non-orthogonality; IIS to handle outliers; tight significance levels to avoid excess retention of irrelevant non-linear functions; an ability to handle more variables than observations; encompassing tests of the preferred non-linear specification. Removing any one of these component would be deleterious. Castle and Hendry (2014b) implement model selection for non-linear dynamic equations with more candidate variables than observations using IIS in an empirical model of real wages in the UK over 1860–2011. They confirm the need for joint modeling of dynamics, location shifts, relevant variables and non-linearities as failing to include any of these features led to included variables that were important when selected in their general model being insignificant in restricted formulations.

22   Testing Super Exogeneity

An automatically computable test is described, with null rejection frequencies that are close to the nominal size, and potency for failures of super exogeneity. Impulse-indicator saturation is undertaken in the marginal models of the putative exogenous variables that enter the conditional model contemporaneously, and all significant outcomes are recorded. These indicators from the marginal models are added to the conditional model and tested for significance. Under the null of super exogeneity, the test has the correct gauge for a range of sizes of marginal-model saturation tests, both when those processes are constant, and when they undergo shifts in either mean or variance. Failures of super exogeneity from a violation of weak exogeneity are shown to be detectable when there are location shifts in the marginal models. The distribution and potency of the test are derived and simulated, with an application to testing super exogeneity for UK consumers' expenditure.[1]

22.1   Background

Parameter invariance is essential in policy models, otherwise the fitted model will mis-predict under regime shifts or structural breaks. Thus, super exogeneity is a crucial requirement for economic policy as it combines parameter invariance with valid conditioning. The Lucas (1976) critique challenged the use of conditional econometric models for policy analysis, exemplified by his syllogism [p.41]:

> 'Given that the structure of an econometric model consists of optimal decision rules for economic agents, and that optimal decision

---

[1] This chapter draws on research originally reported in Hendry and Santos (2010), by permission of Oxford University Press.

*rules vary systematically with changes in the structure of series
relevant to the decision maker, it follows that any change in policy
will systematically alter the structure of econometric models.'*

This is essentially a theoretical claim denying super exogeneity under regime shifts. Thus, the Lucas critique is testable directly via tests of
super exogeneity or indirectly via its encompassing implications. The
fundamental weakness in Lucas's claim is the assertion that "optimal
decision rules vary systematically with changes in the structure of series relevant to the decision maker", which need not apply to contingent decisions, and hence need not affect conditional relationships. To
date, few investigators have found any evidence of induced instabili-
ties following policy regime changes: see Ericsson and Irons (1994) who
overview the literature, and Hendry (1995a) who discusses the interpretation and testing of the critique. However, Psaradakis and Sola (1996)
claim existing tests have low power, and indeed Favero and Hendry
(1992) showed that location shifts were essential for detecting the critique, while Hendry and Doornik (1997) and Hendry (2000b) confirmed
that other shifts in parameters are nearly undetectable. Consequently,
we will focus on tests of super exogeneity when location shifts occur in
the marginal processes. In any case, that is the relevant setting as few
regime shifts are "mean preserving spreads", and almost all involve location shifts.

Most super-exogeneity tests are of cross-linkages between equations,
which need not be conditional relations. Engle et al. (1983) introduced
the three relevant exogeneity concepts, and Engle and Hendry (1993)
proxied the effects of changes in the moments of conditioning variables
on parameter estimates as one test of super exogeneity. Favero and
Hendry (1992) derived a test of the impact of non-constant marginals
on conditional models. Jansen and Teräsvirta (1996) introduced a STAR
model based test, and Krolzig and Toro (2002) proposed a deterministic-
shift co-breaking test of whether breaks cancel between processes, so
some linear combinations are invariant to breaks. Encompassing tests
of the Lucas critique include Hendry (1988) for feedback versus feed-
forward models, who showed that when both of those models are constant, but the marginal process is not, then the feedback model cannot be
derived from any feed-forward structure. However, most tests of super
exogeneity need to be customized to specific settings.

An automatically computable test, like those for autocorrelated errors, say, would be invaluable, and one can be based on impulse-
indicator saturation. Such an automatic test of super exogeneity is one

which can be computed without additional user intervention and with no ex ante knowledge of the timings, forms or magnitudes of breaks in the marginal processes for the conditioning variables, nor how the parameters of the conditional model will alter as a result. Moreover, the conditional model should not need to be over-identified. This can be achieved when the breaks in the marginal models are determined by IIS, using automatic *Gets* to develop congruent, undominated models of their LDGPs: the first stage is shown in section 22.5 to have the desired null retention frequency. Then the significant indicators are added to the conditional model and tested for significance. This second stage also has the desired null rejection frequency (when there are no unit roots), and has power against failures of super exogeneity when location shifts occur, as we now explain.

Section 22.2 formulates the joint system from which the conditional model is derived in section 22.3, leading to the description of the test procedure in section 22.4. Monte Carlo evidence on the null retention frequencies (gauges) is presented in section 22.5. The super-exogeneity test under the alternative is considered in section 22.6, followed by simulations of the power of the test in section 22.7, and compared with the optimal, but infeasible, test in section 22.8. An illustration to UK consumers' expenditure completes the chapter in section 22.9.

22.2 Formulation of the statistical system

We use the same notation as in chapter 6, so let the DGP $D_X(X_T^1, \psi)$ of the T observations on the n-dimensional vector of random variables $\{x_t\}$ be sequentially then conditionally factorized as:

$$\prod_{t=1}^{T} D_x\left(x_t \mid X_{t-1}^{t-s}, \theta\right) = \prod_{t=1}^{T} D_{y|z}\left(y_t \mid z_t, X_{t-1}^{t-s}, \phi_1\right) D_z\left(z_t \mid X_{t-1}^{t-s}, \phi_2\right),$$

$$(22.1)$$

where $x_t' = \left(y_t' : z_t'\right)$ and $\phi = \left(\phi_1' : \phi_2'\right)' = f(\theta) \in \mathbb{R}^k$. If the parameters of the y and z processes are variation free (e.g., Engle et al., 1983, and Hendry, 1995a), then z_t is weakly exogenous for the parameters of interest $\beta = h(\phi_1)$. However, those conditions do not rule out that ϕ_1 may change if ϕ_2 is changed. Super exogeneity adds parameter invariance in the conditional process such that:

$$\frac{\partial \phi_1}{\partial \phi_2'} = 0.$$

When $D_x(\cdot)$ is the multivariate normal distribution and y_t is a scalar:

$$\begin{pmatrix} y_t \\ z_t \end{pmatrix} \sim \text{IN}_n \left[\begin{pmatrix} \mu_{1,t} \\ \mu_{2,t} \end{pmatrix}, \begin{pmatrix} \sigma_{11,t} & \sigma'_{12,t} \\ \sigma_{12,t} & \Omega_{22,t} \end{pmatrix} \right], \tag{22.2}$$

where $\mu_{1,t}$ and $\mu_{2,t}$ are functions of X_{t-1}, and may also shift.

To interpret the parameters of interest $\beta = h(\phi_1)$, we let the economic theory formulation entail:

$$\mu_{1,t} = \mu_0 + \beta' \mu_{2,t}, \tag{22.3}$$

which could be a feed-forward policy rule linking expected values of targets and instruments where β is the reaction parameter, or an agent's decision rule where the $\mu_{i,t}$ are (say) planned, expected, or "permanent" components. In terms of the Lucas critique, in a conditional model, the expectations $\mu_{2,t}$ would be incorrectly modeled by z_t.

22.3   The conditional model

From (22.2) and (22.3):

$$\begin{aligned} \mathsf{E}\left[y_t \mid z_t\right] &= \mu_{1,t} + \sigma'_{12,t}\Omega_{22,t}^{-1}\left(z_t - \mu_{2,t}\right) \\ &= \mu_0 + \gamma'_{1,t} + \gamma'_{2,t} z_t, \end{aligned} \tag{22.4}$$

where $\gamma'_{2,t} = \sigma'_{12,t}\Omega_{22,t}^{-1}$ and $\gamma_{1,t} = (\beta - \gamma_{2,t})'\mu_{2,t}$. The most important implications are that $\gamma_{1,t}$ depends on $\mu_{2,t}$ when $\beta \neq \gamma_{2,t}$, so location shifts in the marginal process are reflected in the conditional, and thereby induce changes in (22.4). Thus, IIS is a natural tool for detecting $\gamma_{1,t} \neq 0$.

The conditional variance is $\omega_t^2 = \sigma_{11,t} - \sigma'_{12,t}\Omega_{22,t}^{-1}\sigma_{12,t}$ and when $\sigma_{12,t}$, $\Omega_{22,t}$ are constant, the conditional relation becomes the conventional regression model for $t = 1, \ldots, T$:

$$y_t = \mu_0 + \beta' z_t + \epsilon_t \text{ where } \epsilon_t \sim \text{IN}\left[0, \omega^2\right]. \tag{22.5}$$

This requires $\beta = \gamma_2$, which is testable if $\mu_{2,t}$ shifts. The parameters of the conditional and marginal densities are:

$$\phi_{1,t} = \left(\mu_0 : \gamma_{1,t} : \gamma_{2,t} : \omega_t^2\right) \text{ and } \phi_{2,t} = \left(\mu_{2,t} : \Omega_{22,t}\right).$$

Three conditions are needed for z_t to be super exogenous for (β, ω^2):

1. $\gamma_{2,t} = \gamma_2$ is constant $\forall t$, which requires $\sigma'_{12,t}\Omega_{22,t}^{-1}$ to be constant;
2. $\beta = \gamma_2$, which requires z_t to be weakly exogenous for β;

3. (β, ω^2) is invariant to a class of relevant interventions C^{ϕ_2} on ϕ_2 in the marginal processes.

Together, 1 & 2 entail that $\gamma_{1,t} = 0$ in (22.4), so that $E[y_t|z_t]$ does not depend on $\mu_{2,t}$. If all three conditions 1–3 are satisfied:

$$E\left[y_t \mid z_t\right] = \mu_0 + \beta' z_t, \tag{22.6}$$

where β is invariant to interventions which change ϕ_2, so z_t is super exogenous for β. This outcome requires $\sigma'_{12,t} = \beta'\Omega_{22,t}$ $\forall t$, so the means $\mu_{1,t}$ and $\mu_{2,t}$ in (22.3) must be interrelated by the same β as the covariances $\sigma_{12,t}$ are with the variances $\Omega_{22,t}$. Under super exogeneity, therefore, the joint density in (22.2) becomes:

$$\left(\begin{array}{c} y_t \\ z_t \end{array}\right) \sim \mathsf{IN}_n \left[\left(\begin{array}{c} \mu_0 + \beta'\mu_{2,t} \\ \mu_{2,t} \end{array}\right), \left(\begin{array}{cc} \omega^2 + \beta'\Omega_{22,t}\beta & \beta'\Omega_{22,t} \\ \Omega_{22,t}\beta & \Omega_{22,t} \end{array}\right)\right], \tag{22.7}$$

so the conditional-marginal factorization is:

$$\left(\begin{array}{c} y_t \mid z_t \\ z_t \end{array}\right) \sim \mathsf{IN}_n \left[\left(\begin{array}{c} \mu_0 + \beta'z_t \\ \mu_{2,t} \end{array}\right), \left(\begin{array}{cc} \omega^2 & 0' \\ 0 & \Omega_{22,t} \end{array}\right)\right]. \tag{22.8}$$

Thus, the parameters $(\mu_{2,t}, \Omega_{22,t})$ can change in the marginal model:

$$z_t \sim \mathsf{IN}_{n-1}\left[\mu_{2,t}, \Omega_{22,t}\right] \tag{22.9}$$

without altering the parameters of (22.5). Deterministic-shift co-breaking then occurs in (22.7) as $(1 : \beta')x_t$ is independent of $\mu_{2,t}$ (see Hendry and Massmann, 2007, and for a related test, Krolzig and Toro, 2002). If z_t is not super exogenous for β, changes in the marginal process (22.9) should affect the conditional model (22.5) through $\gamma_{1,t}$. When (22.3) holds, so $\mu_{1,t} = \mu_0 + \beta'\mu_{2,t}$, then from (22.4):

$$E\left[y_t \mid z_t\right] = \mu_0 + \left(\beta - \gamma_{2,t}\right)' \mu_{2,t} + \gamma'_{2,t}z_t = \mu_0 + \beta'z_t + \left(\gamma'_{2,t} - \beta'\right)v_{2,t}, \tag{22.10}$$

where $v_{2,t}$ is the error on the marginal model:

$$z_t = \mu_{2,t} + v_{2,t} \text{ where } v_{2,t} \sim \mathsf{IN}_{n-1}\left[0, \Omega_{22,t}\right]. \tag{22.11}$$

Thus, tests for the largest outliers $v_{2,t}$ in the marginal process shifting the conditional model via $(\gamma'_{2,t} - \beta')v_{2,t}$ would reveal a failure of super exogeneity. Since IIS implements the former from the evidence presented above, we focus on the ability of significant indicators from (22.11) to reveal such dependence.

22.4   The test procedure

The first stage is impulse-indicator saturation in the marginal processes, automatically selecting over the variables and lags in an extended VAR, retaining indicators at the significance level α_1, where s denotes the selected lag length and with m selected impulse dummies:

$$z_t = \pi_0 + \sum_{j=1}^{s} \Pi_j x_{t-j} + \sum_{i=1}^{m} \rho_{i,\alpha_1} 1_{\{t=t_i\}} + v_{2,t}^*. \tag{22.12}$$

The coefficients of the significant indicators are denoted ρ_{i,α_1} for significance level α_1 in (22.12). Each indicator is kept if:

$$\left| t_{\widehat{\rho}_{i,\alpha_1}} \right| > c_{\alpha_1}. \tag{22.13}$$

The timing of the retained indicators is the only information required for the test. The dependence of the final test on the choice of α_1 is investigated in section 22.5.

The second stage adds the m retained indicators from the marginal models to the conditional equation:

$$y_t = \mu_0 + \beta' z_t + \sum_{i=1}^{m} \tau_{i,\alpha_2} 1_{\{t=t_i\}} + \epsilon_t \tag{22.14}$$

and conducts the F_{SE}-test for the joint significance of $(\tau_{1,\alpha_2} \ldots \tau_{m,\alpha_2})$ at level α_2. Under the null of super exogeneity, the test should be F-distributed, exactly for fixed regressors, approximately in dynamic models as conditioning on z_t implies taking $v_{2,t}$ as fixed in the conditional model. Under the null, indicators are retained in the conditional model when:

$$\left| t_{\widehat{\tau}_i} \right| > c_{\alpha_2}, \tag{22.15}$$

so the probability of retaining that indicator is:

$$P\left(\left| t_{\widehat{\tau}_i} \right| > c_{\alpha_2} \,\Big|\, \left| t_{\widehat{\rho}_{i,\alpha_1}} \right| > c_{\alpha_1} \right) = P\left(\left| t_{\widehat{\tau}_i} \right| > c_{\alpha_2} \right) = \alpha_2, \tag{22.16}$$

since (22.13) holds. This probability only depends on c_{α_2} used in the decision for the conditional, and not on α_1. Thus, the null rejection frequency of the F_{SE}-test on (22.14) should not depend on the choice of α_1 in (22.12), and must not do so if a fixed set of critical values are to be reliable, so we now address that issue.

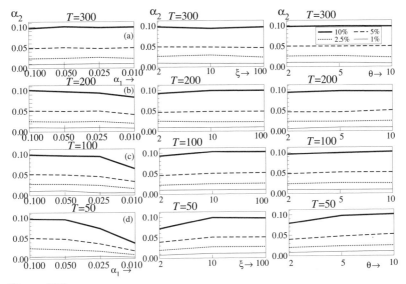

Figure 22.1
Gauges of F_{SE}-tests as α_1, ξ or θ vary in marginal

22.5 Monte Carlo evidence on null rejection frequencies

To check the analysis, we consider three marginal processes in all of which super exogeneity holds as the null. First, no breaks, where we explore the impact of different choices of α_1. Second, a mean shift in the marginal process, denoted ξ, and third, a variance change, denoted θ, both of which are conducted at $\alpha_1 = 2.5\%$. The baseline DGP is the simple bivariate system:

$$\begin{pmatrix} y_t \\ z_t \end{pmatrix} \sim \text{IN}_2 \left[\begin{pmatrix} 2 \\ 1 \end{pmatrix}, \begin{pmatrix} 21 & 10 \\ 10 & 5 \end{pmatrix} \right], \tag{22.17}$$

so $\beta = 2 = \gamma$ and $\omega^2 = 1$. Impulse-indicator saturation in these Monte Carlo experiments uses a partition of $T/2$, with $M = 10000$ replications (using just the sample-split algorithm, not *Autometrics*). Changes in the marginal process occur at $T_1 = 0.8T$ in the second and third cases.

Figure 22.1 records the null rejection frequencies (gauges) of F_{SE}-tests in the three cases (shown in columns) for four different sample sizes, $T = 300, 200, 100$, and 50 (rows), as functions of α_2 (vertical axis). In the first column, the outcomes are for four values of α_1, whereas in the second and third cases they are for three values of ξ or θ respectively. At the largest sample sizes, the lines are flat, showing no dependence of the gauge in the conditional test on α_1, ξ or θ at all four choices of α_2. However, combinations of small values of α_1 with loose values of α_2 are inappropriate at small sample sizes, since if (say) $\alpha_1 = 0.01$ and $T = 50$, under the null no indicators will be retained in many replications so the test cannot be computed half the time, leading to a gauge of 5% when the nominal size is 10%. This is offset when there are shifts in the marginal process, since then indicators are usually retained, explaining the upward drift in the second and third columns at loose values of α_2.

22.6   Non-null rejection frequency

Under the alternative, the test should reject in a variety of situations, and can be automated to make super exogeneity an easily tested hypothesis. Intuitively, significant indicators in (22.12) capture outliers not explained by its regressors, corresponding to the largest values of $\{v_{2,t}\}$, which will enter (22.10) through approximating the term $(\beta - \gamma_{2,t})' \mu_{2,t}$ when $\beta \neq \gamma_{2,t}$.

To formalize this intuition, the analysis proceeds in three steps. First, the non-null rejection frequency of the first stage in the test procedure, namely the potency to retain each indicator in the marginal models, follows from the analysis of IIS in chapter 15. Any retention of irrelevant indicators will lower the potency of the proposed F-test, by increasing the degrees-of-freedom, so the choice of α_1 has to trade off keeping too few relevant marginal indicators against any adventitiously significant irrelevant ones. Secondly, we next consider the main determinants of potency at the second stage, where the significant marginal indicators are added to (22.14) when the marginal model is non-constant due to a single location shift, and weak exogeneity does not hold in the conditional. Thirdly, section 22.7 presents simulation evidence on the potency of the super exogeneity test in that setting.

The central case of a super-exogeneity violation is from a weak exogeneity failure when the marginal models are non-constant:

$$E[y_t \mid z_t] = \mu + \gamma' z_t + (\beta - \gamma)' \mu_{2,t}. \tag{22.18}$$

Here we consider a single location shift in the marginals at time T_1:

$$z_t = \mu_{2,t} + v_{2,t} = \lambda 1_{\{t > T_1\}} + v_{2,t}, \tag{22.19}$$

so that:

$$E[y_t \mid z_t] = \mu + \gamma' z_t + (\beta - \gamma)' \lambda 1_{\{t > T_1\}}. \tag{22.20}$$

The length of the break is $T - T_1 + 1 = Tr$ and let $\mathsf{p}_{\lambda,\alpha_1}$ denote the probability of retaining each relevant indicator in the marginal when selecting at significance level α_1. Hendry and Santos (2010) derived the non-centralities for this unknown break date and form, allowing for the stage-1 pre-test for significant indicators.

Stacking the significant indicators from (22.14) in the vector ι_t, then adding ι_t to (22.18) yields the regression:

$$y_t = \tau_0 + \tau_1' z_t + \tau_2 \iota_t + e_t. \tag{22.21}$$

As the test has an approximate F distribution under the null, the total number of retained indicators matters, and we denote the average degrees of freedom by $Ts = T(\mathsf{p}_{\lambda,\alpha_1} r + \alpha_1)$, although often fewer than α_1 irrelevant indicators are retained on average when the null is false. The potency of $\mathsf{F}_{\mathsf{SE}}(T(1-s) - n, Ts)$ for H_0: $\tau_2 = 0$ in (22.21) depends on

(a) the strengths of the super-exogeneity violations, $\delta_i = (\beta_i - \gamma_i)$;

(b) the magnitudes of the breaks, λ_i, both directly in (22.20), and through their detectability, $\mathsf{p}_{\lambda,\alpha_1}$, in the marginal models, and so on α_1;

(c) the sample size T;

(d) the relative number of periods r affected by the breaks;

(e) the significance level of the test, α_2; and

(f) the number of irrelevant indicators retained, depending on α_1.

Hendry and Santos (2010) treat ι_t in (22.21) as containing all Tr relevant indicators, each with probability $\mathsf{p}_{\lambda,\alpha_1} > 0$. The derivation of the test's non-centrality and its resulting power are described in their paper. Perhaps the most useful expression is for the non-centrality, denoted φ_s^2, when λ is large and $n = 2$, where they show:

$$\varphi_s^2 \xrightarrow[\lambda \to \infty]{} \frac{T(1-r)^2 (\beta - \gamma)^2 \sigma_{22}}{\sigma_\epsilon^2}. \tag{22.22}$$

This outcome uses a χ^2 approximation and lets $\mathsf{p}_{\lambda,\alpha_1} \to 1$ but usefully reflects that potency depends on:

(a) the strength of the violation of weak exogeneity in $(\beta - \gamma)^2$;

(b) the signal-noise ratio $\sigma_{22}/\sigma_\epsilon^2$;

(c) the loss of power from a longer break length $(1-r)^2$ when using IIS; and

(d) the sample size, T.

Moreover, the optimal value of the non-centrality, φ_r^2 for a known break date and form, such that a single indicator variable $1_{\{t>T_1\}}$ is added for the test, is:

$$\varphi_r^2 \xrightarrow[\lambda \to \infty]{} \frac{T(\beta - \gamma)^2 \sigma_{22}}{\sigma_\epsilon^2}. \tag{22.23}$$

Thus, despite adding Tr indicators when nothing known about the failure of super exogeneity, the potency of the IIS-based super-exogeneity test grows rapidly as λ increases, and is close to the optimal value when r is not too large.

22.7 Simulating the potency of the super-exogeneity test

We consider the failure of weak exogeneity under non-constancy when $\beta \neq \gamma$, but $\mu_{1,t} = \beta \mu_{2,t}$ holds in both regimes, with:

$$\mu_{2,t} = \lambda 1_{\{t>T_1\}} + \mu_{2,0}, \tag{22.24}$$

so that:

$$\mu_{1,t} = \beta \lambda 1_{\{t>T_1\}} + \beta \mu_{2,0} = \beta \lambda 1_{\{t>T_1\}} + \mu_{1,0}. \tag{22.25}$$

We allow $\beta \lambda$ to vary by setting $d = \lambda/\sqrt{\sigma_{22}}$ at 1, 2, 2.5, 3 and 4 where β is 0.75, 1, 1.5 and 1.75 when $\gamma = 2$. There are $M = 10000$ replications for $T = 100$ and $T = 300$, with several break points T_1, and different choices of α_1 and α_2. The split-half IIS implementation in the marginal model used a partition of $T/2$

22.7.1 Level shift in marginal: no weak exogeneity

Table 22.1 shows the potencies for $F_{SE}(T(1-s) - n, Ts)$ at $\alpha_1 = \alpha_2 = 5\%$ when $T = 300$ and $T_1 = 251$. As expected, the potencies increase with decreases in β and increase with d. Potencies are never smaller when r diminishes, probably because the degrees of freedom of the F-test are smaller; and are never higher for a more stringent α_2, though they are not much affected by changes in α_1 over the range 0.05 to 0.01.

22.8 Power of the optimal infeasible test

The optimal infeasible test is a step indicator-based t-test matching a known break location in the marginal process. Here we use $\alpha_2 = 2.5\%$,

Table 22.1
Potencies for a level shift at $T_1 = 251$ when $T = 300$

d	$\beta = 0.75$	$\beta = 1.0$	$\beta = 1.5$	$\beta = 1.75$
1.0	0.191	0.152	0.077	0.053
2.0	0.972	0.936	0.528	0.149
2.5	0.999	0.993	0.917	0.338
3.0	1.000	1.000	0.998	0.652
4.0	1.000	1.000	1.000	0.967

Table 22.2
Power of the t-test for a level shift with known break location and form when $T = 100$ with $T_1 = 80$

d	$\beta = 0.75$	$\beta = 1.0$	$\beta = 1.5$	$\beta = 1.75$
1.0	1.000	0.994	0.404	0.083
2.0	1.000	1.000	0.930	0.247
2.5	1.000	1.000	0.973	0.326
3.0	1.000	1.000	0.985	0.380
4.0	1.000	1.000	0.988	0.432

when $T = 100$ with a mean shift at $T_1 = 80$, so that an indicator variable with 20 correct values of unity is always included in the conditional model. Table 22.2 records the outcomes.

Comparing tables 22.1 and 22.2, an automatic test based on marginal impulse saturation loses potency for small breaks relative to this optimal infeasible test. Consequently, Castle et al. (2013) propose step-indicator saturation to detect location shifts in marginal processes as the first stage, and demonstrate much higher potencies.

22.9   Testing exogeneity in DHSY

We now implement the IIS test for the super exogeneity of the parameters of the conditional model in response to changes in the marginal processes for the UK consumers' expenditure model (16.5) in chapter 16. To do so requires building "automatic" models for the LDGPs of the two main conditioning variables, y_t and $\Delta_4 p_t$.

Linear representations with 1-5 lags in c and y, and 1-2 in $\Delta_4 p_t$ with a constant and trend were formulated and selected with IIS at $\alpha = 0.025$

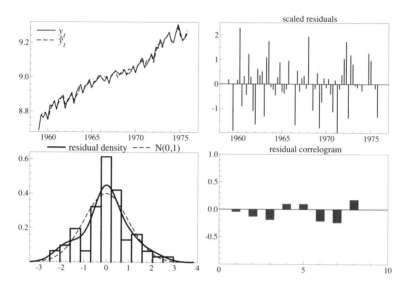

Figure 22.2
Fitted and actual values, residuals and graphical statistics for y_t

using *Autometrics*. The equation selected for y_t over 1959(1)–1975(4) was, retaining both the constant and trend:

$$y_t = 0.87y_{t-1} + 0.43c_{t-4} - 0.49c_{t-5} + 0.0013t$$
$$\quad\;\; (0.08) \qquad\quad (0.046) \qquad\;\; (0.07) \qquad\quad (0.0005)$$

$$+ 0.042I_{59(2)} + 0.050I_{66(1)} - 0.054I_{66(2)} - 0.049I_{68(2)}$$
$$\quad (0.016) \qquad\quad (0.016) \qquad\quad (0.016) \qquad\quad (0.016)$$

$$- 0.042I_{74(2)} + 0.039I_{74(3)} - 0.073I_{75(2)} + 1.63 \qquad\qquad (22.26)$$
$$\quad (0.016) \qquad\quad (0.015) \qquad\quad (0.016) \qquad\;\; (0.7)$$

$$R^2 = 0.991 \;\; F_M(11, 56) = 584.3^{**} \;\; \widehat{\sigma} = 0.015 \;\; F_{ar}(5, 51) = 1.12$$

$$\chi^2_{nd}(2) = 0.90 \;\; F_{arch}(4, 60) = 0.47 \;\; F_{reset}(2, 54) = 0.24 \;\; F_{het}(8, 52) = 1.74.$$

Seven indicators are significant, but no mis-specification test rejects. Figure 22.2 shows the fitted and actual values, residuals and graphical statistics.

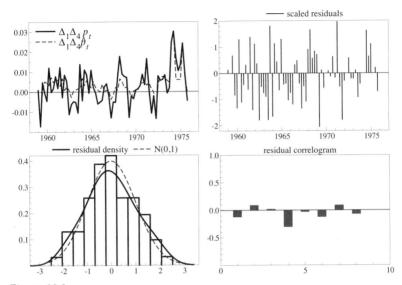

Figure 22.3
Fitted and actual values, residuals and graphical statistics for $\Delta_1\Delta_4 p_t$

Next, the equation for $\Delta_1\Delta_4 p_t$, after I(0) transformations given an almost exact unit root in the model of $\Delta_4 p_t$, yielded:

$$\Delta_1\Delta_4 p_t = \underset{(0.09)}{0.25}\Delta_1\Delta_4 p_{t-1} + \underset{(0.02)}{0.07}\Delta_4 y_{t-1} - \underset{(0.007)}{0.02}I_{59(2)} - \underset{(0.007)}{0.02}I_{72(2)}$$

$$+ \underset{(0.007)}{0.02}I_{74(1)} + \underset{(0.007)}{0.02}I_{74(2)} + \underset{(0.007)}{0.02}I_{75(2)} \tag{22.27}$$

$$(\mathsf{R}^*)^2 = 0.54 \;\; \mathsf{F_M}(7,60) = 9.88^{**} \;\; \widehat{\sigma} = 0.0068 \;\; \mathsf{F_{ar}}(5,56) = 1.88$$

$$\chi^2_{nd}(2) = 0.46 \;\; \mathsf{F_{arch}}(4,60) = 1.26 \;\; \mathsf{F_{reset}}(2,59) = 0.92 \;\; \mathsf{F_{het}}(4,58) = 0.17.$$

Five indicators are significant in (22.27), and again no mis-specification test rejects. Figure 22.3 reports the fitted and actual values, residuals and graphical statistics for $\Delta_1\Delta_4 p_t$.

Overall, therefore, 9 different indicators are significant in these models for y_t in (22.26) and $\Delta_1\Delta_4 p_t$ in (22.27), but none of these indicators was in common with (16.5). Adding the 9 additional indicators to (16.5) and testing their significance yields $\mathsf{F_{SE}}(9,47) = 0.60$, so does not reject the super exogeneity of either y_t or $\Delta_4 p_t$ in (16.5).

22.10 IIS and economic interpretations

Section 16.3 discussed the economic interpretation of (16.5) in relation to general theories of consumption. Here we focus on the additional implications from (22.26) and (22.27).

Several of the indicators in the inflation equation have reasonable historical interpretations as 1974(1) and 1974(2) were at the heart of the first oil crisis. 1972(2) saw a reduction in the rate of purchase tax on "luxury" goods, whereas 1975(2) saw an extension of VAT to a wider range of those goods. 1959(2) is in common with (22.26), and experienced a stimulatory budget. The other indicators in the income equation are harder to pin down, partly because so many events occurred that might affect y, and it is never very obvious why some show up as significant indicators, yet others do not. For example, 1966(1) saw a credit squeeze (but so did 1960(2) which does not show up), yet had a positive coefficient, followed by a downturn next quarter, further tightened in 1966(3), but neither was for the first, nor last, time. 1968(2) was the start of a 12-month wage freeze (as well as student riots in Paris, spreading to many countries), and 1974(2) witnessed increases in personal income tax, which were also raised in 1975(2), but again neither was the first nor last major change in income tax. 1974(3) saw price controls and a reduction in VAT. But there were plenty of other potential events to cause unanticipated shifts in income.

Nevertheless, the evidence in section 22.9 is consistent with treating the contemporaneous values of the conditioning variables in the model of c_t as valid regressors. Such constancy in the face of changing data behavior in the regressors also supports the specification in (16.5). The results reveal 9 different occasions when the regressors shifted relative to their VAR representations, and on all of those, c_t responded in the same way to the changed values of the variables. Thus, (16.5) represents a contingent plan, where consumers reacted to the actual values of income and inflation, rather than (say) their rational expectations.

Conversely, such findings do not preclude an expectations interpretation of (16.5) as discussed in (e.g.) Favero and Hendry (1992), related to recent research on robust methods of economic forecasting discussed in Hendry (2006). Specifically, consider the predictors $\widehat{\Delta_4 y}_{t+1} = \Delta_4 y_t$ and $\widehat{\Delta_4 p}_{t+1} = \Delta_4 p_t$. As shown in section 23.9 below, once a location shift has occurred, these devices quickly revert to the new level, so although they fail to forecast shifts, they do not suffer from systematic forecast failure.

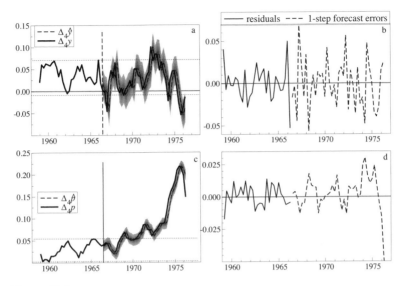

Figure 22.4
Robust forecasts for $\Delta_4 y_t$ and $\Delta_4 p_t$ over 1966(3)–1976(2)

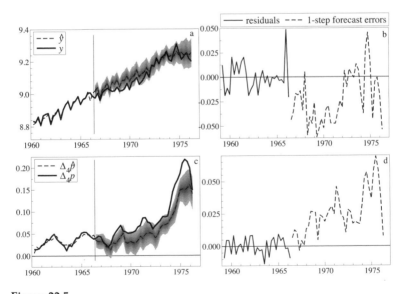

Figure 22.5
VAR forecasts for y_t and $\Delta_4 p_t$ over 1966(3)–1976(2)

Figure 22.4 records their 1-step forecasts over the last 40 quarters of the sample. The vertical solid line marks the forecast origin, and the horizontal dotted lines show the range of data variation prior to the forecast origin: more than half of the outcomes lie outside those bands (the fans are based on conventional standard errors). Despite such substantial changes in the variables to be forecast, there are no systematic forecast failures, albeit that the last forecast for $\Delta_4 p_t$ misses the sharp fall in 1976(2).

That outcome stands in stark contrast to the equivalent 1-step forecasts of y_t and $\Delta_4 p_t$ from a first-order VAR in c_t, y_t and $\Delta_4 p_t$ shown in figure 22.5. Systematic forecast failure is manifest for both variables, especially in the dramatic increase in the forecast errors relative to the in-sample residuals shown in panels b and d.

Consequently, economic agents who used robust forecasting devices to form their views of the future would not have made systematic forecast errors, in contrast to those who might have tried to use a VAR. If so, $\Delta_4 y_t$ and $\Delta_4 p_t$ in (16.5) really represent $\widehat{\Delta_4 y}_{t+1}$ and $\widehat{\Delta_4 p}_{t+1}$, and their super exogeneity provides a clear contradiction of the above quote from Lucas (1976) p.41.

23 Selecting Forecasting Models

Forecasting is different: the past is fixed, but the future is not. Practical forecasting methods rely on extrapolating presently available information into the future. No matter how good such methods are, they require that the future resembles the present in the relevant attributes. Intermittent unanticipated shifts violate that requirement, and breaks have so far eluded being predicted. If no location shifts ever occurred, then the most parsimonious, congruent, undominated model in-sample would tend to dominate out of sample as well. However, if data processes are wide-sense non-stationary, different considerations matter for formulating, selecting, or using a forecasting model. In practice, the robustness to location shifts of a model formulation can be essential for avoiding systematic forecast failure, which may entail selecting from a different class of models that need not even be congruent in-sample: complete success at locating the LDGP need not improve forecasting. However, by transforming a selected congruent parsimoniously encompassing model to a more robust form before it is used in forecasting, causal information can be retained while avoiding systematic forecast failure. The chapter also notes other ways of selecting forecasting models, including model averaging and factor approaches, but focuses on transformations of selected models of the LDGP.

23.1 Introduction

Discovering reliable, accurate and precise forecasting devices has eluded humanity for almost all variables and all times, but has witnessed many ambiguous and dubious claims to the contrary: see Hendry (2001a) and Friedman (2014). Most operational forecasting methods extrapolate current information into the future, so require that future to resemble the present in the ways which matter. If no location shifts ever occurred, then the most parsimonious, congruent, undominated model in-sample would tend to dominate out of sample as well. However, intermittent unanticipated shifts lead to forecast failures. To date, no approach can systematically predict breaks that have not yet happened, although some developments are occurring in economics (e.g., Castle et al., 2010), and many more in other disciplines, such as volcanology (e.g., Sparks, 2003) and earthquake tectonics (see e.g., Hubert-Ferrari, Barka, Jacques, Nalbant, Meyer, Armijo, Tapponnier and King, 2000). Consequently, when data processes are wide-sense non-stationary, different considerations must influence at least one of how to formulate, select, or use forecasting models.

Forecasting is different, and there are four main reasons for that difference. First, Clements and Hendry (2005) distinguish between the predictability of a random variable at a point in time, and its forecastability over a future horizon from a model based on an historical sample. Given an information set, denoted $\mathcal{I}_{t-1}$, a non-degenerate random variable v_t is predictable if its distribution conditional on $\mathcal{I}_{t-1}$ differs from its unconditional distribution. Forecastability concerns our ability to make useful statements about a future outcome, which may depend on the context. Second, a forecasting model may not need to be congruent, as the objective is to obtain the best forecasts, not find the LDGP. Third, once unanticipated breaks become known ex post, they can be removed—but future shifts may still not be anticipated, so the future is more uncertain than the past appears to be. Finally, unlike modeling, testing theories, or policy analyses, parameters and shifts therein do not need to be disentangled for forecasting—an accurate statement about the relevant future value is all that is needed—so there is no obvious objective criterion for selecting devices that will actually provide good forecasts.

The concept of information is also ambiguous in important respects. First, it may denote the contents of the available information set $\mathcal{I}_{t-1}$ on which forecasts are conditioned, namely which variables are included. This then relates to what are the basic set of variables, $\{z_t\}$ from which the GUM, or the class of models under consideration, will be formed. Secondly, it can denote knowledge as to how $\mathcal{I}_{t-1}$ enters the conditional distribution of the variables to be forecast, namely linearly or nonlinearly, how shifts affect that distribution, etc. This sense concerns how the GUM is formulated, with possibly non-linear functions of the $\{z_t\}$, indicators for breaks etc. Thirdly, it may relate to knowing which elements of $\mathcal{I}_{t-1}$ matter, as some variables may be irrelevant. This notion is more about model selection. Switches in meaning can be confusing: predictability assumes both of the first two senses, with the third being irrelevant, whereas forecastability cannot assume the second, and the roles of the first and third are debated. In a broader context, Hendry and Mizon (2014) highlight problems resulting from this ambiguity.

Clements and Hendry (2005) state four provable theorems about the role of information in relation to forecasting. The first three theorems show that in intrinsically non-stationary processes: (*i*) more information cannot worsen predictability (first sense); (*ii*) causal models need not outperform in forecasting even when they dominated in-sample (due to second sense); yet, (*iii*) less information need not by itself induce predictive failure (both first and second). The final theorem only applies to stationary processes and concerns (*iv*) criteria for selecting forecasting models, addressed below, so relates to the third sense. Thus, when processes lack time invariance, theory cannot establish the pre-eminence of more information over less, or its opposite, for forecasting, precisely because the second sense of information cannot apply in reality. The forecasting literature reflects this inability. Many studies offer empirical support for the advantages of using extensive information sets, as in (e.g.) Forni, Hallin, Lippi and Reichlin (2000) and Stock and Watson (2002), whereas others, such as Makridakis and Hibon (2000) and Fildes and Ord (2002), emphasize the benefits of parsimonious models for forecasting. Any approach to selecting models for forecasting has to address this conflict of views, and we follow Clements and Hendry (2001) in considering that the favorable attitude to parsimony in forecasting is due to confounding simplicity with robustness: it happens that in most forecasting competitions, the successful simple models are more robust to past location shifts than their larger competitors. Below, we propose an approach to forecasting that commences from the most general GUM as in earlier chapters, seeks a congruent, parsimoniously encompassing specific representation of the LDGP, then transforms that model into a more robust version–which would in fact be non-congruent if estimated. Thus, there is no real difference in principle as to how to select a model for forecasting, merely a difference in how to use the selected model, and a practical difference in the stringency of the selection criteria given the different objective.

Section 23.2 notes six of the main approaches to selecting forecasting models, then sections 23.3–23.8 discuss those methods in detail. Section 23.9 considers robust forecasting devices, leading to section 23.10 on using selected models for forecasting. In section 23.11, we provide a simulation illustration, followed in section 23.12 by an empirical example, based on a public-sector policy study. Section 23.14 concludes.

23.2   Finding good forecasting models

There are six distinct, but related, approaches to finding good forecasting models. First, prior specification then estimation (discussed in section 23.3); second, conventional model selection from a set of candidate variables (section 23.4); third, model averaging (section 23.5); fourth, factor based approaches to summarize very large data assemblies (section 23.6); fifth, selection of factors combined with a set of candidate variables (section 23.7); and sixth, empirical discovery of the LDGP based on retaining the best available theory, followed by model transformations to robustify the resulting forecasts against systematic failure (section 23.8). We will address all six, and explain their advantages and weaknesses, focusing on the last which builds on the developments described in earlier chapters. The issue of discovery is clearest in the fifth and sixth, where neither theory nor past empirical evidence can determine whether factors suffice to characterize the information relevant to forecasting a future period, nor whether individual variables may still play a key role even after many factors have been included.

An important dichotomy that distinguishes approaches is whether they combine information or combine models. Methods for combining information, in the first sense above, include the GUM (when feasible) and prior specified models (both of which use weights based on their unrestricted coefficient estimates), any selected models (where *Gets* uses bias-corrected estimates for retained variables and zero for eliminated), factors which use principal component (or related) weights, and methods which include both factors and variables. Since *Gets* can handle more variables than observations, all relevant information can be included in the candidate set of variables, and although the GUM will then be infeasible, principal components can help represent a myriad of small influences, as in Castle et al. (2013).

There are many ways of combining models, from simple or weighted averaging of all sub-models, through partial or complete selection of a subset, which are then combined in a weighted average. There are also numerous ways of choosing weights. Since most sub-models of any LDGP will be mis-specified and non-congruent, it is unclear what the properties of weighted averages of many such models are. Conversely, as noted above, one cannot prove that the estimated LDGP is best for forecasting even if no breaks occur, so averaging may help reduce forecast error variances; and if breaks do occur, there seem to be benefits to including some methods that are robust to breaks at or near the forecast origin. Many agencies maintain a suite of forecasting models, partly to average over, but also to help ascertain divergencies between devices which may suggest that breaks have recently occurred.

23.3   Prior specification then estimation

Postulating a theory-based formulation and estimating the unknown parameters thereof by a method that would be optimal under correct specification has been a standard way historically of developing econometric forecasting models. A schematic linear system would look like:

$$y_t = A y_{t-1} + B z_t + C d_t + \epsilon_t, \tag{23.1}$$

where y_t is the n-vector of variables to be forecast given k unmodeled variables z_t and m deterministic terms d_t. The error ϵ_t in (23.1) is treated as an innovation, so its future values are expected to be zero on average. Estimating the parameters $(A : B : C)$ from a sample of T observations, and using "off-line" forecasts $\widehat{z}_{T+1}$ for the future z_t yields the 1-step ahead forecast:

$$\widehat{y}_{T+1|T} = \widehat{A}\,\widehat{y}_T + \widehat{B}\widehat{z}_{T+1} + \widehat{C}d_{T+1}, \tag{23.2}$$

where the subscript $_{T+1|T}$ denotes a forecast made at time T for time $T+1$. The basic approach in (23.2) is exemplified by (say) Klein (1971).

In essence, (23.1) is assumed to be the constant-parameter conditional LDGP with valid exogenous z_t and d_t, and the future outcome is a random draw from the same process. Although (23.1) was thought to be more general than a closed VAR, it may be a special case where the joint process $(y_t : z_t)$ is conditionally factorized as y_t on z_t (e.g., Hendry and Mizon, 1993). In practice, many problems were encountered, including manifest evidence of model mis-specification through autocorrelated residuals—sometimes corrected by fitting an autoregressive process to the residuals—and intermittent forecast failure from parameter changes or mis-forecast $\widehat{z}_{T+1}$, usually fixed by intercept corrections (ICs). ICs simply adjust the previous intercept in an equation, usually by adding the residual from the previous period. While much maligned as *ad hoc adjustments, con factors* etc., intercept corrections do in fact offset location shifts at or near the forecast origin T, when there are too few observations on the shift to allow it to be modeled (see, e.g.,

Clements and Hendry, 1998, who also provide a taxonomy of the main sources of forecast error in closed systems; Hendry and Mizon, 2012, extend the taxonomy to open systems). Even so, apparently naive forecasting devices often outperformed (23.2) on mean-square error measures, as in Cooper and Nelson (1975) inter alia. Finally, the discovery of features outside the postulated framework was not treated systematically, and solutions like autocorrelation corrections are often not helpful, as they are equally a symptom of a parameter shift or an unmodeled nonlinearity: see, e.g., Hendry and Mizon (1978) and Mizon (1995).

Forecast failures around the time of the first oil crisis were misinterpreted as revealing the invalidity of the underlying Keynesian theory from which specifications like (23.1) were derived, leading to very different approaches to obtaining the theory models for imposing on data: such a conclusion would be like NASA deciding Newton's Laws of Motion had to be rejected because Apollo 13 failed to land on the Moon at the forecast time. Unanticipated events outside the framework on which a forecast is predicated (in this case, the explosion of an oxygen cylinder on board the space craft) will often lead to forecast failure (not landing on the moon as predicted), yet need not entail the invalidity of the general theory on which the forecasting model was based (here, Newton's theory of gravity) nor even the forecasting equations themselves (which NASA used moments after the explosion to track the new trajectory of the space craft, later successfully returning the astronauts to Earth).

23.4   Conventional model selection

A perennial issue in forecasting practice is the role of parsimony. The results in Cooper and Nelson (1975), and more recently in the sequence of forecasting competitions (e.g., Makridakis, Andersen, Carbone, Fildes et al., 1982, and Makridakis and Hibon, 2000) are all consistent with the hypothesis that small models forecast best. However, this seems to be due to confounding parsimony with robustness to location shifts, as most small models happened to have robust formulations (e.g., differenced devices: see Clements and Hendry, 2001). Sample means are highly parsimonious but usually poor forecasting devices. Nevertheless, many proposals have been advanced for selecting only a subset of a set of candidate variables with the objective of forecasting more accurately.

The first model selection criteria were in fact designed for selecting forecasting equations: see Mallows (1966, 1973) and Akaike (1969, 1973).

The last of those, denoted AIC and discussed in section 17.5, was based on a penalized log-likelihood which envisaged an infinite, stationary autoregression, so there was a trade-off between the cost of estimating the coefficient of a slightly longer lag and the cost of omitting a non-zero, but small, effect. Akaike (1969) sought to show that the AIC led to an asymptotically efficient selection for 1-step ahead forecasts in that setting. Also Schwarz (1978) proposed a more stringent penalty in a Bayesian information criterion (SC or BIC) that could consistently select a constant-parameter finite-dimensional model as the sample size diverged, and Hannan and Quinn (1979) established the smallest penalty that ensured a consistent selection. Claeskens and Hjort (2003) develop a focused information criterion that aims to be best for a subset of parameters of interest. Campos et al. (2003) map the penalty choices of information criteria to the significance levels of tests that would retain the marginal parameter.

To prove such results as Hannan and Quinn (1979), the model must grow with the sample size at a slow enough rate that its coefficient estimates converge, yet fast enough to eventually nest the LDGP. However, most such selection approaches do not test for congruence, so although they select the best representative in the given class on their internal criterion, that might be a poor characterization of the evidence, which may not necessarily matter for forecasting, but would matter when those criteria are used for other purposes—as they often are (e.g., selecting lag length in an econometric model). Moreover, none of the initial proposals allowed for large numbers of variables relative to the sample size, and most have the odd property of increasing the probability of retaining irrelevant variables as $N \to T$. There are fixes for that defect, as in Hurvich and Tsai (1989) discussed in section 17.5, but such drawbacks of the standard criteria suggest that a more coherent approach may pay dividends. Conversely, within the same general framework, White (1990) establishes the consistency of a sufficiently rigorous test-based selection approach by using *Gets* in a progressive research strategy.

The most important lacuna remains the assumption of parameter constancy around the forecast origin and over the forecast horizon. The latter is impossible to resolve unless the relevant breaks can be predicted, but the former can be attenuated by using forecasting devices that are robust to such shifts. One approach to minimizing the reliance on a single model that might be susceptible to mis-specifications (including breaks), akin to portfolio theory of reducing risk by diversification, has been model averaging, which we now consider.

23.5   Model averaging

There is a long pedigree to combining forecasts from different models, starting with Francis Galton (according to Surowiecki, 2004), then Bates and Granger (1969), through Nelson (1972), to many recent papers including Hoeting, Madigan, Raftery and Volinsky (1999), Raffalovich, Deane, Armstrong and Tsao (2001), Hendry and Clements (2004), and Hansen (2010). A combination of forecasts can outperform, on some measures, all the individual forecasts when there are offsetting biases, offsetting breaks, or diversification across relatively uncorrelated forecasts which reduces the variance of the average. Conversely, averaging without any selection for the set of forecasts involved has obvious drawbacks: by way of analogy, with 10 glasses of pure drinking water and one of a virulent poison, it does not seem wise to mix all of these before drinking, rather than select out the glass of poison. In the extreme of averaging over all 2^N models in a class, as in Hoeting et al. (1999), it is easy to create counter examples where the average is a poor device, so some selection seems essential. This has led to a debate about whether model averaging or model selection is best: see e.g., Jacobson and Karlsson (2004) and compare Hendry and Reade (2006). Since poor averaging or poor selection lead to poor forecasting, good selection is required, and if that is achieved, it becomes less clear why one would wish to average.

Methods of combining models can be summarized by the choice of weights w_m used in the combination, where weighted averaging is carried out using a criterion denoted c_m, scaled by the weights on all selected models, denoted by the set $\mathcal{M}_s \subseteq \mathcal{M}$, the last of which comprises all 2^N possible models, where a weight of zero is attached to unselected models:

$$w_m = \begin{cases} \dfrac{c_m}{\sum_{j \in \mathcal{M}_s} c_j} & m \in \mathcal{M}_s, \\ 0 & m \notin \mathcal{M}_s. \end{cases} \qquad (23.3)$$

Commonly occurring special cases of (23.3) include:

1. an unweighted average of all models, so $\mathcal{M}_s = \mathcal{M}$ and $c_j = 1 \; \forall j$ leading to $w_m = 2^{-N}$;

2. a weighted average of all models, so $\mathcal{M}_s = \mathcal{M}$ again, but for some criterion c_j that varies with a measure of the "goodness" of the model (such as BIC) leading to $w_m = c_m / \sum_{j \in \mathcal{M}} c_j$;

3. the selection of the best single model, so $\mathcal{M}_s$ has a single member, and hence $w_m = 1$ for $m = m^*$, say, and zero otherwise.

In the last case, the single model could be the GUM, the null model, or any formulation in between. The choice of criterion is therefore crucial, and many suggestions have been made, including "Occam's window"— an arbitrary measure of a distance from the best model—as well as various model selection methods.

For procedures such as *Autometrics*, the criterion that indirectly determines the weights in (23.3) is the nominal significance level, α, which can be set tightly, generally leading to a set M_s with a single member, or loosely which can then generate a number of congruent, mutually encompassing models to average over. Indeed, the GUM has $\alpha = 1$, so works extremely well in a constant-parameter world when all variables matter, and badly when no variables are relevant, which is the converse behavior to the null model. Thus, any ranking of methods will vary with the numbers of relevant and irrelevant variables, and the non-centralities of the former (see Castle et al., 2013).

An important difference between approaches lies in what constitutes M, which is often taken to be the 2^N models generated by entering or omitting each candidate linear regressor, whereas *Autometrics* would almost always also undertake impulse-indicator saturation, and often allow for non-linearities as well, so has a vastly larger model set of 2^{N+T+K} for K non-linear terms, from which it selects significant variables. Moreover, as shown in (e.g.) Castle et al. (2010), collinearity between regressors also has an important impact on which models will dominate on (say) MSFE, as we now show.

23.5.1   Collinearity in forecasting models

Consider a constant-parameter conditional linear regression model:

$$y_t = \beta' x_t + \epsilon_t \text{ where } \epsilon_t \sim \text{IN}\left[0, \sigma_\epsilon^2\right] \tag{23.4}$$

with $x_t \sim \text{IN}_k \left[\mu, \Sigma\right]$ distributed independently of $\{\epsilon_t\}$ so that:

$$\mathsf{E}\left[x_t x_t'\right] = \mu\mu' + \Sigma = \Omega. \tag{23.5}$$

It is easiest to consider the case of a known future value x_{T+1}, so that the 1-step forecast is:

$$\widehat{y}_{T+1|T} = \widehat{\beta}' x_{T+1}, \tag{23.6}$$

with conditional MSFE for $\widehat{\epsilon}_{T+1|T} = y_{T+1} - \widehat{y}_{T+1|T}$:

$$\mathsf{M}\left[\widehat{\epsilon}_{T+1|T} \mid x_{T+1}\right] = \sigma_\epsilon^2 \left(1 + T^{-1} x_{T+1}' \Omega^{-1} x_{T+1}\right). \tag{23.7}$$

The unconditional MSFE simplifies to the well-known formula:

$$M\left[\widehat{\epsilon}_{T+1|T}\right] = \sigma_\epsilon^2\left(1 + T^{-1}k\right). \tag{23.8}$$

Thus, for the GUM, or a model that coincides with the LDGP, the forecasting MSFE cost from estimating an additional coefficient is $1/T$, irrespective of the relevance or otherwise of that variable. Moreover, when collinearity stays the same over the forecast horizon as in-sample, that cost remains $1/T$ as follows.

Factorize Ω in (23.5) as $\Omega = H'\Lambda H$ where $H'H = I_k$ and $Hx_t = z_t$, so that:

$$E\left[z_t z_t'\right] = \Lambda, \tag{23.9}$$

and hence the mutually-orthogonal z_t have a diagonal second-moment matrix Λ. Then:

$$x_{T+1}'\Omega^{-1}x_{T+1} = x_{T+1}'H'\Lambda^{-1}Hx_{T+1} = z_{T+1}'\Lambda^{-1}z_{T+1} = \sum_{i=1}^{k}\frac{z_{i,T+1}^2}{\lambda_i}. \tag{23.10}$$

On average, (23.9) entails that $E[z_{i,T+1}^2] = \lambda_i$, so unconditionally:

$$E\left[x_{T+1}'\Omega^{-1}x_{T+1}\right] = E\left[\sum_{i=1}^{k}\frac{z_{i,T+1}^2}{\lambda_i}\right] = \sum_{i=1}^{k}\frac{\lambda_i}{\lambda_i} = k. \tag{23.11}$$

Consequently, matching (23.8), the extent of collinearity is irrelevant to forecasting if the marginal process stays constant, as a linear model is equivariant under orthogonal transformations like H. Indeed, (23.4) is isomorphic to:

$$y_t = \beta'H'Hx_t + \epsilon_t = \gamma'z_t + \epsilon_t, \tag{23.12}$$

which produces identical forecasts. While many forecasting-model selection analyses have used this framework, it abstracts from the four main problems of changes in collinearity, model mis-specification, data-based selection and location shifts. We now consider the first three of these, and return to consider the impacts on forecasting of location shifts in section 23.8.

23.5.2 Changes in collinearity and model mis-specification

First, if Ω changes to Ω^*, which induces a change in collinearity, so that Λ changes to Λ^* with H unchanged then:

$$E\left[\sum_{i=1}^{k}\frac{z_{i,T+1}^2}{\lambda_i}\right] = \sum_{i=1}^{k}\frac{\lambda_i^*}{\lambda_i}, \tag{23.13}$$

and hence:

$$M\left[\widehat{\epsilon}_{T+1|T}\right] \simeq \sigma_{\epsilon}^2\left(1 + T^{-1}\sum_{i=1}^{k}\frac{\lambda_i^*}{\lambda_i}\right). \tag{23.14}$$

Thus, changes in the smallest λ_j induce the biggest changes in $M[\widehat{\epsilon}_{T+1|T}]$, which can lead to dramatic increases in uncertainty. Moreover, if H was also to shift, then γ in (23.12) would cease to be constant.

As it is unrealistic to assume a model coincides with the DGP, we next allow for mis-specification. Partition $x_t' = (x_{1,t}' : x_{2,t}')$, where $k_1 + k_2 = k$, so the forecasting equation becomes:

$$\overline{y}_{T+1|T} = x_{1,T+1}'\overline{\beta}_1, \tag{23.15}$$

where $\beta' = (\beta_1' : \beta_2')$. For simplicity, consider the case where $\Omega = \Lambda$, so is diagonal and hence:

$$E[\overline{\beta}_1] = \beta_1, \tag{23.16}$$

although all the results that follow also hold for non-diagonal Ω. The forecast error at $T + 1$ from (23.15) is $\overline{\omega}_{T+1|T} = y_{T+1} - \overline{y}_{T+1|T}$:

$$\overline{\omega}_{T+1|T} = x_{1,T+1}'\left(\beta_1 - \overline{\beta}_1\right) + x_{2,T+1}'\beta_2 + \epsilon_{T+1}, \tag{23.17}$$

yielding an unconditional MSFE of:

$$E\left[\overline{\omega}_{T+1|T}^2\right] = \sigma_{\epsilon}^2\left(1 + T^{-1}\sum_{i=1}^{k_1}\frac{\lambda_i^*}{\lambda_i}\right) + \beta_2'\Lambda_{22}^*\beta_2. \tag{23.18}$$

Since $\beta_2'\Lambda_{22}\beta_2 = \sum_{i=k_1+1}^{k}\beta_i^2\lambda_i$, letting:

$$\tau_{\beta_j}^2 \simeq \frac{T\beta_j^2\lambda_j}{\sigma_{\omega}^2}, \tag{23.19}$$

then from (23.18) the conditional MSFE is:

$$E\left[\overline{\omega}_{T+1|T}^2 \mid x_{T+1}\right] \simeq E\left[\widehat{\epsilon}_{T+1|T}^2 \mid x_{T+1}\right] + \frac{\sigma_{\epsilon}^2}{T}\sum_{j=k_1+1}^{k}\left(\tau_{\beta_j}^2 - 1\right)\frac{\lambda_j^*}{\lambda_j}. \tag{23.20}$$

The cost of estimation remains $T^{-1}\lambda_i^*/\lambda_i$, and that of mis-specification is also of order $T^{-1}\lambda_i^*/\lambda_i$, but multiplied by $(\tau_{\beta_j}^2 - 1)$. Thus, for the given sample size, one can minimize $\mathsf{E}[\overline{\omega}^2_{T+1|T}|x_{T+1}]$ by eliminating all variables with $\tau^2_{\beta_j} \leq 1$ and correctly retaining those with $\tau^2_{\beta_j} > 1$. Such a model can then forecast better than the estimated LDGP. Changes in collinearity affect forecasts from both included and incorrectly-excluded variables, making it especially invaluable to include relevant and exclude irrelevant if λ^*_j/λ_j is large. The trade-off in (23.20) is central to forecast-model selection: one cannot improve MSFE simply by dropping highly collinear variables if in fact they matter.

Since it cannot be known which variables fall into each category, data-based model selection will be needed to determine that. When there are N irrelevant candidate variables, the GUM will have a cost from that source of $\sigma^2_\epsilon T^{-1} \sum_{j=1}^N \lambda^*_j/\lambda_j$, whereas with *Autometrics* selection, αN will be retained by chance costing on average $\sigma^2_\epsilon T^{-1} \sum_{j=1}^{\alpha N} \lambda^*_j/\lambda_j$. Thus, when N is large, few variables matter or are highly significant, and collinearity changes, then selection will certainly pay. Unfortunately, an "optimal" selection rule is impossible as it depends on features like N, $\{\tau^2_{\beta_j}\}$ and the $\{\lambda^*_j/\lambda_j\}$, all of which are unknown. Given the form of (23.20), one possibility is to select all coefficients with $t^2_{\beta_k} \geq 2$, so variables with large $\tau^2_{\beta_j}$ are usually retained, and smaller eliminated. Such a rule is close to the implicit significance level of $\alpha = 0.16$ in AIC for moderate sample sizes T.

23.6   Factor models

Principal component methods have a long history in statistics and psychology (e.g., Spearman, 1927, Cattell, 1952, Anderson, 1958, Lawley and Maxwell, 1963, Joreskog, 1967, and Bartholomew, 1987), including their application in economics (e.g., Stone, 1947, for a macroeconomic application; and Gorman, 1956, for a microeconomic one). More recently, diffusion indices and factor models are becoming quite widely used for economic forecasting: see e.g., Stock and Watson (1999) and Forni et al. (2000); Stock and Watson (2011) provide an update.

The model proposed by Stock and Watson (1999) considers a large assembly $\{z_t\}$ of potential predictors of y_t that satisfy a factor structure given by:

$$z_t = \Psi f_t + v_t, \tag{23.21}$$

where $\mathsf{E}[f_t v'_t] = 0$ and $\mathsf{E}[v_t v'_t] = \Omega_v$. In (23.21), f_t is a latent vector of dimension $m < n$, so Ψ is $n \times m$ although $n > T$, and so z_t contains a reduced-rank systematic component. The estimates of the f_t are often based on sample principal components, so are mutually orthogonal. Let (possibly in mean-deviations):

$$\frac{1}{T} \sum_{t=1}^{T} z_t z_t' = M_z = H \Lambda H', \tag{23.22}$$

where $H'H = I_n$, so $H^{-1} = H'$ and the eigenvalues are ordered from the largest downwards. Only the first m matter given (23.21), so set:

$$H' = \left(\begin{array}{c} H_1' \\ H_2' \end{array} \right) \text{ and } \Lambda = \left(\begin{array}{cc} \Lambda_{11} & 0 \\ 0 & \Lambda_{22} \end{array} \right), \tag{23.23}$$

where Λ_{11} is $m \times m$, with $H_1' M H_1 = \Lambda_{11}$. Thus, the matrix H_1' weights the z_t to produce the relevant factors, with:

$$H_1' z_t = \widehat{f}_t.$$

Consequently, instead of forecasting by a standard equation of the form:

$$\widehat{y}_{T+1|T} = \widehat{\beta}' z_T$$

say, which would be infeasible in conventional approaches when $n > T$, one uses

$$\widehat{y}_{T+1|T} = \widehat{\gamma}' \widehat{f}_T, \tag{23.24}$$

which is estimable directly. The factors can follow a dynamic process, such as a first-order vector autoregression:

$$f_t = \Phi f_{t-1} + \omega_t, \tag{23.25}$$

where $E\left[f_{t-1} \omega_t' \right] = 0$ and $\omega_t \sim \mathsf{IN}\left[0, \Sigma_\omega \right]$.

23.7   Selecting factors and variables jointly

An algorithm for $N \gg T$ allows an alternative approach to pure factor forecasting methods with extremely large data sets, where an excess of variables is virtually bound to occur. The analysis in Castle, Clements and Hendry (2013) suggests that existing proposals such as Stock and Watson (1998) have potential drawbacks should any individual variables also matter for forecasting. The above selection procedure could be automated, although too many variables and factors might be computationally demanding. The risk of an excess of spuriously significant variables is less relevant in a forecasting context, since the factors anyway attribute some weight to most variables. An obvious additional variant in this setting is to force the first few factors as regressors in all initial models, thereby viewing the approach as one of detecting additional salient effects, as well as possibly replacing the general factors by a subset of relevant regressors, with IIS both to remove outliers and to reduce chance alignment of factors with in-sample breaks.

23.8   Using econometric models for forecasting

Clements and Hendry (1998, 1999) establish the crucial role of location shifts in forecast failure and propose using more robust methods to avoid systematic mis-forecasting. Intercept corrections and differencing offer related solutions, and here we consider the latter following Hendry (2006).

23.8.1   Cointegrated DGP

A vector equilibrium-correction model (VEqCM) for a set of n I(1) variables $\{x_t\}$ is given by:

$$(\Delta x_t - \gamma) = \alpha \left(\beta' x_{t-1} - \mu\right) + \epsilon_t \quad \text{where} \quad \epsilon_t \sim \text{IN}_n \left[0, \Omega_\epsilon\right], \tag{23.26}$$

where $\text{E}[\Delta x_t] = \gamma$ with $\beta'\gamma = 0$ and $\text{E}[\beta'x_t] = \mu$, so there are r cointegrating combinations of the levels. Additional lags are easily incorporated, but (23.26) captures the salient features of the analysis, and is taken to be the LDGP as well.

Location shifts here correspond to breaks of $\nabla\mu^* = \mu^* - \mu$ and $\nabla\gamma^* = \gamma^* - \gamma$ such that for the post-forecast-origin observations when the location shift is dated $T - 1$ for analytical convenience:

$$\Delta x_{T+h} = \gamma^* + \alpha \left(\beta' x_{T+h-1} - \mu^*\right) + \epsilon_{T+h}, \tag{23.27}$$

for $h = 0, 1, \ldots, H$, and hence from (23.27):

$$\Delta x_{T+h} = \gamma + \alpha \left(\beta' x_{T+h-1} - \mu\right) + \epsilon_{T+h} + \nabla\gamma^* - \alpha\nabla\mu^*. \tag{23.28}$$

Then:

$$\begin{aligned}
\Delta x_{T-1} &= \gamma + \alpha \left(\beta' x_{T-2} - \mu\right) + v_{T-1} \\
\Delta x_T &= \gamma^* + \alpha \left(\beta' x_{T-1} - \mu^*\right) + v_T \\
\Delta x_{T+1} &= \gamma^* + \alpha \left(\beta' x_T - \mu^*\right) + v_{T+1}.
\end{aligned} \tag{23.29}$$

Consider 1-step forecasts from the known LDGP at T, given by:

$$\widehat{\Delta x}_{T+1|T} = \gamma + \alpha \left(\beta' x_T - \mu \right), \tag{23.30}$$

which has a forecast error of $\widehat{e}_{T+1|T} = \Delta x_{T+1} - \widehat{\Delta x}_{T+1|T}$ and a bias of:

$$\mathsf{E}_{T+1}\left[\widehat{e}_{T+1|T} \right] = \left(\gamma^* - \gamma \right) - \alpha \left(\mu^* - \mu \right). \tag{23.31}$$

Until the model specification is revised, further step-ahead forecasts, and 1-step forecasts from a later origin, continue to make systematic errors as in (23.31).

23.9   Robust forecasting devices

To avoid such difficulties, a forecasting device that is robust after location shifts is needed. As an illustration, contrast using the so-called naive forecast:

$$\widetilde{\Delta x}_{T+1|T} = \Delta x_T, \tag{23.32}$$

noting that Δx_{t-1} does not enter the LDGP (23.26), so is not even a causally relevant predictor. The corresponding forecast error is $\widetilde{e}_{T+1|T} = \Delta x_{T+1} - \widetilde{\Delta x}_{T+1|T}$:

$$\widetilde{e}_{T+1|T} = \gamma^* + \alpha \left(\beta' x_T - \mu^* \right) + v_{T+1} - \Delta x_T = \Delta v_{T+1} + \alpha \beta' \Delta x_T, \tag{23.33}$$

where from (23.29):

$$\mathsf{E}\left[\Delta x_T \right] = \gamma^* + \alpha \left(\mu - \mu^* \right),$$

so, because $\beta' \gamma^*$ is zero, has a forecast-error bias of:

$$\mathsf{E}_{T+1}\left[\Delta x_{T+1} - \widetilde{\Delta x}_{T+1|T} \right] = \alpha \beta' \alpha \left(\mu - \mu^* \right)$$

and so (23.32) greatly reduces systematic mis-forecasting. Next period:

$$\mathsf{E}_{T+2}\left[\Delta x_{T+2} - \widetilde{\Delta x}_{T+2|T+1} \right] = \alpha \left(I_r + \beta' \alpha \right) \beta' \alpha \left(\mu - \mu^* \right),$$

where all the eigenvalues of $\left(I_r + \beta' \alpha \right)$ are less than unity, so the forecast-error bias falls rapidly.

Conversely, until the VEqCM correctly estimates the new parameters γ^* and μ^*, the same average forecast error (23.31) will persist, so despite its non-causal basis, (23.32) will outperform (23.26). Since most of this book has been about discovering empirical models that approximate the LDGP, it is natural to seek a forecasting device that retains such hard-won knowledge, and differencing the VEqCM has a number of advantages as we now outline. Second differencing removes two unit roots, intercepts and linear trends, changes location shifts to blips and converts breaks in trends to impulses, although differencing exacerbates the induced negative moving average from measurement errors in dynamic equations. Moreover, analyzing a differenced VEqCM will help explain why forecasting devices like (23.32) can be difficult to outperform even when they are a poor approximation to the LDGP.

Instead of the somewhat unrealistic assumption of a VEqCM model that coincides with the LDGP in-sample as in (23.26), consider the more general LDGP:

$$\Delta x_t = \gamma + \alpha \left(\beta' x_{t-1} - \mu \right) + \Psi z_t + v_t, \tag{23.34}$$

where z_t denotes I(0) omitted variables, with both parameter changes and a location shift at $T - 1$, so for $h \geq 0$ the future LDGP is:

$$\Delta x_{T+h} = \gamma^* + \alpha^* \left((\beta^*)' x_{T+h-1} - \mu^* \right) + \Psi^* z_{T+h} + v_{T+h}. \tag{23.35}$$

The mis-specifications and breaks are unknown to the investigator, so the model in use for forecasting is an estimated VEqCM with the same form as (23.30):

$$\widehat{\Delta x}_{T+h|T+h-1} = \widehat{\gamma} + \widehat{\alpha} \left(\widehat{\beta}' x_{T+h-1} - \widehat{\mu} \right). \tag{23.36}$$

All the main sources of forecast error occur given (23.35), as:

$$
\begin{aligned}
\widehat{e}_{T+h|T+h-1} &= \Delta x_{T+h} - \widehat{\Delta x}_{T+h|T+h-1} \\
&= \left(\gamma^* - \widehat{\gamma} \right) + \alpha^* \left((\beta^*)' x_{T+h-1} - \mu^* \right) - \widehat{\alpha} \left(\widehat{\beta}' x_{T+h-1} - \widehat{\mu} \right) \\
&\quad + \Psi^* z_{T+h} + v_{T+h},
\end{aligned}
$$

so comprise:

(a) deterministic shifts: $\gamma^* \neq \gamma$, $\mu^* \neq \mu$;

(b) stochastic breaks: $\alpha^* \neq \alpha$, $\beta^* \neq \beta$, $\Psi^* \neq \Psi$;

(c) omitted variables: $\{z_{T+h}\}$;

(d) inconsistent parameter estimates $\widehat{\gamma}$, $\widehat{\alpha}$, $\widehat{\beta}$, and $\widehat{\mu}$ because of (a)–(c);

(e) estimation uncertainty from not knowing γ, α, β, and μ;

(f) innovation errors $\{v_{T+h}\}$.

Moreover, these errors persist as shown above even when $h > 1$.

Contrast the forecast errors made using the sequence Δx_{T+h-1} to forecast

$$\widetilde{\Delta x}_{T+h|T+h-1} = \Delta x_{T+h-1}, \tag{23.37}$$

where because of (23.35), Δx_{T+h-1} is ($h \geq 1$):

$$\Delta x_{T+h-1} = \gamma^* + \alpha^* \left((\beta^*)' x_{T+h-2} - \mu^* \right) + \Psi^* z_{T+h-1} + v_{T+h-1}. \tag{23.38}$$

Let $\Delta x_{T+h} - \widetilde{\Delta x}_{T+h|T+h-1} = \widetilde{u}_{T+h|T+h-1}$, then:

$$\begin{aligned}
\widetilde{u}_{T+h|T+h-1} &= \gamma^* + \alpha^* \left((\beta^*)' x_{T+h-1} - \mu^* \right) + \Psi^* z_{T+h} + v_{T+h} \\
&\quad - \left[\gamma^* + \alpha^* \left((\beta^*)' x_{T+h-2} - \mu^* \right) + \Psi^* z_{T+h-1} + v_{T+h-1} \right] \\
&= \alpha^* (\beta^*)' \Delta x_{T+h-1} + \Psi^* \Delta z_{T+h} + \Delta v_{T+h}. \tag{23.39}
\end{aligned}$$

All terms in the last line of (23.39) are $I(-1)$, so are noisy, but no systematic failure results. This is because from (23.38), for all forecast horizons, Δx_{T+h-1} reflects every effect needed as it

(a*) incorporates all deterministic shifts γ^* and μ^*;

(b*) incorporates all stochastic breaks: α^*, β^*, and Ψ^*;

(c*) has no omitted variables as $\{z_{T+h-1}\}$ is included;

(d*) has the true values of the parameters after the break; and

(e*) and has no estimation uncertainty.

The three drawbacks of using Δx_{T+h-1} are:

(f*) the unwanted presence of v_{T+h-1} in (23.38), which doubles the innovation error variance;

(g*) all variables enter lagged one extra period, which adds the noise of many $I(-1)$ effects;

(h*) Δx_{T+h-1} does not actually forecast, merely measures the previous state of the system.

The last point may be clarified by the *bus-stop game* analogy in Hendry (2001a)—using just the past state, a volcanic eruption would be forecast only after it had occurred. Using (23.32) at $T - 1$ before any shifts, Δx_{T-1} does not embody those shifts so would not forecast Δx_T, making the same error as in (23.31). There is a clear trade-off between using the VE-qCM in (23.26) to make a genuine, but risky, statement about the future, and the naive forecast device (23.37), which avoids systematic forecast failure after location shifts have occurred.

23.10   Using selected models for forecasting

Such a result emphasizes the major difference between selecting a model of the LDGP for understanding or policy, where it is essential to disentangle and model all relevant variables and all parameter changes, as well as estimate the latter, as against selecting a model for forecasting where only the effects of those changes need to be captured, as Δx_{T+h-1} does one period after a shift. Correspondingly, different selection principles are involved, although that is all too rarely recognized. In part, that is because many economists seek to use the same model for forecasting and policy, as they wish to interpret the forecasts and act thereon. Fortunately, we can combine the *Autometrics* approach to locating a good model of the LDGP with these recent results on forecast failure and its avoidance, to provide an overall strategy: use the VEqCM in (23.26) when the final residual is not discrepant and there is no other evidence of a location shift, and use the differenced version thereof otherwise, as we now explain.

Although the book has focused on the most thoroughly developed setting of individual equations, vector autoregressive systems (VARs) can be selected an equation at a time (in fact, *Autometrics* can also select VARs as systems, but we will not follow that route here). Testing for super exogeneity, as in chapter 22, implicitly requires modeling all the contemporaneous variables as functions of lagged values and deterministic terms, and indeed a VAR was used there for forecasting. Once selected, the individual equations can be expanded to have common lag lengths (say 2) and deterministic terms (denoted d_t), resulting in the VAR:

$$x_t = \Gamma_1 x_{t-1} + \Gamma_2 x_{t-2} + \Gamma_3 d_t + \epsilon_t. \tag{23.40}$$

That provides a congruent basis for system cointegration tests, such as that in Johansen (1995) discussed in section 6.4.1, leading to a reformulation as a VEqCM.

Since shifts in μ are the most pernicious for forecasting, one could use the differenced variant of (23.26), namely:

$$\Delta x_{T+1} = \Delta x_T + \alpha \Delta \left(\beta' x_T - \mu \right) + \Delta \epsilon_{T+1}, \tag{23.41}$$

which can be written as the forecasting device, *after* estimation of the terminal model:

$$\widetilde{\Delta x}_{T+1|T} = \left(I_n + \widehat{\alpha} \widehat{\beta}' \right) \Delta x_T. \tag{23.42}$$

In (23.41), the cointegrating rank restriction is imposed, so (23.42) is a double-differenced VAR plus $\widehat{\alpha}\widehat{\beta}'\Delta x_T$, which re-introduces the main observable from (23.35) in a robust form. It is important to use the estimates from the VEqCM and not re-estimate, and especially not reselect, to avoid choosing over the non-congruent form in (23.41). One or more periods after a location shift, assuming the VEqCM is also the LDGP so consistent parameter estimates are available:

$$\Delta x_{T+h} = \Delta x_{T+h-1} + \alpha \left(\beta' \Delta x_{T+h-1} - \Delta \mu^* \right) + \Delta \epsilon_{T+h}, \tag{23.43}$$

where now $\Delta \mu^* = 0$, so $\mathsf{E}[\Delta x_{T+h} - \widetilde{\Delta x}_{T+h|T+h-1}]$ is:

$$\mathsf{E}_{T+h}\left[\Delta x_{T+h} + \alpha\beta' \Delta x_{T+h-1} - \left(I_n + \alpha\beta' \right) \Delta x_{T+h-1} \right] = 0.$$

Thus, such a DVEqCM misses only for 1 period following a location shift, and does not make systematic, possibly increasing, errors.

The consequences of omitting $\{z_t\}$ are more complicated. Although it was not explicitly formulated as such in (23.35), as well as being I(0), the means of the $\{z_t\}$ must be zero for γ to be the unconditional growth rate of $\{x_t\}$ and μ the mean of its cointegrating combinations. When the $\{z_t\}$ are included in the system with estimated parameters $\widehat{\Psi}$ and future $\{z_{T+h}\}$ need to be forecast, but its parameter shifts are not known, their omission may be less costly than their inclusion (see Hendry and Mizon, 2012, for a complete taxonomy and discussion of this result).

Literally combining all these results suggests the augmented strategy of pooling the forecasts from all the non-pernicious models: the VEqCM, DVEqCM perhaps DVAR, all terminal models selected at a loose significance level by *Autometrics*, and factor forecasts, but not averaging across all 2^N possible models as we now show by simulating a number of cases with and without breaks.

More recently, Castle, Clements and Hendry (2014) propose an extension of (23.41) that averages over several periods to produce "smoother" forecasts. Comparing (23.43) with (23.26) reveals that γ^* is being "estimated" by the one-period change Δx_{T+h-1} and μ^* by x_{T+h-2}. Instead, they suggest using short moving averages of the form $\sum_{i=1}^{4} \Delta x_{T+h-i}$ and $\sum_{i=2}^{5} x_{T+h-i}$ (say, for quarterly data), to reduce the volatility at the cost of slowing adjustment after a shift.

23.11   Some simulation findings

The Monte Carlo study in Hendry and Reade (2006) compares a number of alternative selection and combination approaches. Their constant parameter DGP was:

$$y_t = \beta_0 + \sum_{i=1}^{5} \beta_i z_{i,t} + \epsilon_t, \tag{23.44}$$

where $\epsilon_t \sim \text{IN}\left[0, \sigma_\epsilon^2\right]$. In (23.44), the first five coefficients were set to vary over a wide range of non-centralities, using $\beta_i = \psi_{\beta_i}/\sqrt{T}$, for $i = 1, \ldots, 5$ with $\psi_{\beta_i} = 0.1, 1, 2, 3, 4, 5, 10$, where ψ_{β_i} is the same non-centrality for all the t-ratios of relevant variables. The GUM was:

$$y_t = \beta_0 + \sum_{i=1}^{5} \beta_i z_{i,t} + \sum_{j=6}^{10} \beta_j z_{j,t} + e_t, \tag{23.45}$$

where the second five coefficients were all zero, as was β_0, but all variables entered all models de-meaned.

Eight different selection methods were compared: the DGP (23.44), the GUM (23.45), both without selection; *Autometrics*, where the search is started from the GUM, using both the best selected model and an average of all terminal models found in the tree-search, using BIC; Bayesian model averaging methods (BMAs), both conditional and unconditional where unconditional model averaging is an average over all models; all 2^N models averaged with equal weights or BIC weights.[1]

Figure 23.1 plots the 1-step MSFEs from the experiment as a function of ψ_{β_i}. At most non-centralities, the GUM forecasts are better than averaging. *Autometrics* forecasts have a hump around $|t| = 2$, partly because these simulations did not use bias corrections, but the best and the average of the terminal models have almost identical MSFEs. BMAs also have a hump, but around $t = 4$. Model averaging becomes less useful as the significance of the relevant $z_{i,t}$ increases. Using equal 2^{-N} weights or BIC weights, MSFEs increase exponentially with ψ_{β_i}. Thus, *Autometrics* provides a better, more consistent, performance. When $\psi_{\beta_i} < 2$, model averaging can outperform the GUM, and when $0 < \psi_{\beta_i} < 4$, it can outperform *Autometrics*. When $\psi_{\beta_i} = 0$, *Autometrics* usually selects the null model. As expected from section 23.5.2, it is possible to beat the estimated DGP for small ψ_{β_i}.

---

[1]We are grateful to James Reade for permission to report these result.

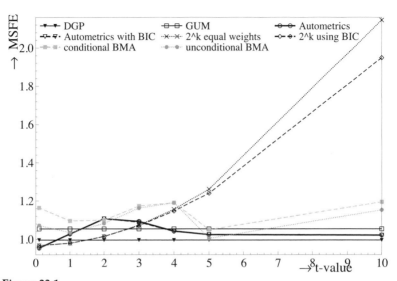

Figure 23.1
MSFEs from alternative approaches

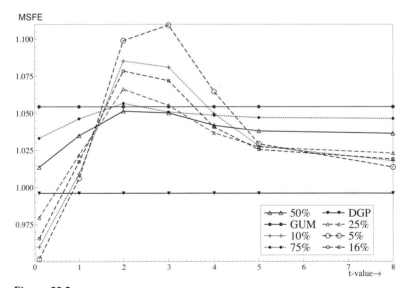

Figure 23.2
Comparative MSFEs for *Autometrics* from varying significance levels

Figure 23.2 shows the effects of varying the significance level, α, on *Autometrics* performance as the non-centrality increases, for a smaller range of non-centralities. As α increases from 5%, the hump diminishes, both in height and range, and by $\alpha = 0.25$ has effectively disappeared. Selection at that criterion level then outperforms the GUM for almost all non-centralities, and has a smaller MSFE than the DGP for $\psi_{\beta_i} < 1$, consistent with (23.20). Looser significance levels behave like the GUM (which has $\alpha = 1.0$), but even 50% generally outperforms the GUM almost everywhere; more stringent selection seems to offer little benefit for forecasting in these experiments, so here parsimony does not pay. AIC is close to the $\alpha = 16\%$ line.

23.12   Public-service case study

The objective in this research for the UK communications industries regulator and competition authority, Ofcom, was to forecast discounted net TV advertising revenues 10 years ahead on quarterly data to calculate the fee appropriate for renewal of the ITV3 licence to broadcast with advertising.[2]

A large number of non-stationary variables needed to be modeled, facing simultaneity, stochastic trends, evolution and structural change, the last of which was most marked in the short period before the forecast origin in 2003, Q2. Among the many breaks affecting some or all the variables were the introduction of personal video recorders (PVRs), new non-terrestrial TV channels, some with and some without advertising as well as Freeview channels, a focus on bar code based advertising, digital broadcasting, internet advertising and marketing websites, e-mail marketing, on-line promotions, etc., leading to greatly increased competition at the same time as audience fragmentation. Thus, both supply of and demand for TV advertising time were seriously affected, but it was manifestly impossible to disentangle the separate effects of these changes on the key variables of the real price per unit of TV advertising time, net advertising revenue (NAR), and audience reach.

Building on the earlier results in Hendry (1992), a VEqCM system was developed by *PcGets Quick Modeller*, which also tried to handle the outliers near the forecast origin. The unmodeled variables, which comprised company profits, aggregate consumers' expenditure, inflation etc., were forecast by an external macroeconomic model and input to the open VEqCM. Forecasts were also made using the DVEqCM, the robust

[2]Reported in www.ofcom.org.uk/research/tv/reports/tvadvmarket.pdf.

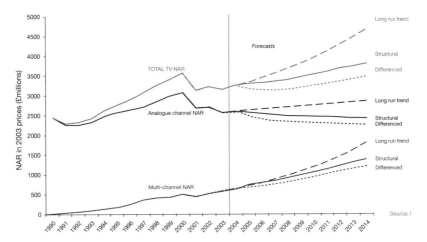

Figure 23.3
Forecasts of TV net advertising revenue, NAR

device described above, as that retained the main causal effects, of importance for the policy analyses (for example, a long-run price elasticity of unity was found unrestrictedly). Finally, forecasts were made using the average across a small group of related methods (not shown in figure 23.3, which was figure 6.5 in the earlier report and is reproduced by kind permission of Ofcom).

At the time of the macroeconomic forecasts in 2003, there was no sign of the impending financial crisis leading to the deepest recession since the 1920s in the UK. Rather, company profitability was near an all time high, consumers' expenditure was growing, fuelled by the credit boom, where houses almost became ATMs, inflation was low, and economists were discussing the Great Moderation. Thus, the macroeconomic environment was benign and favorable to growing TV advertising revenue, as indeed figure 23.3 shows for the long-run trend. Nevertheless, the forecasts for analogue-channel NAR from the DVEqCM showed a distinct downward trend over the decade ahead. In essence, the failure of analogue-channel NAR to have grown in the early 2000s despite that benign environment was due to the set of downward location shifts noted above, and the DVEqCM captured some of the post-break effects, as far as they were embodied by the time of the forecast origin, leading to a forecast of falling NAR.

23.13   Improving data accuracy at the forecast origin

As shown in Castle et al. (2009) and Castle and Hendry (2010b), the automatic model selection tools developed earlier in this book are applicable to improve the accuracy of flash estimates of aggregates like GDP and inflation at the forecast origin. The problem is generally termed nowcasting as contemporaneous information can be used.

A forecast $\widehat{y}_{T+1|T}$ for an aggregate variable y_{T+1} is usually based on y_T, where:

$$y_T = \sum_{i=1}^{N} w_{i,T} y_{i,T} \tag{23.46}$$

when $y_{i,T}$ are the disaggregates, entering with weights $w_{i,T}$. However, there are five important practical difficulties in measuring, rather than estimating (or nowcasting) y_T:

(a) Missing data. Some of the disaggregated contemporaneous data $y_{i,T}$ are unavailable at the time of preparation to construct the aggregate in (23.46).

(b) Changing database. Different components are unavailable in different periods, and tend to be missing on a non-systematic basis. Thus, J_T components are known, but $N - J_T$ unknown, where J_T is not fixed, and the known set changes every period, leading to a need to infill different components in every period.

(c) Substantial delays. Data arrive with varying time delays, and even flash estimates often only appear 4–6 weeks after a quarter has ended. For preliminary estimates of UK GDP, for example, the information is only available up to 24 days after the end of the quarter (see Reed, 2000, 2002). Moreover, different statistical agencies have different trade-offs between the timeliness and accuracy of flash estimates.

(d) Breaks. As stressed above, abrupt shifts can occur, in which case infilling becomes hazardous as relationships between variables, dynamics, and even the weights, all alter.

(e) Measurement errors. Consequently, flash estimates of y_T are subject to potentially major revisions as more disaggregates are observed, providing an unreliable and inaccurate guide from which to compute forecasts, or conduct policy.

As an example, figure 23.4 shows the initial and latest estimates of UK GDP from the *Bank of England Quarterly Bulletin* (Autumn 2005, p.338).

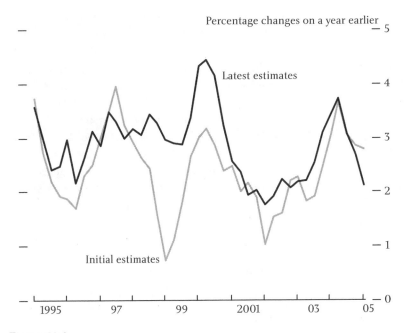

Figure 23.4
GDP outturns: initial and latest estimates

There are substantial, and policy relevant, discrepancies between the flash estimate and the value calculated in mid 2005. Moreover, forecasts based on the initial estimates would have been off target from the outset during most of 1998–2001. Missing disaggregate data are inevitable, so one must estimate what they will be. The crucial issue is how. Often surveys are used to infill the unknown components for a flash estimate (e.g., Clements and Hendry, 2003, and Ashley, Driver, Hayes and Jeffery, 2005), but such a methodology will not work well during structural change. Faust, Rogers and Wright (2007) report that revisions to initial GDP announcements are quite large in all G7 countries.

All these issues point towards a need to nowcast the data at T, namely combine both the data for components that are known with forecasts of components that are unknown, even before trying to forecast $T + 1$ onwards: see e.g., Giannone, Reichlin and Small (2008), Ferrara, Guegan and Rakotomarolahy (2010), Castle et al. (2009), and Castle and Hendry (2010b). Nowcasting is not just contemporaneous forecasting since there are many other sources of contemporaneous data which can be used, as discussed below in section 23.13.1.

To improve over flash estimates, nowcasts must address all five difficulties noted above. Fortunately, the methods of model selection discussed in earlier chapters can be applied to automatically build disaggregate models, which can be used to forecast all the variables that arrive with a delay, incorporating all available near-contemporaneous data, surveys, monthly, or weekly, indicators, etc. Moreover, this can be undertaken with IIS, thereby testing for shifts, and of course, switching to robust forecasts of missing series when breaks are detected. Even when actual values of the relevant variables are available, nowcasts could still be produced, as they can act as early warning signals if they differ radically from the corresponding flash measure. When nowcasts suffer failure relative to available observed disaggregates, their location shifts could also be used to adjust any remaining cognate unobserved disaggregates.

23.13.1 New sources of contemporaneous information

There are a number of new sources of high-frequency data that are available either contemporaneously or near-contemporaneously to guide the nowcasting of the missing disaggregates:

(a) Other disaggregates available close to the forecast origin: e.g., retail sales or RPI;

(b) Covariates at higher frequencies: e.g., new car registrations, construction output, new industrial orders, road traffic, air passenger numbers, energy consumption;

(c) Surveys of business and consumer plans and expectations;

(d) *Google Trends* data (see Choi and Varian, 2012, and Doornik, 2009c);

(e) Prediction markets (see Croxson and Reade, 2013, inter alia).

Mixed frequencies of data could draw on a MIDAS-type of approach (see, inter alia, Ghysels, Santa-Clara and Valkanov, 2004, Ghysels, Sinko and Valkanov, 2007, and Clements and Galvão, 2008), or unobserved components as in Koopman, Harvey, Doornik and Shephard (2004), although a solution using automatic model building is the focus below.

23.13.2 Changing database

The changing database problem, where J_T components are observed and $N - J_T$ are unknown, but J_T changes over time, can be solved by modeling all N $y_{i,t}$ over $t = 1, \ldots, T - 1$ using automatic methods, and forecasting every $y_{i,T}$. That allows comparisons of forecasts and outcomes for the J_T measured values to evaluate forecast accuracy, and forecasts for the remainder. Major discrepancies in the first group suggest a need to rapidly update for breaks, suggesting that impulse-indicator saturation (IIS) should be used on every disaggregate, where significant indicators near $T - 1$ reveal location shifts in some of the observed J_T subset. Such information can be used to adjust forecasts of the remainder and aggregate with data known at $T - \delta$:

$$\widetilde{y}_T = \sum_{i=1}^{J_T} w_{i,(T-\delta)} y_{i,T} + \sum_{i=J_T+1}^{N} w_{i,(T-\delta)} \widetilde{y}_{i,T|T-\delta}$$

where $\widetilde{y}_{i,T|T-\delta}$ is forecast from all the information available at time $T-\delta$, where δ might be zero, or even positive when the end of the period is in the past. Equations like (23.47) described below can be used.

23.13.3 Nowcasts of Euro-area quarterly GDP

For each quarter over 2003Q2–2008Q1, Castle et al. (2009) compute three nowcasts for Euro-area quarterly GDP:

H_1 for the month at the end of the reference quarter,

H_2 for the month after the end of the reference quarter,

H_3 for the second month after the end of the reference quarter.

The forecasts entering these nowcasts are computed by

$$\Delta \widehat{y}_T^{H_h} = \widehat{\beta}' \bar{x}_T + \widehat{\gamma}' \widetilde{x}_T + \widehat{\delta}' \iota, \tag{23.47}$$

where

$\bar{x}_T$ are the retained variables known at T for horizon h,

$\widetilde{x}_T$ the forecasts for retained variables unknown at T for horizon h, and

ι the retained impulse indicators.

Quarterly observations are indexed by t, whereas τ denotes the corresponding monthly index, with $t = 3\tau$. There are three releases available. First, a flash estimate approximately 43 days after the reference quarter, followed by two revised releases in the following consecutive months.

Denote the three releases by the vintages

$y_t^{v_1}$ released at $\tau + 2$,

$y_t^{v_2}$ released at $\tau + 3$,

$y_t^{v_3}$ released at $\tau + 4$.

Table 23.1
Actual RMSFEs for [A], and ratios of RMSFEs to the univariate benchmark
model [A] for [B] and [C]

	[A]	[B]	[C1]	[C2]	[C3]
H_1	0.2951	0.9823	0.4340	0.7994	0.7531
H_2	0.3056	1.2245	0.4808	0.6372	0.6222
H_3	0.1486	1.0372	0.8320	0.8320	0.8320

Survey data has no publication lag, and other data (e.g., industrial production, financial variables) are released with intermediate lags of between 1 and 3 months.

Castle et al. (2009) compute five comparable nowcasts, including two quarterly benchmark models, where all the models are selected recursively using *Autometrics*, so the model specifications and parameter estimates can change with each nowcast origin:

[A]   A univariate benchmark model using only past data on quarterly GDP-growth for all the recent vintages.

[B]   A model also including a range of covariates.

[C1]   Ex post nowcasts, where all the disaggregates are known.

[C2]   Disaggregate-based nowcasts – as in (23.47).

[C3]   A double differenced device – $\widetilde{\Delta x}_\tau = \Delta x_{\tau-1}$.

Table 23.1 records, for the three horizons, the actual RMSFEs for [A], and the ratios to those for the remaining methods, so values less than unity show an improvement. [C1] is infeasible in real-time forecasting, but acts as a benchmark, and [C3] can be used without any additional information or model selection. As can be seen, reductions in RMSFEs result for [C1]–[C3] at all horizons. Indeed, the RMSFE reduction for [C2] at H_2 is very large, reducing the RMSFE relative to [A] by more than a third. Throughout, [C3] is competitive with all other methods. Although this is only one illustration and uses a relatively limited information set, *Autometrics* with IIS applied to nowcast missing disaggregates seems able to both improve accuracy and reduce delays in producing forecast-origin data for real-time forecasting.

In an important sense, we have come full circle. Initial estimates of economic data can have substantial impacts on agents' expectations and plans, influencing economic activity and policy adversely when nowcasts or flash estimates are inaccurate. But in times of economic uncertainty and structural change, nowcasting becomes especially difficult, so a methodology that is robust to such breaks is essential. *Autometrics* can handle location shifts in-sample and at the forecast origin, including all the available information, often more variables than observations, and can accommodate data released at varying times. Thus, a method developed to select congruent parsimonious models of the LDGP from a general initial information set, when combined with the problems confronted in forecasting in the face of location shifts, can be used to improve the accuracy and immediacy of the very data on which such forecasts are dependent at the forecast origin. Since robust forecasting devices both follow from that combined theory, to fully utilize the selected model, and place considerable weight on the forecast origin observations, a more accurate start will translate directly into a more accurate forecast.

23.14   Conclusions

This chapter has addressed ways of using the developments in model discovery in a forecasting milieu, by transforming the selected model, or an average of terminal models, to a more robust form that would alleviate the impact of location shifts after they have occurred. To proceed beyond that, and forecast breaks themselves prior to their occurrence, remains a hope, not yet a feasibility, although some steps are being taken, and in some disciplines, major improvements have occurred in recent years as noted above: see e.g., Sparks (2003) for forecasting volcanic phenomena, and Hubert-Ferrari et al. (2000) for earthquake tectonics. Castle et al. (2011, 2010) respectively analyze the requirements for forecasting breaks in economic data, and during breaks. Also Pesaran et al. (2006) consider ways of improving estimates of forecast-error uncertainty when breaks are likely. Moreover, *Autometrics* with IIS can improve the accuracy and reduce delays in producing forecast-origin data as a key input to real-time forecasting.

In the absence of crystal ball methods to anticipate breaks, especially location shifts, selecting models using a forecasting criterion does not seem a viable activity in economics: best in-sample is no guarantee of best in the next period. Nevertheless, selecting a congruent representation of a well-behaved local data generating process, which embodies the best available consistent theory, based on the approach that has been the focus of this book, and transforming that model to a robust device does seem a feasible approach, and will at least avoid systematic forecast failure.

24 Epilogue

An Epilogue allows authors to recount and explain the plot; it is an end, but not a conclusion. Much research remains necessary to fully develop automatic methods for empirical model discovery with theory evaluation. Nevertheless, comparing our understanding with that of two decades ago, huge advances have occurred, and major strides have been achieved in the computer algorithms that underpin such an approach. Here we summarize the developments described in the book, and present a few final thoughts about the way ahead.

24.1 Summary

Economic analysis reasons about the economy, which together with the measurement process by which economic outcomes are observed, defines the data generation process. But the DGP is too large to model or comprehend, so analyses focus on subsets thereof. Every subset of variables, x, has a corresponding local DGP, namely its joint density over a period $t = 1, \dots, T$, denoted $D_X(x_1, \dots, x_T)$. The properties of the LDGP are determined by the choice of x interacting with what happened in the relevant economy over the sample and how the measurements were conducted. Although theory seeks to specify LDGPs that are relatively complete, constant and interpretable, it can only use models to study them, often highly abstract and greatly simplified.

Chapter 1 provided an overview and introduced some of the key concepts. It explained why understanding the evolution of data processes, testing subject-matter theories, forecasting future outcomes, and conducting policy analyses all involve empirical model discovery: many features of any model lie outside the purview of prior reasoning or existing evidence, especially the occurrence of intermittent, unanticipated location shifts due to many possible events such as wars, technological breakthroughs, financial innovation and so on. Discovery is an essential ingredient of all sciences, albeit occurring in many ways, from chance to systematic evaluation of every possibility. It is covertly present in econometrics, being usually limited to exploring one aspect at a time, but need not be so restricted.

Chapter 2 discussed discoveries and their subsequent evaluations in physical and biological sciences in greater detail to ascertain any common aspects. Despite important differences, seven common aspects could be discerned across a range of scientific discoveries, and were also common to discovery in economics. The complexity of macroeconomic data intrinsically involves empirical discovery with theory evaluation, as simply fitting a theory-based model to data is both hazardous and limits the potential for discovery.

Chapter 3 noted that many criticisms of model selection were only applicable to some approaches, or assumed a level of knowledge where discovery was unnecessary, so neither group of critiques need impugn automatic methods of empirical discovery where many features of models have to be data based. The first route map was displayed in terms of six stages from 1-cut selection to model discovery in a context where there may be more candidate variables than observations, so both expansion and simplification searches are required while retaining, and evaluating, the best available theory.

Chapter 5 considered nine possible criteria for evaluating model selection methods, noting that these can conflict, such as attaining empirical congruence may thwart theory consistency and vice versa. Jointly achieving three practical criteria was proposed: that a selection algorithm should recover the LDGP starting from the general unrestricted model (GUM) almost as often as when starting from that LDGP itself; that the operating characteristics of the algorithm should match the desired properties; and that the selection method should almost always find a well-specified, undominated model of the LDGP. In chapter 14, we added the fourth that the theory model could be embedded in he selection process to be retained without selection when it was a good characterization of the LDGP, so evaluated against a wide range of alternative hypotheses.

The theory of reduction in chapter 6 formalized the notion of the LDGP, and explained why it should be a target for search. Much of the effort of an empirical study must be devoted to theorizing about the relevant joint density to explain the economic behavior of interest, selecting the measured variables, incorporating the historical and institutional knowledge of the epoch, and building on previous empirical findings. These are essential steps in any progressive research strategy. But without an unjustifiable assumption of omniscience, they are insufficient. Empirical model discovery inevitably requires search outside the pre-existing framework.

Chapter 7 described general-to-specific modeling (*Gets*), applicable when the sample size allows the GUM to be estimated. The various steps leading to the formulation of the GUM, the evaluation criteria for checking congruence and parsimonious encompassing, and the role of path searches were all discussed.

Chapter 8 considered a baseline *Gets* approach, denoted 1-cut, which can select a model from any number of candidate variables with just one decision for mutually orthogonal, valid conditioning variables in a sufficiently large sample on a constant process. Commencing from a GUM that nests the LDGP, 1-cut established that model selection need not involve repeated testing, however many variables N there were for $N \ll T$. Thus, selecting variables from a large GUM is tractable, and a false null retention rate (gauge) can be attained that is close to the nominal significance level α. The resulting retention rate for relevant variables (potency) is close to that when selecting from the LDGP.

Chapter 9 focused on the 2-variable, constant parameter, linear regression model that coincided with the LDGP, as that is a setting where analytical distributions are available for post model-selection estimators. Leeb and Pötscher (2003, 2005) have established that large-sample convergence does not hold uniformly, so finite-sample and asymptotic distributions can differ markedly. In the realistic setting that the LDGP is non-constant, high-dimensional and unknown, so model discovery is essential, one cost of search is that uniform convergence will not occur, manifested in the bimodality of conditional distributions for estimated coefficients of both marginally-relevant and irrelevant variables.

However, a cost that can be avoided is pre-test bias in the conditional distributions, as chapter 10 showed, since approximately unbiased estimates of coefficients of relevant variables can be derived. The resulting corrections also drive the estimated coefficients of irrelevant variables towards the origin, substantially reducing their mean square errors (MSEs) in both conditional and unconditional distributions.

Since bias-corrected 1-cut selections match the three evaluation criteria, chapter 11 compared *Autometrics* with 1-cut selection. Despite now exploring many search paths, there was no deterioration in the selection quality, as *Autometrics* outperformed 1-cut on several measures. Importantly, *Autometrics* does not need an orthogonal formulation, so can handle a wide range of models.

The next two chapters, 12 and 13, respectively evaluated the impacts of diagnostic testing and encompassing on the gauge, potency, and MSEs of *Autometrics*. The operating characteristics of the specific misspecification tests used in *Autometrics* to determine congruence were investigated when applied to the DGP, the GUM and the finally selected model, as was the effect of their repeated use as diagnostic checks to ensure that reductions maintain congruence. In each case, the test's simulation behavior matched its reference distribution, with little impact from selection. Since all empirical models are encompassed by the LDGP, it is natural to seek models that parsimoniously encompass a GUM which nests the LDGP. Doing so in *Autometrics* helps stabilize the gauge, by retaining some variables where their elimination in a combination would lead to non-encompassing.

Chapter 14 provided the link between empirical model discovery and theory evaluation by showing that it was almost costless to retain a correct and complete theory model during selection. The key was to orthogonalize the variables that should be irrelevant relative to the theory variables, and only select over the former. Then the distributions of theory-parameter estimators are unaffected by such selection. However, if the theory is not complete, new features can be discovered, and if the GUM is sufficiently general to nest the LDGP, a good model of that should result whereas simply fitting the incorrect theory would deliver inconsistent results.

The analysis in chapters 8–14 was mainly based on *Gets*, where the GUM could be estimated from the available sample. The next step was to allow for more candidate variables than observations, first for impulse-indicator saturation (IIS) in chapter 15, where the candidate regressor set now has $N > T$ members. Developed by Hendry et al. (2008) and extended by Johansen and Nielsen (2009), IIS was first analyzed under the null for a split-sample approach, and showed that on average αT indicators would be retained by chance, which is a small efficiency loss for testing the potential relevance of T variables. The theory generalizes to more, and unequal, splits, and dynamic models, allowing multiple breaks, outliers and data contamination to be handled jointly with selecting from a large set of candidate variables.

Chapter 16 presented an empirical illustration of *Autometrics* compared to an earlier manual study; and chapter 17 undertook a range of simulation comparisons with other approaches, including step-wise regression, earlier multi-path search methods, information criteria (AIC, and BIC), Lasso, and RETINA. *Autometrics* delivered substantive improvements over all of these in many settings; its performance was not greatly affected by having more variables than observations; and although other approaches sometimes outperform, they were not reliable and could also deliver poor results.

Although the aim in *Gets* is to commence from a GUM that nests the LDGP, underspecification remains possible, so chapter 18 addressed model selection in that setting, and when the variables being analyzed provided a poor representation of the economic DGP. Model selection, rather than just fitting a prior specification, may help, and IIS could mitigate some of the adverse effects of induced location shifts when models were mis-specified.

These developments in automatic model selection in turn enable a range of previously intractable problems to be tackled, commencing in chapter 19 with handling excess numbers of variables, $N > T$, based on a mixture of reduction and expansion steps. The implementation in chapter 20 was for IIS to detect multiple breaks jointly with selecting variables. Chapter 21 considered the additional features involved in selecting non-linear models, often with $N > T$ as well as IIS to avoid spurious non-linearity capturing outliers. Then in chapter 22, IIS was used to test for the super exogeneity of conditioning variables, by detecting breaks in models of their marginal processes and testing the relevance of the retained indicators in the conditional model.

Finally, chapter 23 discussed selecting models for forecasting when unanticipated breaks could occur relative to the pre-existing LDGP, so finding the LDGP would not by itself ensure successful forecasting. Instead, since parameter shifts did not need to be disentangled for forecasting, unlike modeling, so there is no obvious forecasting criterion for selecting a viable device, the resulting strategy was to transform the selected model of the LDGP to a form that would be robust to past location shifts. As that chapter noted, improved nowcasting then completes the circle: despite location shifts at the forecast origin, by handling more variables than observations with IIS, and accommodating data with varying release dates, *Autometrics* can be used to improve the accuracy and immediacy of flash data, delivering a more accurate start for forecasts.

24.2   Implications

Despite selecting from a large number N of candidate variables when a smaller number $n < N$ are relevant, where $T \gg N$, so a congruent GUM is estimable:

(a) There is little loss of efficiency from checking many irrelevant variables.

(b) Nearly unbiased estimates of coefficients of retained relevant variables can be obtained while substantively reducing the MSEs of retained irrelevant variables.

(c) Potency in selected models is similar to power in the LDGP at the same critical value c_{α}.

(d) There is some loss from not retaining relevant variables at large c_{α}.

(e) This is offset by a gain from not commencing with an underspecified model.

(f) Theory insights can be embedded in the search process.

(g) Nearly unbiased equation standard errors are delivered.

(h) *Autometrics* tends to outperform other selection approaches, and usually delivers a congruent parsimonious encompassing model.

(i) Many of these implication continue to hold when $N > T$.

(j) IIS has low costs under the null of no breaks or data contamination.

(k) IIS can detect substantive multiple location shifts.

(l) IIS works well for fat-tailed error distributions at tight α.

(m) An automatic test for super exogeneity can be implemented using IIS.

(n) More candidate variables than observations can be handled by expanding and contracting searches.

(o) General non-linear extensions can be selected automatically.

(p) The selection methods are applicable to systems.

(q) Forecasting is different, especially in economics due to unanticipated location shifts.

Chapter 2 delineated seven common attributes of discovery, the initial translations of which were:

1. *framework of ideas*: current economic theory about the LDGP;

2. *going outside*: formulating the GUM to nest the LDGP;

3. *searching*: efficiently selecting a viable representation;

4. *recognizing*: terminating with a well-specified, undominated model;

5. *quantifying*: unbiasedly estimating the parameters of the selected model;

6. *evaluating*: testing new aspects of findings and evaluating the selection;

7. *summarizing*: selecting parsimonious models.

All seven have been achieved in substantial measure. Commencing from a theory insight for which reasonable data exist, a much more general model can be created that embeds that theory by including all the candidate variables, their lags in a time-series context, non-linear functions thereof if needed, and a saturating set of indicators to handle breaks and data contamination. *Autometrics* can efficiently search for a congruent parsimonious reduction, bias correct the estimated coefficients of retained variables, and conduct a range of tests, including checking the validity of conditioning. Empirical model discovery with theory evaluation is feasible.

24.3   The way ahead

Comparing our present understanding of model selection with that of two decades ago, huge advances have occurred, as well as major strides in the computer algorithms that underpin such an approach. However, both theoretical and algorithmic research remains to be undertaken before automatic methods for empirical model discovery are on a really sound footing.

First, the general setting of $N > T$ does not have a complete theoretical basis as yet, although some progress has been made (see Hendry and Johansen, 2014), and the ability to analyze the special case of IIS suggests that a theory may be feasible. Already rather different approaches were used in Hendry et al. (2008) and Johansen and Nielsen (2009), although both depended on the T additional candidates being indicators, so no new information accrued on the variable as the sample size grew. Moreover, the latter highlighted unexpected links with robust statistical methods.

Secondly, it is still not possible to jointly tackle all the issues confronting empirical analyses in economics. For example, finding changes at unknown times in all coefficients in models is not yet feasible; and linear simultaneous systems raise new problems not yet fully addressed, and are not completely resolved for non-linear simultaneous systems even when search is not needed.

Thirdly, better computational algorithms are quite conceivable: to date there has been little research on their development for $N > T$, where both expanding and contracting modes are needed, and full path searches of 2^N are infeasible.

Fourthly, IIS relies on impulse indicators as its basis set, and we are currently researching level saturation, which instead uses a basis set of step functions (see Castle *et al.*, 2013). In time series, such a reformulation may be advantageous, and given the low costs of searching over irrelevant variables, there may be merit in using both indicators and step functions (e.g., Ericsson and Reisman, 2012). Moreover, both types of indicators need greater analysis in cointegrated systems (e.g., Nielsen, 2004).

Fifthly, polynomials are not the most appealing set of functions to use in time series, even when reduced and orthogonalised by principal components, so alternative basis sets, such as squashing functions, deserve careful consideration, although the application in Castle and Hendry (2014b) showed that quadratics and cubics may also have direct economic interpretations.

Sixthly, efficient search strategies also await development. By this is meant such aspects as the order of proceeding, as in searching in an $I(1)$ space till a terminal model is obtained, and then checking cointegration reductions, or first trying to reduce all variables to $I(0)$: see Liao and Phillips (2012) for a method that seeks to do both together. Most macroeconomic data are doubly non-stationary, also exhibiting location shifts, which need to be tackled at the same time. When conducting IIS, or searching over large numbers of non-linear terms, it may be beneficial to retain all linear variables at first, and once breaks and non-linearities are established, do a second reduction across those. Non-linear cointegration is also an active research topic: see e.g., Berenguer-Rico and Gonzalo (2014).

Finally, other observational disciplines offer fruitful applications of the general approach, especially where location shifts occur: a recent example is modeling atmospheric carbon dioxide in Hendry and Pretis (2013) using *Autometrics* with $N > T$ and IIS.

Many issues await further research, promising to extend automatic modeling and its foundations. Let us end with a re-assurance: however far such developments proceed, they will not make economists or econometricians redundant. Instead, as with computers replacing calculators, automatic methods for empirical model discovery and theory evaluation will enhance economists' capabilities.

References

Agassi, J. 1977. Who discovered Boyle's law? *Studies In History and Philosophy of Science, A*, **8**, 189–250.

Akaike, H. 1969. Fitting autoregressive models for prediction. *Annals of the Institute of Statistical Mathematics*, **21**, 243–247.

Akaike, H. 1973. Information theory and an extension of the maximum likelihood principle. In Petrov, B. N., and Csaki, F. (eds.), *Second International Symposion on Information Theory*, pp. 267–281. Budapest: Akademia Kiado.

Aldrich, J. 1989. Autonomy. *Oxford Economic Papers*, **41**, 15–34.

Anderson, T. W. 1958. *An Introduction to Multivariate Statistical Analysis.* New York: John Wiley & Sons.

Anderson, T. W. 1962. The choice of the degree of a polynomial regression as a multiple-decision problem. *Annals of Mathematical Statistics*, **33**, 255–265.

Anderson, T. W. 1971. *The Statistical Analysis of Time Series.* New York: John Wiley & Sons.

Ando, A., and Modigliani, F. 1963. The 'life cycle' hypothesis of saving: Aggregate implications and tests. *American Economic Review*, **53**, 55–84.

Ando, A., and Modigliani, F. 1965. The relative stability of monetary velocity and the investment multiplier. *American Economic Review*, **55**, 693–728.

Andrews, D. W. K. 1991. Heteroskedasticity and autocorrelation consistent covariance matrix estimation. *Econometrica*, **59**, 817–858.

Ashley, J., Driver, R., Hayes, S., and Jeffery, C. 2005. Dealing with data uncertainty. *Bank of England Quarterly Bulletin*, **Spring**, 23–29.

Bai, J., and Perron, P. 1998. Estimating and testing linear models with multiple structural changes. *Econometrica*, **66**, 47–78.

Baillie, R. T. 1996. Long memory processes and fractional integration in econometrics. *Journal of Econometrics*, **73**, 5–59.

Banerjee, A., Dolado, J. J., and Mestre, R. 1998. Error-correction mechanism tests for cointegration in a single equation framework. *Journal of Time Series Analysis*, **19**, 267–283.

Banerjee, A., and Hendry, D. F. 1992. Testing integration and cointegration: An overview. *Oxford Bulletin of Economics and Statistics*, **54**, 225–255.

Bårdsen, G., Eitrheim, Ø., Jansen, E. S., and Nymoen, R. 2005. *The Econometrics of Macroeconomic Modelling*. Oxford: Oxford University Press.

Bårdsen, G., den Reijer, A., Jonasson, P., and Nymoen, R. 2012. MoSES: Model of Swedish economic studies. *Economic Modelling*, **29**, 2566–2582.

Barndorff-Nielsen, O. E. 1978. *Information and Exponential Families in Statistical Theory*. Chichester: John Wiley.

Bartholomew, D. J. 1987. *Latent Variable Models and Factor Analysis*. New York: Oxford University Press.

Bates, J. M., and Granger, C. W. J. 1969. The combination of forecasts. *Operations Research Quarterly*, **20**, 451–468.

Bennett, J., Cooper, M., Hunter, M., and Jardine, L. 2003. *London's Leonardo*. Oxford: Oxford University Press.

Berenguer-Rico, V., and Gonzalo, J. 2014. Summability of stochastic processes: A generalization of integration for non-linear processes. *Journal of Econometrics*, forthcoming.

Birchenhall, C. R., Bladen-Hovell, R. C., Chui, A. P. L., Osborn, D. R., and Smith, J. P. 1989. A seasonal model of consumption. *Economic Journal*, **99**, 837–843.

Blaug, M. 1980. *The Methodology of Economics*. Cambridge: Cambridge University Press.

Bock, M. E., Yancey, T. A., and Judge, G. C. 1973. Statistical consequences of preliminary test estimators in regression. *Journal of the American Statistical Association*, **68**, 109–116.

Boland, L. 2014. Model Building in Economics: Its Purposes and Limitations. Cambridge: Cambridge University Press. Forthcoming.

Bontemps, C., Florens, J.-P., and Richard, J.-F. 2008. Parametric and non-parametric encompassing procedures. *Oxford Bulletin of Economics and Statistics*, **70**, 751–780.

Bontemps, C., and Mizon, G. E. 2003. Congruence and encompassing. In Stigum 2003, pp. 354–378.

Bontemps, C., and Mizon, G. E. 2008. Encompassing: Concepts and implementation. *Oxford Bulletin of Economics and Statistics*, **70**, 721–750.

Boughton, J. M. 1992. The demand for M1 in the United States: A comment on Baba, Hendry and Starr. *Economic Journal*, **103**, 1154–1157.

Boumans, M. A. 2005. Measurement in economic systems. *Measurement*, **38**, 275–284.

Brown, G. 2001. *Count Rumford: The Extraordinary Life of a Scientific Genius—Scientist, Soldier, Statesman, Spy*. Stroud, UK: Sutton Publishing.

Caceres, C. 2007. Asymptotic properties of tests for mis-specification. Unpublished doctoral thesis, Economics Department, Oxford University.

Campos, J., and Ericsson, N. R. 1999. Constructive data mining: Modeling consumers' expenditure in Venezuela. *Econometrics Journal*, **2**, 226–240.

Campos, J., Ericsson, N. R., and Hendry, D. F. 2005a. Editors' introduction. In 2005b, pp. 1–81.

Campos, J., Ericsson, N. R., and Hendry, D. F. (eds.) 2005b. *Readings on General-to-Specific Modeling*. Cheltenham: Edward Elgar.

Campos, J., Hendry, D. F., and Krolzig, H.-M. 2003. Consistent model selection by an automatic *Gets* approach. *Oxford Bulletin of Economics and Statistics*, **65**, 803–819.

Castle, J. L. 2005. Evaluating PcGets and RETINA as automatic model selection algorithms. *Oxford Bulletin of Economics and Statistics*, **67**, 837–880.

Castle, J. L. 2008. Checking the robustness and validity of model selection: An application to UK wages. Mimeo, Economics Department, Oxford University.

Castle, J. L., Clements, M. P., and Hendry, D. F. 2013. Forecasting by factors, by variables, by both or neither? *Journal of Econometrics*, **177**, 305–319.

Castle, J. L., Clements, M. P., and Hendry, D. F. 2014. Robust approaches to forecasting. *International Journal of Forecasting*, forthcoming.

Castle, J. L., Doornik, J. A., and Hendry, D. F. 2011. Evaluating automatic model selection. *Journal of Time Series Econometrics*, **3 (1)**, DOI: 10.2202/1941–1928.1097.

Castle, J. L., Doornik, J. A., and Hendry, D. F. 2012. Model selection when there are multiple breaks. *Journal of Econometrics*, **169**, 239–246.

Castle, J. L., Doornik, J. A., and Hendry, D. F. 2013. Model selection in equations with many 'small' effects. *Oxford Bulletin of Economics and Statistics*, **75**, 6–22.

Castle, J. L., Doornik, J. A., Hendry, D. F., and Nymoen, R. 2013. Mis-specification testing: Non-invariance of expectations models of inflation. *Econometric Reviews*, DOI:10.1080/07474938.2013.825137.

Castle, J. L., Doornik, J. A., Hendry, D. F., and Pretis, F. 2013. Detecting location shifts by step-indicator saturation. Working paper, Economics Department, Oxford University.

Castle, J. L., Fawcett, N. W. P., and Hendry, D. F. 2009. Nowcasting is not just contemporaneous forecasting. *National Institute Economic Review*, **210**, 71–89.

Castle, J. L., Fawcett, N. W. P., and Hendry, D. F. 2010. Forecasting with equilibrium-correction models during structural breaks. *Journal of Econometrics*, **158**, 25–36.

Castle, J. L., Fawcett, N. W. P., and Hendry, D. F. 2011. Forecasting breaks and during breaks. In Clements, and Hendry 2011, pp. 315–353.

Castle, J. L., and Hendry, D. F. 2010a. A low-dimension portmanteau test for non-linearity. *Journal of Econometrics*, **158**, 231–245.

Castle, J. L., and Hendry, D. F. 2010b. Nowcasting from disaggregates in the face of location shifts. *Journal of Forecasting*, **29**, 200–214.

Castle, J. L., and Hendry, D. F. 2011a. A tale of 3 cities: Model selection in over-, exact, and under-specified equations. In Kaldor, M., and Vizard, P. (eds.), *Arguing About the World*, pp. 31–55. London: Bloomsbury Academic.

Castle, J. L., and Hendry, D. F. 2011b. Automatic selection of non-linear models. In Wang, L., Garnier, H., and Jackman, T. (eds.), *System Identification, Environmental Modelling and Control*, pp. 229–250. New York: Springer.

Castle, J. L., and Hendry, D. F. 2014a. Model selection in under-specified equations with breaks. *Journal of Econometrics*, **178**, 286–293.

Castle, J. L., and Hendry, D. F. 2014b. Semi-automatic non-linear model selection. In Haldrup, N., Meitz, M., and Saikkonen, P. (eds.), *Essays in Nonlinear Time Series Econometrics*. Oxford: Oxford University Press. Forthcoming.

Castle, J. L., Qin, X., and Reed, W. R. 2013. Using model selection algorithms to obtain reliable coefficient estimates. *Journal of Economic Surveys*, **27**, 269–296.

Castle, J. L., and Shephard, N. (eds.) 2009. *The Methodology and Practice of Econometrics*. Oxford: Oxford University Press.

Cattell, R. B. 1952. *Factor Analysis*. New York: Harper.

Choi, H., and Varian, H. 2012. Predicting the present with Google Trends. *Economic Record*, **88**, 2–9.

Chow, G. C. 1960. Tests of equality between sets of coefficients in two linear regressions. *Econometrica*, **28**, 591–605.

Claeskens, G., and Hjort, N. L. 2003. The focussed information criterion (with discussion). *Journal of the American Statistical Association*, **98**, 879–945.

Clements, M. P., and Galvão, A. B. 2008. Macroeconomic forecasting with mixed frequency data: Forecasting US output growth. *Journal of Business and Economic Statistics*, **26**, 546–554.

Clements, M. P., and Hendry, D. F. 1998. *Forecasting Economic Time Series*. Cambridge: Cambridge University Press.

Clements, M. P., and Hendry, D. F. 1999. *Forecasting Non-stationary Economic Time Series*. Cambridge, Mass.: MIT Press.

Clements, M. P., and Hendry, D. F. 2001. Explaining the results of the M3 forecasting competition. *International Journal of Forecasting*, **17**, 550–554.

Clements, M. P., and Hendry, D. F. 2003. Forecasting in the National Accounts at the Office for National Statistics. Report no 12, Statistics Commission.

Clements, M. P., and Hendry, D. F. 2005. Guest Editors' introduction: Information in economic forecasting. *Oxford Bulletin of Economics and Statistics*, **67**, 713–753.

Clements, M. P., and Hendry, D. F. 2006. Forecasting with breaks. In Elliott, G., Granger, C. W. J., and Timmermann, A. (eds.), *Handbook of Econometrics on Forecasting*, pp. 605–657. Amsterdam: Elsevier.

Clements, M. P., and Hendry, D. F. 2008. Economic forecasting in a changing world. *Capitalism and Society*, **3**, 1–18.

Clements, M. P., and Hendry, D. F. (eds.) 2011. *Oxford Handbook of Economic Forecasting*. Oxford: Oxford University Press.

Cooper, J. P., and Nelson, C. R. 1975. The ex ante prediction performance of the St. Louis and FRB-MIT-PENN econometric models and some results on composite predictors. *Journal of Money, Credit, and Banking*, **7**, 1–32.

Cox, D. R. 1961. Tests of separate families of hypotheses. In *Proceedings of the Fourth Berkeley Symposium on Mathematical Statistics and Probability*, Vol. 1, pp. 105–123 Berkeley: University of California Press.

Cross, R. 1982. The Duhem-Quine thesis, Lakatos and the appraisal of theories in macro-economics. *Economic Journal*, **92**, 320–340.

Croxson, K., and Reade, J. J. 2013. Information and efficiency: Goal arrival in soccer betting. *Economic Journal*, DOI: 10.1111/ecoj.12033.

Davidson, J. E. H. 1998. Structural relations, cointegration and identification: some simple results and their application. *Journal of Econometrics*, **87**, 87–113.

Davidson, J. E. H., Hendry, D. F., Srba, F., and Yeo, J. S. 1978. Econometric modelling of the aggregate time-series relationship between consumers' expenditure and income in the United Kingdom. *Economic Journal*, **88**, 661–692.

Demiralp, S., and Hoover, K. D. 2003. Searching for the causal structure of a vector autoregression. *Oxford Bulletin of Economics and Statistics*, **65**, 745–767.

Dickey, D. A., and Fuller, W. A. 1979. Distribution of the estimators for autoregressive time series with a unit root. *Journal of the American Statistical Association*, **74**, 427–431.

Dickey, D. A., and Fuller, W. A. 1981. Likelihood ratio statistics for autoregressive time series with a unit root. *Econometrica*, **49**, 1057–1072.

Doob, J. L. 1953. *Stochastic Processes*. New York: John Wiley Classics Library. 1990 edition.

Doornik, J. A. 2006. The role of simulation in econometrics. In Mills, T., and Patterson, K. (eds.), *Palgrave Handbook of Econometrics*, pp. 787–811. Basingstoke: Palgrave MacMillan.

Doornik, J. A. 2008. Encompassing and automatic model selection. *Oxford Bulletin of Economics and Statistics*, **70**, 915–925.

Doornik, J. A. 2009a. Autometrics. In Castle, and Shephard 2009, pp. 88–121.

Doornik, J. A. 2009b. Econometric model selection with more variables than observations. Working paper, Economics Department, University of Oxford.

Doornik, J. A. 2009c. Improving the timeliness of data on influenza-like illnesses using Google Trends. Typescript, Department of Economics, University of Oxford.

Doornik, J. A. 2009d. *Object-Oriented Matrix Programming using Ox* 7th edn. London: Timberlake Consultants Press.

Doornik, J. A., and Hansen, H. 2008. An omnibus test for univariate and multivariate normality. *Oxford Bulletin of Economics and Statistics*, **70**, 927–939.

Doornik, J. A., and Hendry, D. F. 2001. *Modelling Dynamic Systems using PcGive 10: Volume II*. London: Timberlake Consultants Press.

Doornik, J. A., and Hendry, D. F. 2013a. *OxMetrics: An Interface to Empirical Modelling* 7th edn. London: Timberlake Consultants Press.

Doornik, J. A., and Hendry, D. F. 2013b. *Empirical Econometric Modelling using PcGive: Volume I*. London: Timberlake Consultants Press.

Doornik, J. A., Hendry, D. F., and Nielsen, B. 1998. Inference in cointegrated models: UK M1 revisited. *Journal of Economic Surveys*, **12**, 533–572.

Doornik, J. A., and Ooms, M. 2004. Inference and forecasting for ARFIMA models, with an application to US and UK inflation. *Studies in Nonlinear Dynamics and Econometrics*, **8**. Issue 2, Article 14.

Drake, S. 1980. *Galileo*. Oxford: Oxford University Press.

Eddington, C. 1928. *Space, Time, and Gravitation*. Cambridge: Cambridge University Press.

Efron, B., and Gong, G. 1983. A leisurely look at the bootstrap, the jackknife, and cross-validation. *American Statistician*, **37**, **1**, 36–48.

Efron, B., Hastie, T., Johnstone, I., and Tibshirani, R. 2004. Least angle regression. *The Annals of Statistics*, **32**, 407–499.

Engle, R. F. 1982. Autoregressive conditional heteroscedasticity, with estimates of the variance of United Kingdom inflation. *Econometrica*, **50**, 987–1007.

Engle, R. F., and Granger, C. W. J. 1987. Cointegration and error correction: Representation, estimation and testing. *Econometrica*, **55**, 251–276.

Engle, R. F., and Hendry, D. F. 1993. Testing super exogeneity and invariance in regression models. *Journal of Econometrics*, **56**, 119–139.

Engle, R. F., Hendry, D. F., and Richard, J.-F. 1983. Exogeneity. *Econometrica*, **51**, 277–304.

Engle, R. F., and White, H. (eds.) 1999. *Cointegration, Causality and Forecasting*. Oxford: Oxford University Press.

Ericsson, N. R. 1983. Asymptotic properties of instrumental variables statistics for testing non-nested hypotheses. *Review of Economic Studies*, **50**, 287–303.

Ericsson, N. R., Hendry, D. F., and Prestwich, K. M. 1998. The demand for broad money in the United Kingdom, 1878–1993. *Scandinavian Journal of Economics*, **100**, 289–324.

Ericsson, N. R., and Irons, J. S. (eds.) 1994. *Testing Exogeneity*. Oxford: Oxford University Press.

Ericsson, N. R., and Irons, J. S. 1995. The Lucas critique in practice: Theory without measurement. In Hoover, K. D. (ed.), *Macroeconometrics: Developments, Tensions and Prospects*, pp. 263–312. Dordrecht: Kluwer Academic Press.

Ericsson, N. R., and MacKinnon, J. G. 2002. Distributions of error correction tests for cointegration. *Econometrics Journal*, **5**, 285–318.

Ericsson, N. R., and Reisman, E. L. 2012. Evaluating a global vector autoregression for forecasting. *International Advances in Economic Research*, **18**, 247–258.

Farmelo, G. (ed.) 2002. *De Motu Cordis*. London: Granta Publications. (It Must Be Beautiful: Great Equations of Modern Science).

Fasano, A. 2009. Surprises from celiac disease. *Scientific American*, **301**, 54–61.

Faust, J., Rogers, J. H., and Wright, J. H. 2007. News and noise in G-7 GDP announcements. *Journal of Money, Credit and Banking*, **37**, 403–419.

Faust, J., and Whiteman, C. H. 1997. General-to-specific procedures for fitting a data-admissible, theory-inspired, congruent, parsimonious, encompassing, weakly-exogenous, identified, structural model of the DGP: A translation and critique. *Carnegie–Rochester Conference Series on Public Policy*, **47**, 121–161.

Favero, C., and Hendry, D. F. 1992. Testing the Lucas critique: A review. *Econometric Reviews*, **11**, 265–306.

Ferrara, L., Guegan, D., and Rakotomarolahy, P. 2010. GDP nowcasting with ragged-edge data: A semi-parametric modelling. *Journal of Forecasting*, **29**, 186–199.

Fildes, R., and Ord, K. 2002. Forecasting competitions – their role in improving forecasting practice and research. In Clements, M. P., and Hendry, D. F. (eds.), *A Companion to Economic Forecasting*, pp. 322–253. Oxford: Blackwells.

Fisher, F. M. 1966. *The Identification Problem in Econometrics*. New York: McGraw Hill.

Florens, J.-P., and Mouchart, M. 1980. Initial and sequential reduction of Bayesian experiments. Discussion paper 8015, CORE, Louvain-La-Neuve, Belgium.

Florens, J.-P., Mouchart, M., and Rolin, J.-M. 1990. *Elements of Bayesian Statistics*. New York: Marcel Dekker.

Forni, M., Hallin, M., Lippi, M., and Reichlin, L. 2000. The generalized factor model: Identification and estimation. *Review of Economics and Statistics*, **82**, 540–554.

Fouquet, R., and Pearson, P. J. G. 2006. Seven centuries of energy services: The price and use of light in the United Kingdom (1300–2000). *Energy Journal*, **27**, 139–178.

Friedman, M. 1974. Explanation and scientific understanding. *Journal of Philosophy*, **71**, 5–19.

Friedman, M., and Meiselman, D. 1963. The relative stability of monetary velocity and the investment multiplier in the United States, 1897-1958. In *Stabilization Policies*. Englewood Cliffs, N.J.: Commission on Money and Credit.

Friedman, M., and Schwartz, A. J. 1982. *Monetary Trends in the United States and the United Kingdom: Their Relation to Income, Prices, and Interest Rates, 1867–1975*. Chicago: University of Chicago Press.

Friedman, W. A. 2014. *Fortune Tellers: The Story of America's First Economic Forecasters*. Princeton: Princeton University Press.

Frisch, R. 1938. Statistical versus theoretical relations in economic macrodynamics. Mimeograph dated 17 July 1938, League of Nations Memorandum. Reprinted in Hendry D. F. and Morgan M. S. (1995), *The Foundations of Econometric Analysis*. Cambridge: Cambridge University Press.

Frisch, R., and Waugh, F. V. 1933. Partial time regression as compared with individual trends. *Econometrica*, **1**, 221–223.

Garcia, R., and Perron, P. 1996. An analysis of the real interest rate under regime shifts. *Review of Economics and Statistics*, **78**, 111–125.

Gest, H. 2002. The remarkable vision of Robert Hooke (1635–1703): First observer of the microbial world. *Perspectives in Biology and Medicine*, **48**, 266–272.

Geweke, J. F., and Porter-Hudak, S. 1983. The estimation and application of long memory time series models. *Journal of Time Series Analysis*, **4**, 221–238.

Ghysels, E., Santa-Clara, P., and Valkanov, R. 2004. The MIDAS touch: MIxed DAta Sampling regression models. mimeo, Chapel Hill, N.C.

Ghysels, E., Sinko, A., and Valkanov, R. 2007. MIDAS regressions: Further results and new directions. *Econometric Reviews*, **26**, 53–90.

Giannone, D., Reichlin, L., and Small, D. 2008. Nowcasting GDP and Inflation: The real-time informational content of macroeconomic data. *Journal of Monetary Economics*, **55**, 665–676.

Gilbert, C. L. 1986. Professor Hendry's econometric methodology. *Oxford Bulletin of Economics and Statistics*, **48**, 283–307.

Godfrey, L. G. 1978. Testing for higher order serial correlation in regression equations when the regressors include lagged dependent variables. *Econometrica*, **46**, 1303–1313.

Godfrey, L. G., and Veale, M. R. 2000. Alternative approaches to testing by variable addition. *Econometric Reviews*, **19**, 241–261.

Goldstein, R. N. 2010. What's in a name? Rivalries and the birth of modern science. In Bryson, B. (ed.), *Seeing Further: The Story of Science and the Royal Society*, pp. 107–129. London, UK: HarperPress.

Gorman, W. M. 1956. Demand for related goods. Discussion paper, Agricultural Experimental Station, Iowa.

Govaerts, B., Hendry, D. F., and Richard, J.-F. 1994. Encompassing in stationary linear dynamic models. *Journal of Econometrics*, **63**, 245–270.

Granger, C. W. J. 1969. Investigating causal relations by econometric models and cross-spectral methods. *Econometrica*, **37**, 424–438.

Granger, C. W. J. 1981. Some properties of time series data and their use in econometric model specification. *Journal of Econometrics*, **16**, 121–130.

Granger, C. W. J. 1999. *Empirical Modeling in Economics: Specification and Evaluation*. Cambridge: Cambridge University Press.

Granger, C. W. J., and Jeon, Y. 2004. Thick modeling. *Economic Modelling*, **21**, 323–343.

Granger, C. W. J., and Joyeux, R. 1980. An introduction to long memory time series models and fractional differencing. *Journal of Time Series Analysis*, **1**, 15–30.

Granger, C. W. J., and Newbold, P. 1974. Spurious regressions in econometrics. *Journal of Econometrics*, **2**, 111–120.

Granger, C. W. J., and Pesaran, M. H. 2000. A decision-theoretic approach to forecast evaluation. In Chon, W. S., Li, W. K., and Tong, H. (eds.), *Statistics and Finance: An Interface*, pp. 261–278. London: Imperial College Press.

Granger, C. W. J., and Teräsvirta, T. 1993. *Modelling Nonlinear Economic Relationships*. Oxford: Oxford University Press.

Haavelmo, T. 1944. The probability approach in econometrics. *Econometrica*, **12**, 1–118. Supplement.

Haavelmo, T. 1989. *Prize Lecture*. Sveriges Riksbank: Prize in Economic Sciences in Memory of Alfred Nobel.

Hackett, J. (ed.) 1997. *Roger Bacon and the Sciences: Commemorative Essays*. New York: Brill.

Hall, A. R., Rudebusch, G. D., and Wilcox, D. W. 1996. Judging instrument relevance in instrumental variables estimation. *International Economic Review*, **37**, 283–298.

Hannan, E. J., and Quinn, B. G. 1979. The determination of the order of an autoregression. *Journal of the Royal Statistical Society*, **B, 41**, 190–195.

Hansen, B. E. 1999. Discussion of 'Data mining reconsidered'. *Econometrics Journal*, **2**, 26–40.

Hansen, B. E. 2005. Challenges for econometric model selection. *Econometric Theory*, **21**, 60–68.

Hansen, B. E. 2010. Averaging estimators for autoregressions with a near unit root. *Journal of Econometrics*, **158**, 152–155.

Harman, P. M. 1998. *The Natural Philosophy of James Clerk Maxwell*. Cambridge: Cambridge University Press.

Harré, R. 1981. *Great Scientific Experiments*. Oxford: Oxford University Press.

Henderson, J. W. 1997. The yellow brick road to penicillin : A story of serendipity. *Mayo Clinic Proceedings*, **72**, 683–687.

Hendry, D. F. 1974. Stochastic specification in an aggregate demand model of the United Kingdom. *Econometrica*, **42**, 559–578.

Hendry, D. F. 1976. The structure of simultaneous equations estimators. *Journal of Econometrics*, **4**, 51–88.

Hendry, D. F. 1977. On the time series approach to econometric model building. In Sims, C. A. (ed.), *New Methods in Business Cycle Research*, pp. 183–202. Minneapolis: Federal Reserve Bank of Minneapolis.

Hendry, D. F. 1979. Predictive failure and econometric modelling in macroeconomics: The transactions demand for money. In Ormerod, P. (ed.), *Economic Modelling*, pp. 217–242. London: Heinemann.

Hendry, D. F. 1980. Econometrics: Alchemy or science? *Economica*, **47**, 387–406.

Hendry, D. F. 1984. Monte Carlo experimentation in econometrics. In Griliches, Z., and Intriligator, M. D. (eds.), *Handbook of Econometrics*, Vol. 2, Ch. 16, pp. 937–976. Amsterdam: North-Holland.

Hendry, D. F. 1986. Using PC-GIVE in econometrics teaching. *Oxford Bulletin of Economics and Statistics*, **48**, 87–98.

Hendry, D. F. 1987. Econometric methodology: A personal perspective. In Bewley, T. F. (ed.), *Advances in Econometrics*, pp. 29–48. Cambridge: Cambridge University Press.

Hendry, D. F. 1988. The encompassing implications of feedback versus feedforward mechanisms in econometrics. *Oxford Economic Papers*, **40**, 132–149.

Hendry, D. F. 1992. An econometric analysis of TV advertising expenditure in the United Kingdom. *Journal of Policy Modeling*, **14**, 281–311.

Hendry, D. F. 1995a. *Dynamic Econometrics*. Oxford: Oxford University Press.

Hendry, D. F. 1995b. The role of econometrics in scientific economics. In d'Autume, A., and Cartelier, J. (eds.), *L'Economie Devient-elle une Science Dure?*, pp. 172–196. Paris: Economica. Reprinted in English as: Is Economics Becoming a Hard Science? Edward Elgar, 1997.

Hendry, D. F. 1995c. Econometrics and business cycle empirics. *Economic Journal*, **105**, 1622–1636.

Hendry, D. F. 1996. On the constancy of time-series econometric equations. *Economic and Social Review*, **27**, 401–422.

Hendry, D. F. 1997. On congruent econometric relations: A comment. *Carnegie–Rochester Conference Series on Public Policy*, **47**, 163–190.

Hendry, D. F. 1999. An econometric analysis of US food expenditure, 1931–1989. In Magnus, and Morgan 1999, pp. 341–361.

Hendry, D. F. 2000a. *Econometrics: Alchemy or Science?* Oxford: Oxford University Press. New Edition.

Hendry, D. F. 2000b. On detectable and non-detectable structural change. *Structural Change and Economic Dynamics*, **11**, 45–65.

Hendry, D. F. 2001a. How economists forecast. In Hendry, D. F., and Ericsson, N. R. (eds.), *Understanding Economic Forecasts*, pp. 15–41. Cambridge, Mass.: MIT Press.

Hendry, D. F. 2001b. Modelling UK inflation, 1875–1991. *Journal of Applied Econometrics*, **16**, 255–275.

Hendry, D. F. 2002. Forecast failure, expectations formation, and the Lucas critique. *Annales D'Économie et de Statistique*, **67-68**, 21–40.

Hendry, D. F. 2004a. Forecasting long-run TV advertising expenditure in the UK. Commissioned report, Ofcom, London. www.ofcom.org.uk/research/tv/reports/tvadvmarket.pdf.

Hendry, D. F. 2004b. The Nobel Memorial Prize for Clive W.J. Granger. *Scandinavian Journal of Economics*, **106**, 187–213.

Hendry, D. F. 2006. Robustifying forecasts from equilibrium-correction models. *Journal of Econometrics*, **135**, 399–426.

Hendry, D. F. 2009. The methodology of empirical econometric modeling: Applied econometrics through the looking-glass. In Mills, T. C., and Patterson, K. D. (eds.), *Palgrave Handbook of Econometrics*, pp. 3–67. Basingstoke: Palgrave MacMillan.

Hendry, D. F. 2010. Revisiting UK consumers' expenditure: Cointegration, breaks, and robust forecasts. *Applied Financial Economics*, **21**, 19–32.

Hendry, D. F. 2011a. Climate change: Possible lessons for our future from the distant past. In Dietz, S., Michie, J., and Oughton, C. (eds.), *The Political Economy of the Environment*, pp. 19–43. London: Routledge.

Hendry, D. F. 2011b. Empirical economic model discovery and theory evaluation. *Rationality, Markets and Morals*, **2**, 115–145. www.rmm-journal.de/htdocs/st01.html.

Hendry, D. F. 2011c. On adding over-identifying instrumental variables to simultaneous equations. *Economics Letters*, **111**, 68–70.

Hendry, D. F., and Clements, M. P. 2004. Pooling of forecasts. *Econometrics Journal*, **7**, 1–31.

Hendry, D. F., and Doornik, J. A. 1997. The implications for econometric modelling of forecast failure. *Scottish Journal of Political Economy*, **44**, 437–461.

Hendry, D. F., and Ericsson, N. R. 1991. Modeling the demand for narrow money in the United Kingdom and the United States. *European Economic Review*, **35**, 833–886.

Hendry, D. F., and Johansen, S. 2014. Model discovery and Trygve Haavelmo's legacy. *Econometric Theory*, forthcoming.

Hendry, D. F., Johansen, S., and Santos, C. 2008. Automatic selection of indicators in a fully saturated regression. *Computational Statistics*, **33**, 317–335. Erratum, 337–339.

Hendry, D. F., and Juselius, K. 2000. Explaining cointegration analysis: Part I. *Energy Journal*, **21**, 1–42.

Hendry, D. F., and Juselius, K. 2001. Explaining cointegration analysis: Part II. *Energy Journal*, **22**, 75–120.

Hendry, D. F., and Krolzig, H.-M. 1999. Improving on 'Data mining reconsidered' by K.D. Hoover and S.J. Perez. *Econometrics Journal*, **2**, 202–219.

Hendry, D. F., and Krolzig, H.-M. 2001. *Automatic Econometric Model Selection*. London: Timberlake Consultants Press.

Hendry, D. F., and Krolzig, H.-M. 2003. New developments in automatic general-to-specific modelling. In Stigum 2003, pp. 379–419.

Hendry, D. F., and Krolzig, H.-M. 2004a. Resolving three 'intractable' problems using a Gets approach. Unpublished paper, Economics Department, University of Oxford.

Hendry, D. F., and Krolzig, H.-M. 2004b. Sub-sample model selection procedures in general-to-specific modelling. In Becker, R., and Hurn, S. (eds.), *Contemporary Issues in Economics and Econometrics: Theory and Application*, pp. 53–74. Cheltenham: Edward Elgar.

Hendry, D. F., and Krolzig, H.-M. 2005. The properties of automatic Gets modelling. *Economic Journal*, **115**, C32–C61.

Hendry, D. F., Leamer, E. E., and Poirier, D. J. 1990. A conversation on econometric methodology. *Econometric Theory*, **6**, 171–261.

Hendry, D. F., Lu, M., and Mizon, G. E. 2009. Model identification and non-unique structure. In Castle, and Shephard 2009, pp. 343–364.

Hendry, D. F., Marcellino, M., and Mizon, G. E. (eds.) 2008. *Encompassing*. Special Issue: *Oxford Bulletin of Economics and Statistics*.

Hendry, D. F., and Massmann, M. 2007. Co-breaking: Recent advances and a synopsis of the literature. *Journal of Business and Economic Statistics*, **25**, 33–51.

Hendry, D. F., and Mizon, G. E. 1978. Serial correlation as a convenient simplification, not a nuisance: A comment on a study of the demand for money by the Bank of England. *Economic Journal*, **88**, 549–563.

Hendry, D. F., and Mizon, G. E. 1993. Evaluating dynamic econometric models by encompassing the VAR. In Phillips, P. C. B. (ed.), *Models, Methods and Applications of Econometrics*, pp. 272–300. Oxford: Basil Blackwell.

Hendry, D. F., and Mizon, G. E. 1999. The pervasiveness of Granger causality in econometrics. In Engle, and White 1999, pp. 102–134.

Hendry, D. F., and Mizon, G. E. 2011. Econometric modelling of time series with outlying observations. *Journal of Time Series Econometrics*, **3 (1)**, DOI: 10.2202/1941–1928.1100.

Hendry, D. F., and Mizon, G. E. 2012. Open-model forecast-error taxonomies. In Chen, X., and Swanson, N. R. (eds.), *Recent Advances and Future Directions in Causality, Prediction, and Specification Analysis*, pp. 219–240. New York: Springer.

Hendry, D. F., and Mizon, G. E. 2014. Unpredictability in economic analysis, econometric modeling and forecasting. *Journal of Econometrics*, forthcoming.

Hendry, D. F., and Neale, A. J. 1991. A Monte Carlo study of the effects of structural breaks on tests for unit roots. In Hackl, P., and Westlund, A. H. (eds.), *Economic Structural Change, Analysis and Forecasting*, pp. 95–119. Berlin: Springer-Verlag.

Hendry, D. F., Neale, A. J., and Srba, F. 1988. Econometric analysis of small linear systems using Pc-Fiml. *Journal of Econometrics*, **38**, 203–226.

Hendry, D. F., and Nielsen, B. 2007. *Econometric Modeling: A Likelihood Approach*. Princeton: Princeton University Press.

Hendry, D. F., and Pretis, F. 2013. Anthropogenic Influences on Atmospheric CO_2. In Fouquet, R. (ed.), *Handbook on Energy and Climate Change*, pp. 287–326. Cheltenham: Edward Elgar.

Hendry, D. F., and Reade, J. J. 2006. Forecasting using model averaging in the presence of structural breaks. Working paper, Economics Department, Oxford University.

Hendry, D. F., and Reade, J. J. 2008. Modelling and forecasting using model averaging. Working paper, Economics Department, Oxford University.

Hendry, D. F., and Richard, J.-F. 1982. On the formulation of empirical models in dynamic econometrics. *Journal of Econometrics*, **20**, 3–33.

Hendry, D. F., and Richard, J.-F. 1989. Recent developments in the theory of encompassing. In Cornet, B., and Tulkens, H. (eds.), *Contributions to Operations Research and Economics. The XXth Anniversary of CORE*, pp. 393–440. Cambridge, MA: MIT Press.

Hendry, D. F., and Santos, C. 2005. Regression models with data-based indicator variables. *Oxford Bulletin of Economics and Statistics*, **67**, 571–595.

Hendry, D. F., and Santos, C. 2010. An automatic test of super exogeneity. In Watson, M. W., Bollerslev, T., and Russell, J. (eds.), *Volatility and Time Series Econometrics*, pp. 164–193. Oxford: Oxford University Press.

Hendry, D. F., and Starr, R. M. 1993. The demand for M1 in the USA: A reply to James M. Boughton. *Economic Journal*, **103**, 1158–1169.

Hendry, D. F., and von Ungern-Sternberg, T. 1981. Liquidity and inflation effects on consumers' expenditure. In Deaton, A. S. (ed.), *Essays in the Theory and Measurement of Consumers' Behaviour*, pp. 237–261. Cambridge: Cambridge University Press.

Herschel, J. 1830. *A Preliminary Discourse on The Study of Natural Philosophy*. London: Longman, Rees, Browne, Green and John Taylor.

Hoeting, J. A., Madigan, D., Raftery, A. E., and Volinsky, C. T. 1999. Bayesian model averaging: A tutorial (with discussion). *Statistical Science*, **214**, 382–417.

Holmes, R. 2008. *The Age of Wonder*. London: Harper Press.

Holton, G. 1986. The advancement of science, and its burdens. *Daedalus*, **115**, 77–104.

Holton, G. 1988. *Thematic Origins of Scientific Thought*. Cambridge: Cambridge University Press.

Hoover, K. D., Demiralp, S., and Perez, S. J. 2009. Empirical identification of the vector autoregression: The causes and effects of US M2. In Castle, and Shephard 2009, pp. 37–58.

Hoover, K. D., and Perez, S. J. 1999. Data mining reconsidered: Encompassing and the general-to-specific approach to specification search. *Econometrics Journal*, **2**, 167–191.

Hoover, K. D., and Perez, S. J. 2004. Truth and robustness in cross-country growth regressions. *Oxford Bulletin of Economics and Statistics*, **66**, 765–798.

Hsiao, C. 1983. Identification. In Griliches, Z., and Intriligator, M. D. (eds.), *Handbook of Econometrics*, Vol. 1, Ch. 4. Amsterdam: North-Holland.

Hubert-Ferrari, A., Barka, A., Jacques, E., Nalbant, S. S., Meyer, B., Armijo, R., Tapponnier, P., and King, G. C. P. 2000. Seismic hazard in the Marmara Sea region following the 17 August 1999 Izmit earthquake. *Nature*, **404**, 269–273.

Hurvich, C. M., and Tsai, C.-L. 1989. Regression and time series model selection in small samples. *Biometrika*, **76**, 297–307.

Ireland, P. 2004. A method for taking models to the data. *Journal of Economic Dynamics and Control*, *28*(6), 1205–1226.

Jacobson, T., and Karlsson, S. 2004. Finding good predictors for inflation: A Bayesian model averaging approach. *Journal of Forecasting*, **23**, 479–496.

James, W., and Stein, C. 1961. Estimation with quadratic loss. In Neyman, J. (ed.), *Proceedings of the Fourth Berkeley Symposium on Mathematical Statistics and Probability*, pp. 361–379. Berkeley: University of California Press.

Jansen, E. S., and Teräsvirta, T. 1996. Testing parameter constancy and super exogeneity in econometric equations. *Oxford Bulletin of Economics and Statistics*, **58**, 735–763.

Johansen, S. 1988. Statistical analysis of cointegration vectors. *Journal of Economic Dynamics and Control*, **12**, 231–254.

Johansen, S. 1995. *Likelihood-based Inference in Cointegrated Vector Autoregressive Models*. Oxford: Oxford University Press.

Johansen, S. 2006a. Cointegration: An overview. In Mills, T. C., and Patterson, K. D. (eds.), *Palgrave Handbook of Econometrics*, pp. 540–577. Basingstoke: Palgrave MacMillan.

Johansen, S. 2006b. Confronting the economic model with the data? In Colander, D. (ed.), *Post-Walrasian Macroeconomics*, pp. 287–300. Cambridge: Cambridge University Press.

Johansen, S., Mosconi, R., and Nielsen, B. 2000. Cointegration analysis in the presence of structural breaks in the deterministic trend. *Econometrics Journal*, **3**, 216–249.

Johansen, S., and Nielsen, B. 2009. An analysis of the indicator saturation estimator as a robust regression estimator. In Castle, and Shephard 2009, pp. 1–36.

Johnson, N. L., and Kotz, S. 1970. *Continuous Univariate Distributions*. New York: John Wiley. Volume 1.

Joreskog, K. G. 1967. Some contributions to maximum likelihood factor analysis. *Psychometrika*, **32**.

Judge, G. G., and Bock, M. E. 1978. *The Statistical Implications of Pre-Test and Stein-Rule Estimators in Econometrics*. Amsterdam: North Holland Publishing Company.

Judge, G. G., Griffiths, W. E., Hill, R. C., Lütkepohl, H., and Lee, T.-C. 1985. *The Theory and Practice of Econometrics*, 2nd edn. New York: John Wiley.

Juselius, K. 2006. *The Cointegrated VAR Model: Methodology and Applications*. Oxford: Oxford University Press.

Juselius, K., and Franchi, M. 2007. Taking a DSGE model to the data meaningfully. *Economics-The Open-Access, Open-Assessment E-Journal*, **2007-4**.

Keynes, J. M. 1939. Professor Tinbergen's method. *Economic Journal*, **44**, 558–568.

Keynes, J. M. 1940. Statistical business-cycle research: Comment. *Economic Journal*, **50**, 154–156.

King, R. D., Rowland, J., Oliver, S. G., Young, M., Aubrey, W., Byrne, E., Liakata, M., Markham, M., Pir, P., Soldatova, L. N., Sparkes, A., Whelan, K. E., and Clare, A. 2009. The automation of science. *Science*, **324 no. 5923**, 85–89.

Klein, L. R. 1950. *Economic Fluctuations in the United States, 1921–41*. No. 11 in Cowles Commission Monograph. New York: John Wiley.

Klein, L. R. 1971. *An Essay on the Theory of Economic Prediction*. Chicago: Markham Publishing Company.

Klein, L. R., Ball, R. J., Hazlewood, A., and Vandome, P. 1961. *An Econometric Model of the UK*. Oxford: Oxford University Press.

Kongsted, H. C. 2005. Testing the nominal-to-real transformation. *Journal of Econometrics*, **124**, 205–225.

Koopman, S. J., Harvey, A. C., Doornik, J. A., and Shephard, N. 2004. *Structural Time Series Analysis, Modelling, and Prediction using STAMP* 4th edn. London: Timberlake Consultants Press.

Koopmans, T. C. 1937. *Linear Regression Analysis of Economic Time Series*. Haarlem: Netherlands Economic Institute.

Koopmans, T. C. 1947. Measurement without theory. *Review of Economics and Statistics*, **29**, 161–179.

Koopmans, T. C. 1949. Identification problems in economic model construction. *Econometrica*, **17**, 125–144.

Koopmans, T. C. (ed.) 1950. *Statistical Inference in Dynamic Economic Models*. No. 10 in Cowles Commission Monograph. New York: John Wiley & Sons.

Koopmans, T. C., and Reiersøl, O. 1950. The identification of structural characteristics. *The Annals of Mathematical Statistics*, **21**, 165–181.

Koopmans, T. C., Rubin, H., and Leipnik, R. B. 1950. Measuring the equation systems of dynamic economics. In Koopmans 1950, Ch. 2.

Krolzig, H.-M. 2003. General-to-specific model selection procedures for structural vector autoregressions. *Oxford Bulletin of Economics and Statistics*, **65**, 769–802.

Krolzig, H.-M., and Hendry, D. F. 2001. Computer automation of general-to-specific model selection procedures. *Journal of Economic Dynamics and Control*, **25**, 831–866.

Krolzig, H.-M., and Toro, J. 2002. Testing for super-exogeneity in the presence of common deterministic shifts. *Annales d'Économie et de Statistique*, **67/68**, 41–71.

Kuhn, T. 1962. *The Structure of Scientific Revolutions*. Chicago: University of Chicago Press.

Kurcewicz, M., and Mycielski, J. 2003. A specification search algorithm for cointegrated systems. Discussion paper, Statistics Department, Warsaw University.

Kydland, F. E., and Prescott, E. C. 1991. The econometrics of the general equilibrium approach to business cycles. *Scandinavian Journal of Economics*, **93**, 161–178.

Kydland, F. E., and Prescott, E. C. 1996. The computational experiment: An econometric tool. *The Journal of Economic Perspectives*, **10**, 69–85.

Lakatos, I. 1974. Falsification and the methodology of scientific research programmes. In Lakatos, I., and Musgrave, A. (eds.), *Criticism and the Growth of Knowledge*, pp. 91–196. Cambridge: Cambridge University Press.

Lawley, D. N., and Maxwell, A. E. 1963. *Factor Analysis as a Statistical Method*. London: Butterworth and Co.

Leamer, E. E. 1978. *Specification Searches. Ad-Hoc Inference with Non-Experimental Data*. New York: John Wiley.

Leamer, E. E. 1983. Let's take the con out of econometrics. *American Economic Review*, **73**, 31–43.

Leeb, H., and Pötscher, B. M. 2003. The finite-sample distribution of post-model-selection estimators, and uniform versus non-uniform approximations. *Econometric Theory*, **19**, 100–142.

Leeb, H., and Pötscher, B. M. 2005. Model selection and inference: Facts and fiction. *Econometric Theory*, **21**, 21–59.

Liao, Z., and Phillips, P. C. B. 2012. Automated estimation of vector error correction models. Cowles Foundation DP 1873, Yale University.

Lovell, M. C. 1983. Data mining. *Review of Economics and Statistics*, **65**, 1–12.

Lu, M., Mizon, G. E., and Monfardini, C. 2008. Simulation encompassing: Testing non-nested hypotheses. *Oxford Bulletin of Economics and Statistics*, **70**, 781–806.

Lucas, R. E. 1976. Econometric policy evaluation: A critique. In Brunner, K., and Meltzer, A. (eds.), *The Phillips Curve and Labor Markets*, Vol. 1 of *Carnegie-Rochester Conferences on Public Policy*, pp. 19–46. Amsterdam: North-Holland.

Lynch, A. W., and Vital-Ahuja, T. 1998. Can subsample evidence alleviate the data-snooping problem? A comparison to the maximal R^2 cutoff test. Discussion paper, Stern Business School, New York University.

Magnus, J. R., and Morgan, M. S. (eds.) 1999. *Methodology and Tacit Knowledge: Two Experiments in Econometrics*. Chichester: John Wiley and Sons.

Makridakis, S., Andersen, A., Carbone, R., Fildes, R., et al. 1982. The accuracy of extrapolation (time series) methods: Results of a forecasting competition. *Journal of Forecasting*, **1**, 111–153.

Makridakis, S., and Hibon, M. 2000. The M3-competition: Results, conclusions and implications. *International Journal of Forecasting*, **16**, 451–476.

Mallows, C. L. 1966. Choosing a Subset Regression. Presentation, Annual Meeting of the American Statistical Association, Los Angeles.

Mallows, C. L. 1973. Some comments on c_p. *Technometrics*, **15**, 661–675.

Maronna, R. A., Martin, R. D., and Yohai, V. J. 2006. *Robust Statistics: Theory and Methods*. Chichester: John Wiley & Sons.

Mason, S. F. 1962. *A History of the Sciences*. New York: Collier Books. 2nd edn, 1977.

Mavroeidis, S. 2004. Weak identification of forward-looking models in monetary economics. *Oxford Bulletin of Economics and Statistics*, **66**, 609–635.

Mayo, D. 1981. Testing statistical testing. In Pitt, J. C. (ed.), *Philosophy in Economics*, pp. 175–230: D. Reidel Publishing Co.

Mayo, D. G., and Spanos, A. 2006. Severe testing as a basic concept in a Neyman–Pearson philosophy of induction. *British Journal for the Philosophy of Science*, **57**, 323–357.

McLeod, K. S. 2000. Our sense of Snow: the myth of John Snow in medical geography. *Social Science & Medicine*, **50**, 923–935.

Messadié, G. 1991. *Great Scientific Discoveries*. Edinburgh: Chambers.

Miller, P. J. 1978. Forecasting with econometric methods: A comment. *Journal of Business*, **51**, 579–586.

Mills, T. C. 2010. Bradford Smith: An econometrician decades ahead of his time. *Oxford Bulletin of Economics and Statistics*, **73**, 276–285.

Mizon, G. E. 1977. Model selection procedures. In Artis, M. J., and Nobay, A. R. (eds.), *Studies in Modern Economic Analysis*, pp. 97–120. Oxford: Basil Blackwell.

Mizon, G. E. 1984. The encompassing approach in econometrics. In Hendry, D. F., and Wallis, K. F. (eds.), *Econometrics and Quantitative Economics*, pp. 135–172. Oxford: Basil Blackwell.

Mizon, G. E. 1995. A simple message for autocorrelation correctors: Don't. *Journal of Econometrics*, **69**, 267–288.

Mizon, G. E., and Richard, J.-F. 1986. The encompassing principle and its application to non-nested hypothesis tests. *Econometrica*, **54**, 657–678.

Moore, H. L. 1925. A moving equilibrium of demand and supply. *Quarterly Journal of Economics*, **39**, 359–371.

Morgan, M. S. 1990. *The History of Econometric Ideas*. Cambridge: Cambridge University Press.

Musgrave, A. 1976. Why did oxygen supplant phlogiston?: Research programmes in the chemical revolution. In Howson, C. (ed.), *Method and Appraisal in the Physical Sciences*, pp. 181–209. Cambridge: Cambridge University Press.

Nelson, C. R. 1972. The prediction performance of the FRB-MIT-PENN model of the US economy. *American Economic Review*, **62**, 902–917.

Nelson, R. R. 1959. The simple economics of basic scientific research. *The Journal of Political Economy*, **67**, 297–306.

Nielsen, B. 1996. Disco. Mimeo, Nuffield College, Oxford. www.nuff.ox.ac.uk/ Users/Nielsen/Disco.html.

Nielsen, H. B. 2004. Cointegration analysis in the presence of outliers. *Econometrics Journal*, **7**, 249–271.

Nussbaumer, H., and Bieri, L. 2009. *Discovering the Expanding Universe*. Cambridge: Cambridge University Press.

Omtzig, P. 2002. Automatic identification and restriction of the cointegration space. Thesis chapter, Economics Department, Copenhagen University.

Osborn, D. R. 1988. Seasonality and habit persistence in a life cycle model of consumption. *Journal of Applied Econometrics*, **3**, 255–266.

Osborn, D. R. 1991. The implications of periodically varying coefficients for seasonal time-series processes. *Journal of Econometrics*, **48**, 373–384.

Pagan, A. R. 1987. Three econometric methodologies: A critical appraisal. *Journal of Economic Surveys*, **1**, 3–24.

Perez-Amaral, T., Gallo, G. M., and White, H. 2003. A flexible tool for model building: the relevant transformation of the inputs network approach (RETINA). *Oxford Bulletin of Economics and Statistics*, **65**, 821–838.

Perez-Amaral, T., Gallo, G. M., and White, H. 2005. A comparison of complementary automatic modelling methods: RETINA and PcGets. *Econometric Theory*, **21**, 262–277.

Perron, P. 1989. The Great Crash, the oil price shock and the unit root hypothesis. *Econometrica*, **57**, 1361–1401.

Pesaran, M. H., Pettenuzzo, D., and Timmermann, A. 2006. Forecasting time series subject to multiple structural breaks. *Review of Economic Studies*, **73**, 1057–1084.

Phillips, A. W. H. 1954. Stabilization policy in a closed economy. *Economic Journal*, **64**, 290–333.

Phillips, P. C. B. 1986. Understanding spurious regressions in econometrics. *Journal of Econometrics*, **33**, 311–340.

Phillips, P. C. B. 1988. Reflections on econometric methodology. *Economic Record*, **64**, 344–359.

Phillips, P. C. B. 1989. Partially identified econometric models. *Econometric Theory*, **5**(2), 181–240.

Phillips, P. C. B. 1991. Optimal inference in cointegrated systems. *Econometrica*, **59**, 283–306.

Phillips, P. C. B. 1994. Bayes models and forecasts of Australian macroeconomic time series. In Hargreaves, C. (ed.), *Non-stationary Time-Series Analyses and Cointegration*. Oxford: Oxford University Press.

Phillips, P. C. B. 1995. Automated forecasts of Asia-Pacific economic activity. *Asia-Pacific Economic Review*, **1**, 92–102.

Phillips, P. C. B. 1996. Econometric model determination. *Econometrica*, **64**, 763–812.

Phillips, P. C. B. 2003. Laws and limits of econometrics. *Economic Journal*, **113**, C26–C52.

Phillips, P. C. B. 2007. Regression with slowly varying regressors and nonlinear trends. *Econometric Theory*, **23**, 557–614.

Phillips, P. C. B., and Ploberger, W. 1996. An asymptotic theory of Bayesian inference for time series. *Econometrica*, **64**, 381–412.

Popper, K. R. 1959. *The Logic of Scientific Discovery*. New York: Basic Books.

Popper, K. R. 1963. *Conjectures and Refutations*. New York: Basic Books.

Pötscher, B. M. 1991. Effects of model selection on inference. *Econometric Theory*, **7**, 163–185.

Priestley, M. B. 1981. *Spectral Analysis and Time Series*. London: Academic Press.

Psaradakis, Z., and Sola, M. 1996. On the power of tests for superexogeneity and structural invariance. *Journal of Econometrics*, **72**, 151–175.

Qin, D. 1993. *The Formation of Econometrics: A Historical Perspective*. Oxford: Clarendon Press.

Qin, D. 2013. *A History of Econometrics: The Reformation from the 1970s*. Oxford: Clarendon Press.

Raffalovich, L., Deane, D., Armstrong, D., and Tsao, H.-S. 2001. Model selection procedures in social science research: Monte-Carlo simulation results. Working paper 2005/16, Center for Social and Demographic Analysis, State University of New York, Albany.

Ramsey, J. B. 1969. Tests for specification errors in classical linear least squares regression analysis. *Journal of the Royal Statistical Society B*, **31**, 350–371.

Reade, J. J. 2008. Updating Tobin's food expenditure time series data. Working paper, Department of Economics, University of Oxford.

Reed, G. 2000. How the preliminary estimate of GDP is produced. *Economic Trends*, **556**, 53–61.

Reed, G. 2002. How much information is in the UK preliminary estimate of GDP? *Economic Trends*, **585**, 1–8.

Robinson, P. M. 1995. Log-periodogram regression of time series with long range dependence. *Annals of Statistics*, **23**, 1048–1072.

Rothenberg, T. J. 1971. Identification in parametric models. *Econometrica*, **39**, 577–592.

Rothenberg, T. J. 1973. *Efficient Estimation with A Priori Information*. No. 23 in Cowles Foundation Monograph. New Haven: Yale University Press.

Rushton, S. 1951. On least squares fitting by orthogonal polynomials using the Choleski method. *Journal of the Royal Statistical Society, B*, **13**, 92–99.

Salkever, D. S. 1976. The use of dummy variables to compute predictions, prediction errors and confidence intervals. *Journal of Econometrics*, **4**, 393–397.

Sargan, J. D. 1964. Wages and prices in the United Kingdom: A study in econometric methodology (with discussion). In Hart, P. E., Mills, G., and Whitaker, J. K. (eds.), *Econometric Analysis for National Economic Planning*, Vol. 16 of *Colston Papers*, pp. 25–63. London: Butterworth Co.

Sargan, J. D. 2001. Model building and data mining. *Econometric Reviews*, **20**, 159–170.

Schultz, H. 1928. *The Theory and Measurement of Demand*: University of Chicago Press.

Schultz, S. G. 2002. William Harvey and the circulation of the blood: The birth of a scientific revolution and modern physiology. *News in Physiological Sciences,* **17,** 175–180.

Schumpeter, J. 1954. *History of Economic Analysis.* New York: Oxford University Press.

Schwarz, G. 1978. Estimating the dimension of a model. *Annals of Statistics,* **6,** 461–464.

Sims, C. A. 1996. Macroeconomics and methodology. *Journal of Economic Perspectives,* **10,** 105–120.

Sims, C. A., Stock, J. H., and Watson, M. W. 1990. Inference in linear time series models with some unit roots. *Econometrica,* **58,** 113–144.

Smets, F., and Wouters, R. 2003. An estimated stochastic dynamic general equilibrium model of the Euro Area. *Journal of the European Economic Association,* **1,** 1123–1175.

Smith, B. B. 1926. Combining the advantages of first-difference and deviation-from-trend methods of correlating time series. *Journal of the American Statistical Association,* **21,** 55–59.

Smith, G. D. 2002. Commentary: Behind the Broad Street pump: Aetiology, epidemiology and prevention of cholera in mid-19th century Britain. *International Journal of Epidemiology,* **31,** 920–932.

Sober, E. 2003. Instrumentalism, parsimony, and the Akaike framework. Unpublished paper, Department of Philosophy, University of Wisconsin, Madison.

Spanos, A. 1989. On re-reading Haavelmo: A retrospective view of econometric modeling. *Econometric Theory,* **5,** 405–429.

Spanos, A. 1995. On theory testing in econometric modelling with non-experimental data. *Journal of Econometrics,* **67,** 189–226.

Spanos, A. 1999. *Probability Theory and Statistical Inference: Econometric Modeling with Observational Data.* Cambridge: Cambridge University Press.

Spanos, A. 2000. Revisiting data mining: 'Hunting' with or without a license. *Journal of Economic Methodology,* **7,** 231–264.

Spanos, A. 2007. Curve-fitting, the reliability of inductive inference and the error-statistical approach. *Philosophy of Science,* **74,** 1046–1066.

Spanos, A. 2011. Foundational issues in statistical modeling: Statistical model specification and validation. *Rationality, Markets and Morals,* **2,** 146–178.

Sparks, R. S. J. 2003. Forecasting volcanic eruptions. *Earth and Planetary Science Letters,* **210,** 1–15.

Spearman, C. 1927. *The Abilities of Man*. London: Macmillan.

Staiger, D., and Stock, J. H. 1997. Instrumental variables regression with weak instruments. *Econometrica*, **65**, 557–586.

Stein, C. 1956. *Inadmissibility of the usual estimator for the mean of a multivariate normal distribution*. Berkeley: University of California Press.

Stigum, B. P. (ed.) 2003. *Econometrics and the Philosophy of Economics*. Princeton: Princeton University Press.

Stock, J. H., and Watson, M. W. 1998. Diffusion indices. Working paper, 6702, NBER, Washington.

Stock, J. H., and Watson, M. W. 1999. A comparison of linear and nonlinear models for forecasting macroeconomic time series. In Engle, and White 1999, pp. 1–44.

Stock, J. H., and Watson, M. W. 2002. Macroeconomic forecasting using diffusion indices. *Journal of Business and Economic Statistics*, **20**, 147–162.

Stock, J. H., and Watson, M. W. 2006. *Introduction to Econometrics*. Boston, Mass.: Addison-Wesley.

Stock, J. H., and Watson, M. W. 2011. Dynamic factor models. In Clements, and Hendry 2011, Ch. 2.

Stock, J. H., and Wright, J. H. 2000. GMM with weak identification. *Econometrica*, **68**, 1055–1096.

Stone, J. R. N. 1947. On the interdependence of blocks of transactions. *Journal of the Royal Statistical Society*, **8**, 1–32. Supplement.

Stone, M. 1974. Cross-validatory choice and assessment of statistical predictions. *Journal of the Royal Statistical Society*, **B, 36**, 111–147.

Summers, L. H. 1991. The scientific illusion in empirical macroeconomics. *Scandinavian Journal of Economics*, **93**, 129–148.

Surowiecki, J. 2004. *The Wisdom of Crowds*. New York: Doubleday.

Teräsvirta, T. 1994. Specification, estimation and evaluation of smooth transition autoregressive models. *Journal of the American Statistical Association*, **89**, 208–218.

Tibshirani, R. 1996. Regression shrinkage and selection via the lasso. *Journal of the Royal Statistical Society*, **B, 58**, 267–288.

Tinbergen, J. 1939. *Statistical Testing of Business-Cycle Theories. Vol. I: A Method and its Application to Investment Activity*. Geneva: League of Nations.

Tinbergen, J. 1940. *Statistical Testing of Business-Cycle Theories*. Geneva: League of Nations. Vol. II: Business Cycles in the United States of America, 1919–1932.

Tobin, J. 1950. A statistical demand function for food in the U.S.A.. *Journal of the Royal Statistical Society, A, 113*(2), 113–141.

Toda, H. Y., and Phillips, P. C. B. 1993. Vector autoregressions and causality. *Econometrica*, **61**, 1367–1393.

Vining, R. 1949a. Methodological issues in quantitative economics. *Review of Economics and Statistics*, **31**, 77–86.

Vining, R. 1949b. A rejoinder. *Review of Economics and Statistics*, **31**, 91–94.

Visco, I. 1988. Again on sign changes upon deletion of a variable from a linear regression. *Oxford Bulletin of Economics and Statistics*, **50**, 225–227.

Waller, J. 2002. *Fabulous Science*. Oxford: Oxford University Press.

Wang, J., and Zivot, E. 1998. Inference on a structural parameter in instrumental variables regression with weak instruments. *Econometrica*, **66**, 1389–1404.

White, H. 1980. A heteroskedastic-consistent covariance matrix estimator and a direct test for heteroskedasticity. *Econometrica*, **48**, 817–838.

White, H. 1990. A consistent model selection. In Granger, C. W. J. (ed.), *Modelling Economic Series*, pp. 369–383. Oxford: Clarendon Press.

White, H. 2000. A reality check for data snooping. *Econometrica*, **68**, 1097–1126.

Wooldridge, J. M. 1999. Asymptotic properties of some specification tests in linear models with integrated processes. In Engle, and White 1999, pp. 366–384.

Wooldridge, J. M. 2000. *Introductory Econometrics – A Modern Approach*. New York: South-Western College Publishing.

Working, E. J. 1927. What do statistical demand curves show? *Quarterly Journal of Economics*, **41**, 212–235.

Yule, G. U. 1926. Why do we sometimes get nonsense-correlations between time-series? A study in sampling and the nature of time series (with discussion). *Journal of the Royal Statistical Society*, **89**, 1–64.

Zivot, E., Startz, R., and Nelson, C. R. 1998. Valid confidence intervals and inference in the presence of weak instruments. *International Economic Review*, **39**, 1119–1144.

Author Index

Index